*f*P

THE
WRITING
ON THE
WALL

Why We Must Embrace China as a
Partner or Face It as an Enemy

Will Hutton

Free Press

NEW YORK   LONDON   TORONTO   SYDNEY

FREE PRESS

A Division of Simon & Schuster, Inc.

1230 Avenue of the Americas

New York, NY 10020

Copyright © 2006 by Will Hutton

For information about special discounts for bulk purchases,
please contact Simon & Schuster Special Sales at
1-800-456-6798 or business@simonandschuster.com

Designed by Paul Dippolito

Manufactured in the United States of America

1   3   5   7   9   10   8   6   4   2

Library of Congress Cataloging-in-Publication Data

ISBN-13: 978-0-7432-7528-6
ISBN-10:   0-7432-7528-4

To Jane, Alice, Andrew,
and Sarah
And to my mother and father.
He would have liked this book.
I surprise myself at how often I think about him.
He would have liked that, too

Contents

THE
WRITING
ON THE
WALL

Preface

CHINA IS A CONTINENTWIDE COUNTRY WHOSE LAND area is eerily close in terms of square miles to that of the United States. Look at a map and imagine that China's western border was bounded by sea, and the analogy becomes even more eerie. For the Rockies read the Himalayas. For the decaying industrialized northeast of the United States, read the decaying industrialized northeast of China, including Manchuria. For Washington's location, read Beijing. For booming Florida read booming Guangdong province in the southeast. The Yangtze may flow west–east while the Mississippi flows north–south, but each is an enormous river that bisects its country. And for Shanghai, read New York.

Similarities stop there. China boasts a civilization at least 3,000 years old. It is home to 1.3 billion people. It is authoritarian and formally communist. And since 1978 it has burst back onto the world scene in a manner paralleled in scale and speed in world history only by the rise of the United States between the Civil War and World War I in 1914. The open question is whether the twenty-first century is going to be the Chinese century in the way the twentieth century was American and the nineteenth century British. Is the baton of global leadership going to pass from Anglo-Saxon hands, which held so many values in common, to Chinese hands? If so, the implications could not be more profound. The world would have to accommodate a wholly different civilization and values; the character of global institutions, our culture, and obviously the primacy of the English language would be challenged. If China remained communist there would be substantial implications for the organization of western

1

economies and societies. The answer to this question is one of the most important of our age.

The argument in this book is that if the next century is going to be Chinese, it will be only because China embraces the economic and political pluralism of the west in general, and our Enlightenment institutions in particular. I use the Enlightenment as shorthand, to capture the full panoply of institutions, processes, and ways of thinking that were launched by the European Enlightenment and embodied in its quintessential expression, the Constitution and public processes of the United States. The rule of law, the independence of the judiciary, the freedom of the press, the scientific and research processes at independent universities, the very idea of representative accountable government—all those flowed from the great intellectual, philosophic, and political wellspring that we call the Enlightenment. Above all, it endowed western societies with the idea of the public realm and an approach to living whose spirit the great Enlightenment philosopher Immanuel Kant summed up simply: to "dare to know."

What I try to show is that these are not "western" but indispensable components of any well-functioning economy and society. Their lack in China is increasingly showing through in a myriad of dysfunctions and internal contradictions that will have to be confronted. The current economic model is unsustainable, and its unsustainability in turn will have important implications for the capacity of the Communist Party to run China as a single-party authoritarian state.

That is why the simple extrapolations of China's continued growth at current levels for the next forty or fifty years are misleading—and why it is wrong for so many western politicians, business leaders, and opinion leaders to present China as an ominous threat before which the west must change or wilt. This idea is normally a code for the proposition that ordinary Americans and Europeans should accept stagnating living standards and diminished welfare states and fend for themselves in acquiring the education and skills—more and more at their own expense—necessary to compete with China's advancing hordes. Those in the higher echelons of society, meanwhile, can continue to enjoy the trappings of growing inequality.

China is not such a threat. Rather, it is a sophisticated civilization beset by profound and deepening problems that is making a difficult transition from peasant poverty to modernity. It requires our understanding and engagement—not our enmity and suspicion, which might be self-defeating, creating the very crisis we fear. China's vulnerability is not widely understood. Europe and the United States should stay open to China both in our trade and in the realm of ideas.

Above all, we should be confident. The Enlightenment values and institutions that propelled the west past China in the nineteenth century remain no less important today as sources of competitive advantage and social well-being. They lie at the heart of the emerging "knowledge economy." The problem is that they are being neglected, and in consequence they are fading. In the United States, public institutions, representative government, the media, secondary education, corporations, investment institutions, and especially general supports for developing the individual capabilities of its citizens are simply not working as well as they should. Britain is in a very similar position. And in their preemptive war in Iraq, both countries have actively undermined the system of international law and multilateral governance. If we want to persuade China and the world of the virtues of pluralism, Enlightenment values, and democracy, the United States and Britain have to practice what they preach at home and abroad. At present they do not.

This, then, is the heart of the book. After an introductory overview chapter, the next five chapters explore how China has developed up to today, the structure of its economy, and the increasing unmanageability of the contradictions upon which it rests. Chapters 7 and 8 investigate the advantages of economic and political pluralism more fully in theory and trace how they are emerging and their importance in other parts of Asia. Chapter 9 sets out the areas of political, military, and economic tension between the United States and China, and Chapters 10 and 11 use the same framework and criteria through which I look at China to assess the United States, which falls short of the standards it should set itself as a great Enlightenment country. In the Conclusion I briefly examine the Knowledge Economy and set out a prospectus for potential change in our international priorities, processes, and institutions.

The relationship between the United States and China and that between China and the rest of Asia are delicately poised. Yet there are many problems—most tellingly the environment and global warning, which now threaten ecosystems to the degree that we are fast approaching a tipping point where humanity as a species may be in potential danger—that require an international response and appreciation of our shared fate. Both China and the United States must be part of the solution to these problems. My ambition for this book is that it will help tilt the balance toward more international collaboration, a reappraisal of the so-called Chinese threat, and a recognition of the situation as an opportunity and above all a reaffirmation of Enlightenment values and of the importance of economics and pluralism at home. All this is already too long for the preface. Read on—and I hope you enjoy.

CHAPTER 1

The Last Great Powers

A GREAT POWER WILL NEVER VOLUNTARILY SURRENDER pride of place to a challenger. The United States is the preeminent great power. China is now its challenger. The great questions of our time are, first, whether China can translate its potential into reality without democracy and without genuine capitalism; and, second, whether the United States will be wise enough to keep its markets and the wider world system open to China as this Chinese drama plays out, and by so doing accelerate the fundamental reform that must come to it. Our prosperity and even global peace depend on the answers.

Every state in the world may harbor ambitions to have the autonomy of the archetypal nineteenth-century nation-state, but most must come to terms with the constraints of their relatively small size compared with the scale of global markets. Only China and the United States with their continental economies, vast populations, and huge military machines genuinely think in old nation-state terms. They calculate their spheres of military, diplomatic, and economic influence. They are prepared to use military power to secure national ends. Each believes its civilization and culture has a special destiny. The world's future hangs on whether these two powers can resist the temptations of rivalry and find a constructive accommodation that allows them to do business.

For sixty years the United States has overcome its protectionist tradition—no other country in the nineteenth century and the early twentieth century had such tariffs for so long—to lead the development of an open global economy. Flows of trade, investment, and technology have reached an unsurpassed intensity. Growth and living standards have risen remarkably. True, there are disturbing and dangerous new inequalities between countries whose capacity to take advantage of these opportunities varies hugely. But the overall balance sheet is positive. The United States itself is up to $1 trillion richer as a result of globalization.[1] The Asian miracle, including the rise of China, would have been impossible without it.

But within the United States, anxiety has grown about the stagnating incomes and financial insecurity of much of its middle class. Because these afflictions have shown up at the same time as globalization, they are too often said to have been caused by it. In fact, the principal causes lie within the United States (see Chapter 11), including the onward march of new technologies; changing tastes of consumers; an epidemic of mergers, takeovers, and acquisitions; and the increasing unwillingness of American businesses and policy makers alike to accept a duty to care for the American workforce.

Even before 9/11, doubts were voiced in the United States about whether the network of multilateral treaties and institutions that had developed under American leadership since the end of the World War II was still working. Was it right for the United States to be constrained by international law, whether over trade or weapons systems? Since 9/11, the historical American tendency toward unilateralism and suspicion of foreigners has been exacerbated. The expensive, deadly, poorly executed involvement in Iraq is reinforcing the distrust of foreign entanglements; and the threat from Islamic fundamentalist terrorism has spurred calls for clamping down zealously on immigration and sealing U.S. borders. The globalizing economy is blamed by critics for the outsourcing of jobs, causing wage deflation in the United States, and for unfair competition from foreign goods, especially from China, resulting in the largest bilateral trade deficit in 2005 with any single country in its history—$202 billion.

As a result, popular support for the idea that the United States should take the lead in further integrating the world economy is eroding. The congressional majority in favor of international treaties and free trade, always hard to put together, is challenged. The hysterical campaign in 2006 against plans to have Dubai Ports World manage six U.S. ports as a consequence of its takeover of the British company P and O is symptomatic of a new attitude. The United States, however, is not alone in this regard. Around the world, almost no country or trading bloc now looks at the global economy as something that needs to be built and sustained for collective benefit. Rather, it's considered a juggernaut that should exploited to one's own advantage. The World Trade talks aimed at extending trade liberalization were suspended in July 2006, with none of the key actors prepared to initiate concessions for the sake of a collective settlement.

Yet the global economy is not an unstoppable force. What has been made by political choices can be unmade by political choices. If everyone bends, disobeys, and ignores the rules, soon there are no rules. The architecture that sustains the world's growing interdependence is under great strain. It needs to be recrafted and reinvigorated, but this requires preconditions that are lacking—intellectual conviction and a high degree of trust and common values between the great powers.

This is why China's rise is so significant. China's economy in 2006 is nearly nine times larger than it was in 1978: the fourth largest in the world, after the United States, Japan, and Germany. If current trends continue, it is set to become the second largest within a decade.[2] The only comparable rise of an economy as a proportion of world GDP in such a short time is that of the United States at the end of the nineteenth century.[3] Between 1981 and 2001, 400 million people had been brought out of poverty.[4] Between 1978 and 2003, China's average per capita income rose by a multiple of six. The proportion of the population living in towns and cities has doubled to nearly two-fifths. Up to 150 million workers have moved to China's booming cities—the biggest migration in history.[5] It is a head-spinning achievement.

China is the new factor in global politics and economics. No global architecture can be constructed without it. By the end of 2006 it will have some $1 trillion of foreign exchange reserves. The United

States could not be running a current account deficit of $800 billion without consistent selling pressure on the dollar if Chinese purchases of U.S. Treasury bills and bonds were not so high. China is the world's second largest importer of oil. Before 2010, it will be the world's largest exporter of goods.[6] It is, comfortably, the world's second largest military power: the Pentagon believes that China's defense expenditure is up to three times more than the $30 billion China officially declares. The Pentagon's four-yearly defense review stated that the scale of China's military buildup has already put "regional military balances at risk" and that China is the power most likely to "field disruptive military technologies that could over time offset traditional U.S. military advantages."[7] If you are prepared to compare China's output not on the basis of current market foreign exchange rates but on estimates of the real purchasing power of what China produces, then China already is the second largest economy in the world. On this basis it could overtake the United States within twenty years.[8]

The problem is that this new great power is communist, and its rise to power has been masterminded by the Communist Party. The party may have made major ideological changes; it praises only 70 percent of Mao's record, for example, condemning the disastrous Cultural Revolution and the Great Leap Forward in which more than 30 million Chinese died. It now aims to build a "socialist market" economy rather than a planned communist economy. It permitted the dismantlement of 26,000 communes in rural China. Hundreds of millions of peasants are again farming plots on long leases once held by their ancestors. China wants its state-owned enterprises to compete as autonomous companies largely free to set prices as they choose in an open economy.

China's communists have declared that the class war is over. They now claim to represent not just the worker and peasant masses but entrepreneurs and business leaders, whom it welcomes into its ranks. The party refers to this metamorphosis as the "three represents"— meaning that the party today represents, in the ideological categories in which it thinks, "advanced productive forces," "the overwhelming majority" of the Chinese, and "the orientation . . . of China's advanced culture."[9] Party representatives abroad say that the country wants to rise peacefully, not to play power politics or to aim for any kind of hegemony. China has joined the World Trade Organization and is a judicious member of the United Nations Security Council, using its veto largely in matters that immediately concern it, like Taiwan.

Yet it remains formally a communist power adhering to the doctrines of Marxism, Leninism, and Mao. It is a one-party state with no regular competitive elections, no independent rule of law, no freedom of speech, no right of association, and no entrenched basic human rights. Although it condemns 30 percent of Mao's legacy, it praises 70 percent. Difficult as this may be for many foreigners and even some Chinese to accept, a majority of China's 1.3 billion people and its communist rulers regard the communist revolution of 1949 as a significant, important, legitimate event, analogous to the American and French revolutions. The China of 2006 could not have happened without the revolution. Mao's mass murders are condemned, as the French might condemn Robespierre and the Terror; but Mao is seen as part of a process that also included much good, notably a dramatic increase in male and female literacy, and the shattering of the imperial Confucian system, which had held China back for 150 years. Deng Xiaoping, China's great pro-market reformer, did not build contemporary China out of nothing; he built on foundations left by Mao and always aimed to preserve the primacy of the Communist Party.

That foundation is now, however, a profound problem for China, the United States, and the world. It makes China a difficult partner internationally because there is an objective clash of interests over the importance of democracy, the rule of law, and human rights and how they should be represented in the world's architecture. Meanwhile, at home, China's communists, notwithstanding their success to date, are confronting limits regarding how far they can develop a pluralist market economy without also instituting pluralist political institutions. The party leadership has not yet embraced the "soft" institutional infrastructure that accompanies successful capitalism: impartial courts, clear property rights, proper commercial processes for bank lending, independent auditors, accountability to a free press, independent trade unions, effective corporate governance, transparent antimonopoly rules, free intellectual inquiry, and even a properly functioning welfare system. The party is also facing a growing issue of legitimacy. If it no longer rules as the democratic dictatorship of peasants and workers, because the class war is over, why does it not hold itself accountable to the people in competitive elections? Answers are not easy for it to find.

China is confronting an ideological crisis. With the collapse of the Soviet Union, communism in China cannot now justify itself as part of an international communist movement whose success is historically and scientifically preordained. Instead it has to justify itself through its domestic accomplishments as well as its historic role in enabling China to regain the pride and international respect that had been lost ever since the Opium war of 1839–1842. Successful economic development has thus been one strand of policy to legitimize the party; the other has been nationalism.

This latter sentiment has deep roots. Confucian emperors portrayed China as the center of the universe. For that reason, China's reversals during the nineteenth century were felt particularly keenly; by the1870s there was already a patriotic "self-strengthening" movement, aiming to copy foreign methods to recover China's power, and the mood intensified after defeat by Japan in 1895. After World War I, when German concessions in China were handed over to the Japanese as part of the treaty of Versailles, with no regard for China's views, this was felt to symbolize all that was wrong. The spontaneous demonstrations that erupted on May 4, 1919, developed into a loose nationalist political movement that was one of the antecedents of the Communist Party's own official foundation in 1921. Thus today's introduction of "patriotic" education to inculcate pride in China and in the party's achievements builds on long-standing instincts. China has to be permanently on guard against its enemies, who have not essentially changed their spots. "The Chinese people must never again be humiliated by foreign aggressors," runs the official interpretation of history.[10] China must avoid disunity at home and be protected abroad by a vigilant communist government.

The weakness of communist ideology, assuaged only partially by this nationalism, is matched by a growing awareness that the logic of reform is rapidly confronting China with a choice. The current halfway house of trying to retain political control of what is in truth only half a market economy is unsustainable. Is China to accept that economic pluralism, along with an institutional infrastructure to confer political pluralism, is the only way a market economy can flourish? Or can it hold the line and manage today's ambiguities and economic contradictions?

The economy provides an unwelcome answer for the conservative wing of the Communist Party, which wants to hold the line. So far, China has few great companies capable of competing internationally, and almost no global brands. Its private sector consists of a plethora of small transient companies usually dependent on political patronage. China'a state-owned, state-directed, or state-influenced corporations may have the freedom to set prices and wages, but only within limits laid down by the party. Their productivity is disastrous.

The system that has brought China this far is Leninist corporatism rather than anything approaching a proper market economy, let alone a socialist market economy. It is Leninist in the primacy it affords the Communist Party, and corporatist rather than capitalist because it does not foster capitalist economic pluralism. It is neither a communist nor a capitalist economy. The central argument of this book is that for all China's success to date, ultimately the system that the communists have created is structurally unstable. The next phase of China's economic and political development must permit more economic pluralism. But that will set in train a process that must challenge the preeminence of the Communist Party.

The Face-Off

China does not face this conundrum in a vacuum. Its sheer scale forces it into structural tension with the United States. There are three primary flashpoints between the two countries—oil, trade, and currency. Looming over all of them is Taiwan, and the possibility that one day China will test the commitment of the United States to defend Taiwan from a Chinese invasion.

The peak of world oil production is clearly imminent. According to some estimates it is already on us, and if it is not, very few expect it much after 2020.[11] So it is hardly a surprise that the last two great powers eye each other's intentions concerning oil with suspicion. A network of Chinese-financed pipelines is appearing or planned in Canada, Venezuela, Sudan, and Iran that will take oil away from the United States and toward its challenger. Four-fifths of China's oil is transported through the Strait of Malacca between Malaysia and Indonesia. At one end of the Strait is an American fleet at the Changi naval base in Singapore. At the other end, the United States' Indian Ocean fleet operates from Diego Garcia. From Beijing's perspective, the United States has its fingers on China's windpipe; President Hu Jintao makes frequent reference to the "Malacca problem." China wants more oil brought in by pipeline across Asia and by tanker across the Pacific. It also wants a deep-sea fleet to protect its interests. Richard Nixon's former secretary of state, Henry Kissinger, has warned of a potential great-power conflict over oil: this is it.[12] China's "ring of pearls" strategy, developing close relationships with Pakistan, Cambodia, Thailand, and Myanmar (Burma), is designed to give it access to ports for its naval and merchant vessels if hostilities break out with the United States.

However, the most pressing issue between the two countries is over trade and currency. Up to 70 percent of the products Wal-Mart sells are produced in China, to the advantage of the American consumer. Cumulatively American consumers are $100 billion better off, as one authoritative economist estimates, because China's cheap exports have lowered consumer prices in the United States.[13] China's role in financing the United States' trade deficit is critical, as I have already noted.

After 9/11, however, these advantages may not outweigh, in the public mind, the perceived damage from free trade with China. The United States did not become a genuinely open economy until the 1940s, when it became clear that U.S. industry had no serious rivals abroad and there was a strategic interest in accepting imports from Japan as well as the rest of capitalist Asia and Europe. By encouraging trade, the argument went, the United States would advance the cause of capitalism against communism.

But in the mid-1980s there was a ferocious backlash against Japanese imports, and we are now seeing a possible backlash against China. There is no obvious strategic interest in boosting communist China's economic base; indeed, the American public may be unsure that it wants its trade deficit financed by the People's Bank of China or wants to depend on China at all. The forces that want the United States to pull up the economic drawbridge are becoming ever more powerful, drawing on the nation's historical ambiguity about its relationship with the rest of the world and its belief in its own special destiny. Rationality is made immeasurably more difficult by George Bush's warnings that the United States is now in a long war against terrorism.

Non-Americans have difficulty in coming to terms with the contradictions and complexity of American nationalism. The United States, because of its special destiny and difference, is felt to have an obligation to lead others; it can also feel no compunction about using its presumed special destiny to justify behaving astonishingly self-interestedly even when there is a clear global interest in collective collaboration. Global warming is one example. Although the United States accounts for about 25 percent of the world's carbon dioxide emissions, George Bush could unblinkingly oppose the Kyoto Protocol in March 2001 because "it exempts 80 percent of the world, including major population centers such as China and India, from compliance, and would cause serious harm to the U.S. economy." [14] The United States could abdicate leadership, pursue its own interests undeterred by an international treaty, and stand aside from concerns that affect humanity. This stance was and is of serious concern to a significant part of the American public and to the United States' allies. Yet Bush suffered little. He was putting America first.

Public opinion and political leadership in the United States are divided between this protectionist, "America first" tendency and an opposing internationalist tendency that favors free trade and a multilateral foreign policy. Under President Bush, the "America first" strain, which was already gaining ground before 9/11, has become predominant. The reaction to 9/11 recalls an analysis by the American political historian Richard Hofstadter, who identified what he called a "paranoid style" in American politics. There have been periods in American history when conspiracy theories about alien influences, ranging from suspicion of international bankers during the Greenback and Populist era at the end of the nineteenth century to McCarthy's witch hunts in the early 1950s for suspected communists, have given a paranoid, even xenophobic, style to American politics. China is provoking such paranoia as well as the America-first tradition, and the resulting spectacle is not edifying.

The anti-China sentiment that has surfaced in the last two or three years is obvious. Some of the twenty bills introduced in this period, aimed at retaliation against China or its imports, would have disastrous consequences. One bill would impose a 27.5 percent tariff on Chinese imports if China does not immediately revalue its currency, the renminbi, significantly. Another bill would set conditions for expelling China from the World Trade Organization, because—allegedly—China flouts the rules of free trade. Either bill would have an economic impact analogous to a unilateral missile attack. Flows of Chinese finance to support the dollar and U.S. asset prices would collapse; there would be a sell-off in world stock markets; Europe would have to follow the American lead and adopt U.S.-style protectionism to head off a flood of cheap Chinese exports being diverted to the European Union; and the Chinese economy would rapidly slow down with incalculable implications for its political stability.

The scope for miscalculation by either the United States or China is huge. These are two nationalist juggernauts, and the Chinese have very limited room to maneuver in responding to the United States' demands, presented with mounting urgency. In the first place a sudden revaluation of the renminbi would have a very depressive effect on the incomes of the 900 million Chinese living in peasant households, because it would lower China's food prices, keyed as they are to world price levels. It would damage savings, arrest export growth, slow down the economy, and raise the specter of a banking crisis. Second, to call for China to comply immediately with western and best Asian standards of corporate governance, transparency, and accountability is to force systemic change on China. Such change is vital and in my view inevitable, but these reforms must be handled with great sensitivity. Change can and will come; and external pressure should be applied, but not to the point that the fallout causes at least as much pain for the west as it does for China.

Seen from Beijing, the call to revalue the renminbi or transform the Chinese economic system is a de facto act of aggression that will destabilize the government. Seen from Washington, the refusal to become a good international economic citizen is willful neglect of what Deputy Secretary of State Robert Zoellick regards as China's duties as a responsible stakeholder in running the world system. It is an eyeball-to-eyeball confrontation, a great-power game to see who blinks first. The strength of sentiment on both sides should not be underestimated. Only fifteen members of Congress voted in 2005 to allow one of China's national oil companies—CNOOC—to take over the U.S. company Unocal, arguing that concerns of national security were specious, as they largely were; 398 voted against the takeover. In China suspicion of American intentions runs no less high.

Never far beneath the surface of conflict is Taiwan, Japan's former colony, which was commandeered by the Nationalist armies in 1949 and who claimed to have taken the genuine republic of China with them. China wants it to rejoin the motherland, like Hong Kong and Macao; this would remove the last stain of the century of humiliation and, far more important, eliminate an ideological rival. What stands between China and its goal is the U.S. fleet. China continues a military buildup that the Pentagon and senior military analysts agree is congruent only with a projected invasion of Taiwan. The United States maintains substantial military strength in the region, and promises to stand by its understanding with Taiwan in the event of a Chinese attack. The question is whether China will ever choose to test the American commitment.

Underneath the tension lies a greater truth. The two sides are codependent and essentially benefit from their relationship, and the internal difficulties on either side are homegrown—though this political analysis is hard to accept—rather than the fault of the other. Nor should the United States think a Chinese takeover is imminent. It needs to remind itself that as an $11 trillion economy it is still five times larger than China and many times richer in terms of per capita income. It still produces more than one-fifth of the world's output. Thirteen of the world's top twenty brands, and fifty-three of the top 100, are American.[15] The United States leads the world in innovation and patents. Its military power is overwhelming: in 2005, the United States' military expenditure outstripped the combined total of the next fourteen countries by $116 billion.[16] The United States' "soft power" is also overwhelming. This is the country with the Enlightenment inheritance of free speech, free association, rule of law, free thought, and pluralist checks and balances, even if today these look slightly tattered. Some self-confidence and generosity of spirit are in order. China has people, exports, foreign exchange reserves, and enormous potential; it is the only country capable of challenging the United States. But the United States remains in the driver's seat in determining how the challenge will play out and what the final settlement might be.

Indeed, the more China grows, the more likely it is to develop its middle class and an appetite for institutional changes that will make it a more comfortable partner. Alistair Iain Johnston, a China watcher at Harvard, notes that according to opinion polls, China's middle class is already more internationalist than its poor.[17] And the longer the economic reform program continues, the clearer it becomes that China will have to loosen political control. There is already debate within the Communist Party about whether reform has gone too far.

The American interest is to make it impossible for China to turn back. It is not just an economic issue that the bigger and more open China is, the better the prospects for American and western companies to sell in its market. It is that a plural democratic China is more likely to be the stakeholder in the international system that we need it to be. For its part, China has an interest in carrying on with reform and peaceful progress and accepting the logic of where that takes it. These may be objective interests. History, however, is littered with examples of where the temptation not to follow objective interests leads.

Globalization: A Short History

With China's rise, globalization has entered a new phase. Companies, especially from Hong Kong and Taiwan, flock to China, attracted by low wages. Wages for skilled workers are never more than one-fourth of those in Europe and the United States, and on average are one-tenth;[18] wages for unskilled workers are one-thirtieth of those at home. China has a first-world infrastructure of ultramodern ports, highways, and cheap container ship transport, along with factory building costs up to 70 percent cheaper.[19] Also, through the Internet, telephones, and ever cheaper air travel, foreign companies have the capacity to keep in close touch with operations on the ground. The question whether to produce domestically or outsource production to China has become critical in multinationals' strategic planning. Outsourcing precludes the rise of a Chinese competitor (by capturing the same cost structure) and offers an advantage over a company's existing domestic rivals. These are powerful countervailing arguments: there are hidden costs to doing business in China, and advantages to producing close to home. But for manufacturing in well-established technologies with wage costs that are relatively high, China offers great attractions.

The Chinese market itself is an opportunity for western producers. Indeed China is still largely a final assembly exporter, with most of its plants owned and managed by foreigners, and so is still heavily dependent on imports. Nobody knows what the ultimate impact on jobs will be, although gain will almost certainly affect losses, but in both the United States and Britain politicians, unionists, and businesspeople are already predicting darkly that "China is coming," as if globalization is inevitable and the only trajectory is more and more global economic integration. But that is not the lesson of history. Over the course of 500 years, there has been more and more interpenetration of national economies; however, the process has not been linear. Periods of opening have been followed by partial or complete closure as societies have sought relief from competition, immigration, and social and cultural change. In periods of economic and social openness, nothing seems more inexorably natural than interdependence. The journalist and later Labour parliamentarian Norman Angell (who won the Nobel Peace Prize in 1933) made a famous prediction three years before World War I. In a book translated into eighteen languages—*The Great Illusion*—he argued that war would be self-defeating because countries were now so economically and financially interdependent. By contrast, in times of closure and depression, like the mid-1930s, nothing seems more obvious than loyalty to the national unit and the fragility of globalization. The British economist John Maynard Keynes, once a strong advocate of free trade, found himself praising a world of little trade, homespun production, and national rather than international systems of finance.[20] He could no more imagine today's globalization than Angell could imagine war. Both were wrong, as we may be.

The lesson is that globalization is and always has been vulnerable to setbacks. The American historian Harold James describes Europe's first embrace of globalization, arguing that the Reformation, the consequent religious wars, and the creation of nation-states in the seventeenth century were in part a reaction to the disruptive, inflationary impact of Latin American gold and silver, and of the profits from the Asian trade, on the settled societies of late medieval Europe. Martin Luther in 1524 railed against the effect of Indian silks on the culture and attitudes of solid, God-fearing Germans.[21] Although the trade in such luxury goods might have been small relative to European output, its economic and cultural impact was much greater. Venice, then Portugal, then the Netherlands and France were all beneficiaries of long-distance trade. British economic and political history is inexplicable without it. The institutions needed to foster such trade then interacted with the institutional creativity of the Enlightenment to give Europe a decisive advantage over China, which until then had been ahead scientifically and technologically. The result was the industrial revolution.

In the 1820s, a second phase of globalization began, based on the European factory system. This was an era of exchange of cheap manufactured goods produced within national economies for increasingly mass markets. Trade grew at between 3 and 4 percent annually for nearly a century, until 1914—a sustained upward growth that was unprecedented. The architecture and rules of the game were created by the hegemonic power Britain, which insisted on free trade throughout its formal and informal empire, instituted with most of Europe through bilateral trade treaties. Sterling and the gold standard held sway. During this period China's backwardness and insularity became painfully evident. China lacked the institutional and technological wherewithal to participate on anything other than unequal terms.

For all the growth in trade, the years just before 1914 brought increasing strains. The gold standard operated by imposing periods of austerity and growth on economies as gold stocks flourished or shrank. Unemployment jumped violently: these were massive movement of people between countries and even continents. Between 1871 and 1915, 36 million people left Europe for the Americas, Africa, and Australasia.[22] Europe and North America both witnessed powerful reactions against social distress, and Europe saw the birth of socialist parties and eventually communism. Between 1914 and 1950 the global system simply broke down. There was neither the international architecture nor the internal domestic social consensus on which the prewar system had depended, and the world retreated from globalization.

Britain was too weak and the United States too reluctant and inward-looking to enforce rules of the game and sustain a common economic, trading, and financial architecture—and no other country was powerful enough to do this in their stead. In Europe, tariffs on manufactures had been rising ominously toward 20 percent before World War I, except in Britain (which espoused free trade). In the United States, tariffs were over 40 percent. After 1914 tariffs rose again everywhere as countries tried to protect themselves from unemployment, economic slowdown, and social protest.[23] The growth of trade shrank to the lowest level ever recorded, either before or since.[24] Countries retreated into their national economic citadels; exchange and capital controls were imposed. It was an era of depression, war, and a clash between communism and fascism—which in China manifested itself as the communist revolution.

Then, starting in 1950, a third phase of openness began. The leading developed countries were determined to establish a global financial and trade architecture; and at home a commitment to social welfare and full employment helped to construct a more stable social order that could alleviate the pain of adjusting to international competition. The United States instituted and maintained an architecture of trade openness with the dollar as the world's reserve currency and medium of exchange. Tariffs on manufactured imports fell to an average of less than 4 percent. The result was that trade ballooned, achieving an astonishing 8 percent growth rate in the golden years from 1950 to 1973 and subsequently an impressive 5 percent.[25] Multina-

tional companies, with Americans in the vanguard, began multi-
sourcing their production and distribution within a small but growing pool of developed countries; foreign direct investment exploded.

Since the mid-1990s this type of globalization has become even
more vigorous and ambitious. In a sense, it is "true" globalization.
Multinationals have outsourced more production in selected low-
wage developing countries, thereby producing a surge of exports
based on a dramatic cheapening of the price of manufactured goods.
There has been a phenomenal buildup of assets held overseas together with international capital movements amounting to $250 tril-
lion a year—five times world output. Two trends have come together.
The first is the arrival of new information and communication technologies that have reached a tipping point in the intensity, sophistication, cheapness, and scope of exchange of goods, services, money,
and ideas. The second is that these cross-border technologies have
emerged just as the borders themselves have come down. Low average
tariffs are now extending into the less developed countries, as exchange controls melt away.

Crucially, huge countries that were formerly closed have entered
the world system. China has redefined communism to indulge markets and trade; India has decided that openness is a better development strategy than protection; the former Soviet Union repudiated
communism and its former satellites in Eastern Europe joined the
EU. There is a new sense of security among multinationals in the
north and the south alike that they could and should take advantage
of low wages, low transport and communication costs, and low tariffs. A successful commercial strategy now necessitates developing
global capacities, a global reputation, and global brands.

This last phase of true globalization is one in which China, by
virtue of its size and its readiness to be open, has taken a principal role
in intensifying and structuring new interdependencies. During the
Cultural Revolution and the Vietnam war, a growing number of the
Chinese communist elite, including Deng Xiaoping, observed how
China's Asian neighbors were profiting from globalization. Deng's

willingness to champion reform in part originated in a determination to follow the route of the Asian tigers. He has been proved right

But one danger is that the increasing presence of China, along with India, Brazil, and Russia, will destabilize the global system. We could see a rerun of the period leading up to 1914, with internal social strains and a fragmentation of the global architecture. Germany's rise in Europe and the rise of the United States in the world economy between 1870 and 1914 led to tension in Europe and the North Atlantic that in turn led to war and depression. The world system led by Britain was not sustainable; there was no intellectual or political imperative for countries to stay open and keep the peace, given the internal tension that was mounting as a result of rapid industrialization and urbanization—and of German national ambition.

Suppose that China is today's Germany, on a collision course with Asia's top regional power, Japan. Then, does the United States, any more than Britain in 1914, have the economic power, or the political and intellectual conviction, to sustain the present order? Can countries continue to maintain openness and internal stability? Globalization may, historically, advance or retreat. The possibility of another retreat, unless the United States, Europe, Japan, and China are mindful of the dangers, is all too obvious.

The China Effect

The growth of exports from China, always impressive, has recently become startling. For more than fifteen years exports have grown at more than 20 percent a year, with the rate of growth accelerating since China joined the World Trade Organization in 2001. Over the last twenty-five years Chinese exports and imports have each grown from 1 percent of the world's total to more than 6 percent. Not only has China grown very rapidly; it has been exceptionally open to the world. In 1980 the share of trade in China's GDP (exports plus imports) was 15 percent; in 2005 it will exceed 70 percent. The United

States is the only continental economy ever to have matched China's growth,[26] as noted earlier, and it was not as open to trade as China.

The flood of manufactured exports, at what western consumers regard as unnaturally low prices, has been largely directed at the United States, which takes around 40 percent of the total. I have already mentioned the benefit to American consumers, but Europe and Japan have also profited. Another way of looking at this trend is to see how China has lowered the global inflation rate. Dresdner Kleinwort Wasserstein, a major German investment bank, calculates that American inflation over the last few years is 1 percent lower as a result of the competition from China. The U.S. Federal Reserve agrees that China is driving inflation down.[27]

The resulting cheap money has contributed to a housing boom in both Britain and the United States. The Federal Reserve and the Bank of England have been able to keep interest rates much lower than could have been expected, given the growth of credit, because the world prices of manufactured goods have been falling and the growth of wages has been so low. In Britain, the United States, Canada, and Australia, home owners have benefited as the price of housing has soared in response to low interest rates. The deregulated financial systems in these countries are particularly aggressive in marketing money—and home owners are borrowing it widely. Consumers have borrowed against the increase in equity in their homes and spent the cash, reducing savings in both countries to ever-lower levels. The continual rise in consumption has spawned shopping malls, restaurants, and whole new industries that rely on buoyant personal spending; all this in turn has generated new jobs; and the new jobs in turn have made people confident that they can borrow more. The process has kept the economic wheel spinning.

Nor is that all. The mushrooming of the United States' trade deficit has happened at the same time as dollars have poured out of the country to be invested in factories all over Asia and financial assets everywhere while the government has been paying for Iraq and Afghanistan on top of its already vast and growing network of U.S.

military bases and fleets.[28] The U.S. current account has soared to 7 percent of GDP—a record. In more normal times you might expect some weakness in the dollar, and some upward movement in American interest rates as a result.

But no: another aspect of the "China effect" is China's readiness to hold the surpluses it earns from its export trade in dollars rather than sell them back into its own currency, the renminbi. Indeed it is so concerned to maintain the renminbi at a stable rate against the dollar, to promote exports abroad and social stability at home, that it will offer trillions of renminbi to stop it from rising. This has been doubly important since the People's Bank of China, under intense pressure from the United States, adjusted the currency upward by 2 percent in July 2005 (after holding the same rate for more than a decade). The People's Bank may countenance further rises in its new phase of managed floating—whetting the appetite of international financiers for Chinese currency. China's purchases of bonds and bills mean that the price of bonds has risen and their yields have fallen despite the mountainous domestic and overseas debts of the United States (whose international debts now exceed $3 trillion). The low yields on bonds reinforce the trend for money to stay cheap, helping to keep the boom going. The counterpart, of course, is the $1 trillion of China's foreign exchange reserves.

China is also blamed for downward wage pressures in the United States. Median wages in the United States have grown only slowly for a generation; and the argument is that with 760 million potential new Chinese workers joining the global labor market, the impact on the American and European pattern of employment and wage rates will become even stronger.[29] In 2003 China also produced 700,000 science graduates compared with 60,000 in the United States, so it is easy to make the situation seem very alarming. However, despite all the rhetoric, the statistics so far indicate only a tiny effect (see Chapter 11). The more reliable impact may have been to make workforces more fearful and accommodating, anticipating the arrival of China's

hordes; also, examples of successful outsourcing are being exaggerated to terrify workers into accepting lower wages. The rhetorical deployment of China to subdue wage inflation is at this stage more
important than any direct effect.

Still, China is having direct as well as indirect effects on our lives.
The prices we pay for goods, housing, and oil are being shaped by the
big new kid on the economic block. The soaring price of gasoline,
with little immediate prospect of any significant fall, is inexplicable
without the rise in demand from China, now the world's second
largest oil importer. And in 2003 and 2004 Chinese buying drove
world commodity prices to record highs.

China has given new force to the arguments environmentalists
have been making for decades. Debates over how soon oil production
will peak[30] have become more urgent, as has the imminent exhaustion
of copper and zinc reserves, predicted by industry analysts within
fourteen and eleven years respectively.[31] If China continues growing at
the same rate, it will start to press against the limits of some world resources within the next decade. Moreover, its growth is having an impact on the Chinese environment. China is extraordinarily wasteful of
energy. To generate every $1 of GDP, China uses three times more en-
ergy than the global average, four times more than the United States,
and 8 times more than Japan.[32] Pollution is endemic; 400,000 Chinese
die prematurely every year from air pollution. And in addition, China
is chronically short of water.

China is also beginning to flex its muscle as an Asian power. Americans—and Europeans in the peaceful comfort of their EU—have little idea of how edgy and raw relationships are between China and the
surrounding states, or how nationalistic and warlike rhetoric and
sometimes actions can become. China readily entered the Korean
War in 1950; fought India in a bloody border war in 1962; invaded
Vietnam in 1978, with a loss of 50,000 men; and has had skirmishes
with the Russians. Borders are contested; ownership of islands in the
East and South China Sea is not accepted; and old wounds from

World War II and even earlier are unhealed. Asia knows that China wants Taiwan back. The region frequently sounds and feels more like pre-1914 Europe than part of twenty-first century globalization.

For example, in February 2005 Japan formally took possession of the Senkaku Islands, whose control is the key to claiming sovereignty over vast offshore oil and gas reserves. In April 2005 China sent an official warning to Tokyo to withdraw or "take full responsibility" for any consequences. It was the kind of ultimatum a great power might have issued during the nineteenth century. Japan's defense ministry drew up contingency plans to deploy 55,000 troops if China invaded the islands. In September 2005 five Chinese naval ships, including a guided-missile destroyer, were found near the Chunxiao gas field in the East China Sea. Eventually, both sides drew back; but this kind of brinkmanship over a territorial dispute is now almost unknown in the rest of the developed world. The *People's Daily* has declared that the competition for oil resources in the East China Sea is just "the prelude of the game between China and Japan over international energy"[33]

China feels ideologically isolated, encircled by enemies and rivals. These are also challenges at home, even if they are currently submerged. In 1989 China was rocked to its foundations by a coalition of workers, students, and intellectuals like the one that brought down communism in eastern Europe and Russia. The same causes for complaint exist today, arguably with even more force; and a repeat of Tiananmen today might succeed. That is an ever-present fear of China's communist leadership. To understand today's China, we must first understand Tiananmen and its legacy.

The Internal Bargain

Tiananmen was China's own attempted perestroika and "velvet revolution" rolled into one. Not only did the protests convulse Beijing for six weeks in 1989; there were demonstrations in 181 cities, including all the provincial capitals, the major cities, and special economic zones.³⁴ Nearly every city with a university experienced some kind of public march.³⁵ Official records indicate that students from 319 Chinese universities were represented in Tiananmen Square.³⁶ The party itself was divided over how to respond, as was the army; 150 officers openly declared that they would not fire on demonstrators after martial law was declared, and at least a third of the central committee wanted to reach a compromise with the protesters.

At the beginning of the 1980s, China—inspired by Deng—was much more intellectually free and easy than it is today. Political reform and economic reform were more obviously proceeding hand in hand. But there were problems. In 1986–1987 inflation had been rising sharply, and the growth in general living standards had halted, in stark contrast to the extravagant lifestyles of party officials. Corruption was rampant.

In the spring of 1989 a group of students at Beijing University, impressed by the events unfolding in eastern Europe and by Gorbachev's reforms in the Soviet Union, began to wonder if they dared engage in public street protests. The movement was an uneasy, incoherent coalition.³⁷ It included party members from the reformist wing who wanted the pace of reform to be matched by a commitment to social justice; it also included those who wanted to accelerate privatization and market liberalization as well as those who wanted western-style democracy and were agitating for a thoroughgoing change in the regime. The only common ground was a fierce hatred of corruption. Tragically, this was not enough, in the first phase of protests, to let the protesters find an effective common line in their negotiations with the compromisers among the party leaders.

An initial daring march by a motley group of students on the morning of April 27, 1989, with banners proclaiming *"Vive la liberté,"* was not opposed by police gunfire; it spontaneously swelled into a street march of more than 500,000 people that lasted all day. For the next six weeks more than 1 million people manned barricades and blockades, effectively occupying central Beijing. They made their headquarters Tiananmen Square, the vast square outside the Forbidden City that is the public heart of China. Alongside a makeshift statue of the goddess of democracy, the newly formed Beijing Workers Autonomous Federation set up a tent and began to recruit and mobilize workers, copying Solidarity in Poland.

Deng and the party elders—the so-called eight immortals, veterans of the revolution—were furious. They were unafraid to shed blood if necessary to repress what they deemed a counterrevolutionary rebellion. However, the party's general secretary, Zhao Ziyang, the reformer whom Deng had elevated first to the presidency in 1980 and then to the general secretaryship of the party in 1987, was opposed. He wanted compromise, proposing a partial meeting of demands for reform rather than systematic change, and the avoidance at all costs of bloodshed.[38] He had publicly insisted in early May that the "just demands of the students be met" and encouraged extensive news coverage of the events to bolster his position, which he allowed to be understood as a challenge to Deng.[39] As a result the protests grew.

Alarmed at the scale of the demonstrations, the elders finally acted. Zhao lost the argument, his job, and his official reputation; he remained under house arrest until his death in 2005. Martial law was imposed on May 19, and a fortnight later the tanks rolled into Tiananmen Square. However, Deng had to leave Beijing to ensure that army groups 28 and 29, personally loyal to him, would provide the core of the force rather than the uncertain army groups based around the capital. It was a bloody and murderous engagement. The General Office of the State Council reported to the Committee of Elders afterward that 5,000 soldiers and police officers and 2,000 civilians were wounded in the action. Of the 443 dead, 223 were soldiers and police officers, thirty-six were university students, and the rest were ordinary Chinese citizens.[40] At least as many were arrested and disappeared into the Chinese prison system. In sharp contrast to what was to happen in the Soviet Union, the party had reasserted its authority, but at a terrible long-term cost. The image of the anonymous student single-handedly stopping a tank is one of the most arresting of the twentieth century.

The scale of the international response shook the leaders, although privately they congratulated themselves on having shown their willingness to act, irrespective of the views of foreigners. Negotiations over membership in the General Agreement on Tariffs and Trade (GATT, a forerunner of the World Trade Organization), which had begun two years earlier, were immediately suspended; and a European arms embargo was imposed, joining the American embargo, that has continued to today. The pace of inward investment from foreign companies leveled off, and investors were persuaded to return only by being given generous tax concessions that continue to distort and weaken the government's fiscal position.

Equally serious was the crisis of legitimacy at home. The citizens that the party had killed were not just any citizens. Young students have for millennia had a special place in Chinese life as the generation training for China's greater good, and Beijing University is the country's elite institution. The rhetoric applied to defend the suppression—that the event was a "counterrevolutionary riot"—was so obviously a self-serving misdescription of reality that the official language of communism lost any vestigial respect. To call for an official reassessment of Tiananmen has become the most potent and politically challenging declaration in China.

The Communist Party leadership and its 70 million members know that they might not survive another Tiananmen. There would be no committee of elders with revolutionary credentials who could command the loyalty of the military or the personal loyalty of some army groups. The divisions that incapacitated the protesters of 1989 would be unlikely to be repeated; there would be more willingness to campaign for systemwide change as the only way to stem corruption and establish the rule of law. Also, repression imposed as in 1989 would today incur even more international opprobrium; and given China's integration into the world economy, such reaction would make China more vulnerable. The argument for democracy is more strongly entrenched internationally, despite its association with Bush's foreign policy. More states have converted to democracy since 1989, and resisting it seems retrograde.

There is no possibility of an ideological renewal, a "back to basics" reassertion of core communist values such as a modified Cultural Revolution. When that was tried in the mid-1960s, communism was still a live ideology at home and abroad—and even then it failed. The party has now acknowledged that the class war is over, but it finds itself in a catch-22. It resists elections because they would expose it to political competition; but without elections there are no channels except protest through which to express dissent and anger. China's communists confront the same conundrum as the old Confucian emperors. Legitimacy depends completely on continued economic success and urgent appeals to nationalism.

Yet the gap between the booming cities and depressed rural areas grows ever wider. There is a stark contrast between Shanghai, where adjusted per capita income exceeds $15,000 and provides almost first-world living standards, and poverty-stricken Guizhou province in the rural west, with a per capita income of $1,247.[41] Roughly half of China's people, mainly in the rural west, live on comparably low incomes. Income gradually rises toward the coast, but even within the rich coastal cities and provinces there is phenomenal inequality between the migrant workers and the richer middle classes. Eight of China's thirty-one provinces, which comprise 40 percent of its population, have provided almost three-quarters of China's growth since 2000. The UN World Development Report ranks China, with its formal communist commitment to equality, as more unequal than both the United States and Britain.[42]

Regarding employment, the best estimate is that to stave off a potential avalanche of dissent and protest, China has to create 24 million new jobs a year for migrants leaving the countryside, for students leaving schools and colleges, and for people left newly unemployed by the rationalizing of state-owned enterprises.[43] Yet employment is growing by only slightly more than 1 percent a year. Open and disguised unemployment, according to some estimates, is as high as 170 million, or 23 percent of the labor force.[44]

Another problem is corruption. A leading Chinese economist and intellectual, Hu Angang, who has an edgy relationship with the Chinese leadership because of his outspokenness, calculates that in the late 1990s corruption resulted in an economic loss to China of 13.3 to 16.9 percent of GDP.[45]

The number of public protests demanding social justice—especially protests against unfair compensation for compulsory land purchases—has increased significantly. According to official Chinese sources, the numbers involved in public protests increased from 740,000 in 1994 to 3.7 million in 2004. Strikes have risen as well: from 1,909 in 1994 to 22,600 in 2003, with the numbers involved jumping from 77,704 to approximately 800,000. Even the larger numbers are, of course, a small proportion of the total population (1.3 billion). But given the bravery it takes to dissent in an authoritarian state, the fact that some 4 million protesters and 1 million strikers have run the risk is testimony to the growing strength of feeling. The Ministry of Labor and Security has warned that the growing income gap is likely to make the system unstable by 2010 if no effective solutions are found.[46]

The debates within the party about whether to maintain the pace and structure of reform have become increasingly acute. The left has become more vocally critical; a proposed law to enshrine private property rights has been deferred for further consultation. Critics claimed it would undermine Chinese socialism: it was surnamed capitalist, not surnamed socialist.[47] Hu Jintao, China's president and general secretary of the party, has cracked down on the Internet and the media. He praises the communist parties of Cuba and North Korea and eulogizes Mao, using Maoist rhetoric about the danger of bourgeois liberalism in internal party speeches. The returning economic liberals educated at American and British universities are regarded with growing suspicion. Liu Guoguang, onetime reformer and member of the party's standing committee, now says that introducing western reforms into China was a mistake; Liu Guoguang societies are growing dramatically without party opposition. The party's priority is now "harmonious development," lowering inequality, giving rights to migrant workers, sustaining rural incomes, and trying to limit rural protests. Its mounting worry is that if ever the growth machine slows down, it will be in mortal trouble.

The Reckoning

For fifteen years China's economic growth has approached an average of nearly 10 percent a year. Its planners have penciled in a more modest growth rate of 7.5 percent for the eleventh five-year plan, which extends to 2010; but the reality is that the average growth rate the Chinese have become accustomed to must be maintained. China needs to maintain the highest growth rate possible more or less indefinitely if it is to prop up the Communist Party.

This is not possible with the current economic structure. The model that has taken China thus far will have to be transformed, because it cannot withstand the strain of a near tripling of the economy's current size over the next fifteen years. If the current structure of growth continues, by 2020 Chinese exports would constitute nearly $5 trillion, or about 100 percent of its then GDP—and approaching half the likely merchandise exports of the world at that time. But China's export growth has been driven mainly by non-Chinese companies. To reach this total we have to suppose that there are sufficient non-Chinese companies with the capacity to transfer production on such a scale to China, and that western markets have the capacity to absorb such enormous flows of imports. Already 80 percent of American toy imports come from China. So far some 400 of the Fortune 500 in the United States and a comparable proportion of European and Japanese producers have invested in China; in other words, most of those who could move production to China have already done so.[48] Growth projections that extrapolate current trends have to suppose that over the next fifteen years western multinationals in China are going to be able to continue increasing Chinese production and exports at six or seven times the rate of growth of their domestic markets.

This is both a mathematical and an economic impossibility. The law of large numbers is going to apply. To achieve the target, China will have to start exporting under its own steam, with its own companies, its own technology, its own new product lines, and its own brands. But that is equally impossible. At the time of writing, there are no Chinese brands in the world's top 100; and so far only three Chinese companies, all very small—Huawei, TCL, and Lenovo—can be called genuine multinationals. In short, sometime in the next decade export growth from China is necessarily going to subside to more normal levels.

Thus China must be pulled along more by domestic consumption; it must allow investment in its infrastructure to decline relatively, develop indigenous Chinese enterprise, and begin to revolutionize its approach to the use of resources. These are iron laws of economics and, increasingly, of nature. But here is the rub. Chinese enterprise under the current rules has so far shown itself incapable of meeting such challenges. China has developed neither a viable concept of the company nor the institutional network to support it. The vast majority of its state-owned enterprises still have political rather than business priorities; and its plethora of quasigovernmental, local government, and cooperative organizations do not have the balance sheets, the culture, or the organizational capacity to produce at such a scale. Meanwhile its small companies tend to be built around families and kinship relationships (*guanxi*) or to depend so much on corrupt links with officials that they cannot produce on any scale. Many are extraordinarily short-lived. One sign of weakness is that since the mid-1990s each additional increment of capital investment has been producing declining returns.[49] The incentives in the system are soft options, quick returns, and corrupt profits. The party interest trumps building a business.

In comparison with where China started nearly thirty years ago, reform has been extraordinary. It has introduced the "hard" processes of a market economy—free movement of prices, wages, and rents; permitting limited ownership of private property; and recognizing the fundamental role of profit—and it has been open to overseas investors. It has built up state capacity and now possesses the machinery of modern government. It has lowered tariffs and become a genuinely more open economy adhering to the rules of WTO.

But it is not to diminish what has been achieved to argue that it has been comparatively easy compared with what now lies ahead. The party has to recognize that an essential adjunct of capitalism is a morality as vigorous in its own terms as that associated with communism, and certainly more effective. Building a great company is not just a matter of assembling workers, capital, and land and selling the product or service for profit in a market. Long-term success involves the construction of a common culture and shared purpose, which in turn depend upon the establishment of an overriding business aim and organizational reason for existence that binds the company together and relates it to its market and customers. In this respect successful capitalism has a moral dimension.

China has almost no enterprises, no critical mass of executives, and no business tradition that understands this moral facet of capitalism. The "soft" institutions of capitalism are as integral to growth and sustainability as the "hard" processes. If China wants to triple the size of its economy over the next generation, it has no option but to develop them.

The reforms so far proposed in the eleventh five-year plan and under consideration—such as selling shares in the banks to foreigners and trying to professionalize the hopelessly compromised judiciary—are all steps in the right direction and were unthinkable just twenty years ago. But they are piecemeal and reactive. The pace of institutional change must accelerate, and a genuine Chinese enterprise culture must develop; otherwise, some shock will force a sharp deceleration in the growth rate. That shock could be a prolonged water shortage, a further increase in the price of oil, or unilateral tariff increases by the United States against Chinese exports. A relapse into repression at home and nationalism abroad would be likely to follow.

What the West Must Do

Because China must change, it will. The question is what constitutional and political spasms it may experience, and what their internal and global impact might be. Given the inevitability of the outcome, it would be rational to get there peacefully with as few hiccups and alarums as possible. Just as China will need to invent a soft institutional infrastructure, the global institutional architecture—the IMF and WTO—must be reformed. The approaching energy crisis as oil production peaks must bring an international response.

Domestic changes in the west will be required as well. Eventually, the communist leadership will have to accept that China must become a pluralist, representative democracy; similarly, the west will have to accept a major reorganization of its own economic and social structures to accommodate China, and the implications of the international division of labor. The United States and Europe are going to rely increasingly on China and Asia for commodity manufactures and commodity services, and on the rest of the world for food and raw materials.

What this means for the west is an intensified version of its past—a future built not just on science and technology but on knowledge in its widest sense, as everything from the creative and cultural industries to financial services and revolutions in energy. So it should be. The west took a lead over China with a combination of scientific, technological, and institutional prowess; now it has to reassert these skills in order to maintain its place in the global economic order.

However, Western economies will not be able to keep their side of the new global bargain if their own "soft" institutions are not appropriate. In this respect there is nearly as much cause for concern as with China's institutions. The west in general and the United States in particular are failing. The United States needs an economic rebalancing to mirror China's, one that involves spending less, investing more, and boosting exports. Above all it must resist the temptation to close itself to China. The consequences for American living standards and for the implosion of the world trading system that would follow would be awfully self-defeating.

The American economy has always been characterized by tension between its soft institutional infrastructure and the hard processes of its tough market-oriented capitalism—but now the soft infrastructure is weakening. If China needs a free press; corporate accountability; a duty to care for its workforce; intelligent, responsive government; proper concern for equality; and an impartial judicial system, then so does the United States. But the United States' Enlightenment legacy is fraying. The American political system is increasingly compromised by inequality, gerrymandering, and the erosion of the public interest. It is becoming less responsive to public needs. Its media more and more fail in the duty to speak truth to power. American companies and financiers, scrambling for self-enrichment, increasingly deny that they have a duty to care for their workforce. America's social bargain, which promotes social mobility and education in exchange for the acceptance of inequality, has been allowed to decay. And the lack of respect for international law in the response to Islamic terror has been appalling.

This makes achieving the western side of a new bargain much harder. Maybe the world will have to go through spasms or setbacks first. We of course hope not. But to understand how the west might respond, we first have to understand more about China and the character of any potential challenge it might mount. And to do that we have to start with understanding how China, its government, and its culture first began. Which takes us to 1030 BCE.

CHAPTER 2

Pride and Fall

UNDERSTANDING CHINA HAS ALWAYS BEEN A STRUGGLE for the west. Nineteenth-century western critics of China's backwardness and its peasants' poverty were counterbalanced by admirers of its civilization, the quality of its Confucian government, and its astounding advances in science and technology long before Europe achieved them. Now comes a new riddle to superimpose on the old debate. The current western consensus is that political liberty and capitalist success go hand in hand—but here is a communist authoritarian government presiding over an economic success story. Moreover, the Chinese Communist Party was largely shaped by a murderous monster, Mao Zedong. What happened to put a China, long outrun by the west, back into the race?

China's rise, stagnation, fall, and subsequent rise, along with its potential sustainability, constitute a puzzle that is becoming one of the most important to solve. It is made more difficult still by a long tradition of western theorists only too willing to see their own prejudices confirmed by what they imagine to be the Chinese experience. Thus Marx, in the nineteenth century, had to dismiss China as the creature of backward orientalism, in order for his theory to hold. "A rotting semi-civilisation, vegetating in the teeth of time" defined the first, most primitive Asian mode of production, which had not even reached the ancient, let alone the feudal, level of development that was the basis for European Capitalism dynamism and the creation of an industrial proletariat.[1] This framework could hardly explain how China's iron production exceeded Europe's as late as 1750, or how China's agricultural yields had exploded from the eighth to the thirteenth century, when European peasant agriculture languished. It also neglected the problematic truth that Chinese feudalism had mainly disappeared by the fifth century CE.

The German sociologist Max Weber criticized the Chinese for "incomparable dishonesty," "absolute docility," and "distrust for one another," which, together with their lack of the Protestant incentive of a virtuous afterlife earned by saving and hard work, condemned China to economic backwardness.[2] This analysis too was hardly useful in explaining how China had gotten so far ahead of Europe only, later, to fall back. Weber needed to explain how the Chinese had become more docile, dishonest, and distrustful over the nineteenth century. He could not.

More recently American economists, historians, and sociologists have had a similar proclivity to look at China through the ideological prism of conservatism—usually some combination of American exceptionalism and an insistence that because markets and property rights are the route to economic success, a lack of success necessarily means that they did not or could not have existed. The Nobel laureate Douglass North, for example, has stressed the weakness of the system of Chinese property rights, permanently at the discretion of the emperor, as the chief cause of China's backwardness.[3] But as early as the third century BCE China had entrenched, diffused private property rights, which in many ways were better-developed and more sophisticated than either Europe's or America's. Today, for example, an embedded culture of private property and a sense of legal entitlement are provoking protests against the Communist Party when proper compensation is not offered for the compulsory acquisition of peasants' land. North is a pioneer in stressing the importance of institutions to development, but he overemphasizes China's lack of property rights and thus oversimplifies the deficiencies of its institutional structure.

On the other hand, there is a western tradition that is too much in awe of what it sees in China. Marco Polo, the Venetian explorer, arrived there in the thirteenth century and marveled at the skills involved in silk and ceramic manufacture, and at the sophistication of the government. It did not occur to him that no Chinese explorer had spent decades in Venice, although the Venetians' leadership of medieval Europe was no less intriguing. Voltaire, 500 years later, celebrated the disinterested intelligence of the secular Confucian government and its success in creating such an advanced civilization just as, unbeknownst to him, China's Confucian system was being overtaken by a dynamic Europe.

More recently, there is the British economic historian Joseph Needham, whose twenty-eight-volume masterwork, *Science and Civilisation*, details how the Chinese were ahead of Europe in almost every significant invention—the compass, the clock, gunpowder, and the printing press. Needham argued that only China's commitment to harmony and cooperation, contrasted with Europe's addiction to bloody conquest and capitalist acquisition, had prevented China from reproducing Europe's economic success.[4] This thesis ignores the fact that China doubled its land area by conquest under the Qing in the eighteenth century, one of the great imperial landgrabs in history,[5] and Needham fails to explain its sudden conversion to capitalist-style growth today. China remains an elusive intellectual quarry.

Yet it does seem clear that by the early 1800s China constituted 33 percent of the world's GDP, according to the economic historian Angus Maddison,[6] before plunging to around 5 percent in 1950. China had created a political and social system that successfully governed a land area equivalent to Europe or the United States, offering a continentwide order in which the peasant—the key actor in preindustrial China and Europe—was genuinely more prosperous and peaceful, aided by scientific and technological advance that was ahead of Europe's. By preindustrial standards, China had provided the good life to one-fifth of the world's population for the best part of 2,000 years. But throughout the nineteenth century it became more and more dysfunctional; and by the early twentieth century the Chinese system was obviously the principal obstacle to economic and political modernization. To understand today's China we need to understand how and why imperial China succeeded and failed—and how it illuminates economic development in the past and present.

The Chinese Achievement

Imperial China, with antecedents stretching back to the Zhou dynasty 1,030 years before the birth of Christ, lasted from 136 BCE with the first emperor of all China, Qin Shihuang, until the collapse of the Qing dynasty in 1911—one of the world's most extraordinary achievements. Geography, nature, and relative ethnic homogeneity all made the establishment of a common governmental system across a continent immeasurably easier. Nature had been kind. The soil was fertile, rainfall was plentiful, much of the country enjoys a temperate or subtropical climate, rivers are extensive, and crop yields are good. Farming came naturally.

The purpose and basis of the Chinese imperial system was cultivation of the land, raised to the standing of what the historian Kent Deng describes as a "cult of agriculture."[7] As early as 2800 BCE the worship of the land god Shennong was well established, as was *xiangtu,* the idea that establishing a home required the possession of cultivatable land. In contrast to the western antecedents of the word "society," the ancient Chinese word *sheji* has its roots in the veneration of agriculture. *She* means land or earth god, and *ji* refers to millet. Society is based on the land and what land produces. But the Latin word *societas* indicates human relationships, and the western notion of society has to do with citizenship, situated in aggregations of people in cities rather than the isolated countryside. Even as late as the 1780s, only 6 percent of China's then 290 million people lived in cities.[8]

The genius and durability of the imperial system lay in the triangular relationship between the landowning small-scale farming family; the imperial order that protected it, drawing income from rural prosperity; and the Confucian mandarinate who attempted to govern fairly and objectively to boost agricultural production. The English economic and social historian Richard Tawney observed that "the typical figure in Chinese country life is not hired labour, but the landholding peasant."[9] Thomas Rawski comments, "For at least the last millennium, Chinese agriculture has been dominated by a large number of free, small-scale farmers, working under a system of private land-ownership."

By the eighteenth century as much as 92 percent of registered land was privately owned. Among the property owners, smallholders were the majority, with an average farm size of 1.7 acres.[10] European-style feudalism, in terms of land ownership, existed in China, but it was always on the defensive and finally disappeared on any large scale during the Qin dynasty (221–207 BCE). European feudalism would last until the fourteenth century, but the Chinese had left this system behind more than 1,000 years earlier.

The task of successive emperors was to support the fecundity of the venerated land and the incomes of those who owned and cultivated it, and to ensure that the population at large did not starve. And this they did with imagination and energy. By the 1500s China had an unparalleled transport infrastructure of twenty-eight national highways and fifty-three provincial main roads intersecting with a dense system of canals and navigable rivers—the cumulative result of 2,000 years of investment.[11] Private land ownership had been enshrined by Shang Yang (390–338 BCE), an adviser to the Qin dynasty who created a land registry to establish property titles more than 2,000 years before the Declaration of Independence. It proved a masterstroke, motivating peasants to boost production and so equipping the Qin with plentiful food and well-fed armies, thus laying the basis of their dynastic success.

Li Kui, more than 400 years before the birth of Christ, initiated what was to develop into a national system of granaries that stored more than a six months' supply of grain, with minimum prices to guarantee farm incomes and a capacity to buy surpluses for future famine years—a combination of the EU's common agricultural policy and the United States' farm support system. Low-interest loans were available to farmers. In irrigation, famine relief, improved seed types, and farming techniques the Chinese were ahead of Europe by hundreds of years. Needham shows that by the end of the twelfth century the Chinese had invented the compass and sternpost rudder, and by the end of the fourteenth century gunpowder and the mechanical clock—inventions that Europe copied. Taxes were kept low, never more than 10 percent of GDP,[12] largely because there was so little war. Chinese emperors can be seen as archetypal political pragmatists, combining a Republican approach to taxes with a Democrat approach to public improvement.

And for a long time it worked. What Shang Yang had proposed in recognizing title to property was no more than following reality. Peasant families cultivated the land of the forebears they worshipped, developing a virtually unchallengeable sense of entitlement. Their right to farm originated in the legitimacy of their ancestors' first claim and the continuation of the farming tradition. They did not have the feudal European notion that the monarch was charged by God to hold land, thus justifying his absolute rights over it. In China imperial authority might be associated with heavenly purpose, but that conferred no rights over land. Rights came from one's ancestors.

Patterns of land ownership became increasingly sophisticated.[13] Renting, for example, had been supplemented in the early Song period (around 1000 CE) by a system of leasing, which went beyond topsoil cultivation to leases for the exploitation of minerals or for access to water—each right creating its own lively market. Not only could a sublease be bought and sold, but so could any mortgage attached to it. Thus the world's first secondary mortgage market emerged more than 1,000 years ago—infinitely better developed than any comparable financial instrument in Europe.

The system was certainly effective. Although China has less cultivatable land than Europe, and a denser population, agricultural productivity was significantly higher. Historic data on nutrition and daily caloric intake are notoriously difficult to assemble; but Kenneth

Pomeranz—a professor of history at the University of California whose pathbreaking book *The Great Divergence* made him the cowinner of the World History Association Book Prize in 2001—estimates that the average Chinese, at least until the 1800s, was as least as well-fed as his or her European counterpart. We also know that from the Tang period to the Ming period—between 618 and 1644—total grain output averaged about 15 million tons a year, almost twice as much as was needed for subsistence consumption. Not only did the Chinese have a well-established system of property rights and a market in those rights, they also produced a great deal more food per acre. Seven percent of the world's cultivatable land fed between one-fifth and one-quarter of the world's population.

Confucianism in Theory and Practice

All this required predictability and order, provided by the third and most critical leg of the Chinese system—the mandarin official class of Confucian scholars who administered China. The starting point of Confucianism is that the heavenly purpose (*tian*), independent of any particular monarch, is to ensure the well-being of the people (*minben*). The task of the Confucian scholar-official is to interpret in government the day-to-day means of achieving the Confucian goal of perfect harmony (*dao*) and hold the emperor accountable for his decisions. Nothing can be more sacred than the promotion of human well-being: those who are entrusted with governing have to be moral and seek to construct harmony, cooperation, and order all around them. There developed an elaborate etiquette of interpersonal behavior and conduct that was meant to signify adherence to this commitment.

Crucial to the integrity of the governmental and administrative machine was the willingness of the emperor to accept and Confucian officials to offer criticism of his decisions. This was the system of re-monstration and admonition (*jianzheng*). It was taken very seriously and sometimes demanded extreme bravery from the officials concerned. Le Yun of the Northern and Southern dynasties and Hai Rui of the Ming dynasty both brought their coffins to court, recognizing that their challenge might end in their death.[14] In a system in which executive, legislature, and judiciary were one, *jianzheng* was a crucial counterbalance.

Another was the *huibi* system, or law of avoidance. Officials were assigned to provinces and cities other than their own in order to minimize the temptation to favor friends and family; also, it was forbidden for an official to buy land in his hometown. Moreover, there was a systematic rotation: officials were regularly moved on so that they would not be incorporated into local merchant and landlord networks and would not govern in a partisan or unfair way. The design of the system thus reinforced the overriding obligation of the Confucian official to behave with integrity and to administer and adjudicate objectively and impartially, both upward and downward. Among the Confucian virtues, the supreme virtue was *li:* the cultivated, intense self-discipline with which the aspirant scholar or official went about his daily business. But *li* was not meant to be achieved by too great a demonstration of hard work; it was meant to be effortless—a consequence of inner peace reached through inner discipline. The long nails, knotted hair, and elaborate gown of the Confucian gentleman—at once a teacher and exemplar of his creed—signaled that he was above manual labor. What counted was the propriety of his conduct and the scrupulousness of his judgments, in which he had considerable discretion. The essence of Confucian government was that it was executed by men embodying moral purpose rather than a system of impartial rules.

Confucius died in 479 BCE, after some years of wandering throughout China trying unsuccessfully to persuade its vying rulers and warlords to adopt the principles set out in his Analects. His disciple Mencius, who refined the Confucian system, had only marginally better luck 150 years later. It was not until 136 BCE that Confucianism became the official state ideology, offering emperors a source of legitimacy and a code of good government. The emperor could thus acquire an official and administrative class whose secular religion was to further the interests of millions of family smallholders justly and fairly in a spirit of community, harmony, and public-mindedness. The result was to boost their agricultural production, secure their land, and protect them from bullying neighbors, criminals, and arbitrary rule. As the farmer families prospered, so would the empire.

Confucianism was unable to modernize China in the nineteenth century—a criticism made by every shade of opinion from the Communist Party to western intellectuals—and it clung to its apparently otherworldly goals of harmony and virtue. All this has colored our understanding of its achievements. But in practice the economic importance of trade and industry were recognized, even if land ownership and becoming part of the rural gentry offered superior social status. Aspiring Confucian scholars chose to write essays on economic development;[15] once in office they built roads and canals and worked closely with merchants in developing business. The Confucian tradition was much more focused on development than its caricatures would suggest.

The efforts made to legitimize the Confucian bureaucracy were intense and impressive. Competitive written examinations were the key to entry. These were first established in the second century BCE, and they were open to all, even the lowliest peasant. In Europe the first comparable examinations began in 1702; in the United States such examinations began in 1883 and were opposed for some years as a Chinese import and therefore un-American.[16] By the time of the Northern Song dynasty (960–1127) the system had become as fair as possible. Examination papers were kept secret, locked in safe rooms; essays were read by at least two independent examiners only after they had been transcribed into identical calligraphy to avoid bias; examinees were body-searched to avoid cheating; and the emperor himself read the best papers. The penalties for abuse were severe and included death. In 1657 seven imperial examiners found guilty of irregularities were beheaded immediately, their private property was confiscated, and 109 of their close relatives were exiled. So that the bureaucracy would not become self-perpetuating, quotas were established to limit the entry of sons of serving officials.

The process achieved its objectives. As far as can be established the Chinese mandarinate drew its members from across Chinese society. One study found that 83 percent of those who came out on top in the intensely competitive exams—so-called champions—were from lower-class families, with the rest from the upper class, almost exactly mirroring China's social structure.[17] A study of successful applicants between 1015 and 1874 CE found that one village, Liukeng, a tiny backwater in the relatively underdeveloped Jiangxi province, supplied nearly 300 officials, some of whom became ministers and one became prime minister.[18] Far from being a closed caste, China's Confucian bureaucracy was organized as the world's first genuine meritocracy. It offered social mobility and legitimacy, and it kept officials close to the interests of the people—proof positive of the governmental concept of the "people as foundation." The Confucian official has sometimes been described as the embodiment of the impractical and the otherworldly, who achieved his status by committing the Confucian classical texts to memory and writing stylized "eight-legged" essays; the truth is more complex. The structure worked so well for so long because of these officials' dedication to the national cause, the public interest, and the well-being of the people. This vision of how a mandarinate should work was later presented by both Nationalist and communist leaders, even while they criticized it for being antimodern.

The system was an interdependent whole. The emperor relied on his prime minister, imperial secretariat, and liaison office, which in turn linked up to the provincial bureaucracies and magistracies that administered justice, collected taxes, and developed the economy. The family property holders looked to the imperial government to maintain their rights, secure their incomes, and keep order. There were built-in checks and balances. Young officials were the emperor's watchdogs, keeping an eye on the integrity of the older officials who in turn ran the system of remonstrance that kept an eye on the imperial bureaucracy, along with the censorate that inspected it.[19] Administration was relatively decentralized. Successive emperors understood their own place in the scheme of things. Emperor Taizong (627–649 CE) even wrote a book titled *The Norm for Monarchs* (*Difan*), which systematically instructed his descendants in how to behave and govern the country by Confucian standards—and warned them that if they did not they risked revolt and being deservedly deposed.[20]

The trouble was that despite all these efforts, and even the inevitable autonomy in the provinces of so large a continent, formal power lay at the center and Confucian internal checks and balances were an inadequate counterbalance to arbitrary and sometimes just plain bad government. Ominously for today's Communist Party, whose centralized rule by enlightened officials governing for the general good has obvious resonances with China's imperial past, the system was seriously weakened by its lack of institutions and processes that could have held power to account and represented interests and grievances. China's peasants responded in the only way they could; they engaged in periodic sustained and violent protests, so that China has a history of bottom-up rebellion unsurpassed anywhere else in the world.

Revolt came to be understood as a justified, almost legitimate, expression of dissent and anger. It was a kind of institutional cleansing, holding the imperial system to account but stopping short of revolution. The ruler might change, but not the system. The rebellions could be awesome, involving millions of peasants and lasting for decades; two lasted more than forty years, with enormous costs in deaths and loss of output. At least five Chinese imperial dynasties (Qin, Han, Sui, Yuan, and Ming) succumbed to these monumental protests.[21] There were many more provincial and regional rebellions. The structural difficulty was that despite good intentions and moral rhetoric, the network of landlords, officials, and Confucian scholars tended to harden into what became known as the gentry, pitiless and hardheaded in looking after its own interests by tax-farming and imposing the highest possible rents. Meanwhile, the imperial government was too distant to respond(heaven is high and emperor is far away [*tian guo, huangdi yuan*] in the words of an old Chinese aphorism). The salaries of Confucian mandarins were linked to middle-income peasants; and as officials were promoted their salaries fell—the assumption being that the more senior they became, the more they should demonstrate their morality. So they could keep pace with the incomes of the rich landlords and merchants only by tax-farming and accepting bribes.

By the end of the nineteenth century the system not only was challenged by the incursion of foreigners with obviously superior technology and superior financial, communication, and weapons systems but was also beginning to fail on its own terms. As the historian John Fairbank notes, during the Qing dynasty the actual income of a Confucian governor general was as much as 140 times his nominal salary, the difference having been earned by corruption.[22] One-third of China's peasant households were now tenants, most of them renting from a network of landlords who included slightly richer peasants and absentee merchants in far-off cities. It is estimated that at the end of the Qing dynasty (the late nineteenth century) as much as 25 percent of cultivatable land was owned by absentee landlords. As in previous periods of Chinese history resentment directed against the officials and landlords was building up to rebellion, just as Confucius, Mencius, and Emperor Taizong had warned. What was different when the Qing fell was that there was no dynasty in waiting; the imperial system was understood by the governing elite and the governed alike to have reached its end. Rebellion would not just be an institutional cleansing as before; it would be the signal for wholesale change that would culminate in the communist revolution of 1949.

Why Did Europe Overtake China?

Yet the mystery remains. China had markets, technology, sophisticated agriculture, and private property rights. The ingredients that had produced economic success in Europe all existed in China. Anything up to two-fifths of China's agricultural output was traded in any one year—at least as much as in Europe. As we now know, its fleets and seafaring skills were comparable to Europe's; no fewer than seven Ming fleets ranged far across the Indian and Pacific oceans in the early fifteenth century. China could and should have had self-generated industrialization. Yet Europe, not China, was to industrialize and expand overseas. Why?

The answer is that Europe succeeded in creating a network of independent, empowering, nonstate, but nonetheless public institutions that acted as mediators and arbitrators of relationships between the state and the individual. The public institutions might range from scientific associations to the concept of the company, from an independent judiciary to an independent press, but all reinforced a plurality of interests whose experimentation, cross-learning, openness, and competition gave rise to cultural and economic dynamism. They allowed space for a process of rational argument: valuing and protecting the process of justification, marshaling evidence to support or dispute a point of view. Ultimately such values and cultural momentum would make the case for representative government accountable to the people, so that state and government became a discrete part of the same public sphere rather than opposed to it.

The crystallization of these forces in the European Enlightenment is thus the phenomenon that enabled Europe to overtake China with implications that continue today. Rival claims and disputes were settled on their merit in sometimes intoxicatingly fresh and addictive open argument. New institutions developed, in a process and spirit that were independent of top-down fiat, whether by monarch, pope, or Confucian official obeying some ancient textual formula. This was the bursting into life of the eighteenth-century London coffee-houses, the first newspapers, and associations for the advancement of science described by Jürgen Habermas.[23] Their counterpart was the urgent discussion of government in New England town squares in the years before the American Revolution. If the competition between warring European states set in motion the construction of this public space and the accompanying institutions and culture, then the European Enlightenment completed it, beginning the western democratic tradition.

In parallel it ignited the revolution in industrial production techniques that during the nineteenth century would enable European economic hegemony in general and British dominance in particular. Immanuel Kant—as I noted in the preface—summed up the spirit of the philosophical Enlightenment as "dare to know." The economic historian Joel Mokyr of Northwestern University argues that this spirit was transplanted to the economic sphere in a parallel "industrial Enlightenment."[24] Innovation did not stop with individual inventions, as it did in China; what distinguished the industrial revolution was that each invention and scientific advance became the platform for more, in a continual reflexive process, creating waves of technical innovation that characterized the nineteenth century and were at heart of the European miracle.[25] Whereas the Chinese would use mathematics and astronomy, for example, to reconceive how historical ceremonial bronze bells or ancient carriages might be built under the patronage of the emperor, Europeans would use the same techniques to develop means to sail the oceans or cast ever stronger cannons. To dare to know gave an impetus to move restlessly forward. China could not offer the space for those who dared to know to do anything but work within the constraints of what was already around them.

China and Europe both had markets, private property, profit-hungry entrepreneurs, science, and technology. Europe's system became successful capitalism—with its propensity for growth, technological advance, and creative destruction—because of Enlightenment institutions and Enlightenment attitudes. And the Enlightenment itself, by objecting to the irrationality of barriers to trade—monopolies, local tolls, special exemptions and licenses, discretionary taxes—made the intellectual case for the development of first national and then international markets. Adam Smith, father of free-market economics, was doing no more than making the Enlightenment case in the field of political economy.

The Invention of the Public Realm

The advance of this "public" tradition was not a simple process but an interaction of several forces. One of the most powerful was the European proclivity for war, creating a monarchical need for taxes, which in turn created the first faltering public institutions. Europeans were not necessarily more warlike than the Chinese, as Needham suggests; rather, the geography of Europe divided them into an kaleidoscope of kingdoms, duchies, and baronies with different languages, mores, and loyalties, all vying for expansion.[26] For ninety-five years in the sixteenth century and ninety-four years in the seventeenth one major European state or another was at war.[27] China certainly had spasms of warfare, dynastic change, and peasant revolt, but in between there were long periods of relative peace unknown in Europe.

The unintended consequences of preparing for and waging war were far-reaching. To pay for wars, taxes had to be levied and loans raised, serviced, and repaid—and bit by bit this created a new repetitive relationship between governors and governed; taxpayers wanted something in return. Nor was it just a matter of more pressure to raise money because there was more war. The European aristocracy and merchant classes alike were harder to take over and repress because they had distinct power bases, initially from the structure of feudalism and then between 1500 and 1800 increasingly from the profits of long-distance oceanic trade. In Britain in particular early feudalism, followed by the profits from international trade, created power centers that monarchs found hard to coerce. Similar effects were occurring in western France and the Netherlands. It was more rational and cheaper to gain the support of these interest groups by making political concessions to them—in contrast to China, where repression was less costly.[28]

Edward I recognized this political reality by calling representatives of the English shires and towns to attend London's parliament and give him exceptional "grants of supply." The representatives seized this opportunity to present lists of wrongs that should be righted as a quid pro quo. Similar political institutions appeared all over Europe such as the French parlement and the Spanish cortes. If taxation was to rise without civil resistance, then the monarch had to create political space to build consent—and if he didn't, then he risked a political crisis.

As warfare became more intense and expensive, the demand for taxation grew inexorably, and with it the political risk of mishandling the civil reaction. Charles I of England could not subjugate Scotland without taxes that forced the recall of Parliament after eleven years' suspension; this led to the English civil war and to a monarchy bounded by a representative constitution. Louis XVI of France could not pay for a French victory over England in the American Revolution without recalling the parlement; this led to the French Revolution. Both kings paid for their political miscalculation with their heads; both opened the way not merely for more representative government, but for the creation of a public realm.

War also spurred the creation of financial institutions and power centers beyond the state that required superintendence by independent public institutions. The great medieval Italian banking families grew fat by financing war; and the same demand would spur banking families to become the first commercial banks. These could then experiment with lending to the private sector. Economic expansion could be financed from bank loans or—as in the case of England's South Sea Company—from issuing shares on nascent stock markets.

As the financial system developed, it drove the creation of public banks of superintendence and independent courts alike. The Bank of England was established in 1694 and the Swedish Rijkbank in 1688 to superintend the new markets in government bonds and maintain the integrity of the consequent financial system in the wider public interest. Also, loans required collateral, and impartial courts through which to enforce loan contracts if they were not repaid. Europe's emerging representative institutions always insisted not only that merchants, producers, and financiers should have a voice in shaping commercial and contract law, but also that the law should be predictably and impartially administered.

One of the first acts of the Dutch, newly independent from Spain, was to insist that law in the Netherlands was jointly made by king and parliament—and that Dutch courts would be independent of the monarchy. The Restoration of Charles II in England, and the later accession of the Dutch king, William, to the English throne in the Glorious Revolution of 1689, established a similar system in England. English and Dutch commerce required a predictable, independent, impartial legal system adjudicating law that was neither arbitrary nor biased against merchants' interests. The early fight for democracy in both countries was as much a fight for disinterested justice and enforceable contracts as for representative government.

War in China was too infrequent to have the same political and institutional consequences; long periods of peace had the effect of reinforcing the basic political apparatus and its accompanying philosophy, which became more and more difficult to budge.[29] For example, the unwillingness of the Confucian system to pay for more naval expeditions by the eunuch Admiral Zheng He has been taken as proof of its backwardness. But a system consecrated to rural self-improvement and stability did not need to spend a fortune on overseas exploration with uncertain returns—it needed to prioritize financing the internal system of canals and irrigation. The choice was rational. The system was set up to venerate agriculture and family ancestors; as long as it delivered, it was doing its job. And with a powerful emperor behind the 4,400-mile Great Wall, symbol both of its unity and its intent to promote its own objectives undisturbed by others, the priority was to do just that. Its success was enlisting the vast peasantry with a vested interest in the continuance of the system. This halted the processes that might force institutional change. Instead the peasants became guarantors of the status quo.

The state was firmly in charge, so that even while Chinese merchants and bankers enjoyed relative security of property rights, these never led to the creation of autonomous European-style public companies, or to the development of public institutions that were not state institutions, or to a space between individual and state. In Europe, monarchs enfeebled by war had to accept terms imposed on them by banks for loans and the bills of exchange that the banks developed independently. In China, merchants and bankers used bills of exchange created by the imperial government. This is a crucial distinction. Peace locked the Chinese system into stasis, so there was no impetus for institutional development or creativity.

It was further hardened by China's turning away from foreign trade, as part of the same logic. By the late fifteenth century overseas trade was restricted to favor trade on the inland waterway system as the peasants wanted—not only cutting China off from an important source of profit, but also cutting it off from another stimulus to the development of public institutions.

It All Connects

Capitalist development can never be conceptualized as wholly an internal, national achievement of one country or culture without relation to the wider world economy and the opportunities of that economy. This is the insight of the French historian Fernand Braudel into growth in western Europe.[30] In his view Europe's growth from 1550 on cannot be explained without reference to its place in the world economic system. Spain's discovery of gold and silver in Peru:

the Netherlands' domination of the spice trade in the sixteenth and seventeenth centuries; the Venetians' capture of the Middle East and the Silk Road trade; the English and the slave trade, and their later access to raw materials and food from North America—this European story is about groups of merchants profiting hugely through their relationship to the far-flung world economy. They then reinvested in the profitable trade to make more profit still, and their growing imports of key resources removed the constraints on growth.

All this also spurred institutional innovations. The commercial needs of long-distance traders stimulated industrial investment, and their complex linkages demanded the development of new forms of organization—notably the company and the commercial bank as successors to the medieval guilds and fairs. John Maynard Keynes suggested that Francis Drake's *Golden Hind,* completing the circumnavigation of the globe in 1580 with a cargo of gold stolen from the Spanish and worth more than $100 billion in today's prices, effectively paid off all of England's international debt and provided the risk capital for the City of London's first trading and banking institutions, and thus the economic foundation of the British Empire.[31] But London was only following a trail blazed by Genoa, Venice, Cádiz, and Amsterdam.

The profitability of long-distance trade was important in itself, creating a source of surpluses outside the city or emerging state system that could be reinvested. But commercial trade relations also begat production. Merchants wanted to fill their outgoing vessels with goods, offer them for exchange, and bring back the exchanged goods as imports. European vessels would make outward-bound voyages with cargoes of textiles, linen, dyes, mirrors, glass, engines, and clocks; they would return with sugar, tea, spices, cotton, hides, timber, and silk—and, as the trade grew, large volumes of grain and meat. Trade created opportunities for industrial specialization, but it also allowed the trading countries to escape constraints on their own resources, food, and raw materials.

The most obvious example is Britain—the first industrial nation.

In order to industrialize, Britain had to transfer its workforce from agriculture to factories while maintaining the supply of food. It could and did increase agricultural productivity, but it also needed to import food and fuel from overseas—crucially, from North America and later Australasia. Although it was blessed with fast-running rivers in the Pennines that provided water power, and then easy access to coal, it also needed wood to burn for charcoal, wood to construct ships, and wood to build houses and farms. The trade in lumber, sugar, and grain was indispensable for industrialization.

It is also evident that trade, finance, and industry have to be organized. This is another crucial but frequently undervalued part of the development story. Long-distance trade in sixteenth- and seventeenth-century Europe was hazardous. Vessels might not survive the vicissitudes of the voyage, because of piracy, bad weather, or bad seamanship. The outgoing cargoes and the costs of the voyage had to be financed. The prices of the traded commodities fluctuated alarmingly. Also, sea voyages took a long time; for example, the 30,000-mile round trip from the Netherlands to the Dutch East Indies and back occupied eighteen months. First in the Netherlands and later in England, Dutch and English merchants developed the idea of the company as a formal partnership of merchants who would obtain a license to trade from the sovereign, share the risk in financing the trade, and build the organization over time to create a permanent infrastructure to support the trade. This included everything from stocks of key supplies along the trading route, allowing ships to replenish their needs, to armies of clerks who kept an inventory of what was bought and sold.

The formation in London in 1600 of the East India Company and the formation of a Dutch forerunner on which it was modeled are thus milestones in the development of European capitalism. In one sense the early company was still part of the family and guild relationships that characterized economic organization in both medieval Europe and China, with members' or partners' trust based on personal acquaintance. Nonetheless, the company crossed a vitally important line. It moved from a paradigm of personalized relationships to the paradigm of an organization with a personality and life of its own. The company organized the voyage, assumed the risks, and paid the bills; the company owned and developed the infrastructure; and because the company expected to be long-lived, it could be more far-sighted.[32] The company was to grow into the organizational invention • without which European and western capitalism would have been impossible.

It was the apogee of a rapidly developing "soft" Enlightenment infrastructure. Between 1600 and 1750 England gradually put into place the world's first viable soft-capitalist infrastructure—the idea of the company, the establishment of a system of law that could be reliably and impartially adjudicated by an independent judicial system, and the emergence of a financial system that allowed external finance to be raised through both creditworthy, trusted banks and the stock market.

The profits of long-distance trade, imports of vital raw materials, and a coherent soft infrastructure with trustworthy public institutions were essential preconditions for Britain's industrial revolution. But they were not sufficient. Technology and new techniques of production were also necessary, not as onetime phenomena that might stop or even be reversed as they were in China, but rather as the ceaselessly restless driver of industrialization, at the heart of the production process.[33] In effect this was a nineteenth-century "knowledge economy"—the production of knowledge, its initial practical application, and then its subsequent use.

The first European university had been established in Bologna in 1080; and by 1500 Europe had no fewer than seventy centers of secular learning. These became independent engines of knowledge production. But the spirit of science existed not apart from the production system but as its handmaiden. For Joel Mokyr the interpenetration of Europe's "savants" (thinkers) and "fabricants" (manufacturers) was essential to the chemistry of its development.[34]

In Europe, advances in technology were not just national; they were disseminated around the continent. In this respect the printing press was as important as the university. As early as 1500, Europe had 220 presses that had already printed 8 million books.[35] This development, together with Europe's complex dynastic rivalries and wars, meant that European monarchs, whether Hapsburgs or Bourbons, could not establish hegemony as China's emperor had done. Competitive political pluralism was essential to Europe's political momentum and also to its economic momentum. If a technology or scientific advance worked in country A, then countries B, C, and D quickly had to adopt it or else find themselves at an industrial and military disadvantage. The printing presses spewed forth the books and manuals containing the informational gold that could transform industrial and military capacity. Countries that refused to move with the times would find themselves marginalized. Spain's economic decline in the eighteenth century was an awesome warning of the consequences of not accommodating new technologies. Leadership passed first to France and then Britain—with other European countries quickly adopting the factory system, the water-driven looms, and first steam and then coal-driven engines. Europe's pluralism was essential to change: the practitioners of science might find themselves exiled from Catholic Europe, but in Protestant England, Holland, or Germany they could follow where inquiry led, and the results would be eminently reproducible.

These four elements—the pluralism developed by nearly continual war and state competition; profitable long-distance trade and the companies it created; a robust soft institutional infrastructure; and the universalization of technology—kindled Europe's miracle and allowed it to overtake China despite what the two continents had in common and despite China's early leadership. Uniting, underpinning, and embodying all four elements was the Enlightenment, and the public institutions it underwrote. Growth produced its own culture of modernity: a willingness to accept that economic and social systems would not remain static but always evolve. Other propositions also had to be accepted: that the gods or one's ancestors could not provide a compass with which to navigate the ever-changing present; that societies had to find collective responses to change or experience serious dislocation; and that technology and science would relentlessly force the continual aging and obsolescence of what seems indisputably contemporary today and would deliver predictable gains in productivity which are the roots of not only wealth and riches but of military superiority. China, ahead of Europe for millennia, would find by the early nineteenth century that its divinely inspired order was no match for Europe's. The legacy of the resulting turmoil is with us yet.

The Century of Humiliation

At the beginning of the nineteenth century a structural problem emerged in Europe's relationship with China. Europe's demand for Chinese tea, silk, porcelain, furniture, and decorative goods was large and growing—but China had little demand for the products that Europe's nascent factories and mills were producing.[36] The Celestial Kingdom demanded payment in silver and gold, causing a balance-of-payments problem—a flashpoint for Britain, overwhelmingly its largest trading partner. Britain could not expect to support the pound in the world market or maintain its own military, trading, and industrial ascendance after beating France in the Napoleonic wars if its still inadequate reserves of gold and silver were to be transferred to the Chinese.

For most of the eighteenth century the British had preferred to offer another substance in exchange for Chinese goods: opium. A trade that had begun with no more than a few hundred chests in the 1730s had grown to more than 30,000 chests by 1835 and was a source of worsening friction with the Qing dynasty. Within China opium addiction was reaching dangerous levels. Also, there was an increasing shortage of silver to back China's growing economy, lifting the price of silver in relation to other goods—and, as taxes were paid in silver, so raising the real tax burden, with potentially fatal consequences for the regime. In 1838 came the fateful decision: the import of opium was banned.

The British reaction was forceful and was made still more effective by the deployment of a steam-driven battleship, the *Nemesis*, that could operate in water as shallow as five feet. This was a decisive advantage in the bays and river estuaries where the war was waged, and it emphasized China's technological backwardness. The British could win any battle they chose. The peace treaty of Nanjing in 1842 reflected China's reversal and became the most telling symbol of its humiliation. The Celestial Kingdom that claimed to rule "all that was below heaven" and held foreigners in contempt had to allow the destructive trade in opium to continue, had to pay every pound of Britain's war costs and more, had to cede Hong Kong to Britain, and had to allow British merchants to operate freely in its five leading ports. Also, the emperor had to deal directly with emissaries from the British state and accept Chinese being taught to foreigners; and any concession made to any other western power would immediately extend to Britain.

The treaty of Nanjing was the beginning of a series of defeats at the hands of every foreign power that China fought. No fewer than twenty-six treaties[37] followed, in effect opening up the entire Chinese coast and navigable river system to foreigners on their own terms—which might include their own system of education, communications, armed forces, steamship lines, courts, factories, free access, and trading rights. By the 1890s the indebted, militarily weak Qing dynasty was evidently on the point of collapse, prompting a kind of feeding frenzy by the western powers. By 1900 Russia had secured a large part of Manchuria, Japan had colonized Taiwan, Britain added Kowloon to Hong Kong, France expanded its Indo-Chinese empire northward, and Germany seized the Shandong port city of Qingdao and the mineral rights of the surrounding province. China was being carved up, people said, like a melon. The western powers did not need to colonize China; the treaties gave them all they wanted without their having to go to the expense.

If this was not enough the dynasty also suffered a series of violent internal revolts from parts of the empire emboldened by Qing weakness. These revolts did not merely challenge the right of the Qing to rule, but for the first time in Chinese history contested the values and legitimacy of the combination of celestialism and Confucianism that underpinned the empire. The Muslim revolts in the west demanded independence from infidel rule; the Nian revolt in north-central China was fueled by the incapacity of the imperial system to deliver its side of the old bargain, plentiful supplies of food; and, most telling of all, the Taiping rebellion that lasted from 1850 to 1864 embraced Christianity and sought to organize land ownership on egalitarian principles. All despised the Qing for their decadence and the subjugation of Chinese by foreigners: the Boxer uprising between 1898 and 1901 was explicitly antiwestern, killing 200 westerners and wanting to restore China's glory by reinvigorating the integrity of the Chinese imperial system. It was suddued by a largely foreign army whose eight constituents afterward insisted on maintaining their armed forces for protection—another humiliation for China.

The capacity of the Qing to suffer so many simultaneous blows and yet survive for so long was tribute to the continuing resilience and resourcefulness of the Confucian system, despite China's economic backwardness, and the loyalty of so many senior officials and generals to the imperial idea. The domestic rebellions were, after all, subdued. But so many defeats at the hands of foreigners could hardly fail to prompt the most profound soul-searching. China could not match the industrial and technological preeminence of the west or even Japan. The whole edifice of Confucian thought seemed inward-looking and antimodern, locking China into economic and social backwardness with concomitant poverty, misery, and lack of self-respect summed up by widespread opium addiction. In the final days of the dying Qing dynasty, the regime conceded that China needed more representative government, more systematic modern education, a thorough overhaul of its military machine, a fairer distribution of land, and a commitment to industrialization, symbolized by the creation of a national rail network.

However, the collapse of its legitimacy and the accompanying mushrooming of alternative prospectuses to modernize China had gone too far. For example, the newly created provincial parliamentary assemblies became not a constructive force for change, as the Qing hoped, but a forum for dissent. An army mutiny began in the autumn of 1911 and culminated when its forty-four senior commanders insisted that China become a republic. At that point the five-year-old Emperor Puyi and the Qing court, their power base gone, had no choice but to abdicate. China was left with a constitutional and governmental vacuum. The Celestial Kingdom had not just fallen to earth; its prestige shattered, it had evaporated.

CHAPTER 3

Mao's Bequest

CHINA'S URGENT REQUIREMENT IN 1912 WAS TO BUILD A
state that worked. The country needed to be held together, justice and
order offered, and China prevented from being the victim of more defeats by foreigners. The founder and first leader of the Guomindang
(or Nationalists, as I shall call this party from now on), Sun Yat-sen,
put it more ambitiously. China simultaneously had to build a state,
democratize, create order, reconcile competing interests, take on
foreigners, and modernize economically. He even argued for applying the untried precepts of socialism to drive development, because
corrupt Chinese capitalism and its *guanxi* insider networks were
evidently not powerful enough. It was a call that his party never followed up.

The challenge was huge. With the implosion of the imperial center
in the Forbidden City had gone the linchpin of the Confucian mandarinate that had held China together. In the country the landlords,
unchecked, tightened their grip on the land. No longer were they part
of a civilization that purported to generate harmony and benevo-
lence. Into the political vacuum during the 1910s and 1920s stepped a
network of provincial barons or warlords who sustained themselves
with personal armies, paid for by tribute and any profitable trade,
including opium dealing; and who enlisted the old imperial official
gentry to serve them, thus tightening their own grip on the peasants.
Every aspect of the economy—agriculture, industry, finance—was
behind the west and indeed desperately primitive. Public education
and health care were rudimentary. Poverty was widespread, and life

63

expectancy was low, less than forty years. Corruption was endemic. Opium addiction grew exponentially; in 1930, according to one estimate, 20 percent of Chinese agricultural land was devoted to opium production.[1] Secret societies flourished.

Above all, China was violent. In the absence of imperial or democratic legitimacy many warlords held power through force of arms and fear. Zhang Zongchang in Shandong was an extreme example, delighting not merely in murder but in splitting human heads open "like melons" and hanging them on telegraph poles as a warning to those minded to challenge his authority.[2] Others might not go quite so far, but human life was cheap. Lu Xun, China's most influential twentieth-century author, wrote after a student massacre by warlords in Beijing in 1926, "A few lives count for nothing in China."[3] And militaristic Japan was not to be forgotten; its colonies in Korea and Taiwan could be readily used as launchpads for bringing a Japanese colonial empire to China.

Sun Yat-sen, in the years before the collapse of the Qing, had argued for a postimperial Chinese state to be modeled on a western-style division of powers between executive, legislative, and judiciary branches, with an independent non-Confucian civil service dedicated to economic improvement. But none of the preconditions existed. Without them, Nationalist China would struggle to create any kind of legitimate government to counteract the inexorable drift to warlordism, disorder, and hyperinflation—against an international background of beleaguered capitalism, weakening liberal democracy, and invasion by Japan.

Even had political conditions been more favorable, the Nationalists still lacked a prospectus for the economy. The alpha and omega of China's economic problem was its poverty-stricken, unproductive, backward peasant rural economy. The causes—landlordism, inability to raise credit, lack of mechanization, and the tiny size of most plots—had to be tackled, and an agricultural surplus had to be generated. But even if that problem could be solved, there was no national banking system capable of mobilizing the resulting savings into investment. The Chinese banking system was more of a money transmission system than an investment system—there had been no demand for anything else. Companies were family concerns or insider *guanxi* networks; the idea of a corporate organization based on rules and capable of marshaling production resources barely existed beyond Shanghai. Typically, Chinese enterprise hardly reached out beyond the town or province in which it was located. Nor was there any state capacity to step in to do what the banking and investment systems could not. To those Chinese who were burning to create constitutional order and economic prosperity, restore their self-respect, and catch up with the west, the scale of what had to be done on so many fronts must have seemed daunting if not impossible.

Sun Yat-sen, for all his vision of how China should develop, never succeeded in reunifying China's provinces. Chiang Kai-shek, who succeeded him, managed in 1927 to construct a semiunified Chinese republic through force of arms, clever politics, and bringing key warlords into his coalition, but the rest of the task was beyond him. He now had to build state capacity and modernize the economy, with the additional deadly complication of unsuccessfully trying to beat back the Japanese invasion that had begun in 1931 and which by 1937–1938 had captured Shanghai, Nanjing, and Canton. By 1941 Japan had conquered the northern, central, and southern coastal regions of the country, leaving only the remote, mountainous west to the Nationalists and communists. Chiang also had to defeat the communists in what after 1945 became a full-fledged civil war.

This was not necessarily an impossible task. Chinese peasants might hate their landlords, but they hated even more losing their property rights and their links with their ancestors; this was why classic Marxist analysis (and the Communist Party's advisers from the Soviet Union) initially regarded them as too reactionary to be the class base for a communist revolution, and early efforts at radicalizing them within orthodox communist guidelines failed. There was a window of ten or fifteen years from 1927 on when the Nationalists could have won both the ideological and the military argument with the communists if they had been more skillful and capable of building mass support. As it was, the Communist Party's forces and organization were very nearly exterminated by the Nationalists after the Long March in 1935 to the rural redoubt of Yan'an in the provincial west of China and the sustained attack on their organization in the cities; less than 10 percent of those who began the march ended it.[4] As for Japan, after Pearl Harbor and the United States' entry into the war, it was inevitable that Japan would lose. Even after their exile in Sichuan, it was possible that the Nationalists could emerge as the country's prime organizing force.

The insurmountable difficulty was that the prerequisites for such success were a viable state, an enduring political coalition to sustain it, and a workable program of economic development. The Nationalists could achieve none of those targets. To build an effective state, they needed a national bureaucracy; and to begin developing the economy they had to confront some of the interests in their own coalition— warlords, landlords, and the Confucian gentry. As Jonathan Fenby says in his biography, Chiang Kai-shek never had the political strength, the ideological program, or the practical policies that might have begun to approach what was needed.[5]

Chiang could not, as the communists proposed, attack landlords and the gentry to raise agricultural productivity by means of land reform, because they constituted the officer class in his army and raised what revenue he could muster in the country. Nor did he have the resources or the political plausibility to tackle systematic corruption, tax-farming, and the maladministration of justice by his officials. He and the Nationalists might want them to display the Confucian virtues of order, harmony, and self-discipline, but he could offer no compelling moral or pragmatic reason for them to abandon their habits.

Chiang Kai-shek found himself experimenting with a soft version of fascism—again, international influences had an impact on national politics—when he began of the "new life" movement in 1934 to "remoralize" and regenerate China. It certainly showed his recognition of the need for a better political philosophy, but it also showed the Nationalists' own ideological and moral weaknesses. The movement was soon discredited. It issued a stream of petty regulations aimed at improving individual morality—specifying, for example, that the hem of a skirt should fall four inches below the knee—but did nothing against the secret societies, opium dens, and gangsters on which the regime depended.[6]

The lack of effective reform revealed itself in the performance of the economy and public finance. There had been a significant increase in industrial production during the 1930s, with considerable investment in textile and chemical manufacturing from foreign sources; and some of the coastal cities, especially Shanghai, experienced rapid economic growth. But the Chinese had no industrial infrastructure that would enable them to match the Japanese military machine. And the administration was too weak to ensure that the few taxes collected would actually find their way to the republican government in its capital, Nanjing. Every year from 1929 and 1937, before the Japanese overran China, the Nationalist government ran a deficit, which rose from 12 percent of its total spending in 1933 to 25 percent in 1937—an unsustainable amount. Between 1937 and 1943, during the war against Japan, the deficits soared out of control, and the Nationalists resorted to printing money. Inflation reached 300 percent in the early 1940s, and the yuan's international value collapsed.[7]

Meanwhile the communists managed to turn a humiliating debacle, the Long March, into a propaganda success—a sign that after many false starts since their foundation in Shanghai in 1921, they were beginning to learn how to make a revolution in Chinese conditions, and how to become genuinely popular. Whatever happened after 1949, the Chinese communist revolution resulted from a popular mass movement. The Soviet Union under Stalin was savagely cruel, and we know now that communism necessarily leads to authoritarianism. Nevertheless, throughout the Japanese war Mao's base camp in Yan'an was the focal point for a wide range of intellectuals, students, workers, and businessmen who were fleeing from the Japanese and who saw communism as the most effective way of modernizing China and winning the war.

The Appeal of Communism

The Communists had more appeal than may seem obvious today. Capitalism was in disarray; and according to its critics, the prolonged global depression of the interwar years proved that it was inherently flawed. The dominant intellectual theory in the west was that states had to organize economic development. Roosevelt's New Deal in the United States, Stalin in the Soviet Union, and Hitler in Germany were cited as examples. Obviously, then, if China wanted to industrialize, it would have to be state-led and would have to reform rural land tenure. But this implied first constructing a state and political coalition that could confront the landlords and the gentry. The Nationalists could not do this, because they relied on the landlords and gentry; but it was the communists' avowed program. Moreover, the communists' idea was in the long Chinese tradition of changing a regime by mobilizing a peasant revolt.

Communism in China had another and more subtle advantage. It could be understood as a modern transmutation of Confucianism, retaining the Confucian commitment to service, social harmony, and integrity but dropping some of the obviously unnecessary elements.[8] Communism, like Confucianism, promised fairness, incorruptibility, and responsiveness to the preferences and wants of the people. Unlike Confucianism, it celebrated science rather than superstition; progress rather than tradition; economic development; and, importantly for many, equality between men and women. Communism lived, and lives, uneasily with Confucianism: sometimes condemning it, sometimes using it as a source of legitimacy. But in the early days it was a valuable support. For example, Liu Shaoqi, one of the five-strong leadership group with Mao in the early 1940s, drew a parallel in his book *How to Be a Good Communist* between the Confucian scholar and the aspiring communist: each raised his integrity through constant self-discipline and self-criticism. Confucius did not see himself as a born sage. He had gone through a "process of steeling and self-cultivation" to reach an understanding of what was right, and so must the good communist.[9] The thousands of refugees rallying to Mao's banner recognized the continuity between the revolution and Chinese culture, and were reassured. Communism, in short, seemed to combine the best of the past and the best of the future.

Communism also offered a face-saving explanation of China's humiliation—and a solution. China had been a victim of western imperialism, and its quasicolonial status had resulted from a global quest for markets, cheap labor, and raw materials. As John Fairbank, Edwin Reischauer, and Albert M. Craig put it, communism "provided a self-consistent, universalistic and scientific view of the world's history which enabled one to reject the imperialist West in the name of Western 'scientific thought' and explain China's humiliating backwardness as due to her bondage to 'capitalist imperialism.' "[10] A communist revolution in China, along with domestic modernization, would be part of an international defense against exploitation. This alignment between communism and Chinese nationalism still exists today.

So far, so good. But throughout the 1920s and 1930s the problem was how to get the communists' story to correspond to actual conditions in China, and not frighten the people with too much talk about revolution and the abolition of private property. According to Marx, a communist revolution was meant to arise spontaneously from an oppressed working class whose existence and consciousness of its exploitation had been created by bourgeois industrial capitalism. But China had neither industrial capitalism nor an industrial working class outside Shanghai and Canton. If there was to be revolution, it could come only from the peasants, organized and led by the Communist Party—a dauntingly difficult logistical and ideological task. Few would have bet on the communists even as late as 1935.

Understanding how the communists succeeded is fundamental to understanding today's party, and the debt it still owes to Mao, notwithstanding his later failures and his cruelty. There were three important changes to Marx's template. The first change was to follow Lenin and argue that the party would need to be the vanguard of the revolution, which in a peasant society could not be a spontaneous class revolt. Marxism became Marxism-Leninism.

The second change was a departure from orthodoxy. Because peasants were culturally hostile to the maxims of socialization and collectivization, their radicalization would require much more work in the villages by party cadres. The cadres would have to persuade the peasants of the merits of communist ideas; help them articulate grievances; take political action; and then, by helping them achieve their new goals, get them to "own" the revolution. Lenin could use the party in Russia to impose change from above; but Mao developed the concept of the "mass line." "All correct leadership is necessarily from the masses to the masses," Mao wrote. "This means: take the idea of the masses (scattered and unsystematic ideas) and concentrate them (through study turn them into concentrated and systematic ideas), then go to the masses and propagate and explain these ideas until the masses embrace them as their own." [11]

The mass line, as it was developed in Yan'an, had immediate implications from which the third change—another key difference between Chinese and Soviet communism—emerged. Instead of confiscating land into collectivized soviets (the Chinese communists had tried to do this in the late 1920s and early 1930s, and the peasants had resisted), the new approach was more reformist. Land would be redistributed from rich to poor peasants, but property rights would be respected. Taxes would be lowered, as would usurious interest rates. Above all, Mao said, individual party members working in villages had to be extremely responsive to local political conditions instead of behaving as if they were writing an "eight-legged essay"—the classic essay for Confucian examinations. In other words, the party should not rigidly impose communist doctrine where it might not work. Only one-third of the candidates in village, town, and provincial government elections should be communists; another third should be other leftists; and a last third would be more genuine progressives. The aim should be inclusion, decentralization, and the redressing of real grievances. Party cadres had to be responsive, flexible, and unbureaucratic while still developing a communist position. This tough mandate required much education and "rectification."

If the old imperial system had still existed, Mao might have been the leader of a peasant rebellion, but the challenge was now bigger than cleansing the old order. It was to build a new system from the foundation up. Communism provided the ideology, the political script, and guidelines about what to do in power—all validated by being scientific, modern, western, and part of a global movement. Mao's political talent was to see all this, translate it into a Chinese idiom, and make it work in practice. For many Chinese communism became the only viable choice.

The sudden capitulation of the Japanese in 1945 was followed by a full-scale civil war. The Nationalist army was larger but, despite extensive American support, was exhausted by eight years of war against the Japanese. Also, the Nationalists had no political strategy for winning popular support; the state was weak; China's financial position was precarious; and inflation steadily escalated, eventually to more than 6,000 percent in 1948. Mao, who was now the party's undisputed leader—he had been chairman of the Military Council since 1937 and chairman of the Central Committee and Politburo since 1943—rolled out the Yan'an strategy. By developing popular support in areas under their control, the communists could concentrate all their forces—armed by the Soviet Union—at the front line. The Nationalists had to dissipate their own disintegrating forces in quelling village and urban unrest, which was mounting under the strain of hyperinflation. Despite their superior numbers, the Nationalists could not marshal equivalent forces at the front.

Their collapse came sooner than either side had anticipated. The communists controlled the rich province of Manchuria in northeastern China, which gave them a base for taking control of northern China; and the Nationalist armies fell back. On October 1, 1949, Mao

Zedong declared the establishment of the People's Republic of China in Tiananmen Square. Chiang Kai-shek and his armies had fled to the island of Taiwan, which they called the Republic of China, claiming sovereignty over the mainland. The communists insisted that Taiwan should be returned to the motherland; but with the United States protecting Taiwan, the People's Republic has never attempted an invasion. Nearly sixty years later, Taiwan retains all its capacity to inflame mutual enmity.

The Chinese Communist Party had made a seismic coup. It had led a popular communist revolution in the world's most populous country. It faced the monumental work of reconstructing a devastated economy and building state structures—two tasks at which the Nationalists had failed. But the ups and downs that were to follow would be led by a Communist Party profoundly different from others, notably its counterpart in the Soviet Union. It would be a vanguard Leninist party, but characterized by the pragmatism, reformism, democracy, and decentralization of Mao's mass line. Pragmatic reformism would ultimately be its salvation. The question is whether it will ever rediscover its commitment to democracy.

Challenging a 2,000-Year-Old Stasis

The overriding economic challenge for the new communist government in 1949 was to repair the devastation of war and to invest in industrialization, infrastructure, education, health care, and agriculture. Even if China had been an open economy in the early 1950s, it would have had very little capacity to finance investment by borrowing external savings from the international capital markets or institutions like the early World Bank. The funds were not available, and today's sophisticated capital markets did not yet exist. Investment therefore would have to be financed from an increase in domestic saving, and the only route to that destination was from agriculture, which then represented more than 85 percent of the Chinese economy. To produce a surplus, peasants could live on less, work more, or become more productive—or some combination of all three. And that in turn would involve land reform and the reorganization of agricultural production.

The state would have to lead the process; it could not be left to market forces. This was the iron truth that would have faced any government, whatever its ideology. Even the Nationalists began a land reform program on Taiwan to create larger plots and achieve greater productivity—goals that had eluded them in China. The communists would quintuple the 1,600 medium and large state-owned enterprises they inherited from the Nationalists. They would use the state to create a national education system capable of lowering the male illiteracy rate (70 percent) and the female illiteracy rate (which in rural areas was an incredible 99 percent).[12] The state would also develop a health infrastructure to raise life expectancy (from around fifty years). And the state would need to be reorganized so that it could credibly borrow savings rather than print banknotes, if hyperinflation was to be reduced.

Communist leaders knew that this was only a beginning. The goal was radical egalitarianism and elimination of the economic base of class relations. The means would be collective enterprise and the mobilization of investment through planning. The end would be the gradual establishment of the communist utopia. In towns, this would mean the abolition of private capitalist enterprise; in the country it meant abolishing landlordism and even, more controversially, abolishing the property title peasants held for their land. An agricultural surplus would be created to finance the first five-year plan that would deliver economic modernization. Mao, who in Yan'an and before had analyzed the Chinese class system in elaborate detail as a guide to communist strategy to win the war in the country, now undertook the same analysis at the national level. Everybody in China was given a class position on which his or her fate would be determined. Radical egalitarianism had begun.

The land reform of 1950, in which more than two-fifths of China's land was redistributed in a series of nationwide village meetings from those higher up in the class hierarchy to those lower down, was based on this carefully calibrated class position. It was the precursor of first cooperativization and then communization. Hence the nationalization of private enterprise in the towns, and the major initiatives to improve the condition of women in the name of equality. Women, like men, were given the right to petition for divorce, and girls were to be educated alongside boys in the new national education system. Mao declared that "women hold up half of the sky." Even though China was to plunge into the Korean War, supporting communist North Korea against an American-led western coalition in the south and incurring a terrible loss of life, the early, genuine popularity of the revolution was undimmed. Chinese history validated both land redistribution and fighting foreign encirclement; supporting the communists in North Korea was necessary ideologically and for security.

In the first five-year plan between 1952 and 1957, China was to experience rapid economic growth—an average of 9.2 percent. Industrial production more than doubled, with spectacular gains in industries as disparate as bicycles and steel. Advised by technocrats from the Soviet Union, the Chinese maintained the pace of investment throughout the entire five-year period, creating the necessary savings by forcing the newly established cooperatives to sell onefourth of their grain production to the state at low prices. The buildup of communism in rural China was gradual but relentless; small-scale work teams gave way to larger "lower-stage" agricultural cooperatives, which gave way in turn to "higher-stage" cooperatives. The majority of peasants volunteered to participate, accepting that the more they organized themselves collectively, the more their economic position would be improved. By allowing peasants to withdraw income (the amount was based on a combination of the land they had contributed and the work they had put in), by abolishing rent, by supplying cheap credit through new credit cooperatives, and by organizing the process through village leaders, the communists

commanded consent. In the early years they offered a genuine improvement in peasants' incomes, if not in productivity.

At the same time as an agricultural surplus was being forcibly confiscated, industrial investment was being forcibly initiated. Inflation
was brought under control when savers responded to a call to display
patriotism and buy government bonds. The communist revolution
seemed to be bearing fruit.

But already there were problems and tensions. Mao believed that
political will, exercising itself through the permanent dialectic of
political conflict, would drive progress; he believed in political institutions only insofar as they permitted the exercise of that will, and
he saw politics as a succession of conflicts—each transmuting itself
into the next and so propelling progressive change.[13] Thus the cooperatives established during the first five-year plan were political
stepping-stones on the way to true communism; by building on this
political achievement, China would increase agricultural production
and industrial investment.

Mao's colleagues were less certain. Grain production had stabilized at around 167 million tons; the breakthrough to modern agriculture was not happening, and so the prospect of raising the surplus
to fund the next five-year plan was shrinking.[14] There was a limit to
how much cooperatives could raise productivity without fertilizers,
new types of seeds, and mechanization. Also, as the government
began to base members' incomes solely on their work and not on the
historic contribution of land to the cooperative, peasants began to
supplement their meager income by working their ancestors' individual plots more intensively and selling the extra produce on the market. The class of rich and semirich peasants the revolution was meant
to abolish was being re-created while production from the unmecha-
nized, low-technology cooperatives stagnated. Mao wanted to solve
the problem politically by full-scale communization, while other
Politburo leaders—notably Liu Shaoqi—felt that the political justification was inadequate. There had to be a parallel economic effort to

raise agricultural production, and that meant more mechanization and accepting the role of incentives and markets. Liu now began to be associated with an argument which Mao would consider counterrevolutionary and which led to Liu's eventual death under house arrest during the Cultural Revolution.

Another problem had to do with the class of what we would today classify as knowledge workers—scientists, technologists, writers, researchers, and teachers. Sustained economic success would obviously depend on their brains, commitment, and ingenuity; and they would also form the cornerstone of a new communist civil society. The party could try to browbeat them into loyalty to the revolution through ideological training, as it had tried initially, but this was unsatisfactory. Mao wanted to create a genuine communist civil society, in which intellectuals would freely exchange views—perhaps critical, but always within a communist paradigm. This would reinforce communism and the revolution socially and intellectually. By early 1957 Mao was so confident that the achievements of the revolution were obvious, compared with the past, that he said "a hundred flowers" should be allowed to bloom and a communist civil society should begin. For five weeks in May and June, intellectuals were allowed to debate freely what had been and should be happening. But as with Tiananmen thirty-two years later, there was a crescendo of complaint: party officials were criticized for corruption, communist democracy was ridiculed as a sham, and the low standard of living was described as intolerable. Mao responded with a crackdown; 300,000 intellectuals were arrested as counterrevolutionary "rightists" and imprisoned, exiled, or sent to labor camps. Mao complained that his trust had been abused. Debate still rages whether his intent had ever been genuine, or was merely a ruse to ensnare his critics. His subsequent actions suggest the latter interpretation.

This was a turning point. There was stagnation of agricultural output in the countryside, a crisis of legitimacy among the intelligentsia; and a reemergence of the rich peasant class that the party was pledged to abolish. On the other hand, the first five-year plan had matched or exceeded the expectations for industrialization. The Politburo—including, as he would acknowledge later, Deng Xiaoping—came around to Mao's view that the only response was to intensify the political fight. Peasants tempted away from cooperatives and skeptical intellectuals needed to be shown emphatically that more communism was the answer to the Chinese predicament. The party must intensify the egalitarian moralization of the Chinese through communist principles, raise the peasantry to new heights of revolutionary fervor that would permit greater collective efforts, eliminate any signs of a new rich peasant class, and build on cooperatives as the principal economic institution, expecting them to supply their members' needs. The sums in the second five-year plan could add up if the locus of industrialization was moved to newly established decentralized communes. These communes would have the incentive of lifting agricultural production to fund the investment to meet the raised targets for industrial output—a variant of the "mass line" that had won the revolution. The communes, for Mao at least, were also vehicles for constructing the communist civil society that just had been aborted. The inexorable economic and political logic of the situation, and of communist thinking, led to the Great Leap Forward. There seemed to be no other option.

For the next eighteen years Mao never abandoned his conviction that radical egalitarianism would achieve the goals of modernizing China, eradicating forever the legacy of the Confucian gentry, and unleashing the potential of individual peasants, to whom he was romantically if remotely attached. If this egalitarianism required violence and death, so be it. The more the program failed, the more he blamed weak implementation and the opposition of his colleagues, rather than seeing anything wrong with the theory. In any case, he was more and more isolated from reality. The 26,000 communes set up for the Great Leap Forward that were meant simultaneously, through revolutionary will, to raise farm productivity dramatically and develop light industries. Self-sufficient collectives could not deliver all this. They lacked manpower, incentives, equipment, and skills—but Mao, seeing from his special train only fields that were artificially adorned with food crops, would learn only belatedly of the scale of the disaster. The backstreet foundry in which pots, pans, and farm implements were melted into unusable steel, to meet the production targets, was symptomatic of the whole debacle. As for food, after the communes had given their dwindling stocks of grain to the government (which in turn used it to service the debt to the Soviet Union), they did not have enough to live on. Famine, starvation, and death stalked the land; the combination of communization and the mass line had backfired spectacularly. Estimates of the deaths range up to 37 million.[15]

Between 1961 and 1965 there was a brief return to more pragmatic policies. This was when Deng, believing that he was being only as pragmatic as Mao urged, declared, "It doesn't matter if a cat is black or white as long as it catches mice"—a position that was to condemn him, during the Cultural Revolution, to loss of office and exile for being the second "capitalist roader" after Liu. Mao was never reconciled to the peasants' selling surplus produce in the country markets, to their urban counterparts' engaging in small business in towns, or to anyone's deviation from the plan. Deviation constituted a reproach to Mao's belief in communism as a source of cultural and psychic fulfilment and as the road to prosperity and a new society.

The mass violence of the Red Guards during the Cultural Revolution lasted for less than two years from 1966; but the flat-earth political commitment to equality and class warfare continued until Mao's death in 1976, although it was focused mainly on the towns. Private business was still outlawed. But as times became calmer, the investment engine kept propelling state-owned enterprise forward; production quickly recovered, though with declining productivity. All the vocational training schools in the education system were closed until 1978 because they were said to foster bourgeois skills, and the curriculum in general schools was reorganized to focus on ideological and political education.[16] Teacher training was abandoned until 1971; no new undergraduates were admitted to universities until 1972, and no postgraduates until 1978.

Around Mao there could be no public complaint, even though the economic costs were obvious to all. In 1970 Mao's designated successor, Lin Biao, learned that he was to be passed over, and rather than accept this verdict he planned Mao's assassination. The details have never been released, but allegedly he was found out and died in an aircraft crash in Mongolia as he attempted to flee to Russia without sufficient fuel or crew. Mao had now beaten all his political opponents, and China was set on a course of self-sufficient communes, industrialization in heavy industry by state-owned enterprise, and aggressive egalitarianism.

There were two saving graces in an otherwise dismal economic situation. First, peasants' savings had been channeled into investment in infrastructure, education, and industry on a grand scale. Industrial output had climbed more than thirteen times and by 1978 constituted 46.8 percent of national income, compared to 12.6 percent in 1949.[17] The size of the rail network had more than doubled. The proportion of irrigated land rose from 20 percent in 1952 to 50 percent in 1978.[18] Moreover, male literacy had now climbed to 81 percent and female literacy to 45 percent as a result of a generation of educational investment, despite the Cultural Revolution.[19]

Second, Mao's commitment to decentralization was real. Central direction, he recognized, was nonsensical in a country as large as China. In 1970 China's provinces were asked to manage most state-owned enterprises, with the central government running only 8 percent of industrial output. By 1975 provincial and local governments were responsible for about 60 percent of all state investment and for the greater part of the plan; only the production of key commodities like coal, timber, and cement was organized from the center.[20] State-owned industries might have their input, outputs, and prices set by the plan; a report by the World Bank argues that 30,000 medium-size and 150,000 small industrial organizations were largely free of the plan.[21] A new rudimentary form of light industry was emerging in the rural areas; it would take off during the reform period and was unintentionally a great boon.

However, China's advance overall was poor, verging on the disastrous. Per capita income in 1978 was only $210. The growth rate between 1957 and 1978 was only 4.3 percent: the generation of reformers who succeeded Mao doubled that rate—another indication of the waste that took place during the Mao years. Eighty percent of industrial output was in the state sector. More than 70 percent of the labor force worked on the land in conditions of severe poverty. External trade and access to foreign technology were effectively nonexistent; the economy was sealed off from foreigners. The institutions of civil society had been snuffed out; and only the artificial, greatly disliked commune system had taken their place. As Mao lay dying and the leaders of the Communist Party jockeyed for position, they all knew that one way or another policy had to change.

Coming to Terms with Mao

On August 5, 1966, the fifty-year-old headmistress of a leading girls' school in Beijing had become the first victim of the Cultural Revolution. The excoriation of teachers for "rightism," for organizing bourgeois exams, and for being sympathetic to capitalism and the cultural icons of reactionary imperial China had been going on for some months, but in early August its intensity mounted. In a spasm of collective violence the headmistress's pupils, now self-styled "Red Guards" and indoctrinated into believing they were fulfilling Mao's higher purpose, poured boiling water over her. She died from the battering she received from belt buckles and wooden sticks studded with nails. The student leader was honored less than a two weeks later at a review of hundreds of thousands of Red Guards at Tiananmen Gate; she put an armband on Chairman Mao, who told her to rename herself "Be Violent." [22]

Similar abuses would kill up to 500,000 others during the Cultural Revolution. Mao had become convinced that every vestige of China's imperial past and the Confucian gentry class that had suffocated

China had to be irrevocably and violently smashed. Only thus could the revolution escape its tendency to relapse into the temptations of capitalism, stalling the economic and social egalitarianism that he genuinely believed was the route to prosperity and individual well-being. Thus the state, consciously and with no judicial process, systematically encouraged the mass killing of its citizens.

This was only forty years ago—a tremendous event in the history of China and still within living memory. The Communist Party in whose name the killing was done is still in power. South Africa formed a Truth and Reconciliation Commission after the end of apartheid; but in China there has been no honest or sustained attempt to come to terms with the crimes that were committed. Many critics of modern China say that no good can come from evil; but the advances in general well-being—from the reduction in poverty to the transformation in the position of women—suggest otherwise. The reforms that began in 1978 built on Mao's legacy. What sense are we to make of the extraordinary cruelty of his regime? Can there be any gains from such evil? Can China ever become a normal state when the enormity of what was done is not recognized, and when no safeguards have been created so that it might never happen again?

Jung Chang and her husband, Jon Halliday, argue in their best-selling biography *Mao—The Unknown Story* that the Cultural Revolution was further evidence of Mao's deranged amoral lust for power and thus a condemnation of communism, which allowed it to happen. Chang—who also wrote the compelling *Wild Swans,* a story of today's China through the pained eyes of three generations of women—and Halliday did ten years of research to produce a comprehensive indictment. They estimate that 70 million people died as a direct or indirect result of Mao's policies. The Great Leap Forward and the disastrous conditions of workers cynically sacrificed in building dams, railways, and irrigation systems under lethal conditions all are evidence of a callous indifference to human life.

And that indifference sprang from a callous, self-absorbed, immoral human being who treated his wives and children contemptuously, did not even walk the Long March (he was carried in a bamboo litter), owned more than fifty personal estates, and thought nothing of having fresh fish from Wuhan carried more than 600 miles to please his palate. He, and the system which bred him and which still does not acknowledge or offer redress for what was done, are beyond the pale.

Nobody wants to be an apologist for Mao. Even the Communist Party, five years after his death, delivered the famous verdict that he was only 70 percent right. The Cultural Revolution and the Great Leap Forward have had the paradoxical result of delegitimizing Maoist communism and thus were self-defeating even in Mao's terms. But the wider question with which we all have to wrestle is what part of Mao's thought system delivered the good—if any— alongside the acknowledged evil, whatever the relative percentages may be. Or does the scale of the inhumanity and injustice of the Mao era put it beyond the traditional boundaries within which ethical questions are normally discussed?

In the first place, we must recognize, if not accept, the context. Mao was the leader of a revolutionary Communist Party that believed in egalitarianism, collective will, and an ongoing political struggle against reaction as the means to solve China's profound problems. Its civilization had collapsed; it had been despoiled by invasion and civil war; it was economically backward. There was a craving for a complete, decisive rupture with all that had produced this.

China is a proud culture. To plumb such depths was humiliating personally as well as nationally. In the nineteenth century foreigners had treated the Chinese as little better than animals—a reversal of what the Chinese believed the relationship should be. When Mao said that the Great Leap Forward would lead to China's overtaking Britain within fifteen years, he was not just articulating his own deluded personal ambitions—he was speaking for a collective desire to restore China and the Chinese to the proper scheme of things.

For the majority of Chinese the revolution of 1949 ranks alongside the world's other great revolutions. The communist revolutionaries were like the French revolutionaries, who violently ended monarchy and aristocratic government and inaugurated much-needed modernity. A survey published in Beijing in August 1995 by the magazine *Chinese Youth* named Mao Zedong, Sun Yat-sen, and Deng Xiaoping China's three greatest figures.[23] There is respect for his commitment to radical egalitarianism, and an understanding, if not an endorsement, of why he did what he did. Hu Jintao's invocations of Mao today are not empty or ritualistic; they are his way of expressing unease about the values of the market, in contrast to Mao's collectivism.

Maurice Meisner argues that empathy is needed. Communism sought an unalterable break with the past to deliver a future in which everyone could achieve personal fulfillment, genuine equality, cultural depth, and economic prosperity.[24] "Deprived of its ability to inspire hope for the future, the revolution congeals into an image of 'madness' which seemingly transforms it from a problem in history to an aberration outside history," Meisner writes. "And socialism, its ideological motive force, is similarly transformed into a pathological ideological escape from present reality." Unless that is understood, many of Mao's actions seem inexplicable. For the first decade after 1949 most Chinese were behind Mao; what followed in the late 1950s and 1960s is seen not only as a crime against humanity but also as a process through which China reached its present position and its present possibilities. Some elements of the dream of 1949 have been delivered while others have been shown to be impossible and irretrievably compromised. More—even, ultimately, political liberty, the rule of law, and freedom of expression—is expected in future, although such things are uncertain and will have to be fought for.

This raises the question whether any violent means is justified for a morally "good" end—or whether there is a dividing line if the morally good result was unintended. President Truman, authorizing the use of the atom bomb against Japan in 1945, argued that the violent means justified the ultimate end of bringing the war to an earlier end and saving American lives. That has not ended the anguished debate about whether it was right to use such a weapon on civilians, which continues today. In an influential essay of 1918 on what it means to be a political leader, the German sociologist Max Weber observed that political leadership necessarily places politicians in a moral universe where they make decisions about how to achieve ultimate ends—equality or justice or winning a war—whose ramifications may involve moral ills for which the leaders cannot be held to account for in the same way.[25] The "ethic of ultimate ends," Weber argues, cannot be reconciled with the "ethic of responsibility" whereby politicians are deemed to know in advance whether the consequences of their actions will actually be worth whatever progress is secured in the pursuit of an ultimate end. The political leader is in uncharted territory, as he has been throughout history; his vocation damns him to have an ultimate end and he has perforce to strive to achieve it. Truman's action is still intensely criticized even though it led to the ultimate end he wanted.

Communist egalitarianism—the justification that Mao would offer for his action—is a far more debatable ultimate end; we do not share it, so for us, any associated ills have no moral justification. Mao would counter that our view does not matter; his beliefs were sincerely held, and thus he belongs to the same moral universe as Truman even if we do not share his beliefs and values.

But there is an important difference. The American system both before and after the decision to use the atom bomb has held Truman to account for what he did despite the good of the ultimate end—as he knew it would. This meant that the threshold for justification had to be high. And it will be if a similar decision is ever made again, and so the threshold will act as an important constraint. Weber would have approved. However, no such process has taken place in China.[26] Mao was in his own thought bubble while violently rooting out an "infestation" of cultural reaction, as he would put it, that stood in the way of his egalitarian utopia. The authoritarian system permitted only Mao to judge the case and set the threshold for justification of murder; the decision, the results, and the immediate and continuing lack of redress are all wrong. Even Meisner's plea for empathy toward revolutionaries cannot escape these truths. The moral superiority of liberal democracy is that it has a process to hold politicians to account even when they plead that their end justified the means—and it gives civil society some chance of linking, even if imperfectly, the moral universe of ends and responsibility.

This does not mean that good can never come from bad or that communism had zero utility. If good can never come from bad, then it becomes impossible in any circumstance for a political leader to make a decision like Truman's. Weber's point is that we may not like it, but politicians occupy a universe in which such decisions have to be made. Truman's critics must accept that the war probably ended earlier than it otherwise would, even if they think the price was too high. Similarly, we know the negative side of the communist balance sheet: murder, injustice, and economic waste. But even the Mao years cannot be wholly written off. It is true that this was a period of economic futility and famine, and that a tiny Maoist court within the inner government compound of Zhongnanhai in their own secret Forbidden City obsessively played paranoid, murderous, and vengeful political games. But there is also a plus side.

There was a vast buildup of industrial production, extension of the rail network and agricultural irrigation, and a dramatic lowering of innumeracy and illiteracy. Life expectancy rose; and the circumstances of women, as argued earlier, were transformed. Moreover, Mao's commitment to political decentralization was genuine; as a result, state planning and collectivization of agriculture could be reversed more quickly in China than in the Soviet Union when the opportunity for reform came.

There is also a remarkable lack of self-knowledge, and even of history, among some western critics, who seem unaware of how western economies developed from predominantly agrarian communities into capitalist market societies. Too many commentators ignore the degree to which states have had to lead the creation of market economies, and the extraordinary social dislocation and pain involved in moving from a predominantly rural economy to an industrialized one. In his *Social Origins of Dictatorship and Democracy,* Barrington Moore observes that slavery was the core of the U.S. agricultural system in the south before 1865, and that the American Civil War should be seen in part as the dislocation of moving to the wage system on which the industrialized north depended. Indeed, no country has succeeded in industrializing without some pain.[27] Karl Polanyi, in *The Great Transformation,* shows how the nineteenth-century laissez-faire system in Britain—with workers paid in money (rather than food and housing as in feudal times), free trade, enclosed privately owned land, and the gold standard—was created deliberately by the British state.[28] The fact that the Chinese state has had to build capitalism and the market, and that there have been severe costs in moving hundreds of millions of people from a system of low-productivity agriculture built up over 2,000 years to high-productivity industry should not be seen as aberrant. It is, in fact, typical.

Today's China could not have started from nothing in 1978. It build on foundations laid by Mao, not least of which was the experience of the Great Leap Forward and the Cultural Revolution as an approach not to adopt again. The unifying thread was the vanguard role of the Communist Party. Lenin expected it to build communism; instead, it built capitalism—or as Jiang Zemin would have it, the "socialist market economy." The success has been so stunning that just as critics of China's political system have abstracted it from context, history, and the issues of political morality that exist elsewhere, so there is much praise of China's economic system and policy which is similarly abstracted from history and reality.

Andrew Neil, former editor of the *Sunday Times,* cites today's China as evidence of the enduring validity of Hayekian truths about the superiority of markets and economic and political freedom.[29] Sir Digby Jones, former director general of the Confederation of British Industry (CBI), warns the British that an avalanche of Chinese free-enterprise entrepreneurialism awaits them. As we will see, both

Neil and Jones wildly misinterpret what is happening in China. Its economic model is a conflation of markets and political authoritarianism that cannot be sustained. Reform will require genuine economic pluralism. The problem is that China's worrying failure to come terms with Mao points to a wider political incapacity to create independent, pluralist institutions vital for economic development. The party's ducking of the moral consequence of mass murder because it might threaten the legitimacy of the Communist Party, if not addressed, will fatally damage this next economic transition. Just as we need to be hardheaded about the beneficial outcomes of the Mao years if we are to understand today's China, so we need to be equally hardheaded about how the inability to challenge Mao's actions, tradition, and legacy undermines the future. Jung Chang and Jon Halliday are right to insist that before China can move on it must come to terms with the enormity of Mao's crimes; on the other hand neither their comprehensive indictment, in my view, any more than the praise of an Andrew Neil of the subsequent reform program help us navigate the complexities sure-footedly. But then neither do the ideological simplicities and avoidance of the truth by the Communist Party. China, past and present, evokes strong emotions. That increases the importance of seeing through them to the reality.

CHAPTER 4

The Odd Couple—
Communism and Capitalism

DENG XIAOPING (1904–1997) WAS THE INSPIRATIONAL architect of contemporary China, and is thus among the great figures of the twentieth century. He was a canny survivor of the Mao years, but in 1976, when he was a seventy-two-year-old bureaucrat, there was little to suggest his true radicalism. He was known as an economic pragmatist, certainly, but scarcely anyone could have guessed the extent of his ambition for change or his willingness to take risks to advance the cause of reform. He was, after all, an original communist from the 1920s, and had earned his revolutionary credentials as one of the ranking army commanders first in the war against the Japanese and then in the civil war against the Nationalists, when he performed with distinction.

After 1949 he effectively ran one of the six regional bureaus—the southwest China bureau—established to entrench the revolution. He was brought to Beijing in 1952, and by 1956 his combination of organizational skills and political suppleness led to his appointment as general secretary of the party. Between then and 1967 he cast himself as an inscrutable technocrat, effective administrator, and communist loyalist. None of this protected him during the Cultural Revolution. He worked on the floor of a tractor factory under house arrest and was badly scarred by the experience. His eldest son, taken for questioning to expose his father's "rightist" tendencies, had instead thrown himself out of the window and was left partially paralyzed for life. That incident profoundly colored Deng's view of Maoism. Deng reemerged in politics in Beijing in 1973, when Mao recalled him—eventually to take charge of the army. He was the only high-ranking communist Mao could turn to with the standing to stabilize the army; and that fact was a clear signal of Mao's waning ability to find radical recruits who could sustain the Cultural Revolution.

For Mao's allegation was right. Deng was inclined to be a "capitalist roader," and he represented a growing tendency within the upper echelons of the Communist Party. The Great Leap Forward and Cultural Revolution had convinced Deng that Mao's approach to economic development was all wrong. He would say in 1988 that if there was consensus on reform and China's opening up, "This should be attributed to the 10-year Cultural Revolution, the lessons from this disaster are too profound." He also said, "The Cultural Revolution has become our wealth"—without it there would have been no new policies.[1]

After Mao's death, reform had to be fought for. Mao had designated Hua Guofeng as his successor. Within a month of Mao's death Hua arrested the Gang of Four, Mao's leftist clique who had led the Cultural Revolution, accusing them of planning further destabilization. However, Hua could not be the champion of reform. Because he was Mao's designated successor, his own legitimacy depended on Mao's, so he could not repudiate Mao but had to hold the line. The Chinese, he said, should "obey whatever Mao had said and ensure the continuation of whatever he had decided"—a policy that the group around Deng derided as the "whatever approach." With a feeble base, doubtful legitimacy, and a policy that attracted few adherents Hua was in trouble from the beginning.

In any case Deng was a formidable opponent. As a veteran of the revolution he had considerable legitimacy; as a former army commander, regional bureau chief, and general secretary of the party he had an unequaled network to access and mobilize; and he had the better argument. China did not want more of the same. It did not want to follow Mao "whatever." It ached for genuine economic progress, especially because by 1978 its neighbors—Japan, Hong Kong, Taiwan, and Singapore—had established an enviable pattern of economic growth.

Deng had seen peasants and state enterprises respond to incentives in the pragmatic reconstruction after the Great Leap Forward. His initial objective was clear even if the means were not. He intended the Communist Party to retain its iron political control of China—so he closed the "democracy wall" in 1978 and imprisoned the human rights activist Wei Jingsheng when critics began to advocate democratization of China. But he wanted to get the party out of the day-to-day management of communes, state-owned enterprises, education, and agriculture, instead allowing managers to take responsibility and respond to incentives. There should be no fear of re-creating a capitalist class. Rather, the party had to "make practice the sole criterion of truth"[2] and recognize there is no communist virtue in poverty; on the contrary, it is glorious to be rich.

Economic development had to be at the heart of the Communist Party's intent, Deng would say in 1992, or else the party was lost; "it was the only hard truth."[3] Ideological egalitarianism—as in the school system and in the organization of agriculture—had obstructed development. It would have to go.

During 1978 Hua Guofeng was outmaneuvered intellectually and politically, and in December 1978, at the famous Third Plenum of the Eleventh Party Congress, the party committed itself to modernization, broad-based economic development, the rule of law—rather than the class struggle, further peasant collectivization, and heavy industrialization to which Hua had pledged himself. It was a historic and decisive moment. Deng moved fast, and within months his people—many, like him, restored from exile—were in key positions in the Politburo and the state. The Dengists—the "practice" party[4]—had the political momentum, and the conservatives were on the defensive. Reform could and would begin.

What followed was an extraordinary and triumphant vindication of Deng's approach—"crossing the river groping for stepping-stones," as Deng put it. China has made up its own rules and processes at each stage of reform, oscillating between *fang* (opening up) and *shou* (tightening) as it has moved forward, responding to ebbs and flows of confidence and balance between reformers and conservatives.[5] There has been no top-down "big bang" initiation of privatization, price liberalization, or democratization as in eastern Europe,[6] It has been some of the bottom-up movements—like the dismantling of the commune system—that most closely resembled a "big bang."

The centerpiece of economic development has been the ability to maintain investment at a stunning 35 to 40 percent of GDP for twenty-five years (an unparalleled rate, higher than Korea's or Japan's). This was possible because of continued high savings and the single-minded capacity of the state-owned banking system, protected by controls on exchange and capital, to channel the savings to state-owned enterprises and infrastructure. This has entailed serious costs: waste, low productivity, bad loans, and white-elephant infrastructure projects. Also, the banking system has scandalously neglected rural China and is a source of dangerously severe rural poverty (which I discuss in more detail in Chapter 5). But the fact remains. The World Bank estimates that from 1978 to 1998 two-thirds of the 9.4 percent annual growth rate in China's GDP resulted simply from having more machines and infrastructure every year. The proportion of growth attributable to this source rose from 63 percent in the first decade of reform to 67 percent in the second decade.[7] Even today the boom in foreign direct investment has been a relative sideshow; it amounted to $60 billion in 2004 but represented just 10 percent of China's total investment.

In much of the Chinese reform program, there has been a significant element of luck—which has then been cleverly exploited. One example is the continuation of high personal and enterprise savings available for investment, averaging 37 percent of national output between 1978 and 1995; this could not have been anticipated in 1978. Another example is globalization, which has led to greater foreign direct investment over the 1990s and 2000s. This too could not have been anticipated. The main cause—again, unexpected—of high and rising personal savings has been the one-child policy introduced in 1980 to slow down China's population growth and relieve pressure on the land. Urban and rural people have built up their savings because they can rely on no more than one child to look after them in old age, and because of the rollback in the system of social support—the "iron rice bowl"—provided by state-owned enterprises under growing financial pressure. Also, according to Shahid Yusuf of the World Bank, after many decades of austerity the Chinese are keenly aware that it could quickly return, so they have held back from increasing their spending in line with their higher incomes. In fact, the risk of unemployment has been rising. The demographics begin to look less favorable henceforth, as the population ages and people draw down their savings. China is probably at the height of its saving capacity now— but saving, nevertheless, has been crucial in its development.[8]

The regime's pragmatism and gradualism have resulted from a lack of political consensus at the top about what to do, how radically to do it, and in what sequence—together with uncertainty about how specific initiatives would work in practice. There has been as much responding to events, and capitalizing on lucky breaks, as directing them. Almost all the developments in rural China have emerged from the bottom, with the state essentially letting the bottom do what it will as long as it does not obstruct the prime objective: reorganizing and supporting state-owned enterprise, investing in infrastructure, and phasing out planning, all with as few losers as possible. The insistence that the sole test is "practice" disguises an unwillingness to create new constitutional and institutional forms. Focusing on "practice" has involved offering incentives, increasing production, and creating transitional institutions while leaving the current legal, social, and political regime pretty much undisturbed.

When the west sees sound money, balanced budgets, market incentives, and encouragement of small firms, it thinks it is seeing elements of western-style capitalism and an embrace of "free-market fundamentalism." What it is in fact seeing is the Chinese "flexing" their system in ways that do not upset its essential components. Balanced budgets and incentives make macro sense and do not disturb the wider system: indeed budget discipline is a prerequisite for capping inflation, whose social implications the party fears. The real preoccupation of the Chinese is shown by their unwillingness to privatize, to sell majority control of state-owned enterprises to private investors on the stock market, to reduce the party's influence on the banking system, to allow independent trade unions, to develop an impartial judicial system, or to relax capital controls. In these terms, some of the western debate over the virtues of gradualism is beside the point.

China's approach has certainly meant that the mistakes made in eastern Europe and Russia have not been repeated. For example, in Russia premature privatization led to pillaging of state assets before regulations and legal and property rights could be put into place; this has not occurred in China. But it was not economic farsightedness that allowed the Chinese to avoid this mistake. Their eclectic policy has been driven by an overriding political reality: the vanguardist Communist Party must stay firmly in control, keeping hold of the key power levers while managing the reform process so as to minimize the number of powerful losers. This is not free-market capitalism but, as I argued earlier, Leninist corporatism.

In China, more communist institutions have adapted to this policy and proved their economic utility than any western observers would have guessed. Jeffrey Sachs of Columbia University and Wing Thye Woo of the University of California have argued that China was fortunate to start with so much of its labor force in agriculture and with a relatively underdeveloped industrial sector; there were fewer people to feel the pain of restructuring and China could begin afresh.[9] China was also lucky to have Hong Kong and Taiwan on its doorstep, to provide an example of what the Chinese economy could do and to provide an inside track of family and friendship connections within daily commuting distance, showing others how profitable investment in China could be.

But Sachs and Woo concede that the Maoist legacy of decentralization helped. The Chinese plan governed only 1,200 commodities; the Russian plan, by contrast, governed 25 million—so again the Chinese had less to unscramble.[10] This was not so much a result of China's needing less planning because it was a more backward economy, as Sachs and Woo argue. Rather, it resulted from Mao's view that the self-sufficient decentralized unit was the strategic driver in revolutionary success, whether of a guerrilla group or a state-owned enterprise. They could make decisions for themselves, in the light of local conditions, about how best they could further communist objectives. As I remarked in Chapter 3, China's decentralized organization reflected Mao's belief. When Deng, in the initial reform period, gave more autonomy to the provinces over how they spent and raised money and how they could respond to the demolition of the communes, he was operating within precedents and structures established by Mao.

And if the international environment was more benign, Deng had acted to make it so by seeking peace with the United States. On January 1, 1979, the United States and China announced the opening of full diplomatic relations. Washington severed its formal ties with Taiwan; and China agreed to step back from anything but a titular claim to Taiwan, and to accept the United States' rules of the international game for trade, finance, and investment. Although it did not seem so at the time, and is not understood even today in these terms, this represented a de facto victory for the United States in the Vietnam war—in effect, a surrogate war against China. By delaying communist government in Vietnam, with its Chinese backing, until 1975, the United States had bought a crucial decade for the Asian economy to begin its growth—led by exports—and show indisputably that capitalist development was more successful than communist. The normalization of relations included China's buying three American Boeings, allowing Coca-Cola to open a bottling plant in Shanghai, and setting up four special economic zones later in 1980 to attract foreign investment. China had admitted ideological defeat; from now on it intended to develop a market economy, though that economy would have strongly Chinese characteristics. This was a remarkable, unsung success for American policy.

The accommodation was part of Deng's greater plan. He was not content to increase agricultural production and accelerate industrialization by offering incentives to Chinese peasants and managers. He also wanted to reproduce in China the kind of success that Hong Kong, Singapore, and (gallingly) Taiwan had achieved by building up exports through foreign investment and gaining access to foreign technology. Of the four new "special economic zones" established in 1980, tellingly one was in Shenzhen, just across the border from Hong Kong; another was near Macao; and two were across the strait from Taiwan. They were to be tax-free, bounded zones where foreign multinationals (especially Chinese from Hong Kong and Taiwan) could build up export capacity on their own terms. Normalization of relations with the United States gave the Taiwanese and Hong Kong Chinese—the most likely initial investors in China—a green light. Foreign direct investment began to move back into China for the first time since the early 1930s.

Phase One: "Responsibility"

China in 1978 was directly or indirectly run by the state, with party cadres involved in the day-to-day management of every nook and cranny of the country. Apart from 150,000 individual proprietorships representing 1 percent of GDP, the rest was wholly state-owned and state-run. The first step was to take the Communist Party out of management and turn the responsibility over to managers in industry, teachers in education, and so on. Deng focused on the industrial sector. In 1980 he proposed a "factory manager responsibility system" that would "take the Party Committee out of day-to-day affairs and allow it to concentrate on party and ideological work and organisational supervision."[11] Organizations, instead of being subject to detailed planning, would contract with state purchasers regarding how much they would produce and would be given more autonomy to decide how to produce it. In 1984, the "Ten Regulations" allowed organizations to sell any surpluses they produced over and above the targets set by the plan, at prices that could be 20 percent above or below the planned price. To weaken the hold of the party, enterprise managers could make midmanagement appointments. By the late 1980s almost all state-owned enterprises were entering into long-term planning contracts, negotiating prices, promoting on merit, and retaining an increasing share of their profits for reinvestment. Also, managers were able to qualify for bonuses.[12] This was a revolution of sorts; but, as we shall see, it did little to improve the dismal productivity of state-owned enterprises.

Still, it did begin a phased freeing-up of prices. China did not go for a one-off bonfire of price controls; the economic reaction could not be predicted, and if inflation resulted, the social consequences would be dire. The combination of a responsibility system on the land and the "Ten Regulations" meant that by 1985 the prices of 40 percent of farm products, 34 percent of consumer goods sold in shops, and 13 percent of factory products at the gate were free of government regulation.

Deng now wanted to go further. The scope for arbitrage between planned and market prices was sometimes huge, making the whole transition unstable and opening up the possibility of massive fraud. He wanted to move fast to remove the temptation, and introduced a sudden relaxation of prices in 1988. Inflation rose sharply, arousing memories of the hyperinflation of 1949 and a run on the banks. Price reform was dropped almost immediately, but even so there was a rise to double-digit inflation. This was one of the grievances that provoked Tiananmen the following year, and Tiananmen showed the Politburo that it was presiding over a powder keg.

However, by the early 1990s Deng felt politically secure enough to do what he had wanted to do three years earlier: complete the liberalization of prices. By 1995, 78 percent of farm prices, 89 percent of consumer goods in shops, and 79 percent of factory gate prices had been decontrolled.[13] Today virtually all prices have been liberalized, except those for some key utilities and energy. China's degree of price freedom matches that of most industrialized countries which, like the Chinese, regulate key prices.

China's phased decontrol thus involved a dual system of pricing: one within the plan and one progressively set by the market. It has been widely praised as a striking example of successful pragmatism. However, the Chinese had no choice. If the Communist Party was to stay in power, it dared not risk a social revolt. As Qian Yingyi of Stanford University argues, it allowed reform to be phased in so that there were few losers, thus preventing a wider economic and political crisis.[14] Nobody went bust, because inefficient firms could obtain supplies at the planned prices. But at the same time there was plenty of opportunity for efficient firms to expand production to profit from the new opportunities to sell on the free market. In coal and steel, for example, the planned targets were met at the planned prices; but there was also a booming market in coal and steel produced outside the plan, with prices set by supply and demand. However, the longer the dual system lasted, the more corruption took hold: local officials lined their pockets by procuring production under planned prices and selling the products at higher market prices. The People's Liberation Army, with its own network of factories producing a range of goods, some of which could easily be supplied to civilian buyers, was also able to profit illicitly from the reform process. Gradualism was the right policy for reform, but it did not come without costs.

Deng was directing the process in industry, but in rural China the communes themselves seized the initiative, taking the opportunity that the "responsibility system" gave them. Even before the third Plenum in 1978, a group of communes in Fenyang county of Anhui province had persuaded the provincial government to accept that individual peasant households—rather than the commune—would contract to deliver quotas of grain, and that the province would thus get more grain.[15] This would set off a revolution from below, a Chinese-style big bang. The Fenyang arrangement swept through rural China like a social hurricane. Peasants simply closed the commune system down and insisted on farming on individual plots, almost always the plots of their ancestors. By 1983 98 percent of peasant households were individually contracting with their counties or provinces to produce food, sweeping away Mao's detested communes.

Deng called this the "household responsibility system," and nearly 300 million households were operating in this way just four years after the process began. What made the transition happen so quickly was that individual peasant households recognized the system as a way to regain control of land their families had farmed for generations. They might only get twenty-year licenses (later extended to thirty years)[16] but village leaders—and the peasants themselves—knew which land plots were due to them despite nearly three decades of collectivization. Many still retained property titles from the imperial and republican governments, as Li Bozhong of Tsinghua University has shown.[17] As peasants regained their former land, met their contracts, and sold free surpluses on the market, production climbed by 8 percent between 1979 and 1984, and the land was farmed much more economically than it had been under the communal system. Agricultural productivity rose steeply, on some estimates by as much 8 percent per year, and new rice varieties spread rapidly.[18] This was the keystone of the economic reform program. It supported the rural savings that would be deployed for huge investment, and it helped reduce poverty in rural China. There would be difficulties ahead; for one thing, the typical peasant plot is far too small to be the basis of a highly productive agricultural sector in the long term. However, the immediate result was a much-needed uplift.

The fragmentation of the commune system and the return of the peasants to their plots posed a problem for village and local government leaders. What to do with the small-scale factories which every Maoist commune had begun and which produced everything from bicycle parts to buttons and zippers? Now that the communes no longer made organizational sense, and in any case were formally abolished in 1983, who was to own and manage these factories? They could not be privatized, because Beijing was sending out a steady stream of ideological rhetoric against private business and bourgeois capitalism—and because the four newly established state banks (created by breaking up Mao's unitary state bank) were forbidden to lend to private companies. But the factories provided work and were an important source of local supplies. The answer was pragmatic: towns and villages would take them over, manage them, and reinvest the profit in the business or invest it in the community.

Red Hat Capitalists

The boom in "town and village enterprises" (TVEs) took everyone by surprise. Deng, acknowledging that they were "our greatest success," said they had just developed spontaneously: "This result was not anything that I or any of the other comrades had foreseen; it just came out of the blue."[19] They are certainly integral to Chinese development; in 1978 collective enteprise was part of the commune system, but by 1993 TVEs were employing 52 million people—58 percent of all employment in rural industry.[20] By the end of 2005 they employed 135 million people.

These are rural China's metal bashers and suppliers of building materials, clothes, and packaged food—the backbone of the rural economy. Without them, rural unemployment and poverty would be disastrous. Yet according to western economic textbooks, they should not be so successful. Their property rights and legal standing are and were uncertain; for years they were outside the plan and had to scramble for raw materials and supplies. They do not have profit-maximizing shareholders who are willing to risk capital and who want to drive them forward. The result should be indiscipline and waste. Their owners—local governments—should plunder the profits and should have no incentive to make the enterprise grow.

Yet these enterprises have grown, although much faster in southern and coastal China than inland and in the northeast, which are more heavily populated with state-owned enterprise. Despite their disadvantages, they had the aces of being given their equity capital free, and they had strong local franchises. The "tilted playing field"[21] was an incentive to become agile and adaptable. They have been not only a vehicle for the rapid growth of rural employment but also a rich source of revenue to fund housing, schools, and hospitals.

For the first fifteen years of the reform program they were helped enormously by a tax system that encouraged them to keep their surpluses and reinvest these in their own growth and finance local public facilities.[22] In the south and along the coast, where Mao had shunned investing in industry because it would be the first to fall in any invasion, local communities were on their own, with little or no industrial base. Edward Steinfeld of MIT argues that if local officials in these areas did not help their communities, nobody else would. The development of the TVE was a matter of life and death, the only route to economic development and to the provision of local public "goods." It was also an avenue to personal enrichment (by means of a little local corruption).[23] Local communities were made to "eat from a single kitchen," as the Chinese say and were on their mettle rather than "eating from one big pot."

In other parts of China, with more state-owned enterprises (SOEs), the "big pot" tradition could be maintained. Local officials could hold the SOEs for ransom, confident that whatever their trading deficit, the national banking system would come to their aid. In these areas there was less incentive to build TVEs, because officials could plunder the existing state enterprises to build the social infrastructure. In other words, what was emerging was not a new form of capitalist altruism spearheaded by enlightened local government, as some starstruck commentators have argued.[24] Rather, when local government had its back to the wall, it responded creatively; otherwise, it reverted to type—milking state-owned enterprises.

In their heyday TVEs were also a cloak behind which local entrepreneurs—"red capitalists"—could hide their private ambitions, until the late 1990s when banks were finally allowed to lend to private companies and entrepreneurs could "come out." Typically the entre- preneur would make a deal with the TVE, which would shelter him from party investigation for being a capitalist. For example, the first Chinese company to be quoted on Nasdaq in 2002, Qiaoxing Enter- prise Group, spent its first ten years as a supposed TVE in Fujian. Its founder and chief executive, Wu Ruilin, was a "red hat" capitalist; the TVE structure disguised what he was really doing.

However, after 1994 TVEs began a transmutation. In the first place, the tax breaks that supported them were withdrawn as the gov- ernment recentralized taxation: local government became less inter- ested in their development. The TVEs began to turn themselves into much more conventional private firms with only nominal ownership by local government, although achieving that in a Chinese framework without clear property, legal, and incorporation rights remains highly problematic. For the last seven or eight years they have been in an institutional no-man's-land and cannot go forward or back. They proved to be a brilliant institution of transition, but not, unless the party chooses to loosen its political grip, of ongoing economic devel- opment.

Economic reform has been uneven. In the older industrial prov- inces dominated by SOEs, the state continued to lead the economy. In the southern province of Guangdong it was inward investment from Hong Kong and small firms that drove higher growth. And Zhe- jiang, a province across the strait from Taiwan, has emerged as the private-sector capital of China and one of its fastest-growing provinces. In 1998 Zhejiang was the first Chinese province to report that half its industrial output was produced by the pure private sector. Meanwhile the Wenzhou prefecture has been both a showcase and trouble spot, insisting on developing whatever it takes to industrialize and thumbing its nose at party rules. Other provinces want to repro- duce its success.

Mao's strategic ban on investment applied to Wenzhou because of its proximity to Taiwan and its consequent vulnerability to bombard- ment in the event of a war. Thus this prefecture is a dramatic example of how the breakup of the Maoist communes in a dirt-poor part of China meant that without institutional innovation everyone faced poverty or worse. There had to be a conceptual leap. There was no institutional apparatus whatsoever in Wenzhou in 1979 except that of the indifferent, faraway state and, apart from kinship and *guanxi* networks, no civil society. Wenzhou had to create its own structures, all the time kowtowing to the line that its devices conformed to the rules about "collective enterprise." Nor could "banks" be created, even though in a region as poor as this development cannot happen unless there is access to credit; and state banks were forbidden to lend to anything but state-owned or bona fide collective enterprise.

So entrepreneurs in Wenzhou adopted the "red hat" strategy, associating themselves with TVEs or SOEs more aggressively than anywhere else, and—more important—inventing private banking institutions but calling them "money houses" rather than banks. In the early years of reform Wenzhou was home to an increasing number of tiny family businesses. Because Marx had said that the threshold for the exploitative capitalist firm was eight people, the party was happy—in the early years of the reform program—to permit private enterprise up to that limit. Between 1979 and 1987 Wenzhou registered an amazing 190,000 businesses with no more than eight staff members. If entrepreneurs wanted a business to grow, they would need to exceed the eight-person limit; and with company formation banned, the only possible route was some form of affiliation with a TVE.

The forms of affiliation that were invented to solve the problem were and are bewildering. They include mock, artificial "red hat" TVEs and genuine "stockholding cooperatives." In the latter, entrepreneurs would put up capital in an overt cooperative partnership with their workers, who would automatically receive a quarter of the profits as a dividend. In exchange the cooperative would grow beyond Marx's limit of eight. These cooperatives were a halfway house between capitalism and socialism in which workers and shareholders co-owned the company and profits. This was the kind of organizational structure once proposed by the Nobel laureate James Meade to create companies as partnerships of labor and capital, with equal rights to dividends. Meade thought he had invented a building block in what he called liberal socialism, combining the dynamism of profit-seeking capital with the collaborative instincts of socialism. The people of Wenzhou, although they probably have never heard of Meade, might agree.

By 1990 two-fifths of Wenzhou's industrial output was produced by stockholding cooperatives. As Meade had predicted, the workers were just as eager to grow, innovate, and invest as the entrepreneurs. Around Wenzhou, eighteen satellite townships had increased to 110, a tribute to the pace of industrialization.[25] Kellee Tsai of John Hopkins University, who spent two years in the field researching China's informal banking system, reports that this growth would have been impossible without credit.[26] Wenzhou therefore allowed private "money houses"—adaptations of rural cooperative credit institutions and even mutated NGOs, all posing as collective enterprises even if in reality they were private—to get into the credit business. Neglected by Beijing, Wenzhou's officials, local leaders, and entrepreneurs took full advantage of Mao's legacy of decentralization and Deng's remedies: they would take responsibility; they would make practice the sole criterion of truth; and they would glory in getting rich.[27]

Beijing finally forced Wenzhou to close the "money houses" in the late 1980s, but it could not prevent the appetite for innovation, whetted by what was becoming one of the biggest industrial clusters of small firms in China. By 2003 Beijing relinquished its suspicions, and the People's Bank of China designated the city of Wenzhou an official experimental district for financial and banking reforms. Wenzhou, now one of China's richest cities, whose small business *guanxi* networks and quasi cooperatives could not be more different from the declining industrial cities of the northeast dominated by SOEs, had proved both the strength and the weakness of Chinese reform. It was dynamic, but in an institutional, legal, and social vacuum. Sooner or later, if they were to progress further, Wenzhou and

Zhejiang would need the full institutional infrastructure that supports capitalism.

Phase 2: "Made in China"

By late 1991 China's reformers had a significant record of achievement. Rural industry was booming in the form of TVEs; agricultural production was rising; state-owned enterprises were beginning, albeit slowly and belatedly, to improve their performance as a result of the responsibility system; and investment in infrastructure was substantial. But Tiananmen had proved a landmark moment. The conservative crackdown—freezing the reform program, clamping down on the movement of people, renewing hostility toward private business, imposing martial law, and slowing down the economy—had unnerved the country.

Tens of millions of peasants had left the land to find work in the cities during the 1980s, and there was no sign that this migration was abating. The evidence from the previous decade was that nonstate enterprise drove economic growth, and thus should be further supported. Yet the formal ban on private enterprises with more than eight employees remained in force; inefficient SOEs still dominated industrial output; and prices were not yet fully liberalized. Foreign direct investment had stopped growing, and in any case its cumulative total since 1979 was only $25 billion. Thailand, Malaysia, the Philippines, and Indonesia were now repeating the success trailblazed by Japan, South Korea, Hong Kong, Taiwan, and Singapore—a sign of what was possible. Communism had collapsed in eastern Europe and was collapsing in Russia. Unless China could maintain or accelerate the pace of economic development, the writing was on the wall.

So it was that Deng, now eighty-eight years old, made his last significant intervention. In January 1992, weeks after the demise of the Soviet Union and Gorbachev's resignation, he chose to take a "vacation" in seedy, fast-growing Shenzhen, home of China's first stock market and its first special economic zone. This was the beginning of what became known as the southern tour, with Deng traveling in a specially equipped train. He told successive audiences that without development and accelerated reform, the Communist Party was lost. He accused the opponents of reform, echoing a favorite phrase of Mao's, of being like women with bound feet. Reform might mean a little "spiritual pollution" of communist values, Deng said; but whenever you open a window, you let in flies. His presence in Shenzhen, China's foremost capitalist fly, showed that he thought the window should be opened wider. Foreign investment and private enterprise served the cause of development as well as education and scientific research, he declared; China even had to accept that in a race for riches, some people would emerge as winners before others. He challenged officials to say where they stood—and Guangdong, one of the pace-setting provinces in the south that already had been exploiting its proximity to Hong Kong and Macao to grow rapidly, needed little prompting. The party secretary of Guangdong, Xie Fie, replied that with the right policies his province could catch up with the Asian tigers by 2010. Deng approved; little did either know how accurate that prediction would prove to be.

It was a galvanizing political moment. Up until now reform had been considered in terms of responsibility, contracting, price liberalization, and allowing markets only at the margin of the plan. Conservatives had been reluctant but had been mollified because the party was still against private property and private business: state banks were forbidden to lend to private companies in all but exceptional circumstances. The welcome to foreign investment had been guarded; outside the four special economic zones—a fifth was added, but not until 1988—foreign investors had to have a Chinese enterprise as a partner if they wanted to establish a plant in China. The opening of the coastal strip in the 1980s to even limited joint ventures revived such painful memories of the infamous nineteenth-century treaty ports that the party found itself driving the policy through the National People's Congress with 700 abstentions and 300 opposed—an unprecedented degree of dissent. Without Deng and his prestige, progress would have been glacial.

However, the old man wanted to accelerate the pace of reform; and he got it. The new general secretary of the party, Jiang Zemin, seized the opportunity and transformed the party's objective from building a "planned socialist commodity economy"—the outcome of the landmark Eleventh Party Conference in 1978—to building a "socialist market economy," which was agreed on in 1993 at the Third Plenum of the Fourteenth Party Conference. During 1992 the number of industrial and agricultural products whose prices were regulated was slashed. In 1993 production, economic growth, and inflation soared. It was the year of what the Chinese called the five fevers—investment, stock market, real estate, government cadres getting into business, and fast growth.[28] It forced an economic retrenchment: Jiang Zemin had wanted to recentralize government revenues as part of the socialist market economy with a centrally imposed value-added tax, but now this was used as an economic regulator to slow the economy down.

In 1997 a decision was made to "hold onto the big but let go of the small" state enterprise. This has led to a whirlwind of consolidation and redundancy among SOEs. Although western commentators sometimes call "letting go" privatization, it was no such thing, and the Communist Party was careful not to call it that. Even when "let go," management is still beholden to the Communist Party, which continues to make senior appointments; and cash for investment is generated internally or borrowed from state-owned banks. As I explore in more detail later, this is "autonomization" or corporatization rather than privatization, and it takes place within a framework of political control and direction.

For while TVEs and SOEs may be directed by their management teams, ultimately they still dance to the state's tune. Also, although truly private firms that have been founded by entrepreneurs are the dynamic sector in China, the researcher Yasheng Huang of MIT found that during the 1990s their average size hardly grew from around sixty or seventy employees, and those that did grow larger only did so via access to legal and financial structures in Hong Kong.[29] There is still prejudice against lending to private firms, despite the formal relaxations introduced in 1998. The entire structure of ownership, corporate control, and unclear property rights constitutes a strong bias against building a business as understood in the west.

Chasing the Dragon

The pace of reform has been much more impressive in terms of opening up to the outside world. In December 2001 China joined the World Trade Organization, a further tribute to the liberalization initiated by Deng. Average tariffs on imported manufactured goods stood at 43 percent in 1992; by 2001 they had been reduced to 8.9 percent, with virtually all licenses and quantitative import controls eliminated.[30]

The trickle of foreign direct investment has turned into a flood. It nearly tripled to $11 billion in 1992, after Deng's southern tour, tripled again to $34 billion in 1994, and doubled to $61 billion by 2004. In 1992 alone, more than 8,500 new investment zones were created; before Deng's tour there had been only 100. Once the Chinese had signaled that they wanted foreign investment on far less restrictive terms, entrepreneurs in Hong Kong and Taiwan, who had been leading the way since 1979, were joined by western multinationals. There was a rekindling of the "China dream," the lure of a market of 1 billion consumers. The English writer Joe Studwell, editor of the *China Economic Quarterly* and author of *The China Dream,* draws attention to the long tradition of western capitalists who have been captivated by the prospect of China as a market. "If only we could persuade every person in China to lengthen his shirttail by a foot," wrote one nineteenth-century English industrialist, "we could keep the mills of Lancashire working round the clock."[31]

Deng's speech and Jiang's reaction sparked an enormous bullishness about China's prospects. This attitude had been waiting to be reignited ever since Deng took over—and suddenly China did seem to be a new Klondike. In the first half of 1992 the Shanghai stock market rose 1,200 percent. In the autumn of 1993 a group of Wall Street fund managers spent a week in China; Barton Biggs, founder and chairman of Morgan Stanley Asset Management, said, "After eight days in China I'm tuned in, overfed and maximum bullish."[32] He spoke for hundreds of others. Western investment money began to flow into China seriously, but almost everyone was to be disappointed. China might continue growing, but making profits would prove elusive. The Shanghai stock market has yet to fully recover from those heady early days.

The "China play" suddenly became the talk of corporate America, Japan, and Europe. The strategy: locate production capacity in a tax-free zone in China; employ its literate workers at one-thirtieth of the cost of workers in the United States or Europe; coordinate activity by Information and Communication Technology; ship the products in a modern container on a modern freeway to a modern port.[33] And sell them in the west for a colossal margin to boost your profits. Exports would do for now; there was a domestic market that would come onstream, and the advantage would fall to the first mover who could redirect products from the export to the home market when the time came.

A big China deal would reliably move the share price upward—and companies as disparate as General Motors and Microsoft scrambled to be among the first to make such a deal. Production and, increasingly, research in China are key components of most multinationals' strategy; some, like Microsoft, have signaled that they intend research in China to be cutting-edge. *BusinessWeek* estimates that by the end of 2005, 50,000 U.S. firms were doing business of some sort in China.[34]

Nearly 90 percent of foreign investment has been directed to the coastal provinces, particularly in the south; and two-thirds has been in manufacturing. China's extraordinary growth in exports has been propelled overwhelmingly by foreign companies. According to the Paris-based Organization for Economic Cooperation and Development, 55 percent of China's exports are made by foreigners; and generally, the more high tech the industry, the higher the foreigners' share. More than 80 percent of electronic and telecommunications exports are made by foreigners, 70 percent of plastics, and 60 percent of electrical goods.[35] Taiwan and Indonesia are an intriguing comparison: both relied much less on foreign direct investment (FDI) for exports at a similar stage in their development. Only 20 percent of Taiwan's manufacturing exports and 29 percent of Indonesia's were foreign-made.[36]

It should be no surprise that a growing number of western retailers import from China. In the United States Wal-Mart (see Chapter 1), Home Depot, and The Gap all have a growing proportion of sales from exports made in China. Britain's Kingfisher and Tesco and France's Carrefour are other examples, to name but a few.

This avalanche of foreign investment has made China the world's workshop, or at least its mass assembler, of choice and by 2010 (see Chapter 1) will make it the world's leading exporter. A huge number of consumer products have labels saying "Made in China." By 1999 FDI had already employed over 20 million people. The growth in imports is no less spectacular; one feature of China's development since 1992 is the emphasis on openness to both exports and imports—with many of the imports being brought in by foreign investors, reprocessed, and then exported.[37]

The concern within China is that this is a sign of weakness. Wu Jinglian, a researcher at China's State Council of Development Research who is close to the government, represents the internal debate. He observes that when Britain, the United States, and Japan dominated world manufacturing, they had developed and owned the intellectual property of the products they exported. They generated global brands.[38] Japan after a generation of development had developed international companies and brands like Toyota and Sony. China is not in that position today. In 2003 China had no companies in Morgan

Stanley Dean Witter's list of the world's top 250 "competitive edge" companies; it had not one brand in *BusinessWeek*'s list of the world's top 100 brands for 2005–6; and it had only one company in the world's top 300 companies ranked by R & D expenditure.[39] Two leading China-watchers—Peter Nolan at the University of Cambridge in England and Edward Steinfeld at MIT—argue that the way the current international economic and trading system operates makes it very difficult for Chinese companies to catch up. If foreign multinationals can produce at the same cost by operating in China, and if all the obstacles cited above make it hard for Chinese entrepreneurs to grow, then China's place in the world economy is increasingly as a dependent part of the supply chain rather than as a player in its own right. This is not what the Chinese want; nor is it a stable platform for economic growth.

This is certainly the view of Yasheng Huang, who, in his book *Selling China,* argues that the flood of FDI has become a vital source of equity and technology, compensating for the weaknesses in China's own financial and innovation system.[40] China has no system for generating venture capital, and its stock markets in Shenzhen and Shanghai (founded in 1990 and 1991, respectively) are organized not to raise equity capital for new enterprises, but, as I will explore in more detail in Chapter 5, to offer tame investment to cash-strapped SOEs. Foreign direct investment offers the prospect of equity capital that otherwise is not forthcoming, especially in the cities; it also closes the gap in an otherwise dismal record of technological innovation and development. We should be looking at the reasons for the FDI boom—and we should be growing concerned.

So the balance sheet is mixed. We find growth, rising living standards, and a remarkable decrease in poverty; China has managed the reform process with skill. On the other hand, economywide productivity is poor and growing only moderately. China has an estimated 150 million migrant workers living in its cities (the official figure is 112 million), and at least another 200 million more are ready to leave its vast agricultural hinterland. Inequality is growing. Every time the party has let Chinese civil society express itself—whether in Tianan-men, at the "Democracy Wall," or as Mao allowing 100 flowers to bloom—the reaction has been criticism and complaint. Deng's grad-ualism and opportunism, preserving the vanguard role of the Com-munist Party, have taken China this far. The same approach will work much less well in the future. Indeed it may not work at all.

CHAPTER 5

The State They're In

THE CHINESE ECONOMY AND THE CHINESE COMMUNIST
Party are in an unstable halfway house—an economy that is neither
socialist nor properly capitalist, run by a party that is neither revolutionary nor subject to the normal constitutional checks and balances
of even China's own Confucian past, let alone the Asian or western
present.[1] The achievement thus far is impressive: an average annual
growth rate of 9 percent over twenty-five years (nearer 10 percent
over the last fifteen), per capita incomes that have increased six times,
and 400 million people pulled out of poverty. But despite this, the
strains are becoming more evident. Some strains are economic, such
as the capacity to continue to save at high levels, or the cost of acquiring foreign exchange reserves at the current rate. But at least as worrying for the party are the social strains. The great gains in China's
reduction in poverty took place twenty years ago, after the communes
were scrapped. Since then, inequality has been growing consistently.
The World Bank estimates that if the growth in income in rural China
had kept up with the growth in the cities, China's poverty rate would
now be a quarter of the current level.[2] Chinese peasants do not know
the numbers, but they must live with the consequences—and unrest,
disaffection, and anger are steadily mounting.

A proponent of the Communist Party would argue that we are
watching a new economic and political model emerge, the so-called
Beijing consensus.[3] This is a commitment to pragmatic development
policies in contrast to an ideological commitment to markets and privatization. In this optimistic interpretation the Communist Party is

becoming an amalgam of a contemporary Confucian elite upholding a developing Chinese rule of law and a typical Asian nationalist party experimenting with the first elements of Chinese democracy. My own more sober assessment is that economic contradictions, structural defects, and sheer economic waste will lead to worsening decline in the growth rate, which in turn will set off a chain reaction of change in China's economic and political structures. Communism is a doctrine of revolution, class war, and authoritarianism. It has only a very limited ability to abandon the party-state and Leninist corporatism so as to become a successful bureaucratic party accepting constitutional constraints—but that is what must happen. How it will be achieved is the story of the decades ahead.

Progress has been significant. The days of the mass terror of the Cultural Revolution are over; and as urban incomes and employment have grown, so have economic freedom, social mobility, and people's sense of possibility. In 1989 the party justified its action in Tiananmen as a necessary response to a counterrevolutionary riot, clamped down on private business development, and excluded private business-people from party membership. Ten years later, in a constitutional amendment the party accepted "private and individual business" as "an important component" of China's future and was enlisting entrepreneurs as members. Jiang Zemin assumed the general secretaryship of the party in 1989 after the Committee of Elders and Deng Xiaoping dismissed his predecessor, Zhao Ziyang, in the immediate aftermath of Tiananmen. Every general secretary until then had been forcibly deposed by a coup, a purge, or political intervention. But in 2002, as a sign of more orderly times, Jiang stepped down voluntarily, in accordance with a new rule that senior leaders should not renew five-year terms once they were over seventy. Jiang handed power over to a successor, Hu Jintao, who had been chosen by a constitutional party process. This was a milestone: power had been transferred seamlessly, peacefully, and according to constitutional rules.

These developments have prompted the most urgent current debate in political economy. The Chinese Communist Party has made the Chinese state more efficient, financially sound, and better able to regulate the economy that it has created. Also, as Hu Jintao's appointment signified, a constitutionalism is emerging that tries to maintain the predictable rule of communist law even if in practice the most predictable feature is that the party gets its way. Jiang himself said in 2001, "Our party, as the party in power, must pay close attention to the relationship between the party and the masses, and the feelings of the people. Whether the people are for or against it is the basic factor deciding the rise and fall of a political party or a political power."[4] Hu Jintao has been equally aware of this political truth; the party must deliver economically, and it must have a plausible explanation of why it legitimately holds sole power—or else the people will no longer consent to its rule. Hu therefore emphasizes "harmonious development" as one of the three harmonies (the other two are harmony with the world and harmony with Taiwan). This deliberate combination of communism and Confucianism recognizes a need to respond to grassroots concerns about inequality and corruption, and presents Hu as a humane sage-emperor. The formula might work as long as the economy works, but how much longer can the party continue to deliver economically? When will its explanation no longer be good enough?

These two questions are linked. As discussed in Chapter 4, China has become a $2 trillion economy because for a generation the state has channeled freakishly huge savings into investment and because over the last decade the country has made itself the world's greatest assembler and manufacturing subcontractor by giving Hong Kong, Taiwanese, and—increasingly—western multinationals privileges that no Chinese company could hope for. This has created the world's most sustained and most enormous export boom, based on cheap labor and a first-world infrastructure. But the primacy of politics and party over state, economy, and society puts indigenous Chinese enterprise and thus the long-term efficiency of the domestic economy in a cage. Economic progress so far has been achieved despite this impediment. But China is approaching a tipping point. Enterprise must be let off the leash and allowed to move into self-sustaining entrepreneurial maturity; otherwise, there will be a sharp and destabilizing deceleration in the growth rate.

Despite all the talk of economic reform, liberalization, and state modernization, the party-state remains the grand economic puppeteer. Its enterprise marionettes may be allowed longer strings if they are less strategic. But all of them, from the state enterprise bought by management to the company bought by a foreign investment bank, ultimately are manipulated by the party-state. It could not be otherwise. The party runs the state, and the state retains discretionary power to do what it chooses and override any challenge or complaint from any nonstate actor—or indeed from state actors if they cross the will of the party. The distortions are obvious and unsustainable and must be corrected if China is to maintain the growth rate it needs; but this will entail the party's losing control of the state. To analyze China's choices today, we need first to examine how Jiang Zemin responded to the crisis of 1993.

Saving the Party-State

Tiananmen forced a recognition that the party was facing a crisis of legitimacy. The dizzying inflation of 1992 and 1993, in reaction to Deng's southern tour, was no less shocking a reminder of the weakness of China's economic structures. In fifteen years China had moved from a command and control economy in which every production unit was part of the state plan to an anarchic network of autonomous provincial governments, local TVEs, and SOEs that in effect were accountable to no one. These autonomous entities could spend and borrow much as they liked, could rig and protect local markets as they chose, and could fix the court system to get the required decisions; moreover, local communist cadres and officials could help themselves to what they wanted. It made Caligula's Rome look like a Victorian vicar's tea party.

Beijing had no means of organizing an economic tempo that was not the generalized clampdown on which it had insisted after Tiananmen or the complete free-for-all that succeeded it. There were no institutions in government or in the intermediate public domain that could put budget constraints on provincial governments with ambitions to build new infrastructure or on SOEs and TVEs determined to expand, mindless of the financial consequences. There were no independent shareholders who would be concerned about organizational overambition and overstretching; there were no independent auditors to expose excessive indebtedness, or imprudent overlending by banks; there was no independent press to report on generalized excess, corruption, and market rigging; there was no powerful central bank; there was no central system of tax collection or national audit.

Instead, the state banks with their provincial headquarters and the provincial development banks did the bidding of the local communist hierarchy and the enterprises it directed. The People's Bank of China had an office in every provincial capital that was simply coopted for the local cause.[5] Provincial governments were and are jealous of their autonomy and protective of local interests; there were de facto trade wars between provinces. Enterprises and courts were told to favor local interests and ignore claims from outside the province. Markets, as I have argued earlier, are social constructions with contours and dynamics framed by government regulation and law. Their spontaneity has to be shaped; otherwise, they degrade. The United States can look back over its own history of bank failures and growth of federal regulation to find evidence of this long-standing truth. China in 1993 was another example of this logic playing itself out.

In this gadarene rush for growth, exploiting the lack of discipline, investment in state assets jumped by 48.1 percent in 1992 and by 44.1 percent in 1993—in effect doubling over a two-year period. In the first half of 1993 industrial production was up 25 percent. Inflation averaged 17.4 percent over the same period, reaching 21 percent in June.[6] Depositors were withdrawing their money from the banks while bank lending was growing at an unparalleled rate, threatening a financial crisis. Arbitrarily deducting money from workers' pay to invest in government bonds—forced saving—was no longer adequate to finance the ballooning government debt. There were more strikes in factories; and there was unrest in the rural areas, where incomes were not keeping pace with inflation. Jiang Zemin was jostled, when he visited Mao's birthplace, by crowds of farmers petitioning him for relief.[7] An additional cause for protest was the increasing number of central and provincial government agencies that arbitrarily levied fees on villages and enterprises; nearly 10,000 had emerged in Beijing alone. The toxic mix of inflation, inequality, and growing popular resentment about communist corruption was once again threatening the stability of the regime.

The collapse of communism in the Soviet Union seemed to foretell its inevitable collapse in China. After all, inflation had been an important factor in the popular revolts against the Nationalists in 1948 and the communists in 1989; now inflation was back with a vengeance. Revolt against communist rule in some provinces seemed certain. In Japan Kenichi Ohmae predicted that eleven Chinese republics would emerge from China's inevitable breakup and form a new "Federal Republic of China." The Pentagon's Office of Net Assessment assembled a thirteen-member task force to analyze China, and a majority of the members predicted China's disintegration.[8] It seemed all over for China.

But during 1993 Jiang Zemin and his tough-minded prime minister, Zhu Rongji, worked on a reform program to save the party-state. As Jiang declared in December, the party had to "take forceful measures to maintain social and political stability."[9] The inability to check the economy during 1993, when the old techniques—instructing banks to recall loans and instructing provincial governments to freeze infrastructure spending—were both widely ignored, meant that something new had to happen fast. Discipline would have to be imposed, but not by increasing the watchdog powers of the network of intermediate public institutions, which might endanger the hegemony of the party. Rather, it would be necessary to reempower the centralized state. The approach was three-pronged: (1) devise tax-raising powers and processes that would slow the economy and inflation immediately while giving central government more management and spending power; (2) reorganize the financial and legal systems while retaining party control; and (3) give the Communist Party more political authority by reclaiming its power over the provinces, rehabilitating it ideologically, and demonstrably tackling corruption.

The first requirement was for the central government to establish its own nationwide tax base rather than rely on the "contracting system" in which it negotiated with provincial governments for revenue. Under the contracting system, its revenue had plunged to around one-fifth of all state revenues during the previous decade. If the trend had continued, Chen Yuan, deputy governor of the People's Bank of China, warned, China risked "a further loss of economic control and even disintegration."[10] In early 1994 a nationwide value-added tax was introduced to replace the plethora of local product taxes; taxes were earmarked for the center; a new powerful institution was established to oversee tax collection; and broad new powers were given to the National Audit Office to investigate fraud and evasion. The impact was immediate; in 1994 the central government's share of total budgetary revenue jumped to 56 percent, where it remains today. Moreover, the long slide in government revenues as a proportion of GDP—from about 30 percent in 1978 to 10.7 percent in 1995—was reversed; in 2002 the proportion was a modest 18.5 percent. The disintegration of the Chinese state had been averted.

To keep the powerful provinces content, Jiang promised that sufficient cash would be rebated to ensure that their baseline budgets would not be cut in 1994. Then in 1995 he introduced a new system for appointing, promoting, and screening senior party officials that put Beijing unambiguously in charge, trying to limit the existing incestuous spoils and favors system. Interestingly, the Communist Party found itself reintroducing the old Confucian system of avoidance;

as in the imperial era, senior officials are not allowed to govern their hometown or home province, and they are regularly rotated out of an office after a maximum of ten years. There are also more interprovincial transfers: according to Zhiyue Bo, chair of the department of International Studies at St. John Fisher College in Rochester, New York, every province has had a party secretary, deputy secretary, governor, or vice governor transferred either to another province or to Beijing.[11] By 2001, when a new round of appointments to the Central Committee began, the Organization Department of the Communist Party controlled a national system of recruitment from China's provinces, departments, and key SOEs, with the final selection made by the Standing Committee of the Politburo. Beijing's centralized mastery of the party was becoming complete.

The Losing Battle Against Corruption

Jiang set the party on its current course—to shed its revolutionary skin, and become a governing party attempting to be bound by rules and focused on economic development and the people's welfare. The first practical consequence was that the party should no longer be in business itself. Since the early 1940s, the Maoist doctrine of self-sufficiency had meant that not just the army but many organs of government had become producers and profit centers, opening up vast scope for corruption. In the early 1980s the need to develop had been so desperate that no stone could be left unturned. Deng Xiaoping had wanted the People's Liberation Army (PLA) to deploy the massive production resources it had developed to help support growth, but what this had meant in practice was that the army, and many of its generals, became in effect full-time businessmen, using their privileges for self-enrichment. Apart from the factories it owned to produce its own supplies, the PLA ran coal mines, airlines, telecommunications companies, and even hotels. So did the police, government departments, and parts of the judicial system. Nearly all of them prospered by means of rigged prices and uncontested procurement contracts and were proof positive that the Communist Party was both corrupt and corrupting. In 1998 Jiang Zemin ruled that they should all divest themselves of their businesses. "The military must no longer be in business," he declared. "Otherwise, this tool of proletarian dictatorship will collapse, and the socialist state power will change color." Within twelve months more than 30,000 trading enterprises run directly by arms of government were either closed or taken over by third parties, although unraveling relationships in a party-state and making them genuinely arm's-length is almost impossible.

This was the first step of an attempted professionalization and a preoccupation with corruption that increased during Jiang's last five years of office. "If we do not crack down on corruption, the flesh-and-blood ties between the party and the people will suffer a lot and the party will be in danger of losing its ruling position, or possibly heading for self-destruction," Jiang declared 2002, in his last political report to the National Congress. High-level officials were arrested and imprisoned for embezzlement and racketeering; they included the party secretary and mayor of Beijing, Chen Xitong, a member of the Politburo. Cheng Kejie, a vice chairmen of the National People's Congress, was executed for taking $5 million in kickbacks for arranging land deals and contracts for private business. In the financial system the highest-profile casualties have been three of Prime Minister Zhu Rongji's handpicked "can-do commanders." Wang Xuebing, former president of the Bank of China and an alternate member of the Central Committee; and Zhu Xiaohua, vice governor of the People's Bank of China, were arrested and jailed for banking fraud. Li Fuxiang, director of China's State Administration of Foreign Exchange (SAFE) leaped to his death from the seventh floor of Beijing's Hospital 304 while under investigation for involvement in illegal exports of foreign exchange. To put this in a British or American context, it is as if, within the last five years, the mayors of London and New York; the speakers of the House of Commons and House of Representatives; and the chief executives of Goldman Sachs, Citibank, and HSBC, along with governors of the Federal Reserve and the Bank of England, were all imprisoned for fraud and one committed suicide. Add to this convicted high court judges and state governors, and the full scale of the problem becomes clearer.

The anticorruption and Orwellian-sounding Central Discipline Inspection Committee has been strengthened; punishments have been increased; tougher antigraft laws have been introduced, with the burden of proof of innocence now on the defendant; officials have been forced to take responsibility for the behavior of their families and are forbidden to enter business relationships with family members; rectification campaigns have begun; and audits have been introduced so that officials leaving office or being promoted have to pass anticorruption screenings.[12] But for all that, corruption remains deeply embedded. If there are signs that petty corruption is leveling off, reports Sun Yan in *Current History,* large-scale corruption is mounting. The average "take" in the 1980s was $5,000—now it is over $250,000. The number of arrests of senior cadre members above the county level quadrupled between 1992 and 2001.[13] Two examples are particularly significant. In 2005 it was disclosed that $1 billion had been misappropriated or embezzled in Gansu, one of China's poorest provinces, by a ring of forty or more officials. And, as further evidence of the growing scale of corruption and seniority of the offendant, four provincial governors and one provincial party secretary have recently been charged with corruption.

The economist Hu Angang, in his trailblazing book *Great Transformations in China: Challenges and Opportunities,* cites evidence provided by government departments that the annual economic loss between 1999 and 2001 due to corruption averaged from 14.5 to 14.9 percent of GDP. His own estimated range is between 13.3 and 16.9 percent of GDP over the late 1990s alone. Every incident of corruption—smuggling, embezzlement, theft, swindling, bribery— arises in the first place from the unchallengeable power of communist officials and the lack of any reliable, independent system of accountability and scrutiny. There is some truth in the view that in the early years of the reform program the corruptibility of officials gave some flexibility to what was otherwise a highly bureaucratic and monopolistic system, and so might even have contributed to growth. As Samuel Huntingdon has put it, the only thing worse than a rigid, overcentralized corrupt bureaucracy is a rigid, overcentralized honest bureaucracy.[14] But Hu Angang's computations, and the evidence of the depth of corruption at the apex of government, business, and finance, mean that any paradoxical usefulness has long since been surpassed. Corruption to this extent is chronically dysfunctional and even threatens the integrity of the state.

Is Corruption Endemic?

Lu Xiaobo, director of the East Asian Institute at Columbia University, takes the analysis even further. In *Cadres and Corruption* he argues that a postrevolutionary revolutionary party is trapped between its need to become a bureaucracy bound by rules and its revolutionary purpose—to break rules and bureaucracies.[15] As judge and jury for its own cases, abjuring any external scrutiny, communism cannot easily police its own deviant party members. But that is not the only reason corruption is difficult to eradicate. The organization itself is driven into deviance because once the revolution is over, there is an unbridgeable inconsistency between revolutionary rhetoric and the compromises of nonrevolutionary practice. The morality of revolution—that the end justifies the means—becomes a morality that justifies corruption. And when as many as 40 percent of officials are not paid regularly, they seek self-preservation in a morally ambiguous political climate. This reality coupled with the growing opportunity for corruption has characterized China's development. The deviant officials of the deviant party-state can prey on wealth with no ideological discomfort, because of the ambiguity over where the state ends and where, if anywhere, private life begins.

Lu Xiaobo's argument is similar to my own. China has a well-developed concept of the state, but communism cannot permit the concept of an intermediate public domain between state and civil society. In this respect it is the faithful heir to the Confucian tradition of governance with systemic corruption. Absolute power, along with moral exhortation to its official class to refrain from plundering the people, is preferred to offering institutional, legal, or ideological protection from the mendacious official. There is always a tendency toward corruption in authoritarian states; but in a one-party state founded on the doctrine of communist revolution, officials are more powerful and more psychologically predisposed to corruption. I have argued in earlier articles[16] that corruption flourishes where social norms that might induce a sense of shame are weak, where there is a widespread belief that a high income results not from effort or merit but from effectively working the system, and where there is a belief that corruption is a victimless crime involving someone else's money. In China all three inducements to corruption exist in spades. Add the peculiarities of communism, and it is not difficult to understand why corruption is so dominant and so hard to root out.

James Kynge, a former Beijing bureau chief of the *Financial Times,* writes in *China Shakes the World* that in China

> trust is a commodity constantly under siege. Poverty and competition for scarce resources impinge upon it. The ideological vacuum that replaced Communism undermines it. The daily diet of propaganda disorientates it. The venality of officials devalues it. The ascendancy of a value system dominated by money hollows it out. What is left is a society in which describing someone as "honest" can just as easily be a gentle criticism as a compliment.[17]

The costs of this mistrustful, corrupt environment can be very high. Kynge describes a crooked blood bank scheme in Henan in the 1980s that was run with the full knowledge of corrupt local officials. Donors received blood back minus its plasma from a general blood pool that had been infected by HIV-positive blood. This scheme seems to have left as many as 100,000 children orphaned. Yet the enriched officials have arrested AIDs activists, shut down orphanages, and harassed journalists. In another scandal officials allowed companies to sell fake but poisonous milk powder that caused disfigurement and even deaths; and even though officials have been imprisoned, the product has reappeared on the market.[18]

Corruption is part of the system's DNA. Jiang and his successor, Hu Jintao, have thus been impeded despite their rhetoric and their attempted actions. Legislative injunctions have to be implemented and policed by the very system which is corrupt and which disallows any external independent agencies because they would challenge the party's political hegemony. The party begins successive "rectification" campaigns and inquiries, but these are compromised by the fact that the investigators themselves are corrupt, and becoming more so. The climate of psychological warfare creates an atmosphere of fear and uncertainty: corrupt individuals demand even higher bribes because the risks are higher.[19]

Keeping Control

The party's approach to the legal and judicial system is a further illustration of how the logic of its position deforms China's institutions.[20] The judicial apparatus is politicized from top to bottom. Every president and vice president of a court is appointed by the party; and the courts are funded by provincial governments and thus are mindful of the need to keep their patrons sweet. The court bureaucracy works on the same basis as the rest of the government bureaucracy, with a party committee system superintending each rung of the court hierarchy. Judges often make decisions at the instruction of the committee or government, independently of the legal merits of the case; according to one unnamed judge in Shandong, as much as 70 percent of his caseload was influenced by directives from local government and

Communist Party officials.[21] Many judges still have no formal legal training—the majority are retired army officers, only too ready to do the party's bidding. Jiang Zemin's and Hu Jintao's attempts to professionalize the system and bring some objective legal principles into court judgments have made little progress; in any case the preferred route has been Confucian-style moral exhortation and top-down investigations rather than wholesale reform.

The scale of the exposed corruption is stunning. In 2003, 794 judges were tried for corruption (out of a national total of 200,000). In 2003 and 2004 the presidents of the provincial high courts of Guangdong and Hunan were both found guilty of corruption.[22] Progress toward establishing the "rule of law," despite official reaffirmation of the intention, is faltering.

When the party does not or cannot influence the judgment in a case it can use its influence over the police system to decide whether to slow down or not enforce the judgment. Enforcement rates in China are lamentable; for example, only 40 percent of provincial high court decisions are enforced.[23] Provinces are notoriously protectionist, insisting on cumbersome procedures for enforcement by courts outside their jurisdiction; and the lack of a clear system of property rights, with the party-state claiming particular privileges, can make debt enforcement against state organizations close to impossible. The judicial system is an accomplice to the party, compromising the commitment to justice but underwriting political hegemony. Interestingly, there is evidence that the Chinese themselves are increasingly disillusioned, as Minxin Pei of the Carnegie Endowment for International Peace argues.[24] Since the late 1990s the number of administrative litigation cases brought by Chinese citizens has decreased, which has been mirrored by a dramatic decrease in the success rate of litigation cases against the government to about 20 percent. The Chinese are voting with their feet.

As Beijing has sought to control provincial parties and what it considers strategic areas of the economy, it has also tried to control the plethora of national and local social organizations that have developed since 1978. Then China had 100 national and some 6,000 local social organizations. Today there are more than 1,700 national social organizations, like the All-China Women's Federation and the China Charity Federation; and 140,000 local ones. It has more than 125,000 so-called private nonenterprise units and more than 250,000 nongovernmental organizations.[25] Yet under the Regulations on the Registration and Management of Social Organization introduced in 1998, every single one must have a government or party unit supervising its day-to-day operation.

This policy spills into rural China.[26] The obligation of villages to elect their village leaders is portrayed by the party and some observers as a move toward democracy, but the process is managed so that in reality it tightens party control. The village councils from whom the candidates are drawn consist almost wholly of party members screened by the party; campaigning is not allowed, and ballots are less than secret. Party secretaries sit on village councils and are encouraged to put themselves up for village chairs, with the result that overwhelmingly the local party boss also becomes the village chair. Formal power is therefore vested in one person, the party representative—and legitimized by a vote. It is true that peasants have developed a taste for voting, and that village chairs may find themselves torn between what the party wants and what their constituents want. But the party's intention is clear—to legitimize and intensify its control. Notably, voting has not been extended to townships and cities.

Control extends to the media. China now has more than 2,000 newspapers; 2,000 television channels; 9,000 magazines; and 450 radio stations—but they are all under the watchful eye of the party in Beijing or provincial propaganda departments. These authorities issue daily instructions on what may and may not be reported; journalists who digress will be suspended from working or even imprisoned. China is estimated to have imprisoned forty-two journalists, the highest number in the world. Editors know roughly how much slack they have; but recently, under Hu Jintao, there has been a tightening of the leash. The right to *yidi baodao*—to travel independently and report from a nonlocal city—had allowed more aggressive reporting of corruption; but it has been rescinded. Some prominent editors have been fired. For instance, Yang Bin, editor of China's most forceful tabloid, the *Beijing News,* was dismissed in December 2005 for reporting village protests against unfair confiscation of land. Other journalists have been prohibited from publishing.[27] The Committee to Protect Journalists, in its report of 2005 on repression of the media, quotes the government-run *People's Daily:* "[During 2004] twenty-seven censorship agencies permanently shut down 338 publications for printing 'internal' information, closed 202 branch offices of newspapers, and punished seventy-three organizations for illegally 'engaging in news activities.' "

Foreign broadcasters' plans for expansion have been frozen, and as much as $800 million has been spent on screening the Internet and blocking Web sites that contain prohibited words (including "democracy") or stories (90 percent of sites with the words "Tiananmen massacre" were blocked).[28] The party has managed this not by owning media itself—it now funds only two national newspapers including the *People's Daily;* and one newspaper per province—but by exercising raw directional power. The party's instinct is to minimize scrutiny and the information on which it is based. In early April 2003 the Chinese health authorities knew they were experiencing a SARS epidemic, but the media faithfully parroted the line that there were only a few cases. The official response did not change until a seventy-two-year-old doctor, Jiang Yanyong, contacted the foreign media, and the World Health Organization investigated. Two weeks later the Chinese government had fired the health minister and the mayor of Beijing, dramatically raised its estimate of deaths, and started a nationwide campaign alerting the Chinese to the dangers, receiving universal praise for responding so quickly.[29] Emboldened by his success, Jiang Yanyong wrote to the National People's Congress, suggesting that it was now time for Tiananmen to be reevaluated. He was arrested, "reeducated," and has not made a public comment since.

The hope that after SARS China might take a more enlightened attitude to the reporting at least of disease has been dashed. China has 14 billion poultry, one-fifth of the world's total, and is a potential center of avian flu. But when in July 2005 the journal *Nature* published evidence from a Chinese laboratory that avian flu had spread from poultry to migratory birds, the laboratory's work was stopped. Six Chinese journalists who wanted to cover the outbreak were detained and forbidden to continue reporting. Information about infectious disease is classified as a state secret; a journalist who reveals it is deemed to have committed treason—a crime for which the minimum penalty is reeducation and the maximum death.[30] This approach is attracting criticism, and the tremors have reached the west. In February 2006 three of China's most distinguished elders—Li Rui, a former aide to Mao Zedong; Hu Jiwei, a former editor of the *People's Daily;* and Zhu Houze, a former party propaganda chief—published a letter condemning the approach: "History demonstrates that only a totalitarian system needs news censorship, out of the delusion that it can keep the public locked in ignorance," they wrote. Far from ensuring stability, they continued, such media repression would "sow the seeds of disaster."[31]

The desire to control and direct extends across all the structures of the state. Since 1998 the party has tried to remodel, rationalize, and streamline the state simultaneously. The purpose is only partly to save money. Mainly, the party wants to equip the state with structures better suited to regulate and monitor those parts of China's economy, which it no longer directly owns or plans. The giant Soviet industrial line ministries have been abolished and their functions divided. Ownership and direction are now delivered by the State Owned Assets Supervision and Administration Commission (SASAC); and a new network of generic regulatory agencies has been created to superintend areas such as environmental protection, intellectual property rights, and workplace safety. Between 1998 and 2002, staffs in central, provincial, and municipal government have been halved, reflecting the new emphasis on light-touch setting of strategic targets and regulation rather than detailed, daily hands-on management.

Thus Hu Jintao now presides over a state that is better organized, more centralized, and better funded than the China of 1993, which was on the point of disintegration. To the extent that bureaucratic centralization can solve the China dilemma, it has been partly achieved. Economic management is focused in the Ministry of Finance, the People's Bank of China, the streamlined State Development and Reform Commission ("planning," significantly, was dropped from its title), and SASAC. The party in Beijing is in better control of its provincial branches and governments, runs the judicial system, and closely superintends the media and the millions of social organizations. With its direction of police, military, and security services its monopoly of state power is complete.

Ideological Quicksands

Yet despite the budgetary discipline and the more streamlined state structures, the Chinese political system remains haunted by the ambiguities of communism becoming a postrevolutionary party running a postrevolutionary society and an economy in transition to a form of capitalism. The quest is for legitimacy—in Jiang's words, maintaining "flesh and blood ties with the people"—and for continuing to justify communist one-party rule. The Chinese state is not the first among a network of equal public institutions through which, along with competitive elections, civil society could hold it and the communist party to account. It is the Leviathan; at once the executive, legislative, and judicial arms of government; policy maker, lawmaker, and implementer; and judge and jury for all its own actions. Even in 2006 the excuse for this is that the party is the sole legitimate trustee for the victory of the Chinese masses in the revolution of 1949. The ideological reasoning is as follows: Chinese socialist democracy is a democracy of the masses won in the revolution; the Communist Party as the champion of the masses thus democratically controls the state alone to further their interests; and those interests are to build socialism around the canonical thought of Marx, Lenin, and Mao Zedong.

When Deng began his reform program, he insisted that he was conforming to what he described as the four cardinal principles of communism: socialist democracy; the communist party-state; building socialism; and conformity with Marxist-Leninist-Maoist thought. As reform progressed, it became ever more of an ideological stretch to describe how what was happening in reality conformed to the four principles. Socialism was attenuated to include the idea of the socialist market, with every new accommodation justified by Mao's pragmatic insistence that practice had to be the judge of theory. It took all of Deng's prestige to get away with it.

By 2000, as China headed toward full membership in the World Trade Organization, thus accepting by treaty that private business was an important component of the future, the party could no longer pretend that it was implementing the four principles as they might have been conceived in 1978, let alone in 1949. There would have to be an ideological overhaul, not least because by 2001 some 100,000 private businesspeople had joined the party. It could no longer claim that its reason for being was only to represent the worker and peasant masses. On the other hand it would somehow have to stay in touch with the four principles; otherwise, the line of legitimacy back to 1949 would be lost.

Jiang Zemin's answer—his last legacy—was the invention of the "three represents" in February 2002 (see Chapter 1). In effect the party declared ideologically that it intends to represent all China, not just the worker and peasant masses, as a kind of national party, while unashamedly creating a variant of a market economy. As a short-term political necessity the "three represents" were critical modifications. They have allowed the party unapologetically to recruit the once hated capitalists as members and to confirm the direction of economic reform. A twenty-first-century variant of the old Confucian gentry is being re-created, but now reinvented as a class of communist officials, managers of SOES, and private businesspeople who are membrs of the party whose interests, like those of the Confucian gentry, are bound up with those of the centralized state and who are clearly seen as a crucial pillar of communist support. There are some 6 million owners of private firms in China; about two-thirds are former state officials.[32] And in the other direction, about one-fifth of registered entrepreneurs have now become party members—one survey reported a proportion as high as 30 percent, about six times the percentage in the population at large.[33] According to an authoritative survey of private businesspeople who were not members, one-fourth said they wanted to join and half of those had already applied.[34] In other words, the party is inventing a new class of former officials and party members who are running private businesses but who depend on the party and state networks for work, and who understand and benefit from the new ideology. The evidence is all around. In the National People's Congress workers' and peasants' representation declined from 27 percent and 21 percent, respectively, in the early 1980s to 11 percent and 8 percent in the late 1990s.[35] As reform deepens, the bedrock of communist rule is changing. Communist interests are increasingly intertwined with business, on the Asian model; and the communists' roots in the village and farms are dwindling.

The "three represents," like economic reform, are stepping-stones across a treacherous ideological river. But whatever short-term relief this concept has brought, in the longer term it has created a dilemma of legitimacy. The justification for one-party rule is that communism represents the democracy of the masses who have won a class war against capitalists and landlords. Thereafter socialism, involving collective ownership and planning, is to be constructed by the party-state embodying the democratic collective—and justified because the masses are the fountainhead of wealth. But if the party is representing the "broad masses" and in its repudiation of class war is de facto recognizing that wealth comes from capitalists as much as from workers and peasants, it is not building collective socialism, and it has smashed the coherence of its own ideology. It has no intellectual or ideological defense against those who argue that there should be more formal pluralist political representation and more plural public institutions. In these circumstances, why not? After all, the former general secretary of the party, Zhao Ziyang, had openly called for such a development at the Thirteenth Party Congress in 1987. "Different people have different interests and views," Zhao had said; "they need opportunities for the exchange of views."[36] The argument is much more powerful today.

Without institutionalized channels to manage tensions, there is growing restlessness, and even conflict, as people begin to take matters into their own hands. Since 1978 there has been mounting turbulence underneath apparent conformity. For example, during Tiananmen one-third of the leaders of the National People's Congress (NPC), supposedly a rubber stamp, signed a motion asking its Standing Committee to oppose martial law. Throughout the 1990s the party has consistently failed to get its preferred slate of candidates through the provincial elections for the NPC. At the village level, there are vigorous protests when town or provincial officials impose unfair taxes or do not compensate owners properly for land purchased for development. The number of protests is rising sharply, within the workplace and beyond. But so is the number of illegal land seizures against which to protest.[37] In November 2003 the Ministry of Land and Resources reported more than 168,000 cases of illegal land seizure, twice as many as in all of 2002. In 2003 2 percent of China's total farmland was lost to development, and the pace of loss has been accelerating.[38]

Criticism is leveled against corrupt village, county, and provincial governments that have allowed peasants to be fleeced. The more one interacts with government, the more disillusioned one tends to be. To date, distant Beijing has been understood to want to make the system fairer, and it escapes the general censure. Beijing is where citizens go for redress. The *Washington Post* reports one party scholar saying that the number seeking redress has doubled in recent years.[39] But this raises expectations that will not be met; and the inevitable disappointment will leave the people feeling that there is no arbiter on their behalf.

In 1989 Deng Xiaoping could rely on his reputation as a revolutionary hero, the respect of the army, and the standing of the commit-

tee of elders to drive through the repression of the Tiananmen protesters, the imposition of martial law, and the dismissal of Zhao
Ziyang. Otherwise, he would have been unable to override the army's
uncertainty about firing on Chinese citizens and carry out the repression. Hu Jintao is working hard to build up similar relationships, appointing children of the revolutionary leadership to key positions in
the PLA and strictly enforcing China's tight censorship of the media.
But Hu did not fight in the 1940s for the revolution, and so he cannot
command the same prestige as Deng.

Similarly, communist doctrines are incomparably weaker after
nearly twenty years of economic reform driven by concepts mostly
overtly hostile to state ownership and planning. Although the Falun
Gong is regarded in the west as a harmless, eccentric creed that should
not be persecuted, its attraction and threat must not be underestimated. It is seen by both the party and many of its own adherents as offering an idealism that the party lacks; even the former director of the
301st Army Hospital in Beijing has been advising members to join.[40] If
the weaknesses of the system ever threatened economic growth, with
consequential large-scale protests about its legitimacy, there can be no
certainty that the apparatus of state and army—used only reluctantly
in 1989—could be applied with the same force again.

All this weakens the state's capacity. In the World Bank's listing of
199 strong and weak states, China was ranked very low. In 2002, it was
number 186 on voice and accountability; 116 on regulatory quality;
111 on control of corruption; and ninety-four on rule of law. Only
in governmental effectiveness did it score modestly well, ranking
seventy-first.[41] And on all measures the trend has been downward
since 1998. The party is keenly aware of the collapse in idealism, the inability to make communism live as an ideology, and the consequences
for the state. In 2002, 80 percent of the cadre members polled at
Beijing's Central Party School, whose graduates are destined to become members of the elite, somewhat like graduates from Harvard in
the United States and the École Nationale d'Administration in France,
declared that lack of progress in political reform was the most impor-

tant constraint on China's development. Other polls at the school consistently confirm this result. The viewpoint of Zhao Ziyang lives on, and occasionally bubbles up into public view. Li Rui, whose letter I cited earlier, spoke out at the Sixteenth Congress in November 2002:

> Chinese and foreign histories prove that autocracy is the source of political turmoil. As the collapse of the Soviet Union shows, the root cause is autocracy. Modernisation is possible only through democratisation. This is the trend in the world in the 20th century, especially since World War 2. Those who follow this trend will thrive; those who fight against this trend will perish. This rule applies to every country—and every party.[42]

The Central Committee is familiar with the both the unease and the debate. In 2004 it acknowledged that reform had reached a critical state and that the party's "ruling status will not last for ever if the party does nothing to safeguard it."[43] Meanwhile Hu Jintao himself has reasserted that the party "takes a dominant role and coordinates all sectors. . . . Party members and party organisations in government departments should be brought into full play . . . so as to realise the party's leadership over state affairs."[44] In other words, Jiang's formula for strengthening the party and its control over the party-state is to be appled with redoubled zeal as a response to the new complexity and diversity of China; and despite the "three represents," the party's legitimacy in claiming sole rule is unchanged. In 2005 the party issued a "white paper on democracy" making this claim explicit—but the very fact that it chose to write such a paper, and that the paper was so intellectually barren, shows how precarious the ideological halfway house has become. Yet the party needs some justification for its control, whether of village elections or the media. All that stands between it and its own demise is its capacity to deliver economic growth and its control of the army and police. These are thin reeds on which to build long-term hegemony, especially as the economy is beset by the same weaknesses of the halfway house as the polity.

CHAPTER 6

The Economic Impossibility of the Halfway House

THE EMERGENCE OF CHINA AS A $2 TRILLION ECONOMY, after such an inauspicious beginning only twenty-five years ago, is such a giddy accomplishment that even the best can suspend their better judgment. The consensus is that China provides conclusively proof that liberalization, privatization, market freedoms, and an embrace of globalization are the only route to prosperity. For example, Martin Wolf, chief economic for the *Financial Times,* writes in his book *Why Globalization Works* that China is successful because it is the biggest liberalizer, and "all else is commentary." [1] China has made the transition from a planned economy to a more market-based economy, has joined the World Trade Organization, and is so obviously successful that the magic ingredient must be its commitment to markets, the profit motive, and private property. Its intention to continue in the same vein is also obvious. Intellectuals and diplomats, therefore, should discard their reservations about why China has achieved all this, discard any concerns about its future, and recognize it as a full market economy as soon as possible.

But the reality is more complex. If you doubt that, consider Hu Jintao's remarks, cited at the end Chapter 5. This is an economy and society over which the party seeks and so far has maintained extensive direct and indirect control despite a broad liberalization of prices, a rollback of planning, a boom in foreign direct investment, and substantial autonomy among all forms of enterprise. Both the OECD and

World Bank, in their recent reports on China, tread a fine line between acknowledging its impressive transition and expressing serious concern about how much more still has to be done before China becomes a full market economy. The World Bank has been particularly hard-hitting in this regard.

For the party's approach to the economy has reflected its approach to the political system. The streamlining of government structures discussed in Chapter 5—a process that involved halving the workforce—has been reproduced in state-owned enterprises (SOEs). The number of SOEs has been halved, from 300,000 in 1995 to 150,000 in 2005,[2] in pursuit of "holding onto the big while letting go of the small." This is a dramatic transformation that seems to point in the direction of privatization and a reduction in the SOEs' share of GDP. But the SOEs' share of value added has fallen scarcely at all. About 10 percent have gone bankrupt; and there have been mergers, leasing deals, management buyouts, and reorganizations as "shareholding companies."[3] But in almost every such case the resulting shareholding structure of the "let-go" SOEs has been carefully devised, as I wrote in Chapter 4, to maintain the state's controlling interest. Moreover, in an economy where the only source of external capital is bank finance and where only 25 percent of the shares of banks can be owned by non-state shareholders, there are further limits on the ability of even "let-go" small SOEs to operate outside the boundaries set by the party-state.

The party is performing a balancing act. It knows that autonomy increases productivity; and it knows that China's success as an exporter has been built on the technological, branding, and distribution networks of foreign multinationals, which China will need to reproduce itself in order to be a global player. Indeed, the party has repeatedly reaffirmed its ambition to build as many as fifty globally competitive enterprises by 2010.[4] Ever since the amendment to the constitution favoring business (in 1999) and Jiang Zemin's "three represents" (in 2002), the climate has been improving for the private sector. But the party still retains control. China is "half pregnant"; and that is the way the party intends to keep it.[5]

Leninist Corporatization

China's approach to creating firms owned and backed by shareholders—the heart of any concept of capitalism—exemplifies the primacy of political control over private ownership. The "Standard Opinion" delivered in 1992, notwithstanding subsequent Company Acts, remains the foundation document for the formation of companies. It is wholly concerned with how SOEs are transmuted into corporations; there is no detailed provision for a private company to issue tradable shares. It establishes four essential classes of shares: (1) state shares owned by the state or its agencies; (2) "legal person" shares owned by state-authorized social groups, enterprises, or institutions; (3) individual shares owned by Chinese investors or employees; and (4) foreign shares owned by foreigners up to an aggregate maximum of $10 billion (raised from $4 billion in 2005). The transfer or sale of these shares is strictly regulated. How these shares are traded and to what assets and profits respective classes of shareowners are entitled are closely regulated. Until the end of 2006, the 63 percent of shares owned directly by the state (state and legal-person shares) could not even be bought and sold on the stock market, but a new rule allows them to be traded from the beginning of 2007 as long as the buyer is another state or legal person. Only individual A shares can be freely traded by Chinese public investors within China; in addition, this is the only class of share in which investors can build up strategic stakes, and then only on the promise they hold the shares themselves for three years. Foreign-held "special" or B shares can be transferred only if the buyer meets state provisions. But H and N foreign-held shares are more freely tradable: some 60 Chinese enterprises, for example, have issued H shares that are actively traded in Hong Kong.[6]

The key to retaining state control is that this shareholding structure interacts with China's unique accounting structure, which requires different and discrete funds for fixed, current, and special assets. Foreign shareholders are not entitled to any of the fixed assets, and individual shareholders have only a limited entitlement. Fixed assets in effect are to be owned only by state and legal-person shareholders. As a result share valuations on the stock market have depended on the transactions among A, B, H, and N shareholders who have the same claim on current profits and cash (but at the discretion of majority state and legal-person shareholders) but no claim or only a limited claim on the companies' fixed assets. In any case, they constitute a majority of the shareholding, as we shall see, in only a tiny fraction of China's listed firms. Moreover, only half of China's listed companies have ever paid dividends. Thus it is easy to understand the persistent weakness of the Shenzhen and Shanghai stock markets as allocaters and providers of capital and to understand perenially ailing share prices; between 2001 and 2005 share prices halved as disillusioned investors shunned the rigged markets despite the booming economy.[7] If prices recovered in 2006, it was almost entirely because holders of traded shares anticipated being generously compensated for state shares being given the right to be traded—a source of future destabilization. The brutal reality, despite the reforms, is that the Chinese stock market is a creature of the state.

The party has retained control of the former SOEs listed on the stock market while giving them more managerial autonomy and some capacity to raise new capital—the point of the exercise. The World Bank cites a study of 1,105 listed Chinese enterprises in 2001, in which at first sight it seemed that the state had relinquished control of more than 90 percent. However, once the tangled share structure had been unraveled the opposite was the case: the state had de facto control of 84 percent of the listed companies. In 2005 it still retained control of 81 percent.[8] There is evidence that some holders of legal-person shares, notably provincial governments, are becoming frustrated by the lack of dividends and selling to de facto private interests. If so, surrogate private ownership may be higher than a straightforward reading of the numbers suggests. Nonetheless, after more than a decade of stock market development this $2 trillion economy has succeeded in creating fewer than 200 genuine private companies, according to the economists Guy Liu and Pei Sun, who conducted the study reported by the World Bank.[9] Whatever else this is may mean, it is hardly a triumph of privatization. Martin Wolf may be right about the direction of travel, but is it "commentary" to imagine that this is happening any faster than at a snail's pace—or that the party has any other end in mind than retaining its own control?

The process should more correctly be described as "corporatization," and it sharply redefines how the Chinese economy should be conceived. In collaboration with China's National Bureau of Statistics, the OECD carefully analyzed the survey of 2003 of the 180,000 industrial firms with turnovers in excess of 5 million renminbi ($600,000), which together make up 35 percent of Chinese GDP. Of these, 47.7 percent were state-owned or collectively controlled; only 13.3 percent were unambiguously private; 12 percent were foreign-owned companies. The OECD generously identifies the balance, 27 percent, as privately controlled. For example, it counts legal-person shares as nonstate and de facto private, although this is factually and legally incorrect; and it interprets majority control by foreign investors of most joint ventures as meaning that the private sector controls the venture, though this too is unrealistic. Two-thirds of new foreign direct investment is now done as a wholly owned foreign enterprise (WOFE) because foreign investors are not prepared to have a contracting relationship with a minority Chinese partner who provides little of the capital but exerts de facto, and frequently counterproductive, control. It is doubtful that more than one-third of the 27 percent the OECD deems privately controlled would stand up to such a definition under scrutiny. More probably, about two-thirds of China's largest 180,000 enterprises are de facto state-controlled. This conclusion is broadly in line with the results of the study by the World Bank of listed companies, cited above.

China's approach to private ownership means that it is futile to attempt to assess how much of China is public and how much private. No attempt can capture how the party is trying to develop Leninist corporatism. The party-state is at the center of a spiderweb of control.

Political direction is matched by direct control of those parts of the economy that the party considers strategic—telecommunications; energy; transport; iron, steel, and metal production; automobiles, etc. To build an international presence it is encouraging the creation of fifty-seven "business groups" as strategic "pillars" of the Chinese economy—a Chinese version of South Korean *chaebol* or Japanese *keiretsu*. Each group has its own house bank. The two largest groups are in petrochemicals (Donglian and Qilu Petrochemical Groups), and the third largest is steel (Baosteel). The party exerts direct control over the strategic groups. The less strategic the party considers a sector or enterprise, the more it is prepared to loosen its control; but the shareholder and accounting structure is such that at any time the party can regain control if necessary. The genuine private sector has been growing and is the most dynamic part of the economy, with the highest productivity; but in the party-state every private company exists on sufferance. As noted earlier, state-owned banks control the flow of credit; every entrepreneur knows that this flow can be turned off if he (or the occasional she) does not fulfill the party's wishes, and now each, under the latest law, will have an enterprise-based communist party committee (just as SOEs do) on top.

The Spiderweb

The evidence of the spiderweb of control is all around. This control is locking China into a low-productivity, low-innovation economy with a disproportionate number of small-scale enterprises that do not and cannot make the commercial weather. In the World Economic Reform's Business Competitiveness Index of 116 countries, China has slid from forty-second place when the index was first launched in 1998 to fifty-seventh in 2005. Not only is China's absolute performance worse than that of other middle-income developing countries like Brazil and India, but China is also deteriorating faster.[10]

Broadly, the more politicized a Chinese enterprise is, the lower its productivity and performance. The performance of China's SOEs, which control two-thirds of industrial assets, has been lamentable and has hardly improved during twenty years of reform. One in three of their workforces is estimated to be structurally idle.[11] The SOEs are on a financial cliff edge and barely profitable. According to one influential estimate, even the tiniest upward movement in interest rates or the slightest decline in sales would mean that between 40 and 60 percent of their enormous bank debts would not be serviced, rendering the entire Chinese banking system bankrupt.[12] They are overdiversified and unfocused. They spend a trivial proportion of their sales revenue on research and development. Their labor productivity on average is 4 percent of the United States'. Three-quarters of SOEs employ fewer than 500 people.[13] They are commercial and business disaster areas.

The drive to corporatize and consolidate SOEs was meant to address these problems, and to reduce the financial drain on the state. The problem is that organizationally and culturally, even after reform, they are not structured to be as efficient as companies in the western national market economies of thirty or forty years ago, let alone companies in today's more fast-moving conditions. The SOEs were conceived as self-sufficient industrial communes that would provide workers and families with an "iron rice bowl" of support from cradle to grave—nurseries, schools, housing, doctors, and pensions. In many parts of China SOEs remain the sole reliable source of welfare. The huge layoffs of the last five years—involving more than 16 million workers—were politically possible only because in some cities and provinces there is now a rudimentary system of social insurance, even if it extends to only one-third of most urban dwellers and about 3 percent of migrant workers.[14] The many provinces and cities with no social insurance system go to any lengths to sustain SOE employment in order to avert widespread social unrest. Better to have a basket-case SOE subsidized with state bank credits that employs people and provides their families with welfare than no employer at all.

And the party has the means. State, provincial, and municipal governments own state shares and direct legal-person shares, and every SOE has a Communist Party committee to ensure that it does the party's bidding. The system is used ruthlessly, despite the recent moves toward corporatization. The vast majority of SOEs that have been restructured into shareholding corporations retain their party committees. According to Minxin Pei, the same person is both party secretary and chair in about half the firms; and in more than 70 percent of restructured SOEs party committee members have joined the board of directors.[15] Moreover, the State-Owned Assets Supervision and Administration Commission (SASAC), which runs the 196 largest SOEs in conjunction with the party's organization department, decides who will manage which SOE. The SOEs' supervisory boards do not make this decision. In the recent past the CEOs of China Telecom, Netcom, Mobile, and Unicom were arbitrarily swapped around because the party was concerned that the companies were becoming too competitive and wanted to encourage a more collaborative culture.[16]

This is not unusual. Edward Steinfeld provides case studies of the politicization of decision making in three SOEs in the steel industry in his extraordinary book *Forging Reform in China*.[17] Enron, infamously, made profits by inventing sales; similarly, Chinese SOEs invent sales by lending credit to buyers—in effect, the company is borrowing to purchase its sales. One company, Magang Steel, was floated on the Hong Kong stock market, but the party still controlled the company through its shareholdings and the enterprise's party committee. Magang, after its listing, simply bought sales in the time-honored way, expecting its parent holding company to lend it the wherewithal but of course not paying the parent any dividends or interest in return. Twelve months later the holding company went bust and itself had to be bailed out with bank loans. This is a system not of wealth creation but of wealth destruction.

Productivity is 40 to 70 percent higher for enterprises controlled only indirectly by the state, and for town and village enterprises

(TVEs) and private companies where control is more distant from the party, productivity is more than twice as high.[18] Problematically, SOEs have to fund the infrastructure of welfare for their employees; the statistics make a partial adjustment for this. More crucially, once an enterprise under any ownership reaches a reasonable scale, it is inevitably drawn into an universe where business judgments are compromised by political direction. The TVEs and private companies have higher productivity because they are small; but their size means that their contribution to economywide innovation is also small.

A Private Sector Like No Other

Bureaucrats and party officials make decisions not only for the medium- and large-scale SOEs they control directly but also for large private companies. Davin McKenzie, managing director of iVentures, which is based in Beijing, says that almost no private company, however well run, wants to leave the opaque, informal world of *guanxi* personal relationships in which the main aim is to hide revenue, cash, and profits from outsiders' eyes and from potential political direction.[19] Only 1 percent of private Chinese companies subject themselves to independent audit, he claims, and then because they want a listing. The vast majority focus on staying below the radar, underreporting their sales and overinvoicing abroad to keep money overseas—or simply, as he describes it, running even large companies from the "cash box in the back of the Mercedes." Most Chinese companies have three sets of accounts—one for the banks, one for the tax authorities, and one for the management. Outsiders can never believe what they are told, so banks lend only on the basis of hard collateral. Most private firms do not last long; the average duration is about three years. The law of the jungle prevails: you do what you can get away with. China is the counterfeiters' paradise, where intellectual property rights are neither respected nor enforced. Between 15 and 20 percent of all well-known brands in China are fake; two-thirds of the imports confiscated by U.S. customs as fakes were made in China. Counterfeiting is estimated to represent 8 percent of GDP—eloquent testimony to Chinese business strategies and the ineffectiveness of the Chinese legal system.

Inevitably, the private sector devotes much of its strategy to currying favor with the party and key officials, who, as we have seen, are only too willing to trade privileges for bribes. Private companies cannot stand aside from the politicization and corruption and have no choice but to do official bidding, even when it is financially and strategically ludicrous. In one famous case a provincial government twisted the arm of Sichuan Changhong Electric and forced it to sell television sets to a financially suspect distribution company in California. The transaction cost Sichuan Changhong $500 million.

Another case involved the downfall of China's leading refrigerator manufacturer, Kelon Electrical Holdings. By the late 1990s its flair for design and production had carried it from its beginnings as a TVE in Guangdong to $1 billion in turnover. Apparently, this company was partially privatized with H shares quoted in Hong Kong and A shares quoted in Shenzhen. Today it has ceased production after charges of embezzlement and rigging its balance sheet. Despite its share quotes and entrepreneurship, de facto control remained with the Guangdong authorities, who in the late 1990s forced it to buy an SOE that was operating at a loss: a manufacturer of air conditioners. The only way, it seems, that Kelon could manage the shotgun marriage and keep its head above water financially was to manipulate its accounts within China's cavalier financial and political environment. But the Bank of China, smelling a rat, froze new lending in 2004. By August 2005 the end had come for Kelon.[20] An inadequate, soft public infrastructure of auditing, banking, and corporate governance had interacted with the dynamics of Leninist corporatism and de facto state control; the result was the company's destruction.

Kelon is but one of many examples; the risks extend even to China's showcase companies. Haier, based in the coastal city of Qingdao, is one of China's leading white-goods firms. The government delegated management to its man, Zhang Ruimin, at the beginning of the reform process; and he has now built Haier into a $5 billion multinational business, with H shares in Hong Kong and operations in more than twenty countries. Zhang, one of China's favored businessmen, is the most influential private entrepreneur to have joined the Central Committee. But even he could not prevent the SASAC from ruling, in 2004, that despite everything, apparently including significant shareholdings by employees, this former SOE remained controlled by the state. Like Kelon, it once had to take over a company that was making a loss—in this case a drug business—but so far that has not brought Haier down; and Zhang has used his influence to resist other forced marriages. The question remains how much longer it will be before Haier too succumbs to the same endemic weaknesses. The economist Yasheng Huang of MIT is quoted by the *Economist:* "Government shareholders may be passive at first, but once a company succeeds, they interfere. Countless Chinese firms have been driven to bankruptcy or failed to grow big because local governments decided to exercise their legal claims on ownership." [21]

The Chinese companies that can focus on their business undistracted are those whose majority ownership is in the private sector. Huawei is a privately owned multinational that is emerging as a fast-growing manufacturer of wireless equipment and software; and it has a strong commitment to R & D. But even it is not free from the long arm of the party-state. It operates with $10 billion line of credit from the China Development Bank; it has close links with the Red Army; and to win business in China's protected telecom markets, it is reported to have given controlling shares to the provincial telecom companies with which it trades. [22] But without transparency, nobody knows where de facto control comes from. So far the combination of committed long-term bank finance, visionary leadership, and a passion for technology has brought prosperity, and Huawei is one of the main beneficiaries of China's boom in mobile phones. But George Gilboy of MIT, and a longtime senior executive in Beijing, details how political interference has profoundly damaged a successful rival, Julong Technologies.[23] The same fate could lie in wait for Huawei.

China does not have a very dense network of research-oriented, innovative companies, so it cannot afford to be this careless of the examples it does have. Gilboy contrasts China's meager effort to import technology into its production with the experience of the South Koreans and Japanese. When they were trying to catch up with the west in the 1970s and 1980s they spent two or three times the cost of imported high-tech equipment in buying licenses and training key staff members in order to "indigenize" the technology. Today Chinese industrial groups spend less than 10 percent of the value of imported high-tech goods on technological "indigenization."

China's miserable record on patent applications, its parsimonious R & D spending (0.6 percent of GDP, compared with an average of 1.6 percent in OECD), and the insularity of R & D by government and enterprises alike all point in the same direction. Companies' innovation is focused on lowering costs. Edward Steinfeld reports on the World Bank Survey of 2001, in which a mere 7 percent of 1,500 Chinese high-tech enterprises declared that they provided customers with R & D, and only 15 percent designed parts for overseas customers.[24] The rest broadly manufactured products to specifications, designs, or licenses set by foreigners and mostly sold them to customers within their own cities. Their average size was just over 600 employees. These responses eloquently captured the enterprises' provincialism, technological dependence, and emphasis on competing at low costs.[25] Another study[26] reports that localism is, if anything, rising; 72 percent of goods consumed in any Chinese province tend to be produced within that province, and the proportion has recently risen. Sandra Poncet, the author of that study, remarks:

> Barriers to trade between Chinese provinces appear to be closer in magnitude to that on international trade than that on trade flow within a single country. Chinese domestic market integration is low. . . . This evolution underlines the failure of

reforms to promote domestic market integration and the growing division of the Chinese domestic market into cellular submarkets.[27]

I have met one of the officials trying to create a single market on the scale of the EU in the six southern provinces plus Macao and Hong Kong (the so-called six plus two). The difficulties of harmonization exceed those of EU because the differences between provinces are so great; and the talks are hopelessly bogged down. As long as the state sector continues to loom large and provincial authorities feel compelled to shelter it from competition, there is little prospect of any change.

China's R & D is led by the Leninist state. Two-thirds of China's 800,000 research scientists and researchers work in government laboratories, a trend that is likely to intensify with the adoption of some ten to twenty "megaprojects" of up to $1 billion each under China's National Middle- to Long-Term Plan (MLP). When China spends heavily, it tends to get results, whether in stem cells or underwater robots; and it is rapidly rising up the science citation index. But two leading Chinese scientists—Yi Rao, who is codirector of the Shanghai Institute for Advanced Studies and a professor at Washington University; and Bai Lu, who is scientific adviser to the Ministry of Science and Technology of China and a senior investigator at NIH—have complained publicly that politics, as everywhere in China, looms too large. They characterize Chinese research as "rule by man" rather than "rule by merit."[28] Top-down research determined by the Ministry of Science and Technology is wasteful, does not engage researchers' hearts and minds, and does not foster the serendipity and creativity of great science. Less state direction here, as in enterprise generally, would unbottle a great upsurge of energy.

In the west Chinese science and technology are portrayed as a juggernaut that will crush everything under it. Comparisons with India make salutary reading. From 1981 to 1995 China had 537 scientists and engineers in research and development per 1 million people,

compared with India's 151. China also led India in personal computers (three to one) and in Internet usage (four to one). Yet in 2001
India produced one-fourth more software, of which three-quarters
was exported—despite having a much smaller economy than China's.
Not only did China produce less software, but less than 10 percent was
exported, so despite massive investment it trailed far behind India.[29]
The missing link is the soft institutional infrastructure.

China's problems all stem from this incapacity to let the puppet
enterprises off the puppeteers' strings and provide them with the institutional network that would permit more creative pluralism and
endogenous accountability. The lack of such a network is the chief
cause of China's first-order environmental crisis.[30] The pace of deser-
tification has doubled over twenty years, in a country where 25 percent of the land area is already desert.[31] Air pollution kills 400,000
people a year prematurely.[32] Energy is habitually wasted. But the worst
problem is water. One-fifth of China's 660 cities face extreme water
shortages, and as many as 90 percent have problems of water pollution; also 53 percent of the water in major water conduits is unfit for
human consumption.[33] As a result, 500 million rural Chinese still do
not have access to safe drinking water. Illegal and rampant polluting,
a severe shortage of sewage treatment facilities, and chemical pollu-
tants together continue to degrade China's waterways. In the autumn
of 2005 two major cities—Harbin and Guangzhou—had their water
supplies cut off for days because their river sources had been subjected to acute chemical spills and leakages from SOE plants.

Enterprises are accountable to no one but the Communist Party
for their actions; there is no network of civil society, plural public institutions like a free press or representative government, and property
rights to create pressure for enterprises to become more environmen-
tally efficient. Pollution, unless it exists in an international city or a
coastal region trying to attract foreign investors, is in effect cost-free;
to constrain it would slow down development. Local officials, as Elizabeth Economy describes, want and need growth; enterprise does
their bidding; and environmental degradation keeps costs down. But

the wider costs are huge, on some estimates ranging up to 12 percent of GDP.[34] Indeed, it is the same constraint-free commitment to economic growth by provincial and local officials, who only benefit and suffer no consequences for overinvestment, that contributed to the overheating of the economy in 2006. China's environmental crisis, like the crisis in its enterprise and legal systems, is an outgrowth of Leninist corporatism.

If It's So Bad, How Come It's So Good?

In the face of all these problems, how has China managed to grow so fast? The World Bank provides the answers. It estimates that between 1990 and 1998 China's high rate of investment contributed 6.4 percent to the annual growth rate; and migration of workers from rural areas added around 2.1 percent. The increase in the labor force brought the growth rate up to 9 percent. The proportional contributions to growth were very similar in the 1980s. As the World Bank remarks drily, China is gaining relatively little benefit from technological progress by its urban enterprises. They add a mere 0.5 percent to the growth rate.[35] To put it another way, China's growth is pretty much guaranteed by state-driven capital accumulation in the cities financed by state-owned banks using China's vast pool of savings, together with migration from the land. The answer is as simple as that.

At the end of 2004, after a generation of aggressive lending, bank debt stood at $3.7 trillion, about twice China's GDP—the highest proportion of any country in the world. The debt is almost entirely lent by state-owned banks, and the four state-owned commercial banks account for half of it. Nearly all the lending is to support industrial activity. Two-thirds of all lending is focused on SOEs, which raise virtually all their required external finance from the banks.

To put it bluntly, the banking system is the essential and indispensable tool of the Leninist party-state.[36] It is the driver of the growth and enables the party to pay its bills whatever the level of productivity, performance, and profit of the enterprises it supports, and despite any shortfall in tax revenues. The bailout of Magang Steel, for example, is a typical use of the banks. Without control of the banking system both the position of the Communist Party and the structure of the economy would collapse. It should therefore be no surprise that the government has made plain its intention to continue to control the banking system. The maximum stake foreign shareholders are permitted is 25 percent; the maximum any single nonstate share-holder is allowed is 20 percent. As for a private or foreign company considering starting a bank of its own in competition, capital requirements to open a branch network are set prohibitively high.

When the Chinese economy was relatively small, it did not matter much that the basic disciplines of banking—assessing the creditworthiness of borrowers, pricing for risk, and insisting on collateral—did not exist. Nor did it matter much that bankruptcy law was rudimentary and that the politically directed court system prevented predictable enforcement of loan contracts and payment of bad debts. What mattered was ensuring a steady flow of cheap finance to support investment, much of which—for bridges, reservoirs, railways, highways, and steel and cement making—was so obviously needed that complex rate-of-return calculations and pricing for risk were hardly necessary. The SOEs would request a loan; the party would make sure it was granted.

The resulting Chinese growth rate has come at the price of escalating bad debts and nonperforming loans in the banking system, and business recipients who have never had to be serious about putting together a business case for credit, sticking to it, and suffering the consequences if they did not achieve the expected outcome.[37] The lack of hard budget constraints or incentives to make a profit has had dire consequences. China has a "nonpayment" culture; interest on loans, dividends on shares, and the servicing of debt are seen as optional extras rather than business necessities.

The Asian financial crisis in 1997 and 1998 laid bare the scarcely believable nature of the mismanagement of the banking system. Two of

Guangdong's leading banks went belly-up as their racy customers in Hong Kong, where they had expanded their business, got into financial difficulties. This exposed a morass of nonperforming lending the banks had made to the "red chip" state-owned enterprises floated on the Hong Kong stock market. Suddenly the viability of the banking system became an object of close scrutiny. In 1998 the government officially estimated that nonperforming loans stood at $205 billion—25 percent of all bank lending, and about 30 percent of GDP. The unofficial estimates of nonperforming loans were double that.[38] To put the crisis in context, consider that the bad debts in the American savings and loan crisis of the 1980s, the worst financial crisis anywhere in the west since the World War II, were only a quarter of that size. Essentially, the capital at the core of the Chinese banking system had been eliminated; Chinese banks were bust. Nor did they make any profits on their operations that would allow them to rebuild their balance sheets. Without radical action, the party was about to lose its principal economic prop.

The response was prompt. Four asset management companies were set up to which the government transferred $168 billion of nonperforming loans and whose task was to recover as a high a proportion of the debt as possible. To date the government has injected more than $260 billion directly into the banks and asset management companies.[39] The banks were simply instructed to stop lending to over 200 business areas deemed to have too much industrial capacity. By 2002 nonperforming loans had officially stabilized at around $255 billion, and as lending soared dizzily they fell below 10 percent of all lending in 2005.

The crisis had been forestalled, or at least deferred. To help the banks restore their balance sheets, they were allowed to start lending on commercial terms to consumers and private businesses—until 1998, banks could lend only to SOEs, on the narrowest of margins. Today about one-fourth of new lending is directed profitably for car purchases, mortgages, and education and has grown rapidly. However, private companies still get very little access to bank credit. To encourage some basic disciplines, banks have been required to become more sophisticated in their loan appraisal techniques, accounting has become much stricter, and the banks are policed by a newly established, powerful regulator. Even more extraordinarily, foreigners have been allowed to take stakes, including stakes in three of the four big state-owned commercial banks, both to raise money and to bolster the pitifully poor management. The China Construction Bank floated 12 percent of its shares in Hong Kong in October 2005 for $8 billion, which valued it as one the largest banks in the world. Readers will recall that its chairman had been arrested for bribery five months earlier. Over seven years the banking system has seen a genuine overhaul.

Yet the scale of the challenge remains enormous. The China Construction Bank, for example, has over 14,000 branches and 300,000 employees, all of whom have to be trained in basic banking techniques even as all the old incentives for corruption and direction of lending remain in place. According to a leaked report from the China Banking Regulatory Commission, banks commonly ignore the regulations and understate bad loans, a practice that is made worse by poor accounting.[40] The Communist Party, not a bank's board, appoints the chief executive and makes other key appointments. Richard Podpiera, in a paper for the IMF, acknowledges the significance of what the party has tried to do in cleaning up the banks, but reports that so far it has made very little difference to the way business is done. Bank officers do not price risk or take profitability into account when lending, Podpiera says; they simply lend when money is available to be lent, and alarmingly—despite the foreign shareholdings in three of the state-owned banks—their share of lending with more profitable enterprises in the provinces has fallen. Rather, they have lent to sectors like steel, cement, and construction, which have chronic overcapacity and poor profitability. The idea that bad debts have fallen from 45 percent before 2000 to 2 percent after 2000 is too good to be true. Podpiera is skeptical about whether so much can have changed so dramatically in such a short time.[41] Moreover, there are signs that the zeal for allowing foreign shareholdings is diminishing; at the time of writing Citibank's planned takeover of Guangdong Development Bank was encountering stiff opposition.

The possibility of another bank crisis is obvious. The scarcely profitable SOE sector remains the recipient of this avalanche of lending, which is hardly better managed. The SOEs owe China's banks more than $2 trillion; and the World Bank projects that anything up to $1.2 trillion would not be serviced if interest rates rose or sales fell even marginally. Each year the banks add at least another $500 billion to the stock of debt. Now that China is the world's fourth-largest economy, it cannot dare to repeat the crisis of the late 1990s. Officially, China's nonperforming loans amount to about $300 billion; unofficially, they are double that. Indeed, one recent report by the accountants Ernst and Young estimated that in 2005 the real, total nonperforming loans of the banking system stood at $900 billion, of which the four big state-owned banks accounted for $358 billion—twice the official estimate.[42] The report was withdrawn after the Chinese government protested that it was "ridiculous and barely understandable"[43]—a protest that itself testified to the way China is run. Simple arithmetic implies that in a weaker economic climate the total of nonperforming loans could easily pass $1 trillion and climb toward $2 trillion. Even China, with its projected $1 trillion of foreign exchange reserves, could not afford to restructure and pay down bad debts of that magnitude. It would be overwhelmed, the growth process would stall, and social unrest could rise to unmanageable proportions.

China dare not stop growing. For although the banking reforms are welcome, they fall short of what is needed. Only a profitable enterprise sector and an end to political interference and corruption can in the medium term guarantee the health of the banking sector. And these are what China does not possess.

The Ticking Clock

Today China needs $5.40 of extra investment to produce an extra $1 of output, a proportion vastly higher than that in developed economies like Britain or the United States. But twenty years ago,

China needed just $4. In other words, an already gravely inefficient economy has become even more inefficient.[44] China's national accounts tell the same grim story. China had to increase its capital stock by 9 percent every year in the 1980s to produce a 9.8 percent growth rate; but by the late 1990s it had to increase capital stock by 12 percent to produce a lower growth rate of 8.2 percent. Hu Angang calculates that China is now back to the Mao years in terms of the inefficiency with which it uses capital to generate growth.[45]

This astonishing wastefulness is confirmed by Qu Hongbin and Sophia Ma Xiaoping of HSBC Bank.[46] They calculate that the additional output produced by investing the incremental dollar is now below what it was in the late Mao years. Comparisons with other countries at a similar stage of development are equally unflattering. Korea and Taiwan between 1970 and 1980, Japan between 1965 and 1975, and the United States between 1890 and 1910 were all urbanizing and industrializing at about the same rate as China was between 1998 and 2004. China, however, has needed at least one-third more investment than Japan and twice as much as Taiwan and Korea to achieve the same result.[47] However you look at it, the numbers tell the same baleful story. A visitor riding into Shanghai from Shanghai Airport on the new, virtually empty train will recognize the phenomenon: the project was so expensive that it will take 160 years to pay for itself.[48]

The clock is ticking. How much longer can China's current approach to economic development last? One pressure point is the internal economic structure; another is external: China traps every cent of Chinese saving inside China because it needs the pool to be as high as possible to fund its high investment. It also wants to keep the renminbi as competitive as possible to promote exports—even while China earns a current account surplus of about 8 percent of GDP and receives about $60 billion a year as foreign direct investment. The tensions are reconciled by the People's Bank of China buying dollars at the current exchange rate, so there is an explosive rise in China's foreign exchange reserves, now increasing at about $200 billion a year.

The more China moves into the black, the higher its foreign exchange reserves become.

The consensus is that the renminbi is 25 to 30 percent undervalued against the dollar.[49] To put this another way, China's exports are artificially cheap compared with those of other middle-income developing countries, even allowing for its cheap wages. Thus, if the Chinese authorities ever allowed the renminbi to respond to pure demand and supply—to float—it would rise against the dollar; but conversely, that would mean the dollar would fall against the renminbi. China thus would be faced with the elimination of $300 billion of its foreign currency assets (30 percent of $1 trillion of reserves). Olivier Blanchard and Francesco Giavazzi of MIT calculate, in an important paper, that every year that China adds between $200 billion and $250 billion to its reserves, it runs the risk that those reserves will fall by between $60 billion and $75 billion, or about 3.5 percent of GDP, when the renminbi eventually revalues.[50]

Blanchard and Giavazzi calculate that the undervaluation of the renminbi by 30 percent adds 0.45 percentage point to China's growth rate because of additional export growth. Therefore, in any given year, while the People's Bank of China risks losing 3.5 percent of GDP from a potential revaluation, it is adding to the growth rate by 0.45 percent—a good rate of return until the whole fabric unravels. But there is another contribution to growth from the current policy. China is keeping its savings bottled up internally as a crucial part of its growth strategy. If it yielded to pressure from the United States and agreed to float the renminbi, it would want to stop its currency from rising. The best way to do that would be to allow Chinese savers to take their money abroad, supplying renminbi that the world's markets want. But how much would leave China? Blanchard and Giavazzi estimate that about one-fourth would go abroad. Because of the structure of the Chinese banking system, that amount would reduce the growth of its deposit base by one-fourth, and thus its capacity to lend at today's low interest rates. Using the World Bank's numbers, that would reduce growth from investment by one-fourth: about 1.6 percent per year. In other words, capital controls and reserve accumulation are worth about 2 percent to China's growth rate every year—more if you believe that savers would move proportionately more assets into higher-earning overseas assets than Blanchard and Giavazzi estimate.

Nor is that the only consequence. If the renminbi rises, then agricultural prices—which are now keyed to world market prices—will fall. As the renminbi gains in buying power, the world market price translates into lower domestic prices, and lower domestic rural incomes. Abysmally low levels of agricultural productivity mean that rural incomes are barely above subsistence level. A revalued renminbi would trigger a crisis; for example, value added per person is on average a mere $490, compared with $1,040 in the Philippines and $4,851 in Malaysia. This would immediately accelerate the movement of the pool of 300 million agricultural laborers to the cities in search of work, and lower rural savings still further. A revaluation of the renminbi is something the party treats, properly, with great care.

In these terms, China's resistance to pressure from the United States starts to make more sense. But in the summer of 2005 the Chinese government did give way, offering the concession of a managed float and a tiny upward revaluation with the implicit promise of more to come. For acute dilemmas face the Chinese at every turn. If they allow a freer float, as the United States wants, but with the current capital controls to protect the pool of savings, the renminbi will rise, lowering export growth and squeezing rural incomes. The rise can be checked if the Chinese are allowed to move their capital abroad, but this will lower the savings pool at current low interest rates. Either way the growth rate will slow. And that will set off a sharp rise in nonperforming loans, with all the consequences for the banking system outlined earlier.

On the other hand the status quo is equally unforgiving. Already, the capacity of the rest of the world to absorb China's 25 percent export growth is being tested to the limit. The protests about the surge of textiles exported to Europe and the United States in mid-2005 were a storm warning. Western economies need time to adjust to the avalanche of cheap Chinese exports. And the financial by-product of acquiring reserves at this rate is also becoming increasingly difficult. The Chinese are finding it harder to contain the inflationary consequences of money pouring into China; Chinese banks are required to buy government bonds to "sterilize" the cash inflows so they are not lent, but even so the money supply is growing at very nearly 20 percent. In order for sterilization to be effective the banks will be forced to hold a growing proportion of their assets in low-interest-rate sterilized bonds—they already hold $700 billion—but this will directly lower their already low profitability. The government will be forced to raise interest rates to compensate them and check the growth in the money supply, slowing the economy down and pushing some of China's low-profit enterprises closer to the wall.

The financial message is unambiguous. China must stop acquiring foreign exchange reserves at this rate, must allow the renminbi to float, and must allow Chinese savers to move their money abroad so that the potential upward movement of the currency can be slowed. Only thus can China bring down the growth of its domestic money supply, head off the risk of inflation, and slow the momentum of its exports. But this will lower the rate of its economic growth, the rate of saving and investment, and rural incomes—and if nothing changes greatly it will increase the risk of social protest. Every year the decision is deferred is another year in which foreign exchange reserves soar upward, increasing the risk of a huge loss when the revaluation ultimately comes. It's a no-win situation: float and accept a deceleration of growth, or don't float and accept a deceleration of growth. And the deceleration of growth will expose the weaknesses in the banking system, which will force a further deceleration of growth. This is similar to what Japan experienced as a result of banking weakness in the 1990s.

One way or another, China's economic model is certain to begin to change sometime in the next five to ten years. The rest of the world cannot indefinitely absorb Chinese exports growing at their current rate. China cannot continue acquiring foreign exchange reserves at its current rate. Living standards in rural China cannot be allowed to fall much further below those in urban China, for both social and economic reasons. The larger the urban economy grows, the more rural savings it must have to keep on growing—but the rural economy is shrinking proportionately every year.

China must become a more normal economy, with higher consumption, lower saving, and more efficient enterprises. But that will demand major changes in Leninist corporatism. The Chinese Communist Party is faced with a second no-win situation. It can relax its political control to allow the economic reform process to be completed. Or it can retain political control, watch the economic contradictions build, and so create the social tension that may force loss of political control. The party's instinct is to muddle through. The force of events, I suspect, will force more radicalism. Nobody can say with certainty. What you can say is that these choices are approaching—and fast.

Breaking China—Can the Change Be Made?

China needs to take the pressure off investment and exports as the drivers of economic development. It needs to become a more normal economy in which private consumption does more of the work, and so relieve the increasing strains described above. A major report commissioned by the Chinese government from a panel of front-rank Chinese and foreign economists concluded that consumption had to rise from its current 50 percent of GDP to 60 percent.[51] So much is common ground. The issue is how. The problem is that persuading the Chinese to save less, consume more, and to make enterprise more productive is not just a technical issue. It goes to the heart of Leninist corporatism.

The problem in raising consumption is that the habit of saving is very deeply embedded, largely because China's health, pension, and social security system is so weak. As discussed in Chapter 4, the chief explanation of high personal saving is the interaction of China's chronically weak, patchy welfare system with the one-child policy; saving is needed for health, income in old age, and education, and there is no wider support available from either family or welfare. The intention of the next five-year plan—to improve rural incomes, welfare, and health care—is hard to fault, but it starts from so low a base that it is hard to credit. For example, until the 1970s health care in rural China was provided by the communes and covered 90 percent of rural areas. When the communes collapsed, so did rural health care, which by the late 1980s covered only 5 percent of rural areas. The government has made no serious effort to compensate; only 15 percent of the health budget is allocated to rural China, although this is where 900 million people—70 percent of the population—live.[52] Worse, the only way health care could be sustained in the countryside was for doctors who used to work for the communes to charge fees, but peasants do not have the money to pay. The quality of health care has nose-dived. In 2001 a study of 400 village clinics found that two-thirds did not keep medical records and that only half of the surgical equipment was sterilized.[53]

Even with costs and thus prices cut drastically, the National Health Service survey conducted by the Ministry of Health in 1998 conceded that 37 percent of farmers who fell sick could not afford medical treatment, and 65 percent of peasants were refused admission to hospitals because of their inability to pay.[54] The system is better in the towns, but still hardly comprehensive. Only 12 percent of individuals in rural China are insured, and the proportion in urban China rises only slightly above half, to 54 percent.[55] In the World Health Organization's report for 2000, the overall performance of China's health case system in 1997 ranked 144, placing China behind India, Indonesia, and Bangladesh. For "fairness," China was ranked only 188 (by contrast, India was forty-two). So it is understandable that peasants save so aggressively.[56]

The story is similar with regard to education. Much of China's improvement in literacy and numeracy is a legacy of the Mao years, and progress has largely stopped. China, having made great strides between 1949 and 1976, will not meet UNESCO's goal for literacy in 2015.[57] As with health, the central government has not stepped in to make good the loss of the "iron rice bowl"—the system of care formerly provided by the communes and the state-owned enterprises. Townships foot four-fifths of the education bill, obtaining the money from a mix of fees, taxes, and charges. In the rural areas, the schools have to charge fees—with the inevitable result that the poorer the area, the poorer the education. Low-income countries spend on average about 3.4 percent of GDP on education; China spends only 2 percent—forcing large areas of the country to make do as best they can.[58] Peasant families save for their children's education because they must.

Also, China's population is aging. Ten percent of today's population is over sixty; and by 2015 the proportion will have risen to 14 percent. Yet there is no national pension system. Children have been legally required to take responsibility for their aging parents; and because most families have only one child, the potential burden is considerable. Fear of what will happen to them in old age impels urban and rural Chinese alike to save intensely. And with the one-child policy the ratio of elderly people to the working population can only rise. In the seventy years between 1970 and 2040, China will have gone from a country where every "elder" over sixty was outnumbered by six young people to one where there are twice as many elders as children.[59] It is a phenomenal switch.

Then there is the lack of property rights, and its complex linkage with saving and spending rates. Consumers in western societies have lower savings in part because they borrow against the collateral in their housing assets. This happens more in Britain, the United States, and Scandinavia than in Germany and France, but the trend is apparent everywhere. Communist China still does not acknowledge private property. Houses and apartments in towns are available on seventy-year leases, but typically rural smallholdings are available only on thirty-year leases, if at all. China also lacks a national land registry, and this situation aggravates the unclear property structure. Chinese consumers thus have no backing from their property and face life's hazards—aging, poor health, unemployment, and educating children—largely on their own. Nor can Chinese workers look to a labor union to advance their interests, protect them from arbitrary layoffs, or secure real wage increases.[60] The unions are directed by the All-China Federation of Trade Unions, and are creatures of the party—so another piece of China's soft infrastructure is lacking. Small wonder that saving is so high. Recent moves to allow collective wage contracts and give unions a role in arbitrating disputes may be welcome, but as David Metcalf and Jianwei Li of the London School of Economics[61] report hollow collective contracts are not collective bargaining. Chinese workers are not effectively represented and remain at the mercy of their managements.

To move to a lower-saving, higher-spending economy requires solving these conundrums. Solutions will necessarily involve the party in having to concede property rights, allow independent labor unions, and impose the taxes needed to finance a more comprehensive welfare system. But the party does not dare to move on even one front. To permit private property is to empower Chinese civil society as well as to repudiate the ideological base of communism. To permit independent labor unions is to lose control of the workforce and create a base for ideological competition. And to raise taxation is to invite taxpayers to want to hold the government that spends their money to account. As Montesquieu famously observed, the compensation for despotism is modest taxes. In the same way that the Chinese business sector needs an Enlightenment soft infrastructure to move to higher levels of productivity, so Chinese society needs it to save less and spend more. Welfare systems, freedom of association, representative government, and enforceable property rights are not simply pleasant options. They are central to the capacity of a capitalist economy to grow to maturity. Without them China will be condemned to live with its economic contradictions—but sooner or later these will become unsustainable. Indeed, the dangerously overheated economy in 2006, refusing to slow down despite interest-rate increases and

Beijing's exhortations, pleading, and instructions, shows how increasingly difficult it is to manage an economy where normal constraints do not apply and the independent institutional power to enforce normal accountabilities is close to nonexistent. China is in a dilemma very similar to the one that Jiang Zemin confronted in 1993. Why that should be so is what we examine next.

CHAPTER 7

The Democratic Graces

TWENTY YEARS AGO REAGANISM AND THATCHERISM WERE at a peak in the United States and Britain; they were responses to the perceived economic and social dead end into which these countries had plunged in the 1970s. What these creeds sought to accelerate was more animalistic, go-getting individualism, more personal responsibility, more personal reward, and less dependence on the state. Their critique was similar. Western capitalism had become too soft; it was too influenced by labor unions, state subsidies, and regulatory busybodies. Above all, the state got in the way of private property owners, businesses, and entrepreneurs, forcibly exerting their proprietorial and managerial rights to create wealth. Inflation and slow economic growth were symptoms of a deeper malaise. Prometheus had to be unbound. Workers and citizens alike had to realize that there were hard budget constraints, and hard choices. To revive western economies, profits would have to be higher, incentives greater, prices and wages more flexible, and the scope of personal ownership enlarged. In particular in Britain privatization of nationalized industries and weakening of trade unions would presumably open the way to greater productivity and growth.

Chinese reform had similar antecedents. By the end of the 1970s there was an analogous Chinese impatience with the state as an agent of economic development, even if the Chinese state was a model apart from anything in the west. The pro-market reforms of the last thirty years took much the same trajectory as those in the west and China has now arrived at a corresponding fork in the road. Everywhere, applied experience and severe intellectual examination are making the explanation of capitalist success more complicated and nuanced than the simple account advanced in the 1980s. Just as the west, as I shall argue, is rethinking what works and why, so the challenges to policy and institutions in China are moving beyond Deng's brave but simple concepts of 1980 about loosening planning and celebrating markets and wealth.

The free-market economic propositions that made such advances in the 1980s are being challenged and modified. To make the case that perfectly competitive markets would arrive at a perfect point of balance, the so-called neoclassical free-marketeers had to make some highly doubtful assumptions about human behavior and attributes: for example, that people process information and assess risk with scientific precision and form preferences in a state of nature, uninfluenced by culture, history, or each other. As soon as the utopian free-market economic model is peopled by human beings who each possess different amounts of information and who make false guesses about the unknowable future—i.e., real people—it quickly becomes obvious that even in theory markets cannot be left to their own devices. They reflect the universal human tendency to undervalue future costs and benefits and overvalue the immediate; in short, they are myopic. They do not automatically create public goods. There are externalities—external consequences of private activity—ranging from environmental costs to traffic congestion, that the price mechanism does not automatically capture. Equally, there are spillover benefits from private activity, like undertaking R & D, that the price mechanism also does not capture. Markets create winner-take-all and loser-take-all effects that increase inequality. In sum, human beings are far too fallible and unreliable in identifying their own best interests for price signals in markets to be the only means of coordinating what they do.

Moreover, unlike the predictions of the free-market textbooks, economic life is saturated with the truth that the more one does, the more accomplished one becomes and the more one learns. This cumulative learning and raised skill then translates into a capacity to produce at lower cost. The larger scale at which a firm produces, the more its returns tend to increase and the more it becomes easier for it to monopolize its market. Unless counteracted, there is, in short, an inevitable tendency to monopoly in market economies with all the unfair and inefficient market, political, and social power it implies. The best argument for markets is not the argument of the 1980s that they are unimprovable and always deliver best outcomes; rather, it is that they are the best way to sustain plural societies and economies. It is an interpretation that requires much more complexity in how markets are to be conceived and governed than that offered by free-market theorists.

If the debate among economists has become more sophisticated, so has the debate among practitioners—who have had twenty years' experience trying to make free-market solutions work in what came to be known as the Washington consensus. There have been successes; arguably, globalization, the intensification of trade flows, the rise of Asia, and the great reductions in poverty are attributable to a better understanding, and an embrace, of market solutions. But there have also been failures. In too many countries, for example, privatization has been tantamount to embezzlement: handing over state assets to political cronies and insiders at bargain prices. The most scandalous example is the creation of the Russian oligarchs. Financial deregulation has too often meant little more than allowing the financial system to lend freely while paying few of the costs in terms of wider credit growth, reduced savings, or clashes with other policy objectives. The proximate cause of the Asian financial crisis of 1997 and 1998, for example, was rapid credit growth (in turn caused by financial deregulation) colliding with the policy objective of lowering inflation by pegging currencies to the dollar. Mountainous speculation, another feature of deregulated financial markets, caused devaluation and economic retrenchment: GDP fell by 13 percent in Indonesia, by 10 percent in Thailand, and by 7 percent in South Korea. Some adjustment might have been necessary, but this speed and ferocity almost certainly were not.

Even the economic development process has been rethought because of weaknesses in application of the theory. When the Washington consensus was in its glorious pomp at the time of the collapse of the Soviet Union, the view was that the underdeveloped world stayed underdeveloped because of its resistance to the magic of markets and its attachment to statism. As a result there was an unfocused, universal belief in liberalization, privatization, price stability, and deregulation whatever the particular circumstances of any country and with little interest in how specific policies were sequenced. In some countries it might be human capital constraints that were limiting growth; in others, weaknesses in the physical infrastructure; in still others, high real interest rates caused by high investment demand and low saving. As the economist Dani Rodrik of Harvard argued, instead of forensic examination of what the diagnostic signals were saying, the Washington consensus became a kind of spray gun in which everything was tried in the hope that a generalized movement toward markets would be beneficial.[1]

Today there is a new sobriety—a recognition, for example, that geography, climate, and disease constrain development and that more forensic analysis is required. In *Guns, Germs, and Steel* Jared Diamond showed that innovations which worked in temperate Europe and northern Asia did not travel to Africa; even the animals and crops could not be reproduced.[2] Other analysts have shown that disease severely limits the scope for gains in agricultural productivity.[3] Achieving basic levels of education and health, and accepting the necessary public expenditure, may have better payoffs than market liberalization. In these contexts, just unleashing markets is hardly likely to start the development process. And for many landlocked poor economies, such as Bolivia in Latin America, Burundi and Rwanda in Africa, and Laos and Mongolia in Asia, their own physical isolation and low demand from neighboring countries limit their growth options.[4] Profits from long-distance trade, as discussed in Chapter 2, are important to development; but such profits presuppose both goods and partners with which to trade. Invocations of free markets which neglect the hard truths of geography are of no help to anyone.

The emerging consensus takes this into account. In particular, it is now understood that the quality of a country's institutions are as important to development as the strength and diversity of its market processes. John Williamson, the man most closely identified with formulating the Washington consensus, regretfully acknowledges the mistakes of the 1990s:

> [My] emphasis would have been different; I would have focused much more generally on institutions. . . . The major advance of the 1990s stemmed from recognition that the central task of the transition from communism to market-based economies involved building the institutional infrastructure of a market economy. This realisation was complemented by a growing recognition that bad institutions can sabotage good policies.[5]

It is a recognition that the reliable weathervane of the international consensus, the well-intentioned but self-regarding World Economic Forum, accurately reflects. It produces an annual Global Competitiveness Index in which businesspeople rank more than 100 countries. Market efficiency and macroeconomic rigor, once the heart of the conservative revolution, are now only two of nine "pillars of competitiveness." The other seven are the quality of public institutions; the quality of infrastructure; health; primary education, higher education, and training; technological readiness; business sophistication; and innovation.[6] Reaganism and Thatcherism, it may be objected, never overtly dismissed these other pillars; on the other hand, neither philosophy stressed them. The Reaganites and Thatcherites held that individuals, entrepreneurs, businesses, and managers must be empowered; markets were magic; and the state must as far as possible stand aside.

No such clarity is available today. The new stress on the role of institutions in development and growth may seem to widen the argument and deepen our understanding, but in truth it muddies the waters. Generally institutions are regarded in one of two ways. First, they may be said to support growth because they undergird a particular type of Anglo-Saxon capitalism—e. g., tradable property rights enforced in independent courts, powerful stock markets, or "light" regulation that does not inhibit market efficiency. Second, they may be collapsed into a list of desirable "good" institutions, with little sense of whether they are the cause or the outcome of successful development. Are independent media, good transportation infrastructure, a strong innovation system, and even efficient, transparent government causes or effects? And if any of these are causes, how and to what degree can they be created?

We alternate between a catchall view of institutions, because they all count, and the view that because the American business model is presumably best, any developing or developed country had better create institutions like those in the United States as part of a general commitment to "liberalize." This thinking comes close to being a circular, nonfalsifiable argument: markets are best, so institutions that support and complement markets are obviously crucial. This wishful reasoning, typical of the Washington consensus or the World Economic Forum, is certainly more sophisticated today than in the past, but it still falls short of the rigorous noncircular logic we need.

Which Institutions Matter, and Why?

Dani Rodrik is one of the creative thinkers about the role of nonmarket institutions in the effective functioning of a market economy. He identifies a wide range of nonmarket institutions, such as labor unions and social insurance systems, that help the market to function better even though that is not their primary purpose.[7] Rodrik is on the right road, but we need to go further. Efficient markets require complementary market and nonmarket institutions. In fact, sustainable, legitimate, high-growth capitalism needs institutions whose values and mission are in tension with and sometimes opposed to markets and market values, in order to keep the markets honest. They are nonmarket institutions precisely because they have different values, different mechanisms of accountability, and different purposes. Their clashes with the values of markets are not technical but are felt passionately and arise from a clash of vocations.

Consider the values and origins of the distinct network of institutions with a public vocation whose purpose is not capitalist success but which play an indispensable role in driving capitalism forward. Justice and the rule of law are grounded in the insistence that right and wrong have their roots in reasoned justification in the light of evidence judged before universally applicable principles enshrined in law. Justice cannot be bought and sold. Another example is the university, an institution committed to the acquisition and dissemination of knowledge; scholarship has to follow reason and truth rather than commercial advantage. Even the media, although they may need to make a profit, have an independent vocation to report and comment on objectively observed reality. They are an indispensable component of transparency and accountability in both the private and the public sphere. Nor were welfare systems ever conceived as "market-supporting"; rather, they were created as instruments of social solidarity, basic insurance against the risks of life, and means of securing equal opportunity. Welfare may help to manage social conflict and protests when firms are involved in tumultuous competition and technological change, but its moral force comes from a different wellspring. Labor unions want a voice in the workplace and better working conditions, and have proved a crucial mechanism in making workplaces less exploitative, more humane, and frequently more productive; yet the right to strike and even the unions' right to exist resulted from a prolonged political battle. The tension as much the complementarity between market institutions and such nonmarket institutions impels capitalist development and growth.

Nonmarket institutions are direct or indirect descendants of the Enlightenment—a result of at least two centuries of historical development. They create and sustain accountability, transparency, the process of justification, the acquisition of knowledge, and the capacity of ordinary citizens to participate in social and public life. One way or another they make up the concept of "publicness" and the public sphere. If they are crucial to the functioning of the capitalist economy, they are no less crucial to the functioning of representative government. Charles Taylor of Northwestern University, McGill, and Oxford—one of the most influential philosophers in the English-speaking world—in *Modern Social Imaginaries* identifies the separation of public sphere and government as one fundamental quality of an effective democracy. The public sphere is where "society can come to a common mind about important matters," he writes; and because the debate is not just sounding off but an attempt to arrive at a reasoned collective judgment, the government ought to listen and respond. This is where a sovereign people thinks out aloud; it is self-consciously outside power and does not exercise power itself—rather, it is listened to and plays a crucial role in defining the limits of governmental action. This legacy of the Enlightenment underpins not just representative government but the institutional pluralism that in turn underpins the good economy and society. To describe these values and the institutions they have created as "nonmarket" is to denude them of their lifeblood, rob them of their historical context, and accord them a technocratic instead of a moral and political foundation.

China, as I have argued, needs the gamut of such nonmarket institutions. But getting them is not a matter of organizing a technocratic transplant or copying. It is a matter of revolutionizing Chinese nonmarket spheres and in particular accepting the idea of a public sphere that is independent of the state and the Communist Party.

This is where the political and the individual are conjoined. Communism purports to enlarge individual choices and enrich individual lives through collective action. Mao believed the communist proposition of the Great Leap Forward: the creation of communes would enfranchise peasants and, more importantly, expand their imagination. It would give them an opportunity, for example, to write poetry that they had never experienced before. Some did, notwithstanding the wider inhumanities and mass deaths. But the experience of the last forty years of reform has shown the Chinese that expanding the imaginations does not necessitate a suffocating daily compliance with communism. Nobel prize–winning economist Amartya Sen, echoing Mao but proposing very different means to achieve the same end, has declared that the objective of development is not just material wealth but the substantive freedom and capability "to choose a life that one has reason to value."[8] This is a common urge among all peoples, rich and developed or poor and undeveloped.

So here is a mechanism, plural public institutions; and here is a consequence, human happiness. Enlightenment institutions need Enlightenment people to breathe life into them; modernity has to be won by real people who are prepared to imagine a life that they themselves want to make and are prepared to act on that concept, leaving behind the universe in which preferences are inherited and fixed. Nic Stern, a former World Bank adviser who is now chief economic adviser to the British government, argues that this involves a mental shift from the traditional to the modern.[9] What societies have to demand and governments supply is the tools to do the job—and that first requires even better proof of why and how pluralism works.

The Pluralist Advantage

The Great Leap Forward was admitted to be a disaster, a utopian top-down master plan for China, forced on a civil society that was powerless to resist. So was the aggressive implementation of the Washington consensus and financial liberalization that was forced on much of the world. Latin America's protracted stagnation in the 1990s,[10] Asia's financial crisis later in the decade, and Russia's reform program imposed severe but avoidable costs on one-third of the world's land area.

When utopian grand ideas do not respect the complexity of real human communities, there is serious trouble.

James Scott of Yale University, in his book *Seeing Like a State,* discusses some of the twentieth century's debacles, ranging from Soviet agricultural collectivization to Le Corbusier's schemes for new urban communities like Brasília. He argues that they have in common an overriding of the diffused wisdom and practice of many plural actors in favor of a grand plan.[11] In a way, this is obvious; what is intriguing about Scott's analysis is his demonstration that the disasters have similar pathologies. First, grand-plan thinking needs stylized aggregated facts, so that complex reality becomes standardized. What animates the planners is a passionate confidence in what Scott calls "high modernist ideology"—the idea that science and rationality, by revealing how nature and human society work, allow them to be mastered. Le Corbusier, the introducers of calamitous western agricultural techniques into Tanzania, the authors of the Washington consensus, and Mao himself are linked by the same thread. But the combination of modernist ideology and stylized facts becomes deadly when they are in the hands of an authoritarian state willing to coerce its subjects, and when there is a prostrate civil society unable to resist the plans. China's tragedy, as with Russian collectivization, was that communism was uniquely powerful and coercive in implementing its modernist ideology, and civil society uniquely weak. The result was murderous havoc. Mao recognized that the lack of accurate feedback from the local communes allowed the Great Leap Forward to continue for too long unchanged; and in his own terms he did want better socialist democracy to inform the planners so that the center could be more responsive to the local. Scott's retort is that the problem is more than faulty design; it is inherent to the grand designers' way of thinking about the world.

Scott argues that states have to respect what he calls "metis"—the fabric of institutions, knowledge, and practice that societies have developed to solve problems, live together, and propel their economies. He describes this as a wide array of "practical skills and acquired intelligence in responding to the constantly changing natural human environment." Scott is thinking along the right lines; but if his idea is taken to extremes it is a de facto prohibition on government action. For governments have to act as well, and are necessarily imperfect; and as much as we may deplore Maoism, sovietization, or the clumsy implementation of the Washington consensus, these philosophies were responding to genuine economic and social concerns that had reached a crisis. What was wrong (over and above the obvious intellectual mistakes) was the arbitrary ideological intervention—and, in the case of communism, the totalitarian imposition. We can acknowledge this and still acknowledge that society, while respecting "metis" and the plural institutions which create it, has to find some way of acting collectively in order to capture the benefits of public goods and avoid the expensive externalities of some private actions. The holy grail is to combine them both in order to achieve both social coherence consistent with plural action.

Even Birth Control Is Better Controlled Democratically

Even a policy that at first sight seems best implemented by an authoritarian state will, on closer examination, be seen to work best if the system respects pluralism and "metis" and so wins cultural ownership of ideas. An intriguing example is the contrast between China's approach to birth control and the approach taken by some Indian states.

Fertility in China has certainly fallen since the one-child policy was introduced in 1982, and the target of stabilizing the population has been broadly achieved. However, there have been terrible costs: abortion, female infanticide, and a gross imbalance between the sexes. (Chinese couples want a boy rather than a girl, and the manipulation means these are 120 male births for every 100 female births.) With an illegal trade growing in prostitutes and forced brides, there are increasing questions about the sustainability of the policy. In 2004,

President Hu Jintao asked 250 senior Chinese demographers to study whether the one-child policy should be revised.[12] The projection is that by 2020 as many 40 million men could be unmarried with no sexual outlet. In the past, such a situation has been a source of economic and social instability; and the regime fears that this result could happen again.[13]

The one-child policy may be reaching the limits of administrative sustainability. Systematic intrusion into the intimacy of hundreds of millions of couples is beyond even the Chinese state; the quality of the 400,000-member birth control bureaucracy is patchy; and the policy of bulldozing or dynamiting the homes of couples with more than one child is gradually being abandoned because of its brutality and lack of legitimacy. Instead, China has gradually been moving away from coercion and moving toward a policy based more on fines, tax penalties, exhortation, and education about birth control.[14] However, it does not dare abandon coercion altogether, because there is so little cultural ownership of the need for small families. Despite rising prosperity and female empowerment, the birthrate might bounce back upward again. Nor is there any prospect of the distrusted bureaucracy and distrusted organs of state propaganda winning such cultural ownership; nor of plural communities in civil society doing the same job, because they are so weak. Coercion finds itself at a dead end.[15]

In fact, as Amartya Sen has argued, the fall in China's birthrate might have been expected anyway, given the rising per capita income, the education of women, and the rising literacy. (These are all the best predictors of lower fertility.) Sen discusses how the birthrate in the literate, rapidly developing Indian state of Kerala, where women have been increasingly as well educated as men, has actually fallen faster than the rate in China since 1979.[16] The plural communities of Kerala—schools, women's birth control advocacy groups, expanding companies, and families themselves—have voluntarily and spontaneously constructed a culture of greater female empowerment that, along with higher living standards, has motivated women to have fewer children. Sen also points out that there is no evidence in Kerala of increased abortion of female fetuses or murder of infant girls, as there is in China. The intervention in Kerala has been less heavy-handed from the beginning, working with the grain of Kerala's civil society, so it has won ownership of the notion that families should be smaller while respecting the pluralism of its society. The outcome is both better and stabler than China's.[17]

This is tribute to democratic pluralism in the broad sense I have used throughout this book: not just voting but the entire network of institutions and processes in which representative government nests. The obvious case for democracy is that it delivers sovereign government of the people, by the people, and for the people; and despite all its problems of implementation it is the least bad way of guaranteeing liberty. In fact, the case is more profound. In *Why People Obey the Law,* Tom Tyler, a professor of psychology, marshals evidence that the more people have participated in forming the law, the more likely they are to accept its rulings even if they disagree with a particular outcome. Process matters. People want to participate; they want procedures to be neutral and consistent; they want to be treated with dignity and respect; and they want to be sure that the lawmakers have considered their needs and concerns.[18] China's birth control policy fails to meet all four criteria, so its illegitimacy is guaranteed—and the many attempts at evasion are inevitable. In Kerala, by contrast, birth control was felt to be more legitimate.

The Economic Case for Democratic Pluralism

There is growing statistical proof that democracy and economic advantage are closely associated. Consider *The Democracy Advantage: How Democracies Promote Prosperity and Peace,* written by Morton Halperin of the Open Society Institute together with Joseph T. Siegle of the University of Maryland and Michael M. Weinstein, director of programs at the Robin Hood Foundation.[19] They argue that democracies, understood as states with a network of democratic institutions rather than just representative government, tend to have more interests involved in government decision making, to be more open, and to have more accountability. Whatever the shortcomings of a particular democratic system, at least politicians have a dramatic incentive to meet citizens' preferences: they could get kicked out of power in an election. The democratic institutions may be rudimentary and incomplete, but over a period of decades democracies tend to manage their resources more effectively and accommodate themselves better to necessary economic and social changes. Halperin and his colleagues test the thesis as rigorously as possible.[20] They find, for example, that since 1960 poor democracies have grown 50 percent more rapidly than nondemocracies on average, so that the Baltic countries, Botswana, Costa Rica, Ghana, and Senegal have done much better than, say, Angola, Syria, Uzbekistan, or Zimbabwe. The social dimensions of development—access to drinking water, girls' literacy, health care—are better in democracies. Life expectancy is typically nine years longer in poor democracies than in poor autocracies; the likelihood of finishing secondary school is 40 percent higher; infant mortality rates are 25 percent lower; agricultural yields are about 25 percent higher. And so on. According to Halperin and his colleagues, "95 percent of the worst economic performances over the past 40 years were overseen by nondemocratic governments."[21]

The numbers are hard to dispute. Democratizing countries are less vulnerable to both internal and external conflict. In sub-Saharan Africa, one of the world's black spots of intense conflict, either internally or externally or a combination of both, democratizers have been only half as likely to experience civil conflict as others.[22] The only exception to this worldwide rule is in parts of Asia, where authoritarian Singapore and China have been successful. By contrast democratic Japan, Thailand, and now India exemplify the thesis—and Singapore, like Hong Kong, has the British legacy of an independent judiciary. South Korea and Taiwan, even in their authoritarian periods, were significantly pluralist. As for China, the next phase of its growth will probably also be accompanied by more pluralism.

The process at work here is often inadequate and always imperfect, but more frequently than not fosters better government, more pluralism, and better decisions. Herd behavior, groupthink, and conformism all menace the quality of decision making in government or private-sector organizations. The more diverse the interests that are represented at the table, the less likely it is that groups will commit themselves to a decision or conform with an approach that is self-defeating or plain wrong. Cass Sunstein, a professor of jurisprudence at the University of Chicago, argues in *Why Societies Need Dissent*[23] that societal pressure to conform stifles the multiplicity of voices that are needed to articulate views other than the group norm—and that groups tend to reach lowest-common-denominator decisions acceptable to all that are either second-best or downright wrong. Democratic systems make fewer such mistakes than others but even so are prone to the same biases.

Sunstein's list of bad decisions attributable to conformist thinking includes Neville Chamberlain's appeasement of Hitler, the disaster at the Bay of Pigs, the infamous corporate debacles of the early 2000s—Enron, WorldCom, and Tyco. He also includes the Nazis' invasion of the Soviet Union, the Watergate cover-up, Ford's ill-fated Edsel, and NASA's failure to stop the launch of the *Challenger*. In every case the decision makers maintained a course of action that was wrong, ignoring the dissenters. There are two powerful forces that reinforce each other to create such conformity, Sunstein argues—cascade effects and the tendency of groups to polarize around more extreme decisions. Because information is costly to obtain, once a few individuals have agreed that a particular course of action is right, other participants in the process either have to be very confident or have to know a great deal more in order to challenge them; there is a cascade of alignment behind the core decision makers, motivated by a fear of being ostracized by other group members. Sunstein argues, for example, that many Republicans voted for Bill Clinton's impeachment not because they thought it was right but because by falling behind their leadership they would not be penalized.

Similarly, one paradoxical consequence of deliberative discussion is that the group gets persuaded by argument to coalesce around not just a favored course of action but its most extreme form. There is a race among broadly like-minded people to demonstrate that they are not cowardly and are committed to the same cause. The more persuasive the leading proponents, the more these dynamics move the group to an extreme position. This concept makes the development of Islamic fundamentalist terror more understandable; the group is moved to an extreme position because everyone competes to demonstrate his or her strength of commitment to Islam.

Decision making needs the grit in the oyster—the passionate dissenter who, with institutional safeguards, can oppose an emerging consensus and force the group to reevaluate what it is doing. It needs, in short, genuine pluralism. This point is made by James Surowiecki, who has seized on the intriguing and apparently contrary insight that the average of aggregated individual decisions is often right and therefore calls his book *The Wisdom of Crowds*.[24] Building on the "jury theorem" developed by the French mathematician de Condorcet, he shows how such averaged decisions prove to be astonishingly accurate when those expressing an opinion have independently made up their minds—whether about the weight of a cow or the location of a sunk submarine. The wisdom of crowds emerges from comprehending the universe of possible outcomes in all their original diversity and then averaging them.

Pluralism thus improves the quality of deliberative decision making; and as a process it also provides crucial safeguards for the whole system by offering insurance against mistakes. Decisions are made in a context of uncertainty, fallibility, and complexity, which grows more uncertain and unpredictable when the consequences depend on events in the distant future. Some decisions have nearly immediate consequences; others may take years to prove their worth. But all decisions require delicate judgments about whether the supporting conditions will hold about whether and how a changing world might alter them. The value of plural decision making from the point of view of the whole economy and society is that although one individual decision is almost certain to be wrong, one decision among a multiplicity is likely to produce the right answer. One famous example from the business world was the rivalry between Sony's Betamax and JVC's VHS.[25] It was not obvious that the VHS would triumph as a video technology over the technically superior Betamax; each company perforce had to back its own technology, and JVC outmaneuvered Sony by allowing other producers to license the VHS, "going plural," even if it suffered some loss of revenue. Sony emerged as the relative loser. This was bad for Sony but good for the whole system because experimentation took place which ensured that the technology capable of faster diffusion would dominate. The problem with authoritarian planning is that necessarily it has to choose which idea to back, so that as a system it lacks the protection of a multiplicity of diverse decision makers.

The case for pluralism does not stop here. Within the United States, the urban geographer Richard Florida has linked the economic growth of cities to their diversity and thus to the creativity of their populations, using the presence of gay adults as an indicator. Five metropolitan areas with the highest gay population—Washington, D.C.; San Francisco; Austin; Atlanta; and San Diego—are among the fifteen top high-tech cities.[26] Similarly, Stanford Research International has developed the "waterholing" technique to maximize the creativity of organizations by designing a problem-solving process that rests on diversity. Groups are established whose membership is as diverse as possible—with different talents, genders, ages, sexual orientations, and skills sets—to get the most serendipity and thus creativity. Early evidence indicates that this process delivers results.[27] Richard Lester and Michael Piore argue in *The Missing Dimension* that innovation cannot simply be commanded from the top down.[28] They differentiate between goal-oriented analytic research and more discursive, open-ended "interpretative" research. The latter results from the conceptual thought and unexpected connections that develop when diverse researchers, with diverse minds, come together. It is "fluid, context-dependent and undetermined"—in fact, reminiscent of Scott's "metis." Genuine innovation almost always comes from ambiguity and fluidity—the kind of creativity Stanford Research International's waterholing principles try to capture—rather than from goal-oriented projects. Goals may be vital in developing the innovative results of interpretative research but rarely are themselves a source of innovation. In short, pluralism works.

The Paradox: Governing Pluralism

Whatever its intellectual and practical advantages, pluralism is not easy to create or sustain. Economists have long been aware that to maintain competitive markets the state has to set limits on monopolies and unfair trading, and—critically—has to ensure that incumbents in markets can be easily challenged by new entrants. The U.S. government's Sherman and Clayton acts of 1890 and 1914, respectively, outlawed monopoly and predatory pricing. This legislation, together with the activism of the Supreme Court and the government, especially during the New Deal, created a climate in which existing American firms are wary of colluding to restrict entry, price unfairly, or exploit monopolistic power, because they could incur the whole panoply of lawsuits, fines, and governmental intervention. They police their own conduct, knowing that if they stray beyond the line they could get badly burned, although recently the line of restraint has been fraying.

Taking on dense concentrations of private power is politically and technically hazardous; governments have to prove market abuses and spend political capital in wrestling with private companies that protest their innocence and use the courts to defend their interests. Over the last twenty years the U.S. federal government has been more

indulgent of the concentration of corporate power; apart from the famous case against Microsoft, there has been much less activism than
in the first sixty years of the twentieth century. Between 1945 and
1960, for example, the federal government demanded that over 100
leading corporations license patents they had acquired in order to get
the technology into the marketplace rather than sit on them to prevent others entering the market. Little such activism is evident today
in either the United States or Europe.[29]

Indeed pluralism is more generally under assault, and one of its
most dangerous enemies is the market process and market values. Enforcing competition is crucial to the vitality of the market economy;
but giving privileges to markets and incentives over every other aspect
of a plural economy and society is paradoxically an anticompetitive
act to which economists seem curiously blind. The media, education,
research, law, and politics, for example, are all spheres where nonmarket values need to be nurtured if these functions are to stand in
tension with capitalism and sustain the accountability and justification processes that are at the heart of great companies. According to
Lester and Piore, U.S. corporations, under pressure from Wall Street,
are so hungry for profits that they insist on goal-oriented, commer-
cialized research. This commercial research is killing off interpretative
research, which requires time and different structures. A good example is the once great Bell Labs, now part of AT&T. The new hegemony
of markets and corporate values is driving Bell Labs toward groupthink, homogeneity, and sterility and away from pluralistic research
and thought. Innovative research needs the protection of the university, with its Enlightenment vocation of creating and disseminating
knowledge, if the advantages of pluralism are to be captured.

Research is not alone. The media in western societies are crucial to
accountability. They gather and disseminate the information without
which public debate and the accountability of private and public actors are impossible. However, throughout the west, and especially in
the United States, the media have been increasingly adopting entertainment values. Their defenders say that this makes news more ac-

cessible and appealing—but the transformation in the content of news, documentary, and current affairs programs; the scheduling of broadcasts; and the declining budgets suggest a different agenda. In a quantitative study of media content, John Zaller observes that between the 1970s and 1990s, the proportion of material about government, education, and politics in local news programs in Pennsylvania (which he considered representative of the United States) had fallen from 54 percent in 1976 to 15 percent in 1992. Over the same period, programs he describes as "sensationalistic" or human-interest rose from 25 percent to 48 percent. There has been further deterioration in news programs since the early 1990s. Human-interest stories on television have always been a way to attract viewers; but now we have reached a tipping point in which such stories are crowding out information that public-spirited citizens need to know. During the U.S. presidential campaign of 1968, candidates could expect to speak on camera for an average of forty seconds without interruption. Two decades later, the average was just nine seconds.[30]

It seems obvious that the government must respond to these challenges to pluralism. But this is not easy in a culture where "government" is seen as inherently bad. Nor is it obvious how to respond, because the forces at work are very complex, and the government does not want to lower pluralism by an intervention aimed at increasing it. The media are a classic example, because one determinant of their content is internal pluralist competition, aided by new delivery platforms like the Internet and satellite and cable television. However, another determinant is a less pluralistic trend: increasing concentration of media ownership, and the demand by today's capital markets for ever-increasing profits, which forces private media to adopt aggressive commercialization just to stay alive. Wearing one hat, the government wants competition; wearing another, it wants a vigorous public realm; wearing still another, it wants any intervention to leave the media independent and plural. One way or another, ideas must be developed and a view has to be taken about how the balance is to be regained. Simply praising competition or pluralism is not enough.

On a deeper level, principles must be offered to allow these dilemmas to be navigated.

In an important paper, Andrew Dunsire of the University of York conceptualizes government action in a plural society as continually tipping the balance. He draws a useful analogy: the various institutions, actors, and communities in an economy and a society are held together in tension, rather as the rigging of a yacht holds masts and sails together. If one part becomes too strong or too weak, it puts the whole system of interdependent checked and balanced tensions out of kilter. The state, as the custodian of the whole, must do something that is corrective but is not so interventionist that it will destroy the capacity of the system to function by itself again once the balance has been retipped.[31] Dunsire lists a variety of interventions available to government, ranging from straightforward subsidy through law to "light touch" rebalancing of power. There is no a priori "right" way for the state to respond except, if it wants to sustain social pluralism and interdependent tension, to proceed cautiously and not damage the communities whose interaction are part of the society's health.

The strictures I have made against authoritarian government should not be interpreted as a generalized attack on all government. Rather, government in a pluralist society must respect the governed, not coerce them or subject them to top-down plans. The possible solutions to the issue of the media thus include, for example, increasing grants to public service broadcasters like the BBC or like PBS in the United States; reintroducing the American "fairness rule"—abolished in the 1980s—under which broadcasters ensured that individual programs were fair; reducing concentrations of ownership within the media sector; and placing a regulatory obligation on newspapers to report within certain guidelines. How the government should respond will depend on politics and on its own ideology; there are many options. The larger point is that pluralism does not just happen; it is a precious quality that has to be protected and nurtured. China has a long way to travel.

CHAPTER 8

The Soft Infrastructure
of Capitalism

PLURALISM IS NOT GUARANTEED. ITS ENEMIES ARE PUBLIC
and private monopolies. Its ally is the variety of pressures, lobbies,
and interest groups that come from a vigorous, independent civil society. The underpinning of such a civil society is not only a state that
understands the need to keep rebalancing forces, but the empowerment of ordinary citizens with the minimal necessary material living
and educational standards to give them the capacity and coinage to
participate actively and sustain the pressure to stay plural. Poverty
and ignorance drain pluralism of its support. As western societies
gave their citizens the franchise in the nineteenth century, the citizens
used it to insist on more social and educational spending—which in
turn helped the economies to become richer, with more vigorous civil
societies, which in their turn sustained the growth of pluralism.

To get to that point, however, there had to be a number of preconditions. One was the Enlightenment's creation of the public realm
and its commitment to an egalitarian enfranchisement of the citizens.
Citizens became infected, as Arjun Appadurai argues, with a "capacity
to aspire." [1] This is a complex phenomenon. The capacity to aspire is
rooted in material and intellectual capability. One reason that widespread property ownership is important—and was an early advantage of the United States—is that it confers a sense of autonomy
and allows control over a minimum level of personal material well-
being. This is also why universal education is important: it endows

individuals with the intellectual capability to turn aspiration into reality—and become vigilant citizens.

Something equally important is afoot, today. Economic and social dynamism originates, as the economist and theorist of risk Robert Schiller has argued, with individuals who are prepared to take risks. And taking risks is more likely when there is a material cushion to guard against the consequences if the risk goes wrong. If there is insufficient protection, people become wary and conservative:

> Fearing to venture out into the rapids where the real achievement is possible, brilliant careers go untried because of the fear of economic setback. . . . [Instead] we tend to work cynically, treading water, staying in an unsatisfactory job, pretending to achieve.[2]

This is not just about welfare systems, levels of education, and degree of property ownership. It reaches into the marrow of a society. Lack of protection penalizes risk-takers; protection encourages them. For example, the United States has a lenient approach to bankruptcy.[3] The more a society permits a fresh start, the more genuinely it allows risk and dynamism. There is nothing mystical or culturally unique about the United States per se that endows American culture with its strong can-do ethic; that ethic evolved naturally from a combination of property ownership with the egalitarian spirit of the Enlightenment—and from the way the United States underwrites and encourages risk.

One pillar of this spirit is private property. The urge for the security of individual property ownership and for the fair distribution of land is a universal instinct; and has been an issue in all civilizations. More notably, it is a precursor for rapid economic development. In Asia after World War II, Japan, South Korea, and Taiwan all benefited from major programs of land redistribution. In Japan the program was led by the U.S. military authorities; in Taiwan it was led by the fleeing Nationalists; and in South Korea it was made possible by the retreat of Japan as a colonizing power. In all three countries the combination of equitable land reform and a strong commitment to education reproduced the foundations of the growth experienced in the United States a century earlier.[4] Interestingly, China found its way to a similar position in the early 1980s when peasants regained de facto control of their plots of land and were much better educated after the massive Maoist investment in radically improving their literacy and numeracy. China, in this respect, has two of the preconditions for a plural society: a long tradition of private property ownership and a powerful cultural commitment to education. But it lacked and continues to lack Enlightenment values and institutions.

Property rights are thus crucial in transforming peasant societies into self-sustaining modern plural societies—not just economically but psychologically.

This is an insight developed by Hernando de Soto, the Peruvian economist, who has argued that the best means of giving peasants a material and psychological impetus to challenge tradition and stop accepting poverty is to give them formal control over their informal property rights, and then construct financial institutions that will offer credit with the property as collateral.[5] He estimates that throughout the undeveloped world $9.3 trillion of "dead" capital is locked up in squatted land and favelas over which the occupiers have de facto but not legal property rights. If this estimate is accurate, the amount is twenty times greater than all the cumulative foreign direct investment since 1989.[6] In countries as disparate as Peru and Egypt the assets of eight out of ten people play no part in the formal economy. If governments could find ways of legally defining occupiers' rights, a new vista would open up. Peasants would own property and have collateral against which to borrow. They would even have the simple asset of a reliable address, so there would be a greater likelihood that utilities could get their bills paid; and this would make the economics of extending power and water to peasant cities more favorable. Registering voters, the indispensable precondition for democracy, becomes easier and more reliable. Property, economic, and political enfranchisement go hand in hand.[7]

However, de Soto needs to go further, as his more recent writing concedes. Property rights are a necessary but not a sufficient condition for sustained development and a plural society. For example, without independent courts and a body of law, property rights are stillborn. And courts and law require, as we have seen, a process of legitimization in which some form of deliberative, representative democracy is essential. Nor is the legal system just about courts and judges; if these are to work they have to be part of a wider culture that understands that clashes of interests are best adjudicated using general principles such as justice and objective evidence. This process—the idea of justification—lies at the core of a successful, active legal system.[8] It is where the Enlightenment ideal of reason and pluralist practice intersect. I may have disputes and conflicts with my rival, competitor, family, or neighbor, but I am prepared to seek justice within what I understand to be an independent and objective framework. More profoundly, my acceptance implies reciprocity; we are playing by the same rules, and each of us has faith that the other will respect them.

Justification, reciprocity, and collaboration in creating shared rules are thus crucial to pluralism. They cannot just be imported into underdeveloped countries. Each country has to learn them by resolving its own pluralist conflicts and building up its own institutions to incorporate these values. Seen through this prism, however, the scale of the challenge facing communist China, then, becomes apparent. China has relied on communism to bulldoze the country to economic modernity—justification and reciprocity did not enter the picture. Now they must.

Understanding the Human Proclivity for Cooperation, Equality, and Justice

Learning, adaptation, and the creation process are the sine qua non of a pluralist society. These processes sustain competition, compel empowerment, and continually repopulate the plural economy and society. To adapt and create requires social interaction within and between institutions, firms, and actors. Learning is not just a matter of individuals responding to material incentives in markets—the vision of the neoclassical economists. It is a matter of communication between macro and micro communities: each must be able to understand what is being said, to process it, and to act. For example, a firm whose products are selling badly needs to be able to interrogate its customers and workers for an explanation, process what it has heard, and decide on a course of action.

A firm, like other institutions, can never be conceptualized merely as a bundle of transactions, though both communist and free-market theorists assume that it can. The firm is neither the black box of communist planners' imagination, turning inputs into outputs; nor the Pavlovian institution of free-marketeers' imagination, responding slavishly to prices. Rather, adaptation and responsiveness in the marketplace depend on the mutual trust among those delivering information, those processing it, and those who will later act differently because of it. Firms are sites of social acts and social exchange, which depend on reciprocity and mutual respect operating within processes that are understood to embody those values. A firm can no more escape the reality of its social makeup than any other social actor. Neither communist theory nor free-market theory comes close to comprehending this insight.

Of course the better the process of social exchange the better its quality, pleasurablity, and effectiveness. So far so good. But there is an umbilical link between effective process and equality—and it has to do with an elemental human characteristic, the pleasure that we take in the well-being and happiness of others. We have what the economist Adam Smith called moral sentiments: a desire to reciprocate and collaborate with an understanding that general well-being is a collective good from which we all benefit materially and psychically.[9] We want the regard of other human beings, a shared sense of purpose, and the pleasures of friendship. The underpinning of a good social process requires the acknowledgment of these truths, which is easier the readier we are to reciprocate; and our readiness in turn is more likely when there is less social distance between the parties—which in turn happens more when the parties to the process are equal. Social distance makes reciprocity harder. Social interaction is impossible without the expectation of reciprocity. And that in its turn depends on equality. Professor Richard Wilkinson of Nottingham University argues that the more inequality, the more feelings like dominance and subordination, superiority and inferiority become prevalent.[10] Human beings want respect, but are not in a position, materially or psychologically, to earn it if the economic and social gap between them becomes too wide. Equality and reciprocity are thus mutually reinforcing. If they are in short supply, it becomes impossible to construct well-functioning communities, and pluralism is diminished.

This is the heart of the conundrum over values facing a pluralist society. Of course there is a need for individualism, materialism, and response to incentives; firms are trying to make money, and so are their directors and employees. But if adaptation, learning, and cooperation are to take place, then the opposing values of reciprocity, trust, and altruism must also exist. This is a matter of economic efficiency. If, for example, firms have to monitor and enforce every aspect of every contract, then the transaction costs will overwhelm them. This is not liberal hand-wringing, but part of the gospel of one of the toughest advocates of free markets. Alan Greenspan is former chairman of the U.S. Federal Reserve. In the aftermath of Enron, he observed:

In virtually all transactions, we rely on the word of those with whom we do business. . . . A reputation for honest dealings with a business or financial corporation is critical for effective corporate governance. Reputation and trust were valued assets in freewheeling 19th century America. . . . I hope and anticipate that trust and integrity again will be amply rewarded in the marketplace as they were in previous generations. There is no better antidote for the business and financial transgression of recent years.[11]

This not just a question of trust between firms; it is also about trust within them. Firms have to trust their employees with secrets, with ideas, and even with having the best interests of the firm at heart: employees have to trust each other and, indeed their employer. This social capital exists beside the professional competence the firm must possess if it is to succeed; the better it can talk and communicate with itself, the more productive it will be.

This may seem to challenge the received wisdom of decades of economics in which the core assumption is that individual self-interest is the only reliable guide to action. In fact, new interdisciplinary thinking has begun to support the view that human beings are more than simple pursuers of self-interest.[12] This thinking combines insights from social and evolutionary psychology about how human beings really behave with more sophisticated models of economic interaction, especially game theory. Humans are not hardwired to calculate only their own advantage, distrust others, and cheat if they can in the pursuit of self-interest; they are more complex. We are neither the economically self-interested beings of classic economics nor the altruists and cooperators imagined by Jean-Jacques Rousseau or Karl Marx, frustrated by the shortcomings of the wider economic and social system. Banally, we are a combination of both. We are wary cooperators because we understand the rewards, but our cooperation is conditional on reciprocation by others, whom we are ready to punish if they cheat.

Some behavioral psychologists and economic theorists specialize in setting up "games" between individuals to see which strategies the players adopt in a variety of settings. These analysts tend to agree that it is best to think of human beings as conditional reciprocators.[13] Essentially, cooperation pays off, in part because it meets other human needs and in part because it guards against the risk that we may need help at some time in an unknowable future. Moreover, if we want others to cooperate with us, we have to be fair. This adherence to fairness is observed in experiments like the "ultimate game." In this game, two individuals are shown $10, and one has to make an offer to the other about how the money should be shared. If the offer is accepted, they both keep the money. Typically the proposer suggests an even split, $5 each. Typically responders reject anything less than $4 because it is unfair—even though both them end up getting nothing.[14] The "tit for tat" strategy in game theory, outlined by the economist Robert Axelrod, leads to very similar results.[15] Essentially, if I apply "tit for tat" I respond cooperatively with you until you defect, and then I punish you by defecting. Because both sides know this is likely to happen, they continue cooperating.

Some behavioral psychologists argue that humans are inclined to cooperate because of the structure and cognitive complexity of the brain. The orbitofrontal cortex, the temporal cortex, and the amygdala allow us to estimate time, recall reputation, delay gratification, and detect cheaters; these structures separate out human beings from other animals and give humans a proclivity to co-operate.[16] Others, notably Samuel Bowles and Herbert Gintis, believe that human emotions have a "prosocial" bias to make cooperation more likely.[17] Contempt, anger, and disgust, for example, prompt individuals to punish free riders; gratitude and honor incline us to reward altruists; sympathy, compassion, and empathy encourage contributions toward the public good; and other emotions such as guilt, shame, and embarrassment persuade us to avoid cheating or to repair its effects.[18] The era of the hunter-gatherers lasted from 100,000 years ago until the beginning of the agricultural age less than 12,000 years ago, which in evolutionary terms is scarcely the blink of an eye. Biological evolution is a slow process, the evolutionary behavioral psychologists remind us; and many of our cognitive and emotional functions were extraordinarily useful when human beings would perish without cooperation. Even the most skilled hunter could return from an expedition with only a few or no kills because of bad luck; this possibility made pooling the yield from any one hunt more rational. Equally in the fluid hunter-gatherer world of population collapses, sudden disease, or the need to move on, human beings had to have cooperative skills to manage their encounters with the strangers they would inevitably meet, and with whom they would want to collaborate.[19]

Dan Kahan of the Yale Law School builds on these insights to show that too much stress on individualism is counterproductive, imperiling the benefits of the cooperation for which we instinctively quest.[20] When group members believe that others are behaving cooperatively, they are more likely to be motivated by honor and altruism and more likely to contribute to the public good, even without material incentives. But if they believe that someone else is shirking or cheating, they relapse back into individualism. For example, an incentive can itself become an organizational cue signaling that at least some members are not inclined to cooperate voluntarily: if everyone were inclined to cooperate, the incentive would be unnecessary. Thus incentives can crowd out altruism by making it impossible for individuals to show that they would have behaved altruistically without an incentive. What makes people fill in their tax forms honestly, Kahan says, is not exhortation or an advertising campaign; on the contrary, the more people are alerted to the opportunity to cheat, the more they will do so, assuming that others will. Rather, the best predictor of honesty is interaction with others who plan to behave honestly.

Interaction is greater when equality is greater. Wilkinson traces the close links between deteriorating social relations and unequal societies. These societies tend to have lower levels of trust, more violence, less involvement in community life, lower turnout in elections, and more discrimination against women and minorities. He cites more than fifty studies showing that rates of violent crime and homicide are higher where income inequalities are greater—in some places there is a tenfold difference in homicide rates related to inequality. From Robert Putnam's *Bowling Alone* to Ichiro Kawachi and Bruce Kennedy's study *Social Capital: Income Inequality and Mortality,* the evidence in the United States is unambiguous: the more equal the state, the more trust. In the most equal of states, Kawachi and Kennedy found, only 10 to 15 percent of the population feel they cannot trust others; in the more unequal states, the proportion rises to 35 to 40 percent.[21]

This impacts on economic performance. William Easterly, Jo Ritzen, and Michael Woolcock maintain that too much income inequality in less developed countries leads to malfunctioning, poorly designed economic and political institutions, which in turn lead to lower economic growth.[22] They argue that even well-intentioned politicians in fractured, unequal societies cannot easily build coalitions for reform. This is because people have to trust governments to deliver long-term benefits to offset inevitable short-term costs—and the lower the social cohesion, the harder it is to persuade losers that there will be long-term benefits. Rich and poor alike try to avoid taxation. Poverty and inequality, in short, tend to beget more poverty and inequality. Social cohesion and social capital turn out to have strong economic payoffs—a result confirmed in a plethora of articles and statistical tests.[23]

The charge that inequality is offensive morally, socially, economically, and in human terms thus takes on new life. The foundation of human association is the idea that human life has equal worth and human beings are equally entitled to political, economic, and social rights which will allow them to choose a life they have reason to value. But without powerful countervailing forces, the accident of birth will always predict the rights to which one effectively has access and thus one's capacity to choose a life one values. The issue is to what degree. In most western societies, social mobility is declining, as it is in most less developed countries. That makes it more urgent to reach some agreement on the minimum entitlements and capabilities society will guarantee to offset the increasing importance of birth. The philosopher John Rawls and economist Amartya Sen agree on the need for a social safety net to ensure a basic standard of living, basic human rights, equality of opportunity, and the accountability of political decision makers. Most moral and political philosophers will accept that society has such obligations in the broad areas identified by Sen and Rawls. The questions are to what degree these obligations exist and how to persuade the better-off members of society that it is in their interests to acquiesce in the redistribution of income and opportunity in order to provide what Rawls calls an "infrastructure of justice." These questions need to be asked everywhere.

The answers are brutal, if subtle. Inequality is the enemy of pluralism, and pluralism is the friend of the good economy and society. Wilkinson cites the first page of Alexis de Tocqueville's *Democracy in America* and the "enormous influence" of what de Tocqueville called the "equality of conditions" on the workings of American society. It influenced lawmakers, governors, and governed; but beyond that, "its empire expands over civil society as well as government: it creates opinions, gives rises to sentiments, inspires customs and modifies everything it does not produce."[24] De Tocqueville hit the nail on the head. Equality of conditions is crucial to pluralism. China and the west neglect it at their peril.

Justification and the Classic Idea of the Company

The company animates the plural economy. Companies are a necessary (though not a sufficient) condition for successful capitalism. But a company is a complicated mechanism. It is at once a profit-seeking machine, necessarily ruthless in eliminating obstacles; and a living community peopled by complex, simultaneously self-interested and altruistic human beings. When people walk into their place of employment, they do not leave behind their sense of fairness or their responsiveness to being respected and trusted. Companies have to accommodate these sentiments and respond to their expression; indeed the highest-performance companies are those that manage to combine the hard and soft dimensions of successful business.

A high-performing company, whether in the United States, Asia, or Europe, has to find a way of creating the social capital and trust that allows its employees to share a language, respond flexibly and quickly to daily business challenges, and understand what the company is trying to do. Jim Collins and Jerry Porras, in *Built to Last*, their best-selling study of seventeen "visionary" American companies and one Japanese company, found that companies which endure over time, pick themselves up after setbacks, and successfully take over other companies and integrate these into their own have a strong sense of organizational purpose. Collins and Porras call this a "reason-to-be." What is important about GE's success, for example, has been its powerful sense of shared purpose and its strong "core ideology"—as much as Jack Welch's presumably aggressive leadership in pursuit of quarterly profits.[25]

The notion that a company has a purpose or vocation is not new. It was the cornerstone of the original idea of the company. A group of companions would come together to share risk in an enterprise and would petition the crown for a license to trade. The license would set out the function or purpose of the company, and its accompanying obligations to the crown, representing civil society. Companies were first routinely established in England and the Netherlands, as organizations that would exist over time to solve the problem of how to create the infrastructure for long-distance trade—but they were more than that. The East India Company in 1600 received a monopoly license to undertake England's trade in Asia, but it accepted as a quid pro quo that it would carry the cargoes in English vessels, undertake the defense of its fleet, expand England's political and commercial influence, and pay duties to the crown. The right to trade was accompanied by obligations—the core notion of what we would now describe as corporate responsibility. And the company had an explicit purpose, which was not to maximize profits. In the case of the East India Company, the purpose was to trade in Asia, and it would seek to maximize profits from that trade. This is a subtle distinction, but it is enormously important in how the company is conceptualized and how it constructs its internal and external relationships. The company builds its internal social capital and external reputation and brand around its declared purpose, to which discharging its mission accountably and publicly is central.

For most of the following 300 years, incorporation in Britain, America, and Europe required the company's founders to declare what the function of the company would be and faithfully follow it. This principle has been weakened in the United States and Britain since the so-called shareholder value revolution of the 1980s, which asserted that the sole purpose of a company is to maximize profits. Still, what the great western and Asian companies have in common remains a commitment to what they do. Boeing, for example, was founded to build airplanes, and although this ethos has been strained by the shareholder value revolution, it continues to exist.[26] Unilever was founded to build great "everyday things for people everywhere."[27] Sony was founded to establish a place of work "where engineers can feel the joy of technological innovation and be aware of their mission to society, . . . to apply advanced technology to the life of the general public."[28] Incorporation reinforced the purpose and the accompanying ethos, and provided a compass to help the leaders navigate through technological and market challenges.

From the beginning, the company would issue an annual written public statement of its activities, and thus would be held accountable by shareholders and public authorities for its actions. With the introduction of regular audits to provide accounts for bankers and other creditors, the process became more formalized. It became still more formalized again when companies' shares were listed on public stock exchanges and companies earned the privilege of limited liability. Investors wanted an accurate, comparable, and verifiable flow of information on which to base investment decisions; and the quid quo pro for directors being offered limited liability for corporate debts was that they provided accurate information about the companies' affairs to the public authorities. Companies, in short, are and were at the heart of an iterative justification process providing evidence on which they were to be publicly judged—hence the notion of a public company.

The public company, in the business domain, accepts that it must justify itself to its investors and the wider public; democratic justification becomes a unifying element in the world of markets and democracy alike. Public companies, therefore, are both market and nonmarket institutions. In their external affairs this should now be obvious, because the company continually interacts with the key constituencies that will determine its future, notably government and shareholders. Also, it will be constantly processing information from the marketplace about the strengths and weaknesses of its offering. But the description of companies as market and nonmarket entities also extends to internal relationships. For example, wages do not capture the entire relationship between employer and employee as they would if the company were wholly economic and market-based. The other dimension is how the employee is motivated, is communicated with, and adopts the company's objectives as his or her own. Workers hold management accountable for keeping their internal promises. This can be done formally through collective bargaining, information, and consultation—the fundamental raison d'être of labor unions—or it can be done informally through one-on-one conversations or whatever structures the company provides for such exchanges. High staff turnover is often a sign not only of dissatisfaction with any particular market wage but also that management has been unable to manage the nonwage, psychological part of the employment contract.

Channels for much interaction and justification vary with history, culture, and nationality; but whatever the channel, the larger point is that the company deliberates with its own staff and its external shareholders and stakeholders. In Germany the process may be organized with union members, bank creditors, and large investors formally represented on company boards. In the United States the process may be largely through transparent disclosure of information to the capital markets. But one way or another, there is a deliberate two-way flow of debate involving judgments about the appropriateness of the chosen means to achieve the declared ends. The process involves collecting and assimilating evidence and—as far as possible—using reason to form a collective judgment about how to proceed. In other words, the idea of justification—the exposure of reasoned judgments to other reasoning in an attempt to get the best and most correct answer—which is at the heart of deliberative democracy, independent media, and justice, also turns out to be at the core of the classic concept of the company.

Because the process cannot begin without a shared idea of what the company is trying to do, the great companies are those that, over time, maintain a clear concept of their reason to be. Largely, they do this by managing the relationship with their shareholders and stakeholders so successfully that all parties to the deliberation understand what is to be achieved and contribute to that goal. Danger arises when companies overemphasize any particular dimension of their operations. Porras and Collins's objection to maximizing shareholder value is not that companies should avoid it; plainly, the pursuit of profit is a key corporate goal. Rather, their objection is that profit may displace the corporate reason to be, so that the company neglects its own function and becomes merely a profit seeker. This may work in the short run, but it never works for long, according to Porras and Collins. A great company that makes airplanes, automobiles, or soft drinks has a vocation to be in its particular business. Once it admits that it is indifferent to its line of business and that its only criterion is short-term profit, it in effect torches its justification process, its social capital, and the unique capabilities it has developed over time. It is on the road to perdition.

The Work Foundation (declaration of interest: I am the chief executive), an independent, not-for-dividend British business think tank and consultancy, has found in a survey of some 3,000 companies that what drives business success is the capacity to blend five key clusters of business activity.[29] Companies need to engage their employees, satisfy their shareholders, manage their external networks responsibly, innovate, and respond to the market. In other words, they have to respect market and nonmarket impulses simultaneously and holistically. Companies that can perform this balancing act have measurable and significantly higher performance than those that cannot—a British validation of Collins and Porras's insights. Successful companies have powerful processes of justification and accountability; but those processes cannot exist if the company does not declare a purpose by which to be held to account—and that purpose has to be more than simple profit maximization. Companies are sophisticated, subtle, and moral organizations. Small wonder China has found it difficult to create enduring ones.

Asia Is No Different

In the early 1990s Mahathir Mohamad of Malaysia and Lee Kuan Yew of Singapore were passionate advocates of the notion that Asia's economic success had its roots in distinctive Asian values—a blend of Confucianism and Buddhism. Authoritarian government was different in Asia from elsewhere in the world, they argued; it used its power to promote general economic and social welfare, in keeping with the Confucian tradition, and overrode sectional, pluralist interest groups that might obstruct the general good. Democracy got in the way of this disciplined mobilization of resources. The Asian belief in the family allowed the development of high-trust, long-term business groupings that aimed to build enterprises over time. This belief also meant that Asia could spend less on welfare systems, because the family undertook many of the welfare responsibilities provided by the state in the west. A Confucian work ethic and belief in self-development contributed to a strong impulse to educate and train, and to work hard after such training. Thus the Asian model consisted of low taxes, low welfare, high education, high savings, high investment, business building, entrepreneurialism, and authoritarian Confucian-minded government. In the Bangkok Declaration of 1993, Asian governments supported the notion that Asia was different; its stance on human rights had to be judged by Asian standards and culture.

After the Asian financial crisis and the retirement of both Mahathir Mohamad and Lee Kuan Yew from active office, the case for Asian values lost its chief champions and part of its underlying justification.[30] Confucian authoritarian states, just like any other states, could make policy mistakes that led to economic calamities; and these mistakes could work their way through the economic system with noticeable similarity as well. Family capitalism, which had looked like an asset before the Asian financial crisis, looked remarkably like crony capitalism afterward. The argument then became subtly different. It is not that Asian values implied a radically different approach to capitalism; rather, Asia has different variants of democracy, law, human rights, and capitalism instead of alternatives to them.[31]

The desire to assert "Asian difference" is understandable. The new countries established after European decolonization wanted to declare their nationhood and identity—and to declare that while they might borrow from the west, they still retained an Asian core. Amartya Sen, in his new book *Identity and Violence,* describes this desire as the product of the "dialectic of the colonized mind": it becomes tragically impossible to see past the grievances and resentments of colonization to recognize any intrinsic worth in western values and institutions—or of any analogous function played by their Asian counterparts. There were also reasons of practical politics. In particular, Singapore needed to establish a personality distinct from Malaysia, of which it had been part, and justify one-man rule. Similarly, Malaysia needed to assert its identity. China, associating itself with the movement, was also anxious to show that western-style democracy was foreign to Asia. Interestingly, one of the most vigorous critics of this theory of Asian values is Kim Dae-Jung, the democratic victor in South Korea, who says that distinct pro-authoritarian Asian values are a myth. His view is also taken by Lee Teng-Hui of Taiwan.[32] Democracy and capitalism, they argue, have the same essential attributes and appeal everywhere. What defines Asia is its diversity in moving toward these qualities, rather than its denial of their usefulness.

The trouble with this debate is that it sets up two straw men. Western culture is much too complex to be diagnosed simply as individualist and materialist. For a start, as I have argued throughout this book, it incorporates the Enlightenment tradition of the public realm. But that rationality coexists with a strong religious Christian and collectivist socialist tradition that proponents of Asian values ignore or underestimate. Nor are western societies hostile to the ideas of social capital and the community. Arguably, they have succeeded because of their ability to create the social capital that sustains economic and social pluralism. Equally, a value system like Confucianism has cross-cutting trends. It can be as accommodating to individualism as western philosophies; indeed, family dominance can be too strong and *guanxi* family networks corrupt and closed. Cultures in all civilizations reflect the same tension between hard and soft, individualistic and altruistic. Look more closely at Asia, and you will see universal rules in operation.

For example, the heart of Japan's postwar economy, like China's, was its capacity—for more than thirty years—to mobilize very high savings for infrastructure and manufacturing investment. A large proportion of the output was then exported to the United States, which was prepared to have an otherwise unacceptable trade deficit for the sake of strategic ends. Of the three great principles of successful capitalism—pluralism, building capabilities, and justification processes—Japan had weak pluralist institutions and weak justification; but as mentioned earlier, land reform and a long tradition of the importance of education had produced citizens readier to think and act for themselves after 1945. Japan wanted to leave authoritarian militarism behind and start anew. The industrial mobilization was organized by the Ministry of International Trade and Industry (MITI), which ensured that chosen or "guided" industrial groups received the technology, finance, grants, and freedom from competition to invest on an enormous scale. Between 1960 and 1970 Japan's national income doubled, as had been planned.

Yet Japanese firms were never wholly creatures of government, however close the relationship to government might be. And although Japanese banks made long-term loans to permit investment on a scale rarely matched in the west, they were also highly activist in ensuring that a company pursued the growth strategies it promised—and they would ruthlessly replace any management team that failed. The justification process to external shareholders, government, and the public might be weak and transparency effectively nonexistent; but inside the *keiretsu* or *kigyo shudan,* networks of interlocking cross-shareholdings between banks and group members, companies were and are held accountable for the success of their strategies. Moreover, the company was and is recognized as a core, autonomous social unit, not just a network of transnational market contracts—a community of employees ambitious for themselves and their company, overtly committed to promoting corporate goals. This is a far cry from today's Chinese companies, and much closer to a Japanese variant of the classic western company. Indeed Japan's success has forced a re-examination in the west of what it means to be a company and organize high-performance production.

The economic boom went on until it reached a climax during the late 1980s, with record levels of bank lending to construction and property, sky-high property and share prices, and the emergence of overcapacity in key industrial sectors such as consumer electronics and automobiles. The lack of proper accountability in the banking system; the insider crony networks of lenders and borrowers; the intimate and frequently corrupt involvement of the government bureaucracy in so much of the economy—in short, a lack of economic and political pluralism, together with weak accountability (an uncanny parallel with today's China), finally undermined the Japanese miracle. As the yen appreciated, growth slowed down and share and property prices collapsed. The Japanese banking system was essentially bust, holding at least 43 trillion yen of nonperforming loans ($325 billion, but government estimates range up to $650 billion) that it should never have made.[33] Fifteen years of negligible growth followed, as the financial system has wrestled with its huge losses (no fewer than six insurance companies have collapsed, and banks have merged and restructured). There have also been fifteen years of small-scale reforms, which cumulatively have begun to create a Japanese-style plural soft institutional infrastructure and better legal and justification processes. Bank and stock market regulation has been beefed up and made more independent of the central bureaucracy.

Prime Minister Koizumi was reelected in 2005 by appealing directly to voters over the heads of the governing party's faction leaders. He asked for support in taking on vested interests, and he has been part of a strengthening of Japan's process of democratic accountability. Freedom of public information, unheard of in the early 1980s, was established nationally in 1999, although it does not include Japan's notorious public enterprises, which continue to have privileged access to government funding and are subject to little scrutiny.[34] Shareholders' rights have been augmented. Official guidance of public companies has been constrained. The legal system is being reformed; trial by jury has been established for criminal cases; there is a two-year time limit on first-instance criminal and civil trials; and the number of trained lawyers has been doubled, with a third expected to be women. Some 20,000 NGOs have been established under a new law permitting their formation.[35]

Gradually, Japan is developing the sinews of economic and political pluralism. Company accounts are more detailed; banks more careful and aloof in their lending; regulation is more transparent. Hard processes have been addressed alongside the "soft" processes. The labor market has also been less closely regulated. Lifetime employment has receded, and "nonregular" workers without the same entitlements and costs now constitute 30 percent of all Japanese employment—up from 18 percent in 1990.[36] Japan remains authentically Japanese; and the political system is in thrall to one party and to the malfunctions and systemic corruption that flow from this reality. But as an imperfect and incomplete pluralism begins to take hold, Japan looks less like a country that is a paradigm apart from the west, and more like an Asian country expressing a need to develop its people's capabilities, establish justification and accountability, and create soft "Enlightenment" pluralist institutions. The first sign of accelerating economic growth is testimony to the success of the transformation.

There is a similar story in India, Asia's other giant. Since the early 1990s India's growth has averaged more than 6 percent, even though its investment levels are half of those in China. In other words, India's fast-growing companies—such as Infosys in software, Ranbaxy in pharmaceuticals, Bajaj Auto in automobile components, and Mahindra in car assembly, succeed in getting more growth per dollar of investment than their Chinese counterparts. If companies are not held to account by the 130-year-old stock market—many are unquoted and private—then a more independent banking system, with new powers to enforce loan covenants, does the job. India has inherited from the British an independent judiciary with a strong culture of upholding the rule of law. Its argumentative tradition, identified by Amartya Sen as a major strength, can be traced back to the Rig Veda, India's oldest sacred text, which questions the very existence of a divine entity.[37] Sanskrit "has a larger volume of agnostic or atheistic writings than in any other classical language."[38] This tradition combines with the British-style legal system to give India strong justification and accountability processes. India's corporate governance is among the best in Asia.[39] In a survey by the *Far Eastern Economic Review* India had more companies ranked for their leadership performance than any other Asian country.[40]

India has a democratic political system as well as genuine changes in government—which, given its 1 billion people, twenty-nine independently-minded provinces, and six religions, is a remarkable achievement.[41] Its left-wing parties are closer to "old Labour" in Britain than to Asian communists, and have tended to be more strongly committed to promoting social welfare and alleviating rural poverty than to engaging in class war and expropriating private property. As a result of Nehru's foresight in developing the Indian Institutes of Technology and Management, Bangalore has more IT engineers than Silicon Valley, and India's universities produce 3.1 million graduates a year. India also has independent media and a lively public sphere. In short, this is an Asian country with economic and political pluralism, an educated middle class, and a strong tradition of justification.

Still, two problems are its lack of openness and its weakness in developing its people's capabilities, in part because of the caste system. Its tariffs average 22 percent; its $4 billion of foreign direct investment is only a small fraction of China's; its exports are one-eighth of China's and growing less rapidly. The long decades of attempted autarchy after independence in 1947 have left their mark, together with a legacy of clumsy state regulation, stubborn fiscal deficits, and rickety public infrastructure. Also, the level of illiteracy in rural India remains appalling. Forty-four percent of Indian workers are illiterate; and 55 percent of Indian women are illiterate, compared with just 13 percent of Chinese women. India is, however, making an overdue attempt at female education.[42] Although the Indian constitution forbids discrimination on the basis of caste, between 150 million and 200 million untouchables continue to live mostly on the margins of society—and in rural areas literally on the margins of the villages.[43] Old prejudices die hard, and the development of a genuine labor market encompassing every Indian remains elusive. Service-sector employment is proportionally lower than in comparable countries, and India has focused skill development on a narrow cohort of acceptable castes.

Is India an embodiment of Asian values as its pace of industrialization accelerates? Is its development attributable to principles different from those identified in this chapter and Chapter 7? Hardly. Capitalist success entails managing the interplay between hard capitalist processes and soft institutional processes. A country can avoid this for as long as a generation, but ultimately reality will emerge. India and Japan are plotting a more pluralist future. China will inevitably follow suit.

But the view persists that Asia is special. For instance, Joshua Cooper Ramo, a consultant based in Beijing, argues that China represents a new "Beijing consensus" about how to pursue development. There are three key factors, according to Ramo. First, China has embraced technological innovation rather than basing its growth on cheap labor. Second, it stresses equity and sustainability in its growth priorities. Third, it has been prepared to strike out on its own with its own experiments, true to its own Chinese destiny, rather than adopt western examples and rules as necessarily better. China, Ramo says, is admired throughout the less developed world because of its ideas about how growth can be organized to offer a viable alternative to the "Washington consensus."[44]

Ramo is right in saying that the Chinese leaders now stress technology, equity, and sustainability in their rhetorical declarations of their aims for the economy and society. But in reality, indigenous Chinese enterprise has competed largely on the basis of low wages, has copied technology, and has disregarded environmental costs throughout the reform period. Moving to an alternative model without substantial institutional reform will be beyond it. Any other narrative is implausible, whatever the official goals declared for the future may be. China has been innovative in managing its gradual transition from communism; and although inequality has grown dramatically, the commitment to universal education, including women, has had economic benefits. And China does insist that its jurisdiction as a self-determining nation-state should be respected—an insistence which has given it the self-confidence to make its own way.

This does not constitute a new consensus or a refutation of the need for economic and political pluralism. Ramo's claims, like Lee Kuan Yew's or Mahathir's, cannot survive close scrutiny. The more we examine the postwar Asian miracle and today's China, the more obvious it becomes that economic development, and in particular the evolution of successful firms and financial systems, follows universal rules, even in the context of particular individual states with their unique histories and cultures.

Western capitalism succeeds because its institutional framework permits more such companies; the weakness of China's Leninist corporatism is that it can hardly get to first base. There is no constitutional framework to allow China's companies to develop their own corporate identity; there is no tradition of justification that companies can build on as a process to strengthen themselves; there are no institutions through which such values could be created or expressed. China's weaknesses, however, expose the current dangers in the western system. The western consensus still does not acknowledge the subtlety of company building, the crucial role of the wider institutional complex, and the danger of consecrating companies to the sole cause of maximizing shareholder value. Neither the Beijing consensus nor the Washington consensus has a real grip on the dynamics of successful capitalism.

CHAPTER 9

Of War and Peace

NO COUNTRY IS AN ISLAND. COMMUNISM IN CHINA would not have begun without the rise of communism in the rest of the world; its subsequent success was part of a worldwide communist advance over the first half of the twentieth century. Similarly, the last twenty-five years of successful Leninist corporatism would never have taken place without the special character of globalization, opening up unparalleled opportunities for foreign direct investment, transfer of technology, growth of trade, and economic development without ever challenging China's right of peaceful sovereign self-determination—in other words, communist authoritarian rule—within its frontiers. Deng accurately saw the character of the emergent international system and how it could be turned to China's advantage. "Peace and development," he pronounced, "seem to be the trend of the times."[1] China could play the same economic cards as the rest of rapidly growing east Asia and use the consequent growth, ironically, to entrench and legitimize communist rule, which the rest of the world would not challenge. Openness in the current climate would not mean de facto colonization and humiliation as it had in the past; rather, it would be a way to make up the time lost during the Mao years. Deng was right.

He was nonetheless careful to present openness as essentially nationalistic. He told the Twelfth National Congress of the Communist Party in 1982 that opening not only was indispensable for economic modernization but also would achieve two other aims: strengthening China so that it could challenge the hegemony of foreign powers, notably the United States; and furthering the cause of bringing Taiwan back to the "motherland."[2] China's identity would not be changed by engaging with foreign multinationals and technology, but its capacity to meet its destiny would be vastly enhanced. Like other reformers in China's history—such as Li Hongzhang, who masterminded the abortive self-strengthening movement between the 1860s and the 1890s[3]—Deng believed that China could adopt western forms of modernization *(yong)* without having to import the culture and essence *(ti)* that created them. Communist China would remain communist China, but it would require a foreign policy that did not disturb the international system from which it intended to profit.

Deng's advice after Tiananmen was that China should "observe developments soberly, maintain our position, meet challenges calmly, hide our capacities and bide our time, remain free of ambition, never claim leadership."[4] China should not attempt to be a hegemon; it should never practice power politics; and it should never pose a threat to its neighbors or to world peace. These are mantras that Chinese officials continue to repeat. China's foreign policy, as Foreign Minister Li Zhaoxing has declared, is designed first and foremost to serve economic development, following Deng's injunction.[5] Moreover, its rise is to be peaceful, in the famous formulation by Zheng Bijian, chair of the China Reform Forum.[6] But rising peacefully did not imply that China would forgo its proper interests; rather, it would seek to pursue and resolve them peacefully. Thus although China has felt the need both to sound and to act more aggressively nationalistic in the years after the collapse of international communism, it has operated within Deng's maxims and the doctrine of the peaceful rise. So after the presumably accidental bombing of the Chinese embassy in Belgrade by the United States in 1999 and later the midair collision between a U.S. EP-3 spy plane and a Chinese fighter in the South China Sea in 2001, China allowed an upsurge in nationalist street protests to accompany its own diplomatic response but quickly curbed the protests when they threatened to get out of hand. The communist leadership did not believe that either issue damaged Chinese interests seriously enough to be worth threatening China's basic foreign policy. The objective is to be sufficiently nationalist to assuage domestic opinion and legitimize communist rule; to pursue carefully calculated national interests; and not to challenge an international system that is fundamentally friendly to China's development.

This is a tightrope that is increasingly difficult to walk as China becomes larger. The United States, as a hegemonic power, cannot be certain what China means by eventually regaining its "rightful place" in the world, however unmenacingly it tries to behave at any particular moment. In the view of a pragmatist like John J. Mearsheimer, a professor of political science at the University of Chicago, China and the United States are destined to clash militarily, and the United States has an interest in doing all it can to forestall China's becoming economically rich enough to challenge it. He draws an analogy with the Germany of Kaiser Wilhelm II and imperial Japan just before Pearl Harbor. They were rising powers whose developing might precipitated war, and war with China is similarly inevitable.[7] Others, such as Avery Goldstein at the University of Pennsylvania, argue that China is different because—unlike Germany under Wilhelm or imperial Japan—it is not part of a wider coalition of states ready to challenge the United States. Also, there are areas of collaboration as well as competition between the United States and China; and an international system based on open markets makes war less necessary to secure vital interests. Comparisons with the nineteenth century omit a key difference; in an era of nuclear weapons, rising states have to be a great deal more circumspect in how they challenge the hegemonic power militarily. The United States has formidable hard and soft power compared with China, whose regime might collapse if any potential conflict—even one in Taiwan—went wrong. Goldstein concludes that the United States should remain watchful while holding China accountable for continuing to improve its international behavior.[8]

China is keenly aware of the American debate; its best strategy is to pursue its national interests in a way that makes Mearsheimer look wrong, while striking a suitably nationalist note for domestic ears.

So far both sides have managed the relationship, but there are vast possibilities for mistakes and miscalculations; furthermore, the party could lose control of the nationalist sympathies it has unleashed. As a good international citizen, China became a signatory of the Comprehensive Test Ban Treaty in 1996, condemned India and Pakistan for testing nuclear weapons, did not devalue the renminbi during the Asian financial crisis, has (along with the United States) put pressure on North Korea to freeze its nuclear missile program as a member of the six-party talks, and is establishing the ASEAN-China free trade zone. It has used its veto in the UN Security Council only five times, and two of those vetoes were over Taiwan. All to the good—and all consistent with the doctrine of peaceful rise. China even dispatched $60 million of relief to the victims of the tsunami and publicly demoted Major General Zhu Chenghu after his unwise warning to the Americans that China could and would aim missiles with nuclear warheads at its cities.[9]

On the other hand, China's size, economic growth, hunger for resources, and military buildup can hardly be ignored. Its ambition to reintegrate Taiwan into China is undimmed. It is suspicious of Japan's intentions and of Japan's alliance with the United States. Its anti-Japanese rhetoric is unrelenting. Moreover, China's good citizenship stops at the issue of human rights. It has assembled a majority coalition in the UN to prevent the western powers from making motions condemning its actions. It has portrayed itself as a victim whose internal frictions—characteristic of any state—are being exaggerated by the west and described as systemic violations of human rights so that westerners can infringe on its right of self-determination. To give way would be to hand the United States a propaganda coup and would serve as a precedent for further incursions into states' freedom of action and sovereignty across the third world, in the name of human rights.

This is a stance that many authoritarian third world leaders, such as Robert Mugabe of Zimbabwe, find congenial, excusing them from making the economic and political reforms the west urges. When the

EU and the United States made representations to the UN Security Council about Mugabe's slum clearance program of 2005, which left hundreds of thousands homeless, China left the room. Mugabe has been feted in Beijing and is now an honorary professor at the Foreign Affairs University there. Zimbabwe gets Chinese arms; China gets favorable mining concessions from Zimbabwe. The African Union expelled François Bozizé of the Central African Republic from membership in 2003 after a violent coup; China gave him a $2.5 million interest-free loan and welcomed him on an official visit.[10] China's championing of "Asian values" is part of the same crusade; communism, far from being aberrant, is one more way that different Asian values express themselves and is thus excusable.

Western governments and business have largely let China off the hook. American business is anxious to have a foothold in China for low-cost production, to protect its international competitive position and build its share in what is already one of the world's largest markets. It has urged successive U.S. administrations to look at China's problems through the eyes of the Chinese communist rulers and not to push issues of democracy and human rights too far. The business-people argue that the first priority is to feed China's hundreds of millions; human rights and democratic freedoms will evolve naturally later and are in any case the preserve of the Chinese people, not of outsiders. This, for example, was the consistent argument of Maurice R. Greenburg, chairman of American International Group, which is one of the world's largest insurance companies and was an early and well-connected front-runner in developing its Chinese business interests. British business echoed the argument in the period before the handover of Hong Kong to China in 1997. When Governor Chris Patten opened up the appointed legislative assembly to universal suffrage, China saw this (correctly) as putting it in a very difficult position after the handover. Either it would have to abolish the council, to a predictable storm of international criticism, or it would have to accept the council and the explicit challenge to China's concept of socialist democracy. British business, a powerful faction within the

British Foreign Office, and the communist government put intense pressure on Britain to reverse Patten's position; Prime Minister John Major—to his credit—resisted and supported Patten.[11] The democratized Legislative Council was preserved.

In the grand scheme of things, this was only one, albeit significant, reverse amid a general advance. Its importance is that it suggests a lack of sustainability in China's position. China accepts pluralism, the rule of law, and accountability abroad, however imperfectly expressed, while denying them at home, a position it has formalized with regard to Hong Kong, applying the formula one country—two systems. Moreover, since the fall of the Soviet Union democracy has become the new international gold standard—the desirable political structure to which more and more states are moving and which is the best way of exploiting globalization. In 1988 two-thirds of states were nondemocratic; today two-thirds are democratic.[12] China is increasingly an outlier. The more it grows and the more economically powerful it becomes, the more its identity as a one-party authoritarian state intent on remaining so—complying with the international system because that system serves its interests rather than builds and upholds it—will become ambiguous and difficult to manage.

The Writing on the Wall

So far China has defused tension and exploited the system of which, arguably, it is one of the biggest beneficiaries. China's problem is that its objective interest is to buttress the international system from which it benefits; but this means associating itself with values, institutions, and process that directly challenge what it practices at home. Yahoo, Microsoft, and Google are part of the cultural yeast of globalization; yet each has been at the receiving end of China's Internet firewall of censorship, which, whatever security advantages it might bring, has been a severe propaganda setback. Equally, no trading partner can afford subsidies like those China gives to its state-owned enterprises. The larger China becomes, the more it will be subject to intense scrutiny about its trading practices.

Nor is the democratic question going to become easier to finesse. It is no accident that globalization has been so closely associated with the spread of democracy. If states want the benefits of trade, foreign investment, transfer of technology, access to saving, and reciprocal rights for their own enterprises to enjoy the same benefits, then they have to accept that there are attendant rules. Moreover, certain dynamics develop. It can seem very attractive, for example, partially to privatize a state-owned enterprise to foreign investors; but afterward there are demands for higher standards of transparency and accountability—part of the democratizing agenda.

This process, for example, is now indirectly at work as China seeks foreign shareholdings in its banking system. China wants western banking know-how and better banking standards because it is trying to avoid the high proportion of nonperforming loans that it had in the 1990s—such loans would now be unfinanceable and would threaten the entire economy with a meltdown of the financial system. But that means accepting much higher standards of corporate governance and reporting together with constraints on using the banking system to further the ends of the nation-state. China certainly obtains foreign investment in its financial system, hard currency, and skills in an asymmetric deal heavily loaded in its favor; but it has had to concede a degree of transparency and accountability that is more consistent with democratic capitalism than Leninist corporatism. I repeat one crucial argument: to raise the productivity of Chinese enterprises and rebalance the Chinese economy toward more normal levels of consumption, saving, and investment while maintaining current rates of economic growth vital to generating jobs and ensuring social stability, China will have to accept more economic and political pluralism, and the process of justification and accountability that go with it. Deng's assumption, like Li Hongzhang's, that China can enjoy the economic advantages of the west without accepting the substantive processes that create them will prove wrong.

China is thus a cockpit both for the emergence of democratic pressures and for resistance against them. The west needs to judge over what time period, how smoothly, and how inevitably China will march toward the distinctive mix of capitalism and democracy that is emerging in parts of Asia like India and Japan, and how to use its small leverage to advance the process. The danger is that now that China is a $2 trillion economy, substantively behind only Japan and the United States (on current trends Germany will have been over-taken during 2007), it therefore has options for autonomous action to shape globalization that might suit its interests but not those of the west. Chinese communism and Chinese nationalism are an uneasy coalition; the more nationalism gains an upper hand in an authoritar-ian state, the more China will want to behave according to its own cri-teria. China is perfectly capable, for example, of invading Taiwan, obstructing any international action concerning Iran, or refusing to accept international protocols regarding climate change. The power it will necessarily confront above any other is the United States. The hope and aim must be that the story has a happy ending; but there is plenty of scope for it to turn out otherwise.

Flashpoint 1: Trade and Finance

The United States is the anchor and driver of globalization, but its domestic coalition favoring globalization is weakening and becoming ever more fragile. The question is whether the avalanche of Chinese exports which dwarfs any of the flows from China's predecessors, but without any of the strategic necessity that justified free trade in the past, is going to force the United States away from its free-trade, open-market policy. After all, China, unlike Europe or Japan, is communist. In 2005 the United States had the largest bilateral trade deficit of any country in history. It imported about $240 billion of goods from China and exported a mere $40 billion back, so the trade deficit was just over $200 billion. This represents a ratio of six to one. C. Fred

Bergsten, director of Washington's Institute for International Economics, points out that the ratio is twice as bad as the ratio at the peak of concern about Japan's export flood in the 1980s.[13] And with Chinese exports growing at some 28 percent in 2005, there is little sign that the ratio—or the deficit—will do anything but get worse.

Six industries have lobbied Congress and won special protection—textiles, clothes, wood furniture, color television, semiconductors, and Louisiana shrimpers. They are harbingers of more to come; the Department of Commerce has begun some seventy antidumping proceedings against Chinese imports. Seizures of Chinese counterfeit goods are increasing dramatically. In the summer of 2005 Senator Charles Schumer of New York managed to get a two-to-one majority on a procedural vote calling for a 27.5 percent tariff on all Chinese imports unless the Chinese revalued the renminbi. The Chinese conceded the 2 percent upward movement in July 2005, together with a more flexible framework for making subsequent revaluations; few expect more than small annual movements, for the reason I have set out—the risk of a destabilizing economic and social shock from a sharp revaluation is too high. Yet on his state visit to Beijing in the autumn of 2005 George Bush received a promise from President Hu Jintao that China would eliminate its trade deficit. The problem is that without a dollar devaluation against the renminbi of about 30 percent (see Chapter 6), there is not the remotest chance of such a correction. In May 2006, when Hu Jintao came to Washington on a visit that deliberately was not described as a state visit, the deficit was higher and the renminbi was unaltered. By the time this book is published, Charles Schumer and Senator Lindsey Graham have promised to reintroduce their bill if there has not been a further revaluation.

A formidable institutional apparatus is being constructed whose interest is to oppose the growth of Chinese imports. A warning of the congressional mood has been the three annual reports of the cross-party U.S.-China Economic and Security Review Commission, established as part of the deal to allow China into the World Trade

Organization. It has used its position to put together an impressive body of analytic evidence supporting its basic stance: that, as it said in its report of 2005, "over the last year, on balance, the trends in the U.S.-China relationship have negative implications for our long-term national economic and security interests."[14] China, it argues, is pursuing a twenty-first-century mercantilist policy as part of its ambition to be a great power with commensurate military capacity, boosting its high-technology sector through huge government spending, and subsidizing export growth and foreign direct investment—the centerpiece of which is the persistent undervaluation of the renminbi. Cumulatively, the United States has lost 1.5 million jobs between 1989 and 2003, it claims from Chinese exports; a further study reported that some 100,000 jobs were lost in 2004.[15] Interestingly, neither study makes any effort to estimate compensating growth of employment in the United States' service and knowledge industries as a result of higher consumer spending and lower interest rates, in turn resulting from cheap Chinese import prices. In the commission's universe the traffic is all one-way. There should be an across-the-board tariff on Chinese imports if China does not revalue the renminbi; and the commission warns of the strategic dangers if China acquires U.S. companies.

Three years ago the commission represented the hawkish wing of American views of China, but it has increasingly become more mainstream. Democrats are concerned about blue-collar jobs and human rights; everybody is concerned about the strategic threat; and everybody opposes China's buying any but the most innocuous companies. The *Economist* reports Gary Hufbauer of the Institute for International Economics as saying that there are twenty draft anti-China bills in the congressional hopper, among which the most menacing would rescind China's "permanent normal trading status" that was the precondition for its membership in the World Trade Organization to go forward.[16] Actually, a unilateral attempt by the United States to suspend China's membership in the WTO would be illegal. But that has not deterred its two sponsors, Byron Dorgan of North Dakota and

Lindsey Graham of South Carolina. In February 2006 the Bush administration created a China enforcement task force within the U.S. trade representative's office to monitor the growth of Chinese imports—something that never happened at the height of the hysteria over Japanese imports in the 1980s. The administration warned darkly of countermeasures and antidumping suits if China did not heed American concerns. In April 2006 Timothy Stratford, assistant U.S. trade representative, said that the trade relationship with China lacked "equity, durability, and balance in the opportunities it provides." [17] The United States reserves the right under the Trade and Competitiveness Act of 1988 to initiate, either alone or with the IMF, action to force a country to readjust its currency if the currency has been manipulated to produce a material trade imbalance. So far the U.S. Treasury has ruled that China is not manipulating its currency, but it is under intense pressure to change its ruling—a precursor to a potential full-scale trade and financial war.

China's problem in formulating a response is threefold. First, revaluation of the renminbi has profound economic and social consequences. Second, without a broad move to western and the best Asian standards of corporate governance, transparency, and accountability, China will never be able to prove before the World Trade Organization's investigations that it is not subsidizing state-owned enterprises through its banking system or that its allegedly private corporations are not puppets of the Communist Party—accusations that will stand because they are substantially true. When China was smaller, it could escape international censure; but as the emergent world's number one exporter it will have to comply with the rules of transparency in order to show that it is competing fairly. The attempt to draw the sting of criticism because so many of its exports are produced by foreign companies is working less and less successfully; American politicians do not make this distinction. And, third, even if China manages these two problems, its last problem is insoluble: it is formally communist.

It is this that will make China's attempts to repeat what the Europeans and Japanese have done—buy American companies—so toxic. For a generation the United States has financed its monumental trade deficit by allowing foreigners to buy its assets—Hollywood studios, Ben & Jerry ice cream, Sohio. Foreigners have $1.5 trillion invested in the United States, and until recently this fact has created a surprisingly small political backlash. Europeans and even the Japanese have been seen as surrogate Americans who ultimately are not challenging American interests and who in any case allow reciprocal purchases in their own countries by Americans. China, following the doctrine of peaceful rise, has so far held the mountain of dollar foreign exchange reserves it is acquiring through its trade surplus and rigging its currency in U.S. treasury bills, but the risk-reward ratio is looking increasingly silly from its point of view. It receives a derisory interest rate and risks a capital loss as the renminbi is revalued; it badly needs to acquire American companies and assets both in the United States and throughout the world that will offer better returns and better protection against currency movements. Yet China's total stock of overseas foreign direct investment was $44.7 billion at the end of 2004—about 5 percent of its current stock of foreign exchange reserves.[18] Cumulatively Chinese investors have bought perhaps 900 small U.S. companies worth in all $1 billion; and Lenovo bought the personal computer division of IBM for $1.25 billion.[19] It is doubtful that the total value of Chinese-owned American companies is more than $3 billion.

It was already difficult enough for China to buy into the United States before 9/11. But now, with the intensely hostile reaction to Dubai Ports World acquiring a management interest in six U.S. ports, it is close to impossible. If CNOOC's bid for Unocal aroused security concerns, the threshold has become very low. According to the Congressional Research Service, Unocal accounted for only 0.8 percent of the United States' production of crude oil and natural gas liquids and 0.3 percent of U.S. consumption; it is hard to characterize the potential change of ownership as "threatening the national security of the United States"—which would require it to be blocked. On the other hand CNOOC could top Chevron's bid of $17.7 billion only because it had access to cheap credit from a state-owned banking system that was indifferent to the underlying strength or weakness of its balance sheet. And there is no escaping the fact that the ultimate owner of an American oil asset would have been the Chinese Communist Party.

The United States is becoming increasingly nationalist about foreigners in general and especially the Chinese. The Exon-Florio amendment of 1988 authorizes the president to block foreign takeovers if they threaten national security; and between 2003 and 2006 there were six reviews and five withdrawals under threat of review—more than in the previous ten years combined. China's companies are not like BP, VW, or Sony; they are the arms of a communist authoritarian state or intensely influenced by it. If China came shopping for companies and assets in the United States in a major way, the reaction would be ferocious. And unless China changes, such a reaction would be partly justified.

Flashpoint 2: Resource Wars

The oil price of $50 per barrel in 2004 and its rise to over $70 during 2006 is more than a cyclical upward spike after which the oil trade will return to normal. The emergence of China as the world's second-largest oil importer with the most rapid growth of oil demand underlines a long-term change in the imbalance of oil demand and supply, of which the latest oil price rise has been the most significant manifestation. The world is making a transition to a period when oil and gas are more likely to be expensive, with alarming moments when they may become very expensive indeed. At a time of international terrorism, when oil pipelines and transshipment ports are targets, shocks to prices can come as much from unexpected falloffs in supply as from demand. The investment banking firm Goldman Sachs, for example, warns that oil could experience a "superspike" of up to $105 a barrel sometime over the next few years.[20] Oil prices at these levels, driven by demand rather than by artificial limits on supply (such as those imposed by OPEC at the time of the Yom Kippur war in 1973), ring a tocsin about how much longer finite oil reserves can last, given the present rates of demand and energy efficiency. After another thirty or forty years, there simply will not be enough identified, readily accessible oil under the ground to meet the United States' current and anticipated demand for oil together with the surge in demand coming from China in particular and, if growth continues, from India and the rest of the world. By 2030, China will import as much oil as the United States does now. The U.S. Geological Survey takes the Panglossian view that there is sufficient oil to meet demand at least until 2040, when production will peak; others observers, such as the International Energy Agency, concede that peak production could come as early as 2017.[21] But whether one is an optimist or a pessimist, the end is in sight. Chevron's warning that the era of cheap, plentiful oil is over[22] is shared by most senior analysts and industry watchers. (See footnote 11 in Chapter 1.)

The importance of the politically unstable Islamic Middle East as an oil supplier is going to grow. Today two-thirds of the world's oil reserves are in the Middle East; but the rapidity with which oil is being exploited in Africa, Russia, the United States, the North Sea, and South America means that by 2020 the proportion of global oil reserves in the Middle East will have grown to 83 percent.[23] Moreover, much of this oil passes through the Strait of Hormuz between the Gulf of Oman and the Persian Gulf. The strait is twenty-one miles wide at its narrowest point, and the Iranian island of Abu Musa is near its entrance—manned by Iranian Revolutionary Guards reportedly equipped with Silkworm antiship missiles.[24] Even today they could wreak havoc on world oil supplies and prices: 17 million barrels of oil flow through the strait daily. By 2020 Iran, or any committed terrorist group, would be in an even stronger position.

The threat is live. Al Qaeda's leaders Osama bin Laden and Ayman Al-Zawahiri have said that the Saudi Arabian oil infrastructure is a target. The Abqaiq oil processing facility in Saudi Arabia, the massive complex that removes impurities from two-thirds of the kingdom's oil production before it is pumped to the coast, has already been the object of an unsuccessful suicide bombing mission in February 2005. A former CIA operative, Robert Baer, estimates that the facility's output of 6.8 million barrels per day could be reduced to 1 million in the event of a "moderate to severe attack." [25] Nor is the Suez Canal any less vulnerable. About 1.3 million barrels of oil move through it daily, and it is 300 yards wide at its narrowest point. Terrorists have so far restricted their attacks to Egyptian vacation resorts; an attack on the Suez Canal would produce much more damage for the west.

Also, there is the evidence that higher oil prices and revenues are likely politically to freeze the oil-producing states with authoritarian, repressive political regimes. Michael Lewin Ross studied 113 countries between 1971 and 1997 and found that the oil producers were more resistant to democracy.[26] An authoritarian government with significant oil revenues has more revenue to pay for internal repression; it has less need to justify its actions to its citizens, because it does not have to tax them; and by having a less developed, less diversified economy, it experiences less pressure to open up to the forces of economic and political pluralism. The same phenomenon is observable from Indonesia to Nigeria. Ross's findings dovetail with research by Jeffrey Sachs and Andrew Warner; resource wealth, they find, holds back the process of industrialization and modernization because the spillover effects into the rest of the economy are much lower from exporting oil than from exporting manufactures.[27] Other research, examining forty-seven civil wars between 1965 and 1999, found that once an economy hit a threshold of around one-fourth of its GDP originating in a commodity like oil, there was an irresistible tendency for rival groups to fight for control of the spoils. Civil war became much more likely.[28]

Oil, in short, is something of a curse. And, as Iran is vividly demonstrating, it has plenty of destabilizing implications for power relationships within the international system. Iran wants to build nuclear reactors; the United States is opposed because these would give Iran the possibility of developing military nuclear capacity. Iran's delegate to the International Energy Agency, Ali Asghar Soltanieh, has described Tehran's view: "The United States has the power to cause harm and pain," he said in March 2006, "but the United States is also susceptible to harm and pain. So if that is the path that the U.S. wishes to choose, let the ball roll." [29] The logic is merciless. Global demand for oil is currently about 85 million barrels a day; global supply at maximum production is only slightly higher. Iranian oil exports—2.7 million barrels a day—are a crucial swing factor. If for any reason they were suspended the price of oil would rise sharply. If the United States attacks Iranian nuclear installations, and Iran retaliates by either stopping its exports or attacking oil tankers in the Strait of Hormuz, the United States and the west would be in the middle of mayhem as far as oil prices were concerned. Fortified by this knowledge, and China's support, Tehran is happy to face down almost any threat from Washington.

Because of these challenges, Chinese and American leaders have become alert to the risks, and to the need to develop energy policy at the highest level. This is well-established precedent. Few British or American readers will have been alive when the United Kingdom grabbed the oil-rich parts of the former Ottoman Empire after World War I in order to make sure it had secure oil supplies for its oil-dependent fleet. More recently, the United States led the operation to liberate Kuwait from the Iraqi invasion in 1989, in part because of concerns that Iraq would control too much of the world's oil reserves. The open question is whether states will revert to historical type or will continue to rely on the global market system.

The auguries are not good. In May 2005 China established a new State Energy Office that reports directly to the State Council, the highest executive body in the country. President Bush, in his State of the Union address of 2006, declared that one strategic objective was to lower the United States' dependence on imported Middle Eastern oil. His intervention followed a simulation called "Oil Shock-wave" chaired by senators Richard Lugar (Indiana) and Joe Lieberman (Connecticut). Its purpose was to assess what the United States could do to mitigate the price and supply effects of a small interruption in oil supplies due to, say, a terrorist attack on a major Middle Eastern supplier. The answer was almost nothing. Robbie Diamond of Securing America's Energy Future (SAFE), one of the chief sponsors of the event, declared: "This simulation serves as a clear warning that even relatively small reductions in oil supply will result in tremendous national security and economic problems for the country. The issue deserves immediate attention." [30]

China is of the same opinion—and its diplomacy is increasingly driven by the need to make sure that it has dependable, diversified, secure oil reserves and the means to get them to China. As the deputy chief of the Chinese general staff, General Xiong Guangkai, has acknowledged, the competition for oil has become "fiercer": Xiong argues that China's energy problem needs to be taken "seriously and dealt with strategically." [31] That means less reliance on the Middle East,[32] less transportation of oil via sea-lanes policed by the U.S. navy, a bigger Chinese navy to protect Chinese tankers, and more oil brought overland by pipeline from central Asia. The American buildup of its naval base at Changi in Singapore, allowing it to patrol the Strait of Malacca, between Malaysia and Indonesia, through which 80 percent of China's imported oil moves, is regarded with particular suspicion. The channel is 500 miles long and less than two miles wide at its narrowest point. With India modernizing its military facilities on the Andaman and Nicobar islands at the northern end of the strait, China feels sandwiched in and strategically vulnerable between the attentions of the Indians and Americans. Hu Jintao has referred a number of times to what he describes as the Malacca dilemma. "Certain powers," he has declared, "have all along encroached on and tried to control the navigation through the strait." [33] There is no mistaking whom he means.

For decades the doctrine of peaceful rise has meant that China has tried to secure energy and raw materials without confronting the

United States and the west. China's long-standing willingness to deal with states that the west regards as pariahs is in part a practical and ideological refusal to make judgments about countries' domestic policy. (That is their concern, and China is not going to set a precedent for closer scrutiny of its own internal arrangements.) It is also in part a recognition that dealing with a Sudan, Angola, Iran, or Uzbekistan allows China to avoid direct confrontation with western interests. Indeed the United States, tacitly, has considered China's readiness to access oil from pariah states helpful. However, as China has grown larger, the sheer scale of its needs has forced it more and more to intrude into areas that the United States regards as its own sphere of influence. China has also moved from noncommittal engagement with pariah states to openly supporting them. The relationship with the west, therefore, is becoming steadily tenser.

Take China's courtship of Canada. In April 2005 Petro China and Embridge signed a memorandum of understanding to build a $2 billion "Gateway" pipeline to move oil from Alberta to the Pacific coast. Yet only four years earlier Dick Cheney, the vice president of the United States, had declared that Canada's tar sands were part of the U.S. energy security. Venezuela in South America sells 60 percent of its oil to the United States. President Hugo Chavez, in Beijing in December 2004, declared that he now wanted to put Venezuelan oil "at the disposal of the great Chinese fatherland" after 100 years of American domination; and in 2005 he signed deals to allow the Chinese to explore for oil and gas. Like the Canadians, the Venezuelans want to build a pipeline to the Pacific coast, which in their case they reach via Colombia. They reached an agreement in principle with Colombia in July 2004. Conspiracy theorists can portray the two moves as China darkly intruding into Uncle Sam's backyard; the fair-minded can see that Canada and Venezuela as major oil exporters need to be able to offer their Asian customers the opportunity to load their tankers inexpensively on the Pacific coast. Both stories are congruent with the facts.

Saudi Arabia, holder of the world's largest oil reserves, supplies

16 percent of China's imports and is an object of assiduous Chinese courtship—again, a direct challenge to the United States' traditional sphere of influence. In 2004 Chinese companies were given exploration rights, and China has reciprocated by offering the Saudis preferential partnership rights to build oil refineries in China that can refine heavier Arabian crude. For the moment Saudi Arabia knows that its long-term security and its defense interests lie with the United States. But Islamic militancy is increasing, and Saudi Arabia has its own strict Wahhabi sect, which is now in total control of the Saudi education system. The Saudis are facing explosive growth in the numbers of young people seeking work (Saudi Arabia has one of the highest birthrates in the world) and are having difficulty meeting this demand. For such reasons, it might one day make sense for the Saudis to align with a power that is less controversial in Islamic eyes. Already, that reality has begun to mean that China has diplomatic opportunities to confront the United States which were not available even five years ago.

In Iran, the Chinese have been given rights to exploit the giant Yadavaran oil field and are examining the feasibility of a pipeline project to link the transport of Iranian oil to pipelines from central Asia. As I have discussed, Iran is particularly problematic. China has used its veto in the UN Security Council to block attempts to bring Iran's nuclear program under the U.S. inspection regime, and has sold C-801 and C-802 antiship cruise missiles to Iran which could be used against American naval vessels in the Persian Gulf. Suddenly China's foreign policy looks less benign—perhaps indicating that its moves in the Americas should be reinterpreted. In the Sudan, China has persistently obstructed international efforts to sanction the government over the genocide in Darfur, which has killed some 2 million people. In Uzbekistan, China has refused to allow an international investigation of President Karimov's bloody suppression of dissent. Thus an ominous picture emerges of China developing a foreign policy that is actively hostile to human rights and to international law: all it wants is oil. Deputy Foreign Minister Zhou Wenzhong (now China's ambassador to Washington) said when asked about genocide in Darfur: "Business is business. We try to separate politics from business, and in any case the internal position of Sudan is an internal affair, and we are not in a position to influence them." [34]

If this is the state of affairs in 2006, tension is only going to rise. Note, too, that competition over resources is not confined to oil. China's trade with Africa has quadrupled since 2000. The main target has been oil from the Sudan and Angola, but China has also been in this market to secure supplies of platinum from Zimbabwe (hence the relationship with Mugabe discussed earlier), copper from Zambia, tropical timber from Congo-Brazzaville, and iron ore from South Africa. China has bought natural resource companies in Australia and Canada, gold mines in Bolivia, and coal mines in the Philippines; and it is developing soy production in Brazil. Australia, an important ally of the United States in Asia—George Bush characterized it as the United States' deputy sheriff in east Asia—is sedulously courted. Australia even acknowledges that its support could not be automatically assumed in any resistance led by the United States against a potential Chinese invasion of Taiwan. [35]

All this is congruent with a peacefully rising economic power. The interdependencies of trade foster the interpenetration of the world economy; and although China may be boosting its secure sources of energy and raw materials, it is also massively benefiting the world by lifting prices and itself providing an enormous market for imports. Those are not the concerns. Rather, the worry is that China will— sometimes consciously and sometimes just because of its sheer bulk and its authoritarian character—find itself undermining the framework in which globalization has taken place. This is partly a willingness to have all states share minimum common norms regarding the rule of law; and partly a willingness to accept that security is provided by the United States. China chafes under these constraints already; it watches the United States picking and choosing which international laws to obey, and it sees no reason not to copy. The world issue will come if the chafing ever transmutes into an active challenge.

Flashpoint 3: Strategy and Defense

There are plenty of running sores and territorial disputes in Asia, but the most dangerous is Taiwan. Captured as a Japanese colony in 1894, it was repossessed by the Nationalists in 1945 and was where they fled after their defeat by Mao. China has never accepted Taiwan's claim to the status of a sovereign state and has effectively blocked its international recognition ever since 1949. Chiang Kai-shek ran Taiwan as a militarized authoritarian state. He died in 1975, a year before Mao; and after that there was a democratic unfreezing as part of a Nationalist strategy to create a Taiwanese identity and unity in defiance of Beijing. In 2000 the opposition party, the Democratic Progress Party, founded in 1986 as part of the democratizing process, won the election. It has been in power since then.

Taiwan has not been controlled by Beijing for more than 100 years, and now it is run as a Chinese democracy—two facts that madden the communist government. In its view Taiwan is an integral part of the People's Republic of China. Its flourishing as a democratic, capitalist territory that dares to call itself the Republic of China is a constant reminder that the revolution is not yet complete; that there is a rival and successful alternative economic and social model for dissident mainland Chinese to compare and copy in their critique of communism; and that the century of humiliation is not yet completely revenged. Hong Kong has been returned by the British and Macao by the Portuguese; but because Taiwan was a Japanese colony during China's period of weakness, the foundation was laid for today's regime, and no prospect of a handover is in sight. If an invasion did not risk impelling the United States to intervene on the side of Taiwan, it would have been made long ago.

The Taiwanese, meanwhile, are increasingly frustrated by their semistatehood. The Democratic Progress Party (DPP) is committed to fight for the completion of Taiwanese democracy in a full-fledged Taiwanese state. The party has been the beneficiary of Taiwan's steady move toward economic and political pluralism—freedom of the press, a two-party democratic system, and the rule of law. In 2004 President Chen (a member of DPP) proposed two referenda—one on strengthening Taiwan's defenses and the other on opening talks with China. If passed, they would have laid the basis for a larger referendum on Taiwan's independence. China regarded the proposals with deep dismay, as a provocation. A boycott by the Nationalists and opposition from the United States meant that the necessary 50 percent quorum was not reached. But the episode reinforced Beijing's belief that a movement toward full statehood is under way in Taiwan and, if unopposed, will gather momentum. In 1992 only 17.3 percent of the population regarded themselves as Taiwanese, but by 2003 the figure had jumped to 43.2 percent. This trend, too, confirms Beijing in its view that the relaxation begun in the mid-1980s could easily lead to Taiwan's declaring statehood, even if only 10 percent of the Taiwanese want independence "as soon as possible."[36] Another sophisticated poll of the Taiwanese found a substantial increase in those prepared to risk independence even if implied war, and only 3 percent supporting reunification with China.[37] The use of the local Minnan dialect has soared, effectively displacing Mandarin. The Examination Yuan, the government's top examination agency, has omitted Chinese history and geography from future civil service exams. The cultural changes are profound. If Taiwan ever succeeded in winning consent for independence within its own democratic rules, it would be very difficult for the world to withhold recognition. That would be a severe diplomatic and political reverse for Beijing.

Beijing is using every tool it can find to resist. It encourages crossstrait trade and investment, so that Taiwan has a growing stake in the mainland: China has now supplanted the United States as the number one destination of Taiwanese exports. It supports those forces in Taiwanese politics that favor the status quo, such as the mayor of Taipei, a future Nationalist presidential candidate, Ma Ying-Jeou. In 2005 it passed an antisecession law in which it reminded Taiwan that it would regard a claim for statehood as secession, which it reserved the right to resist militarily. Also, it consistently builds up its military forces. Rear Admiral Eric A. McVadon, a seasoned, experienced China watcher who is the current director of Asia Pacific studies at the Institute for Foreign Policy Analysis in Washington, argues that there is only one way to interpret China's priorities for defense spending. China is not seeking to become a rival superpower but rather is seeking to reclaim Taiwan and repel any Japanese and American reaction.[38] McVadon explains the military "concept" that China's investment supports. It will use short-range and medium-range ballistic missiles, in particular the mobile DF-21, to overwhelm Taiwan's air defenses and offensive missile capacity. It concentrates on accurate medium-range missiles because it wants to attack U.S. carrier groups and surface vessels at sea, which it expects would be sent to support Taiwan. China is investing in submarines, particularly those of the Russian Kilo class and their lethal weapon system the SS-N-22 missiles, because it wants to be able to deploy antiship cruise missiles against the United States from submarines in addition to its land-based efforts. The naval and air-force investment, again, makes sense only as essentially second-wave operations after the missile systems have done their work; and again in the context of expected retaliation by the United States.

This is a formidable and growing armory. But even so, an attack on Taiwan together with preemptive attacks on potential American and Japanese retaliation would be a huge logistical challenge; and although China has engaged in fourteen joint exercises since 2000, according to the Pentagon, it is still a long way from the kind of coordination that the United States achieved in Iraq. Indeed the Pentagon Report of 2005 on China's Military Capacity[39] endorses McVadon's analysis: although it acknowledges that China is building up long-range road mobile intercontinental missile systems—the DF-31—it nonetheless describes China's posture as essentially "active defense" focused primarily on Taiwan. However, the scale of this more limited buildup is increasingly impressive. In the Pentagon's words:

The pace and scope of China's military build-up are, already, such as to put regional military balances at risk. Current trends in China's military modernization could provide China with a force capable of prosecuting a range of military options in Asia—well beyond Taiwan—potentially posing a credible threat to modern militaries operating in the region.[40]

The question is whether China will act. From the Chinese point of view, to regain Taiwan would be a great boost to domestic legitimacy, would remove a potential ideological threat, and would also open up military options not present at the moment. The Pentagon quotes General Wen Zongren, political commissar of the elite PLA Academy of Military Science, as saying that resolving the issue of Taiwan is of

far-reaching significance to breaking international forces' blockade against China's maritime security. . . . Only when we break this blockade shall we be able to talk about China's rise. . . . To rise suddenly, China must pass through oceans and go out of the oceans in its future development.

On the other hand, an attack on Taiwan would be a massive risk. Taiwan has a well-equipped modern air force and 350 fourth-generation fighter planes such as the F-16 and the Mirage (twice as many as the British RAF). The Chinese air force may be more than 1,000 planes strong, but it can field only less than 100 fourth-generation planes. The airspace over Taiwan permits operational airspace for around 300 aircraft; Taiwan would give a good account of itself, especially as it could expect assistance from Japan and the United States.[41] An amphibious attack on Taiwan would also be fraught with hazard. In 2001, the International Institute for Strategic Studies observed that "it would take around 800–1,000 large landing craft nearly 2 weeks to transport the required 30 infantry divisions to Taiwan. At present, the Chinese Navy could move one, perhaps two divisions.[42] The landing craft would have to run the gauntlet of the Hsiung Feng III, a highly sophisticated supersonic antiship missile. But while the balance of military risk and advantage suggests that China would not dare an invasion at present, it is outspending Taiwan by ten to one on arms. Taiwan is actually reducing its spending—confident that China will not invade and that it can rely on the United States. After all, an unsuccessful Chinese invasion would probably constitute a lethal blow to the Communist Party's standing and prestige. It would also be a green light to other restless parts of China— Tibet, Xinjiang, and Inner Mongolia. They, too, could then try their luck against a diminished regime.

Even if an invasion of Taiwan succeeded, the change in the world's perception of China would be decisive. China could no longer pretend to be engaged in a "peaceful rise," and some of its moral authority as a challenger to the United States would be lost. Nor could it be certain that it would win a long war against a broad Asian alliance including the United States and Japan, aimed at the restoration of Taiwan's status. Such a defeat would represent a more extended and dramatic humiliation than failing to take the island. The best strategy for China if it wants to reintegrate Taiwan is to do so within a democratic, pluralist China based on the rule of law—the very structure opposed by the Communist Party. For what may be best is not necessarily what will be pursued. Indeed a Communist Party with its back against the wall could decide that invasion was one way out of its troubles.

What Should America Do?

American diplomacy in Asia should be aimed at keeping the temperature down, keeping the lines of communication open, and constructing an unthreatening environment in which China can move in a pluralist direction. Instead, it does the opposite. It overaccentuates its preoccupation with bilateral military and security relationships;

underplays its commitment to fostering strong multilateral regional groupings, which it almost casually neglects; and incites fierce nationalistic rivalry between Japan and China. As a result whatever its warm words about "engagement" or inviting China to be a "responsible stakeholder" in the international system,[43] China believes that the real aims of the United States are containment, encirclement, and blocking China's rise. China is, of course, partly right. The United States cannot make up its mind whether to contain or engage China, and by default it has found itself applying a foreign policy more in keeping with the nineteenth-century German statesmen Bismarck than with the enlightened United States that created the postwar international settlement and supported the formation of today's European Union.[44] This is a historic mistake that could all too easily topple the United States into conflict it does not want and does not need. Allowing the Pentagon to define the interests of the United States and the west will inevitably mean that the focus is on defense and security, bilateral alliances, and coalitions of the willing. Whether having a spat with South Korea's president Roo Moo-Hyan or showering favors on Japan's prime minister Junichiro Koizumi, President Bush shows that approbation will be conferred on those who do his exact bidding.[45] Regional security, regional alliances, and multilateralism are seen as the soft option. This view could not be more wrong.

The management of the United States' relationship with Japan, and thus with China, is fraught with difficulty. Japan is a capitalist democracy that is deepening its commitment to pluralism and the rule of law; it has apologized twenty-one times for what it did in China between 1931 and 1945. Within Japan the state is receding in importance, and increasingly there is a genuine marketplace of ideas and opinions. The coalition in favor of freezing defense expenditure at 1 percent of GDP is very powerful. However, Japan is a key regional actor, and the second-biggest economy in the world, and there is every reason why it should adapt its constitution to permit more overseas activism and offer greater input to global security initiatives, especially within the United Nations. Over the last two years Japan has begun to flex its muscles. In February 2005, a joint statement by Washington and Tokyo explicitly linked, for the first time, the alliance's interests with peace in the Taiwan Strait. After Prime Minister Koizumi won the election in October 2005, the governing LDP has proposed retaining Japan's permanent renunciation of war as a constitutional obligation but amending it to allow Japan's Special Defense Force to join collective efforts at defense beyond Japan. The United States broadly supports the initiative; it wants Japan's support in its international adventures, and it will need Japan's Special Defense Force if it ever has to intervene in the Taiwan Strait.

Asians regard these moves with suspicion. For China's communists they prove that Japanese militarism is just below the surface. China even objected to Japan's participation in sending 600 noncombat soldiers for support operations in Iraq. Lee Kuan Yew of Singapore has likened the idea of Japan's participation in peacekeeping operations supervised by the UN to giving liqueur-laced chocolate to a reforming alcoholic: a needless lure which could entice Japan back to bad old habits.[46] And Japan does not help its own case. In the spring of 2005 when China and Japan were squaring off over the Senkaku Islands (see Chapter 1), tension also mounted between South Korea and Japan over the Dokdo (or in Japanese, Takeshima) Islands: about 0.08 square mile, or fifty acres, of land. Heavily armed Japanese and Korean naval vessels were dispatched to an ocean face-off. The dispute is still unresolved.

Japan is more and more self-assertively nationalistic, confident of the United States' defensive nuclear umbrella. Koizumi's annual visit to the Yasukuni shrine to commemorate 2.5 million dead Japanese soldiers, unfortunately including fourteen convicted war criminals, is hardly an act of emollience notwithstanding his protest that the visit is private and that it is wrong to distinguish among the dead. Even within Japan the visit provokes outspoken criticism. Japan's war record—of comfort women; slave laborers; the notorious Unit 731, where human experiments were undertaken; and the slaughter at Nanjing—is still not accepted or confronted by some on the nationalist right, whose textbooks (in particular, Atarashii Rekishi Kyokasho) omit these crimes.[47] All is grist to the mill of the Chinese Communist Party, which is looking for evidence of growing Japanese militarism and nationalism.

From China's perspective, the United States' bilateral military alliances with Japan and India and its network of military bases do not look like "engagement." When Defense Secretary Donald Rumsfeld said in Singapore in 2005 that he did not understand which enemy China thought it had in mind to justify its growing military spending, that was disingenuousness of the highest order. Readers have only to cast their eyes back over the various quotations from Chinese officials in this chapter to get a sense of how China feels. Although it promotes ASEAN + 3 (the ten members of the Association of South East Asian Nations plus China, Japan, and South Korea[48]) as a multilateral regional economic and security forum, China can hardly fail to notice Washington's reluctance over any form of multilateralism except the Association for Pacific Economic Cooperation (APEC), which the United States leads and which is little more than a talking shop. And when China collaborates in the "six-party talks" (United States, North Korea, South Korea, China, Japan, and Russia) to address the issue of North Korea's nuclear capacity, it observes the United States' double standard, because the United States takes an accommodating approach to India's civil nuclear program. Concerning North Korea, the United States is careful not to institutionalize any mechanism that would give China a formal international role. If America wants to play Bismarckian politics, why should not China?

The answer is that for the time being China gets too much out of the international system to rock the boat. China carefully appraises the advantages. It keeps close watch on how its "comprehensive national power" is developing—a term the Chinese Military Academy defines as "organic integration of capacities of subsistence, development, and coordination."[49] Each year there is a detailed appraisal of the Chinese coordination system, assessing the ability of the Chinese political leadership to unify and coordinate; and of China's "hardware," including all its physical factors, and then its software—its "ideational ethos" and intelligence. This is a conscious analysis of the totality of China's power capacity.

Chinese nationalism is, if anything, growing, as a consequence of massive domestic propaganda. In September 1994 the Central Committee of the Chinese Communist Party, advised by the Central Propaganda Department, issued an "Outline for Conducting Patriotic Education." The outline established patriotic education from the nursery school to the university as a key party aim, and it has been delivered with scant regard for historical truth. Zhao Suisheng argues that Chinese history has been oversimplified and that inconvenient truths—such as the expansion of the Qing dynasty, the violence of the Boxers, and Chinese atrocities during the war against Japan—are downplayed or ignored.[50] There is no mention of China's recent wars. There is intense paranoia and distrust of foreign intentions. Beijing's failure to be chosen as the site of the Olympics in 2000 was depicted as an anti-Chinese plot—though this is now conveniently forgotten as the Beijing Olympics of 2008 approach. The message is unambiguous. China has to be on permanent guard against its enemies. It must avoid disunity at home, and it must be protected abroad by a vigilant communist government.

Patriotic education has built on a proclivity ever present in the population at large—defiance aimed against the allegedly predatory foreigner. This attitude is attributable to a lack of confidence in China, its culture, and its achievements. The *China Can Say No* books of the 1990s were best sellers with little official inducement. In August 2005 China presented an e-signature petition with 46 million names to UN Secretary General Kofi Annan, opposing Japan's being offered a permanent seat on the Security Council—a reform that the Chinese government implacably opposes.[51] Communist leaders know that General Secretary Hu Yaobang's championing of reconciliation with Japan in the 1980s contributed to his ousting; and even Mao is sometimes accused of being soft on Japan.[52] Yet this genuine nationalist feeling together with the party's own nationalist rhetoric locks it in a foreign policy trap. It cannot give ground or change stance even when doing so may be in its own objective interest. All this makes the conventions of normal diplomacy very difficult. For instance, Jiang Zemin's state visit to Japan in 1998 was in Japanese terms a public relations disaster—Jiang felt obliged to hector Japan on its conduct, only to be criticized at home for being insufficiently tough.

The consequence is that as Japan becomes China's largest trading partner, diplomatic relations are—to repeat—very difficult, with both populations in a cycle of deepening mistrust. China believes it has a rightful, proud place in the world and that its destiny is to recover this place. Its leaders, however, having chosen to ride the nationalist tiger, could easily find that it rounds on them—forcing them or their successors into warlike actions to match their words. The single most important counterweight is the United States. The least good way to respond is to go head-to-head with China and thus vindicate and exacerbate its paranoia. The United States needs to wean itself from the "seductive but nonetheless destructive simplicity" on which it is currently set.[53] The smarter policy is to build China into the world system and genuinely offer it the possibility of co-managing the system for mutual benefit. Assessing the likelihood of that is where we go next.

CHAPTER 10

It's the Enlightenment, Stupid

THE UNITED STATES IS NOT A NATURAL CANDIDATE TO support an open world trading and financial system, even if it is an enormous beneficiary in terms of lower interest rates, cheaper goods, vast inward flows of savings, smarter organization of production, and higher living standards. The problem is not only that those who lose by any dislocation from imports are more obvious and shout louder than those who gain—the latter being diffused through the entire population—or that the United States has a long-standing and powerful protectionist tradition. Rather, the problem is that at the heart of the United States' relationship with the rest of the world is an ambivalence which has deepened since the collapse of the Soviet Union. The pursuit of its national interests involves preaching multilateral openness in trade and finance and simultaneously claiming the scope to act unilaterally with regard to security, the military, and diplomatic relations. Economic openness may be a strategic necessity, but it sits uneasily beside America's protectionist instincts and traditions—all against a background of fear that the middle class is collapsing and opportunity is declining.

The United States is not alone in its ambivalent attitude to trade. An open trading system tempts every country to pursue strategic trade policies that are much more mercantilist in their rationale than their rhetorical obeisance to free markets and openness would suggest. The United States' strategic interest is to keep the system open in order for its multinationals to sustain their global brand leadership and growth prospects. China, by pegging its exchange rate to the dollar and being open to foreign investment, is strategically boosting its export sector and thus the momentum of industrialization. Japan's prosperity depends on having a large manufacturing sector that needs strategic access to the Chinese, American, and European markets. Nor are members of the European Union innocent. France, for example, has established ten strategic sectors in which it refuses to allow foreign takeovers. All genuflect to the rules-based openness of the trading system as regulated by the World Trade Organization. But they believe in it more because it is the means to secure their strategic, mercantilist aims than because of any desire to create gains in which everyone would share. Thus the suspension of the Doha round of trade talks in July 2006 aimed at further liberalization—an ominous moment for the world system and a tribute to those underlying attitudes.

The United States now finds that its own strategic trade policy—openness—is being exploited by a potential superpower rival that is using its growing economic strength to support communism or, more accurately, authoritarianism. Deng's policy of opening to reinforce the legitimacy of the Chinese Communist Party is working precisely as he anticipated. The United States is beginning to reexamine whether the pursuit of its national interest should mean remaining strategically open, or whether it should revert to the system of the nineteenth century. The latter option is a real and growing temptation; and the more communist China seems to benefit, the more urgently the question will be asked. The United States could escape back to its nineteenth-century protected laager is the siren call: it does not have to engage with the world. But if Deng and the Chinese seem to have won the first round, this is a much longer-term contest. The United States needs to have more confidence that its democratic Enlightenment institutions are vital to growth. If it can stay open, it will be rewarded by the ultimate achievement of transforming communist China and growing richer at the same time. Openness works, and protection was never the real reason why the United States grew—indeed, protectionism may have restrained growth. To embrace this proposition, the United States will need to have a better understanding of its own past as well as the present.

American Trade Nationalism Was Ever Thus

The United States is a country on a continental scale. Whatever the differences among the founding fathers of the United States, what united them was their keen awareness that the new country could and should declare independence from more than George III. The New World should operate according to different principles from the Old World, and one of its principles would be that a single-continental-scale economy had prospects and options that no single European national economy had. For a start, the United States had a nearly inexhaustible supply of fresh land to settle. It was not just the farmer on his homestead who could be self-sufficient and independent; so could the country. Protectionism is but one by-product of a wider belief in the particular and providential destiny of the United States. America was big enough to go its own way. It could declare independence from British free-trade policies if it chose, and still prosper.

From the beginning, then, the debate about trade was not ideological but strategic, concerning what kind of country the United States wanted to become. For Thomas Jefferson, republican and religious virtue lay in farming, and farmers needed the cheapest machinery and the maximum access to foreign markets—hence his bias toward free trade. Alexander Hamilton, the first secretary of the treasury, under Washington, instead championed an idea which has run through economics for 200 years: that not all forms of economic activity are equally important to the life of the nation, and that states should therefore accept the economic hand dealt to them by the free market. It may be true, as nineteenth-century British theorist of free trade David Ricardo maintained, that if Portugal and England trade their port and cloth and specialize in what they are best at, then both are better off. But England, as Joan Robinson argued in the twentieth century[1] and Alexander Hamilton in the eighteenth, gets the better of the bargain. It becomes a textile manufacturer and achieves the consequent technological and strategic advantages. Portugal meanwhile is locked into being an agricultural country, with a reduced chance of capturing the dynamic advantages of a developing industrial base.

Manufacturing matters more than agriculture, Hamilton said, because it inevitably deploys more machines. He cited England's advances in textile manufacture. Machines embody scientific and technological advance and so are a primary means of generating wealth. Also, a country with a strong industrial base is more likely to be able to defend itself. But there is a problem. Young countries that want to create industries face incumbents who have the advantages of producing at scale. The scale advantages make their unit costs very much lower, and thus almost impossible for a young industry to compete against. In a classic exposition of what economists call the infant-industry argument, Hamilton argued that the only solution was tariff protection. It would allow the prices of industrial goods to become high enough to let American producers get started. There might be short-term pain, but the long-term prize would be a rapid industrialization. Hamilton did not want to pick winners, or get the state involved in production. Within the United States he was as laissez-faire as Jefferson. He wanted to bias the general prices of industrial goods upward to give American producers the financial headroom to justify investment in early factories.

American protectionists never made the case for generalized governmental or state intervention in the economy. They were on the side of the private sector and an American internal market. They observed that England had been protectionist in the eighteenth century, and its growing commitment to free trade in the nineteenth was no more than a self-interested attempt to kick away the ladder by which it had reached economic strength. If other countries could not protect their industries, then the advantage would always lie with English companies—which, in effect, could never be challenged. Protection was a way of simultaneously financing the federal government—Hamilton's other preoccupation—at the expense of foreign producers and giving American producers a head start. And there was an implicit understanding that as the United States grew in area, eventually its multiple industrial producers would have the advantage of continent-wide production on a scale at least equal to that of the English. They would have a parallel opportunity to specialize in what they were good at. There would be plenty of American competition and incentives to become efficient. Protection would not create expensive, sleepy monopolies. The United States could be committed to free-market principles internally, but it could afford to be pragmatic about whether those same market principles worked for it abroad.

Hamilton, killed in a duel in 1804, never lived to see his ideas given general application. Up until the war with the British between 1812 and 1814, the young United States was broadly Jeffersonian in its attitude toward trade. But the burning of Washington; the flooding of the U.S. market by cheap British industrial goods; and the British Corn Laws, which imposed a high tax on imported grain, were wake-up calls. In 1816 the United States introduced its first hefty tariffs; and in 1824 it transmuted them into a generalized tariff on imported industrial goods. That tax averaged 35 percent and would stay in place until the disastrous Smoot-Hawley tariffs of 1930, which averaged 48 percent and precipitated the Great Depression. No other industrialized or industrializing country has ever had such high tariffs for so long. German and French tariffs during the nineteenth century never topped more than 15 percent, and Japanese tariffs even in the 1930s did not go above 30 percent.[2] Historically the United States was the undisputed king of protectionism.

If Hamilton was the intellectual author of the American system, Henry Clay was its passionate political architect. In 1824, as speaker of the House, Clay gave a famous six-and-a-half-hour address in favor of protectionism. "The measure of the wealth of a nation is indicated by the measure of its protection of its industry," he said.[3] Clay argued that the United States' vast and fertile lands offered security against too much power falling to manufacturers. The diversity of a country as large as the United States would also allow everyone to benefit from the construction of a genuinely American system. The agricultural south might benefit from free trade, but it could not be allowed to call the shots for the whole country.[4]

In the years preceding the Civil War, the intellectual and strategic arguments seesawed. Democrats, representing the laissez-faire south, argued that tariffs should be high enough to raise the desired revenue, but no higher; and so they chipped away at the tariff system. After the Civil War, the Hamiltonian tariff system was reinvigorated. From 1867 to 1930 tariffs rose steadily toward the peak achieved by the Smoot-Hawley Act. As economic growth averaged 3.5 percent between 1890 and 1930, a causal relationship between growth and protection seemed obvious.

In fact the story was much more complicated. Over the 1870s and 1880s the American economy swung from boom to bust. For almost half the years between 1873 and 1898, the United States suffered severe depressions. The key point is that the historic importance of protection in advancing U.S. interests in the past has been vastly overstated by the protectionist lobby—and the dangers of retreat today are understated. High tariffs might have coincided with solid growth, but they were not its principal cause. The raw economic data, as the economist Douglas Irwin demonstrates, hardly prove the protectionist case. Between 1870 and 1914 American economic growth was propelled by massive population growth and investment—growth in productivity was very similar in America and in free-trade Britain.[5] Indeed the fastest growth in productivity was in the service sector that was unexposed to trade; there, employment rose from 30 percent of the workforce in 1870 to 43 percent in 1910. Protection had little or nothing to do with this. Irwin thinks that making imported capital goods expensive may even have hindered the growth of the service sector and slowed American growth in general.

The drivers of growth were domestic, as were the difficulties. As the continental economy linked up, the frontier closed down, the great factories in New England and the midwest spewed out their products as if the helter-skelter expansion of the previous two centuries was continuing undimmed, but the American consumer could not keep up with the pace of potential production. The 1890s were a turbulent decade of falling prices, rising unemployment—reaching more than 16 percent in 1894—and growing unrest among workers.[6] In 1892 Carnegie broke a strike at his vast Homestead steel plant in Pennsylvania, aided by a three-mile wall and the state militia. Two years later, in the summer of 1894, George Pullman broke a strike at his locomotive and carriage factories in Chicago, using federal troops sent in by President Cleveland. These two defeats represented a watershed for the American labor movement. They were symptomatic of the times.

Earlier in 1894, Jacob Coxey had marched from Ohio to Washington trying to gather distressed unemployed workers into an "army" to protest against falling wages and unemployment. His army numbered only about 500, but it signaled a willingness to take to the streets and shook the American establishment. That same autumn William Jennings Bryan, arguing that silver should become legal tender alongside gold in order to boost effective purchasing power, made a strong run for the presidency. The system was not working; discontent was palpable.

The proposition that prosperity and well-being lay in self-sufficiency, protectionism, and looking inward was aggressively challenged. According to an emerging intellectual consensus, unless America could find a new way to continue the frontier tradition and harness the energies of its people, social upheaval might result. Frederick Jackson Turner caught the mood in his famous essay "The Significance of the Frontier." He argued that to sustain a concept of space and ambition, which was at the root of the American sensibility, the frontier now had to be extended overseas. Foreign trade should replace land as the spatial anchor of the republic. Turner's ideas became influential; even Theodore Roosevelt expressed his indebtedness.[7] American expansionism, however, would be distinct from European expansionism. The aim was not to create an overseas empire but to export the American idea—and a fervent belief in Christianity. The United States would create a commercial network overseas that, as the British historian Niall Ferguson puts it, would create dependence on the United States rather than domination by the United States. Its trading partners would benefit by having access to American goods, values, and ideas.[8] Following historian Charles Maier, the ascendancy the United States sought (and seeks) is post-territorial—"to project power, exert influence and enjoy prestige far beyond traditionally bounded jurisdiction."[9] America's open-door policy for China would of course benefit the United States; but the growing wave of American missionaries genuinely hoped to bring benefits to the Chinese as well.

The expansion of American trade would also entail a broad expansion in its merchant and military navies. Alfred Thayer Mahan in *The Influence of Sea Power upon History,* another influential work of the 1890s, insisted that the United States now had to develop the sinews of its naval power if it wanted to exercise influence overseas.[10] The lesson was heeded. In the 1880s the United States was a trivial naval power, but by 1907 its intense naval building program had carried it to the rank of second in the world, after the British. The United States had to protect its vital sea-lanes as it began to look outward. Thus as protectionism reached its apogee, a strategic argument was emerging that would ultimately change the United States' trade policy. Even President William McKinley, who was responsible for the highest tariffs in the nineteenth century, had begun to argue that there might be a case for lowering tariffs if other countries reciprocated. American industry no longer needed protecting. This was the theme of McKinley's last speech before he was shot in 1901.

When the Democrats won the presidency in 1932, they blamed protectionism for the disaster that had befallen America—developing an economic and political argument that had been gestating for more than forty years. Although the argument in favor of reciprocal tariff cuts fell short of calling for a full free-trade system, there was nonetheless a recognition that protection had led nowhere. The strategic interest, now that U.S. companies were clearly among the most innovative and productive in the world, was to develop a policy of reciprocal tariff cuts to help them boost their overseas sales. The Reciprocal Trade Agreements Act (RTAA) of 1934 empowered the U.S. government to cut tariffs by 50 percent if a trading partner reciprocated; and by the end of the war bilateral agreements had been agreed on with twenty-five countries. The United States' policy was changing.

Like Britain before it, the United States was gaining enough confidence in its industrial strength to drop its long commitment to protection. The way was being paved for the settlement that would come after World War II. Britain, meanwhile, as its share of world trade slipped to 14 percent in 1913, compared with 24 percent in 1870, found itself more willing to accept the protectionist case. The leading Conservative politician, Joseph Chamberlain, had first made the case for "imperial preference" in the early 1900s. In 1933 the British government, presiding over a network of small- to medium-size producers in the hard-pressed traditional industrial sectors, finally gave way and started a system of tariff protection within the British Empire. Britain, having kicked away the ladder for others in the 1840s and 1850s when it insisted on low tariffs for all, was now rediscovering the virtues of protectionism as it became industrially weaker—just as the United States was becoming strong enough to abandon it. Strategic interests came first for both.[11]

The Golden Era of Free Trade

After World War II the United States' first reaction was to try to make sure that German and Japanese reconstruction was as limited as possible. Essentially both countries would be ruralized and their capacity to wage war would be removed forever. But the march of events turned the tide. The Soviet Union's ambitions to extend communism were obvious, and Chinese communism was getting the better of the tired Nationalist armies. It was becoming a strategic imperative for the United States to ensure that western Europe and the rest of east Asia did not fall under communist government. There was a real prospect, in the postwar years, that most of the Eurasian landmass and the newly independent nation-states emerging from European decolonization would constitute a communist bloc, whose economic and military power could challenge the United States. As it was, the Soviet Union and communist China constituted a formidable prospect, and there were strong communist parties in Italy, France, and southern Europe.

The United States' response was in some respects chosen for it. It had to preempt any direct military challenge by promising mutually assured destruction through nuclear retaliation. It would fight local wars like the one in Vietnam, to limit communist gains and buy time. And it would organize and support the buildup of Europe, Japan, and other Asian powers into robust capitalist democracies not prone to communist temptations. For nearly thirty years, from 1947 to the Trade Act of 1974, the United States embraced free trade as whole-heartedly as the nineteenth-century British had.

The decisive year was 1947. In March the United States decided to reverse the ruralization strategy in occupied Japan and instead committed to develop the Japanese economy along with the economies of Korea, the Philippines, and eventually French Indochina as part of an Asian capitalist bulwark against communism.[12] In June the Marshall Plan was initiated to reconstruct a prostrate western Europe (in today's prices, more than $100 billion was sent) and provide it with vital convertible currency to pay for imports. In July George Kennan wrote a famous essay in *Foreign Affairs* (under the pseudonym X) urging a policy of "containment" of the Soviet Union.[13] And in October the last piece of the jigsaw puzzle was put into place with the establishment of the General Agreement on Tariffs and Trade (GATT), in which every signatory agreed to extend whatever reciprocal tariff arrangements it had agreed on bilaterally to every other signatory. The signatories also agreed to an across-the-board 20 percent reduction in tariffs as a down payment on their future intentions. In effect the reciprocal agreements under the United States' RTAA would be extended multilaterally, and new signatories such as Japan and Germany would be able to shelter under the U.S. trade umbrella. The GATT was the trade tool that would deliver the economic dimension of the geopolitical strategy.

Yet even at this high-water mark of the strategic case for free trade, the U.S. Congress ferociously resisted proposals to set up an International Trade Organization as an autonomous body to police the GATT. Arthur Vandenberg, the ranking Republican on the Senate Foreign Relations Committee, had already told Truman that the only way to get congressional agreement for the Marshall Plan was "to make a speech and scare the hell out of the country." [14] To reverse more than 100 years of protection and establish an international organization to regulate the new trade system was a leap too far. Congress could accept conditionally extending the RTAA as long as the United States reserved the right to retaliate against unfair trade. It could not accept a commitment to free trade that entailed abiding by the objective rulings of an international body in trade disputes. It wanted the United States to have the right to act independently and in its own interests.

Still, the evident superiority of U.S. industry made free trade easier to sell. John Foster Dulles opined that while the Japanese might be able to export shirts, pajamas, and "perhaps cocktail napkins" to the U.S. market, little else was possible for them. [15] So it was that until the mid-1970s the United States refrained from using the leeway that a suspicious Congress had insisted on in 1947. It indulged both Japan and Europe. Japan was allowed to peg the yen at a supercompetitive level against the dollar, thereby boosting its exports. Until 1975 the U.S. government supported Japan in every claim against it by individual American companies complaining that they had been damaged by unfair Japanese competition. The United States even allowed Japan to protect its market against foreign imports; and Japan was allowed to use 42,000 western technology patents without challenge.[16] The story was similar in Europe. Article 24 of GATT permitted the formation of customs unions and regional free-trade areas if other states allowed them, and the United States condoned the formation of the European Iron and Steel Community in 1952. Subsequently, it approved the initiation of the quintessential expression of a regional trade bloc, the European Economic Community (EEC). American negotiators, during the "Kennedy round," which sought cuts in industrial tariffs of about 35 percent, accepted that the EEC could maintain the Common Agricultural Policy. They also accepted that fifty-eight developing countries could continue to rig their domestic markets and still have access, under the terms of GATT, to the U.S. market.

American policy was more successful than even its most ardent proponents could have hoped. In 1950 European output per person-hour worked was about half of American output. By the mid-1970s the gap was rapidly closing, and by the mid-1990s it had almost closed. The situation was similar in Japan. Rapid economic growth, rising employment, and booming trade brought an ideological legitimization of capitalism that reversed its delegitimization in the interwar period. Communist parties in western Europe were in retreat. In Asia by the end of the Vietnam war the "tiger economies" of Singapore, South Korea, Hong Kong, Taiwan, and the Philippines proved that open trade and pro-market economic structures were the precondition for a rate of economic growth that was plainly faster than the rate in the communist world. The ideological tectonic plates were shifting—of which one was the rise to power of Deng Xiaoping.

The Era of Rising Trade Tensions

In the mid-1970s the United States suffered the first oil shock. The growing competitiveness of Europe and Japan was now reflected in a stubborn U.S. trade deficit, which meant that it was becoming increasingly onerous to allow a growing number of foreign holders of dollars to exert their right to convert dollars into gold. Economic growth slowed down. Inflation soared. Unemployment rose. And in Washington the postwar consensus began to break down. The Republicans, seeing an opportunity to reverse what the Democrats had done in 1932, argued that the United States had to return to more self-interested economic policies. It should move away from trying to create a global commons abroad, and retreat to calculate its own narrow interests while challenging the liberal consensus at home.

Not that the United States had ever wholly repudiated protectionism. The Buy America Act of 1933, insisting that federal and state government place orders for key supplies with American producers, had never been repealed. Indeed, it was under this act that the Pentagon had justified focusing its postwar spending wholly on U.S. industry. The United States closely monitored exports of any high-technology goods that might be incorporated into the defense industries of the communist bloc, even through third parties. And for some years there had been a growing consensus that the burden of maintaining the dollar as the world's anchor currency, linked to gold, was placing too much strain on the U.S. economy. The United States should float the dollar and manage its economy just as it chose.

The year 1974 was a watershed. Convertibility into gold had been formally abandoned in 1971, and the United States had walked away from the so-called Bretton Woods system, with exchange rates pegged to a predictable value of the dollar. Now the United States abandoned all the capital controls that had been intended to support the dollar's role as the linchpin of the international financial system. The value of the dollar would henceforth be set by the markets, and the United States would be free to pursue whatever economic policy it thought best for itself rather than be hamstrung by international obligations. The Trade Act of 1974 backed up the move to a supposed new hardheadedness, as if the former policy of attempting to boost liberal capitalist democracy worldwide by being generous had been soft. The

United States empowered itself unilaterally to reinstate tariffs if imports from any country suddenly rose. Under Section 301, if U.S. exporters complained of any discrimination against them, the United States reserved the right to take unilateral punitive action. This move was a destructive challenge to the concept of multilateral reciprocity that is at the heart of the world's free trade. If the United States chooses, it can act by itself.

The change of direction has persisted with growing intensity. Japan, once cosseted, over the 1980s became an object of intense American pressure to revalue its currency and open its markets. Under the Structural Impediments Initiative of 1989 the United States required Japan to consider every aspect of its economic structure—from the retail distribution system to the supply chains of firms—as essentially reformable. The goal was to increase the reciprocal access of American goods to the Japanese market. By the early 1990s the combination of U.S. trade hawkishness and a sharply rising yen was the most important contribution to ending the long postwar Japanese boom.

Financial liberalization was another area where the United States demonstrated its new focus on its own strategic interests. Here it had the wit and vision to see that manufacturing, which had been widely regarded as the heart of the process of creating wealth, was giving way to services. This was an embrace of the future that some commentators have called a "revolution in social ontology."[17] Opening up the world to America financial institutions and telecommunications companies might seen obvious now, but then it was a leap in the dark. Nonetheless, the United States pushed for liberalization and deregulation. In 1982 Citibank and Federal Express founded the Coalition of Services Industries, which consistently pressed the U.S. Department of Commerce and U.S. trade negotiators to liberalize world service industries to competition from American business. Between 1972 and 1985 the 1,000 largest U.S. banks increased their dedicated spending on telecommunications from 5 to 13 percent of their operating expenses. The progressive liberalization of both permitted the development of twenty-four-hour global financial networks. By 1985 Citibank had linked its offices in ninety-four countries and was trading $200 billion daily in the foreign exchange markets. The company needed telecoms deregulation as much as capital market deregulation to pull off the coup.[18]

For the multilateral trade institutions, the choice was stark. If they did not accommodate the United States' strategic trade ambitions, then the United States would achieve its ends without them—so it was better to keep some multilateralism than none at all. The GATT could not launch a round of tariff reduction negotiations without support from the United States. When the "Uruguay round" of reducing tariffs and opening markets began in 1985, the United States insisted that intellectual property rights, service-sector trade, and in particular telecommunications were on the agenda. The strategy was to bypass what the Reaganites saw as the statist International Telecommunications Union (ITU), the intergovernmental agency that regulated international telecoms business. Four years later the ITU submitted to the GATT talks, recognizing that the United States was going to drive through liberalization of telecoms and that its only chance of saving even minimal regulation was to work through GATT.

In 1990 GATT ruled that American multinationals should in principle have access to all the service markets of its signatories. Four years later the United States used GATT to force the European Union to agree to open all its communications (post, telephone, and telegraph) to competition. In 1995 the United States forced through a framework agreement (trade-related intellectual property, TRIP) that subsumed all earlier treaties in order to enlarge the enforcement of intellectual property rights. In effect the U.S. Patent Office—as the gatekeeper of exercising patents in the world's largest market—would become the world regulator of patents in the information age, and American rules would become the global standard. This was an extraordinary achievement; and according to John Braithwaite and Peter Drahos it resulted from the coordinated lobbying of fifty key

American executives and was a tribute to the capacity of American business to get the U.S. government to act in its interests, and of U.S. trade diplomacy to fulfill its mission.[19] In April 1996 the U.S. delegation walked out of talks held by the World Trade Organization (WTO, the successor to GATT), insisting that telecom liberalization should become global. A year later the WTO gave in and opened up seventy countries to U.S. telecom companies on the United States' terms. With the World Bank and IMF insisting on telecoms deregulation as the price of every structural adjustment program, the United States was succeeding at deregulating global telecoms in the 1990s, just as it had deregulated finance during the 1970s and 1980s. In 2005, the value of U.S. service exports amounted to $323 billion, nearly 40 percent of the value of merchandise exports and generating a surplus of some $65 billion.

At home there has been rising hawkishness over dumping, the practice of exporting products into other markets at below economic cost. Since 1980, the United States has led the world in the number of antidumping suits brought against foreign exporters.[20] And ever since 1980, as Bruce Blonigen has pointed out,[21] the average fine has been increasing by 2.5 percentage points a year. In the early 1980s fines averaged 15.5 percent of the imputed difference between a "fair" price and the actual price, and by 2000 they had quadrupled to more than 60 percent. Not only that; the U.S. International Trade Commission is increasingly likely to find injury—the rate is up from 45 percent in the early 1980s to 60 percent in 2000. The United States' trading partners are becoming increasingly vociferous at the one-sidedness, injustice, and mounting costs of the U.S. approach and wanted to put this issue on the table in the "Doha round" of trade talks begun in 2001 and which have now collapsed. The House of Representatives voted 410 to four before the first meeting, insisting that the president should not agree to any major revisions of antidumping practice.

That vote is of a piece with the wider American approach. The United States, like Britain in the run-up to the introduction of "imperial preference," is finding that as its relative economic power wanes, sustaining a coalition in favor of trade openness becomes harder. So the debate over trade increasingly focuses on security. Industries considered crucial to national security—semiconductors, high-definition television screens, steel, and supercomputers—are strategically supported.[22] Amendments are proposed (the Shelby and Inhofe amendments) to expand the definition of national security under the Exon-Florio Act, (which give the president of the United States the power to block foreigners buying American companies, if they impair U.S. national security) supported by the administration. Foreign ships are forbidden to move from one American port to another, even in extreme conditions like the hurricane in New Orleans. And so on. Security, to paraphrase Samuel Johnson, is the last refuge of the protectionist scoundrel.

The United States, more economically challenged and genuinely concerned about terrorism, feels weaker and less able to make unilateral concessions for the common good. As the trade expert Jagdish Bhagwati argues, free trade has to be increasingly justified by reference to reciprocity and fairness.[23] The United States is ratcheting up its demands for reciprocity; the Structural Impediment Initiative against Japan is a classic example. It demands not so much reciprocal cutting of trade tariffs as sweeping across-the-board economic change. This is twenty-first-century reciprocity in which the United States wants to require its trading partners to have economic and social structures like its own if they want the right to trade with it.

In short, trade is becoming more politicized and more dominated by one-sided concerns to maximize immediate strategic advantages. American lawmakers are doing no more than following U.S. public opinion. According to a recent survey, 84 percent of the public wants the United States' top foreign policy objective to be the protection of American jobs.[24] In this atmosphere, China's cheap labor is seen not as a natural advantage from which both sides benefit but as an unfair excuse to dump goods in the United States. Everywhere, it's the same story. If the United States is going to allow free trade, then there has to be an overt strategic reason, as in the creation of the North American

Free Trade Area in 1993. That initiative, by bringing Canada and Mexico under the same free-trade umbrella, consolidated North America into a strong regional trading bloc in a world of blocs. Even in 1993 this was a knife-edge decision requiring the lobbying effort of four American presidents (Clinton, Reagan, Bush, and Carter) together with an enormous effort by American business to overcome the protectionist lobby and win a very tight vote. And if a country does not play ball—if New Zealand does not allow U.S. ships carrying nuclear weapons to dock at its ports, or Chile does not back the UN resolution to go to war with Iraq—it finds itself paying or threatened with trade penalties.

Today the coalition in favor of NAFTA would be impossible to assemble. American businesspeople and much of the political class may understand the benefits of free trade to the American business model and to the wider American public, but they are also wary of being on the wrong side of a new antiforeign populism. Populist feeling is reaching unexpected heights. Fifty-eight percent of Americans agreed that Congress acted correctly in opposing the acquisition of six U.S. port terminals by Dubai, with 41 percent saying they watched it closely—only 2 percent less than watched the Iraq war closely.[25] This episode ranked seventh among political stories attracting most interest since the mid-1980s, exceeded only by such controversial issues as court rulings on the pledge of allegiance (2002), the debates surrounding Clinton's health care plan (1993), and whether to lift the ban on gays in the military (1993).[26] American commitment to a rules-bound, open trading system based on free trade is weakening. The old-time religion of protection is making a comeback.

The Enlightenment Legacy

Yet it was never protectionism that stimulated America but rather the nation's pluralism and its Englightenment institutions. The difficulty is that even Americans find it hard to discern this truth, which is buried under a general celebration of liberty. Liberty, in the American narrative, is the sun under which everything flourishes. Liberty permits individuals' hard work, courage, and application to produce wealth and happiness. Government should not get in the way; nor should it tax the fruits of hard work. If unfair foreign competition puts hardworking Americans at a disadvantage, then it should be stopped. Liberty and the American dream are linked; they make for a pleasingly coherent story because the United States is so successful. The great conservative counterrevolution of the last thirty years has been grounded in its brilliant capacity to exploit these cultural icons to support its own cause.

And liberty is indeed crucial to the American story, but not in the way the story is conventionally told. American liberty has been advanced within a highly sophisticated Enlightenment political infrastructure. The danger from excessive private power has been as well understood as the danger from excessive public power.[27] The founding fathers' concept of checks and balances in government has been an essential guarantor of pluralism; and free speech, the rule of law, argument, debate, and justification are part of the warp and woof of U.S. institutions and culture. Also, the United States has cherished a deep conviction that all men and women are born equal. In reality, the United States has always been an unequal society, but as Benjamin Friedman of Harvard argues in *The Moral Consequences of Economic Growth*, there has been, until recently, sufficient prospect of mobility and change to construct a conceptual equality—a belief that even if my circumstances are inferior to yours, there is a very good chance that our children might change places.[28] Moreover, the republic was lucky in having considerable ability to generate cultural support for this view: for three or four generations after its founding, there was almost limitless free land. Settlers could get an equal stake and so had a chance of moving upward and becoming individually empowered. The Louisiana Purchase, the acquisition of Florida, the annexation of Texas, and the securing of Oregon, between 1800 and 1850, added 2 million square miles of land to the country. Whether with the decision in 1785 to grant land ownership absolutely "fee simple," so that the ownership was unqualified, or with the Homestead Act of 1862 entitling any settler to claim ownership after five years' tenure, the U.S. approach has been that everyone has a right to property. It has been a crucial social safety valve.

Look at the United States through the same lens with which I have analyzed China, and you will see an economy and society characterized by pluralism, diversity, and investment in individual capabilities. Moreover, every nook and cranny is characterized by accountability, scrutiny, and justification. Whether in the crystallization of the concept of the company, the acceptance of the rule of law, the commitment to education, or the normative acceptance of the need for a free press, this country is the living embodiment of the link between the Enlightenment and economic growth that is at the heart of this book. It is true that in the first decade of the twenty-first century these institutions are atrophying through neglect and willful disparagement of their importance, in particular by American conservatives. But it is hard to imagine that they will never be rediscovered.

I have already mentioned that Alexis de Tocqueville, touring the young republic in the mid-1830s and trying to understand the particular forces in its dynamics, identified what he described as "equality of conditions" as the central feature animating its economy and society. American egalitarianism even in the 1830s never had the leveling-down character that European egalitarianism would assume. Rather, it was an aspirational egalitarianism in which all citizens—equipped by property ownership, education, and the enfranchisement conferred by the Constitution—could aim equally high. Americans had both the mind-set—the willingness to embrace the modern and abandon tradition, imagining a life they would construct for themselves—and the capacities to act on their will. The Enlightenment public sphere was the essential component of this culture, enfranchising everyone and entitling everyone, as de Tocqueville wrote, to participate in public debate and deliberation. That in turn imparted a sense of self-esteem and self-confidence in the pursuit of one's private affairs. Public engagement and never-ending argument leavened what otherwise might have been a culture of egoism, argued de Tocqueville, and transmuted it into a culture in which egalitarianism and individualism enriched each other. Self-interest was not only a matter of bettering oneself; it was also a matter of ensuring that there would be a vigorous public life and opportunity for others. American intellectuals, for example, whether natural rights republicans, Jeffersonian liberals, or land reformers, have simultaneously championed the right of an individual to own property and wanted to see property fairly distributed.[29] This same impulse—wanting the best for oneself and for others—prompts much of American civic activism.

Commitment to education was also intimately connected with egalitarian culture. In 1830, for example, nineteen of the then twenty-four states had given every man the vote, and each made education a high priority. As early as 1874 school districts were allowed to raise public funds for not just primary but also secondary education.[30] Universities were established in every state, generously endowed with hundreds of thousands of acres—an act of farsightedness and commitment to higher education from which the United States is gaining ever-greater dividends. The proportion of GDP going to tertiary education is currently twice that of the European Union.[31] Egalitarianism went into the marrow of what was taught and how it was examined. Claudia Goldin of Harvard, the leading authority on the history of the U.S. education system, notes:

> If the American system is characterized as open, infinitely forgiving, lacking universal standards, and academic yet practical, the European system was closed, unforgiving, with uniform standards, and academic for some and industrial for others. One was egalitarian; one was elite.[32]

By 1900 the educational gap between the United States and the rest of the industrialized world was very wide—but so was the extent of the franchise. European countries came to democracy later, and to mass education later. The United States had mass secondary education for both boys and girls, and the curricula and exams were structured so that every child had an opportunity to find a subject in which he or she could at least pass if not excel. Its pupils fed a mass college system that also had no parallel, and its universities were emerging as intellectually preeminent in the world. When Truman signed the GI Bill in 1944, giving every GI the right to a college education, Britain was just about to enact its own education bill, which gave each British teenager the same access to secondary education that was already fifty years old in the United States.

This investment in individual capability led the world, and it drove growth in productivity first in agriculture and then, later in the century, in industry. American industrialists—the Carnegies, Pullmans, Fords, and Rockefellers—could organize and coordinate production on a scale unknown in Europe because as a precondition they had the people with the skills and educational background capable of engineering and managing the often complex logistics. Without corporate organization of production this could not have happened. Crucially, the speed and facility with which the American corporation developed as an organizational, financial, and legal entity also sprang from the Enlightenment infrastructure of the United States. Within a generation of the signing of the Constitution the corporation was a common part of American life; entrepreneurs were petitioning states to form corporations with a declared purpose and formal rights for investors because under the Constitution, companies had the same legal rights as individuals to own land and develop their business.

To produce on the enormous scale that the U.S. internal market permitted meant raising vast amounts of risk capital and loans. Doing so in turn required transparent financial accounts, management, and processes in which governments, banks, and investors could be confident. The corporation, with its complex accountability networks, solved the problem. But this expression of capitalism was rooted in the United States' Enlightenment approach to accountability, the rule of law, and justification. Shareholders could pursue their rights under the law. Companies had to deliver what they promised or explain why not. That accountability contributed to the dynamism of American capitalism.

Nobody would or could pretend that industrialization in the United States was anything other than turbulent and often brutal. This, after all, was the era of the robber barons and vast private fortunes. But another Enlightenment principle informed it throughout—a deep belief in the pluralist requirement to set up countervailing power to limit monopoly and check arbitrary private power. The twenty-nine-year quest to break up the Standard Oil Trust, which had been founded in 1882 with a virtual monopoly of U.S. oil and refinery production, finally succeeded in 1911. This was a result of Enlightenment institutions and culture in action: the application of the law in the Sherman Antitrust Act and the Supreme Court's final judgment; the muckraking, campaigning journalism of a free press that exposed Standard Oil's nefarious practices and blatant profiteering; the instinctive sense that private monopoly was as problematic as state power; the insistence that notwithstanding its private character the company is nonetheless a public actor; and of course the belief in competition. All contributed to the spectacular breakup, one of the most celebrated in American corporate history.

The growth of vigorous independent journalism in the United States during the second half of the nineteenth century and into the twentieth century played an indispensable role in keeping the system more honest and creating American successes.[33] The number of independent newspapers quintupled between 1870 and 1910. The press in New York challenged Tammany's control of the city and state. And it was the muckraking tradition, along with Upton Sinclair's novel The Jungle, that gave the United States its first proper regulation of food and medicine in the Food and Drug Act of 1906. The press was the arm of the citizen in holding private and public power to account, an irreplaceable watchdog policing scandal and corruption alike. It developed singularly high standards for evidence, and for balance.

The Radio Act of 1927, reflecting the Enlightenment culture, required licenses to be distributed on the basis that licensees served the "public convenience, interest, or necessity." In 1949, the Federal Communications Commission adopted the doctrine as a formal rule.

Pluralism Works

All these forces combined to share in, guide, and foster the emergence of an astonishingly vigorous capitalism and propel it in the direction of serving a wider interest. Thus the Interstate Commerce Act of 1887 set out to ensure that trusts and corporations did not abuse their power across state lines, in particular in the setting of rail prices. In 1903 Theodore Roosevelt persuaded Congress to establish the Department of Commerce and Labor, to ensure better regulation; a separate Department of Labor was created in 1913. Rail regulation was introduced by the Hepburn Act of 1906. The Federal Trade Commission was created in 1911 to prevent fraud and misleading practices. The Federal Reserve Act of 1913 aimed to bring stability to the banking system. The Clayton Antitrust Act of 1914 outlawed monopoly and unfair price discrimination. Private power had to be institutionally challenged and regulated in order to try to make the pluralist system regulate itself more effectively as a pluralist system—a concept that even extended to labor law. By 1896 Pullman and Carnegie had broken strikes, and Pullman had introduced yellow-dog contracts under which workers promised not to join a union; but despite this, in *Veghelan v. Gunther* in 1896 Justice Holmes wrote: "Combination on the one side is potent and powerful. Combination on the other is the necessary and desirable counterpart, if the battle is to be carried out in a fair and equal way." [34] In other words, trade unions were also a legitimate part of American pluralism—and indeed the Clayton Act explicitly excluded trade unions from its definition of anticompetitive combinations.

The corporation whose rise Alfred Chandler charts in his book

The Visible Hand thus had antecedents in this Enlightenment architecture.[35] Companies were developing and multiplying in Britain and Europe, but it was in the United States that they most rapidly developed their public character and scale. In 1832 the McLane report found only 106 manufacturing firms with assets greater than $100,000; by 1917 there existed more than 278 firms, each with more than $20 million in assets.[36] The twentieth-century American corporation would prove to be the most restless and dynamic driver of capitalism so far devised.

The United States had created a sophisticated system of justification and accountability without which the modern company could not have developed. Systematic audits, for example, promised integrity of financial affairs so that ownership could be dispensed among external investors and traded in company shares. That in turn allowed companies to operate at scale, coordinating production and distribution all over the United States. By the early 1930s, when Adolf Berle and Gardiner Means first observed that the management of a company and those who owned it were now divorced and separate functions, the modern company was truly born.[37] Shareholders now held management to account for the stewardship of a company's assets, its trading prospects, and the pursuit of its goals. Although this would lay the foundation for future problems when shareholders insisted their only aim was short-term profit maximization, at the time it was a revolution. An Enlightenment principle of accountability was at the heart of the capitalist process. The company had come of age.

Until the early 1970s the economic history of the United States is a story of this turbulent interaction between its Enlightenment architecture and associated culture mingling with egalitarianism and liberty on the one hand, and the driving energy of dynamic capitalism on the other. Episodes such as the suing of IBM and AT&T by the Department of Justice for abuse of their market position, and Franklin Roosevelt's overhaul of banking and securities regulation after the Wall Street crash, were ongoing efforts to maintain economic pluralism and keep private power accountable. Roosevelt's New Deal,

Truman's Fair Deal, and Johnson's Great Society were presidential initiatives to sustain the educational opportunities and stake in society that free land and basic education had provided in the nineteenth century. In the nineteenth century the Army Corps of Engineers had been vital in creating the national transport infrastructure, which was the precondition for mass production; in the twentieth century the tradition was carried on by 50,000 infrastructure projects began under the New Dealers and the postwar construction of the interstate highway system.[38] And no story of the Internet or the array of recent innovations such as nanotechnologies and magnetic resonance imaging is complete without reference to government funding.[39]

The United States had not arrived at its preeminent position by an exercise of pure liberty as the conservative Reaganite counterrevolutionaries and later neoconservatives have argued. Rather, liberty had been exercised within an Enlightenment constitutional framework that always included conceptual egalitarianism, which provided the tension between the ambition and appetites of the propertied rich and their accountability to society. This is not the egalitarianism of income or opportunity; rather, it is the equality of self-esteem, self-worth, and possibility. My circumstances in life might be different from yours today, but there is no obstacle of title, birth, accent, or social rank that would prevent my children from occupying the same place as you, or a higher place, because the Constitution and the expansive geography put us on the same footing and offer us the same possibilities. It was never markets and the price mechanism alone that created the United States; it was their fecund interaction with its Enlightenment infrastructure and the culture that flowed from it that formed the American genius. And it is that which is in peril today.

The American Condition

Imagine a twenty-four-hour parade of all Americans, with their height corresponding to their income. For the first four hours and fifteen minutes the spectators would see only very short people of five feet or less—those with incomes of no more than $20,000. Over the next nine hours there would be a progressive doubling in height; and over the following seven and three-quarters hours another doubling. You would have watched for twenty-one hours before you saw twenty-foot giants, people with incomes of $80,000. Another two hours and fifteen minutes would pass before you saw another doubling in height. In the last forty-five minutes the rate of increases in height would start to accelerate. Fifteen minutes before midnight individuals 200 feet high would be walking by, representing incomes of $400,000. In the last ninety seconds of the parade there would be individuals 400 feet tall, and then in the last seconds America's richest would pass by—21,750 feet tall.[40] They would be Himalayan beside the earlier molehills.

This is what is implied by inequality—and inequality in the United States is not just a matter of income but today also involves opportunity, life chances, neighborhood, and the experience of work. It is concerning work that the fears and anxieties of ordinary Americans are becoming most acute—and this is where their experience has been most rapidly changing. Over the last twenty years, according to an analysis by Louis Uchitelle in *The Disposable American,* 30 million American workers have lost their jobs because of downsizing and economic restructuring. As many as 30 million more have taken early retirement or left the labor market, never to return, for the same reason.[41]

Nor is that the only adverse impact on them. There has been a collapse in the value of pension benefits, as corporations wind up the old defined benefit pension, which gives retired workers a fixed proportion of their final salary, and replaced it with 401k plans that pay out much less. It may be true that with rising life expectancy, low interest rates, and a stagnating stock market, the defined pension benefit was insupportably expensive. But from the point of view of the average American worker, this is a lowering of his or her lifetime income. According to one calculation, every man, woman, and child in the

United States would need an additional $28,000 of assets to compensate for the lower income in retirement.[42] Then there is the fact that 45 million Americans do not have health care coverage.[43] And we should not overlook the 34 million people who work full-time for less than $8.70 an hour, the hourly wage necessary for a family of four to rise above the poverty level.

The middle class is also a subject of concern. There is a growing national preoccupation with the disappearing middle: the income of the typical two-child couple is hardly rising in real terms, and the number of middle-income households is steadily shrinking.[44] And while the great American middle class is under siege, a tiny elite of plutocrats prosper. As Thomas Piketty, director of studies at the École des Hautes Études en Sciences Sociales (EHESS) in Paris, and Emmanuel Saez, of the University of California, have shown in a path-breaking work, income distribution is slowly but surely returning to levels seen only during the "gilded age."[45] Economists use a measure of inequality called the Gini coefficient—the proportion of income earned by the top 10 percent of the income distribution over the bottom 10 percent—to compare inequality between countries. At 0.41 the Gini index of the United States outstrips that of Japan and Europe (0.25 and 0.32, respectively) and is only fractionally lower than China's (0.45).[46]

The growth of inequality is matched by a decline in social mobility: Americans are less likely today than a generation ago to move out of the socioeconomic group into which they were born. For example, boys from the bottom three-quarters of the socioeconomic scale were less likely to move up in the 1990s than in the 1960s. By 1998, the *Wall Street Journal* reports, only 10 percent of sons of fathers in the bottom quarter (defined by income, education, and occupation) had moved into the top quarter. Twenty-five years earlier more than double that proportion—23 percent of lower-class sons—had managed the move.[47] The exit rates from poverty tell the same story. Families with children are much more likely to stay poor in the United States than in Europe. The economist Gosta Esping-Anderson estimates that after three years American poor families are five times more likely to stay poor than their British, German, French, or Spanish counterparts.[48]

And there is a racist aspect to the figures. Seventeen percent of the children of poor white parents but 42 percent of the children of poor black parents stay at the bottom.[49] And as I reported in *A Declaration of Interdependence,* access to college is becoming ever more unequal. In 1979 a student whose family was in the top quarter of the income distribution was four times more likely to get a college degree than someone from the bottom quarter; by 1994 the likelihood had grown to ten times more. With regard to exit rates from poverty, the chance of moving upward from one's family, or the chance of going to college, the United States has become a more immobile, sclerotic society.

Americans expect better. Seventy-one percent of Americans believe that the poor have a good chance of escaping poverty; only 29 percent believe that they are trapped there. By contrast Europeans, living in more socially fluid societies, are nonetheless much more pessimistic about the chances of mobility. Only 40 percent believe the poor can escape their fate, and 60 percent believe they are trapped.[50] The utopian ideal of America—that through hard work you can achieve your place in the sun—is being confounded by everyone's actual daily experience. Benjamin Franklin was born the fifteenth son of a candle maker and retired at forty-two with enough of a fortune to comfortably pursue a life of politics and scientific inquiry. The opportunity for such mobility is retreating, and this is beginning to affect not just American society but the American imagination.

The Wheel Turns Full Circle

Against this background it is hardly surprising that globalization is regarded with growing alarm and has become widely debated. Lou Dobbs devotes part of his show *Lou Dobbs Tonight* on CNN to a fight against the export of American jobs. The claim is that 400,000 or 500,000 a jobs year are lost to outsourcing and relocation of production—and he likes to name the corporations and state governments that are guilty.[51] Meanwhile *American Prospect*, the magazine of the intellectual left, carries a polemic by a former candidate for the Democratic presidential nomination, Ernest Hollings, in favor of reviving the American protectionist tradition.[52] The columnist Tom Friedman of the *New York Times* titled his recent book *The World Is Flat*. But unlike Lou Dobbs or Ernest Hollings, Friedman is not a protectionist. Rather, he is an apostle of the new order. Protectionism would be self-defeating, he argues, damaging to the rest of the world and only a short-term escape from reality. The best response is to embrace change as an opportunity, to "upskill," and to concentrate on industries whose advantage is based on brain power, agility, and high value added rather than those based on low wages.

I am on the same side of this argument as Friedman, but I think the entire exchange should be cooled down. The impact of globalization is vastly exaggerated by him as much as by Dobbs and Hollings. It is true that the future of western economies—Britain and Europe as much as the United States—will be much more biased toward knowledge industries (broadly defined to include high-tech manufacturing, education, and the creative and cultural industries) and the service industries associated with them. And it is also true that education and skills are going to be more important in the future. But that is because of important trends within our economies driven by the usual forces of technological change, which are changing consumers' tastes, leading to higher disposable incomes and the secular growth of knowledge-based goods and services. It is alarmist, counterproductive, and intellectually wrong to associate the ills of western industrialized societies with globalization and with foreigners. Look more closely at what has been happening, especially in the United States, and the proposition begins to seem more ragged.

Every week the United States loses and creates 500,000 jobs. In any given year about one-fifth of the country's jobs have been eliminated but another one-fifth have been created. Some of this is due to the march of technological change; some is a result of restructuring to be better equipped to meet new tastes and preferences. It was ever thus and it is comparatively small changes in these very large numbers that can change the economic condition in the United States from being "job-rich" to "job-poor." But foreign trade has a minuscule impact. The most exhaustive and impartial inquiry into the impact of foreign trade on American jobs estimates that 226,000 jobs are lost annually—and the authors of the study believe that it is a high estimate.[53] As for China, calculations using the model built by the Economic Policy Institute, which is very hawkish on trade, can attribute only 2.24 million lost job opportunities to Chinese imports between 1989 and 2005. That is a little more than 100,000 a year.[54] As for offshoring, its impact is even smaller. The National Bureau of Labor Survey in 2004 identified 956,327 job losses from mass layoffs; only 16,073 jobs moved abroad.[55]

Globalization and the trade deficit do have an impact on the pattern of employment in the United States, and there may be a greater impact from offshoring in the future. But trade effects cannot begin to explain the totality of what has happened in the recent past—and certainly not the 60 million job losses attributable to downsizing and restructuring between 1984 and 2004 cited by Louis Uchitelle.[56] Nor does the avalanche of gloomy material about the impact of trade on U.S. employment mention the improvements in efficiency that derive from trade. The economists Scott Bradford, Paul Grieco, and Gary Clyde Hufbauer, who have used four different models for estimating trade effects, believe that $1 trillion of American GDP is the result of global integration.[57] Also, the United States has enjoyed a sustained consumer boom for most of the last twenty years, with only shallow recessions. We cannot explain that boom without recognizing the importance of sustained low interest rates and strong capital inflows—features of globalization that work to the advantage of the United States.

The relative rise of services and decline in manufacturing is inexorable, with or without trade. According to the Current Population Survey provided by the U.S. government, blue-collar and administrative support workers fell from 56 percent of all adult workers in 1969 to 39 percent in 1999.[58] The biggest compensating jump in employment was recorded for professional, managerial, and technical occupations, up from 22 percent to 32 percent over the same period. That rise reflects the growing importance of applying cognitive and judgment skills in an increasingly complex workplace. The growth in sales jobs—up to 12 percent from 8 percent—reflects not just a growth in American consumption but a growth in more complex and multiple products for which consumers seek sales advice. The increase in pure service occupations (cafeteria workers, janitors, security guards)—up to nearly 14 percent from 11.6 percent—also reflects the reality that some categories of jobs are physically rooted in place. It is structural change that is creating these changes, and trade is only a relatively small part of the story.

Nor is the divergence of wages and incomes within these fast-growing occupations due to the fact that the market values certain kinds of skills more highly in an era of globalization. If that were true, one would expect a rise in inequality to be associated with rising productivity. In fact the opposite is the case. The most rapid growth in inequality in the United States was between the late 1970s and the mid-1990s, when growth in productivity was falling. Skill was having little impact on underlying productivity in those years, but there was still a growth in inequality. If it were true that skills are driving income differentials, then we would expect the earnings of skilled workers to rise. But as Ian Dew-Becker and Robert Gordon of Northwestern University show,[59] between 1989 and 1997 (the latest date for which we have figures) the earnings of computer scientists and mathematicians rose by 4.8 percent, those of engineers dropped by 1.4 percent, and those of CEOs rose by 100 percent. What has driven the growth of inequality over the last thirty years is not the wage and salary income of the top 10 percent as a whole, which has grown hardly faster than the average, but that of the top 1 percent. The dramatic gains have been won by a tiny number at the very top. Income at the ninety-ninth percentile rose 87 percent between 1971 and 2002, they estimate; at the 99.9th percentile it rose 181 percent; and at the 99.99th percentile it rose 497 percent. Paul Krugman, writing in the *New York Times,* estimates that the last 0.001 percent are now earning more than $6 million on average.[60]

What has been taking place is a redistribution of income from the bottom 99 percent to the top 1 percent. This is not about skills and the development of the knowledge economy driving income disparities in an era of globalization. It is about market power, failures of corporate governance, and the increasing capacity of winners in today's society to take all. "Virtuous circle" effects are now so quick to be established, in industries as disparate as investment banking and football, and have such dramatic impacts on sales and profits, that those considered responsible can name their remuneration.

In short, it is not possible to offer a satisfactory account of job insecurity, rising inequality, and the acceleration of downsizing without recognizing the substantive changes that have taken place in the United States' own economic structures, institutions, and processes over the last twenty-five years. Those include the decline in labor union membership, the new priority given to maximizing shareholder value, the decline in impartial news media, and malfunctions in the political system. The circuit breakers and systems that used to stand in tension with the American market system, and so provided forward momentum, creativity, and underlying legitimacy for ordinary people, have been systematically undermined and scrapped. The embedded checks and balances in the economy, society, and polity have grown weaker as the United States has neglected its Enlightenment tradition. Americans' blues are largely homegrown.

CHAPTER 11

Born in the U.S.A.

THE RETREAT FROM THE AMERICAN ENLIGHTENMENT
tradition is a world event to rival the emergence of China. What began
in the 1970s as a conservative campaign to revitalize American capitalism has grown into something of a monster. Arguably American
capitalism by the late 1970s did need rebalancing, away from the
structures that had grown up over the previous thirty years; but today
some of the conservative authors of the revolution have themselves
become dismayed as they watch the flight from Enlightenment values. The former neoconservative Francis Fukuyama recently argued
that over the long term, multilateralism and the rule of law are better
ways of securing U.S. interests than preemptive unilateralism. The
former chairman of the Federal Reserve, Alan Greenspan, is concerned about the scale of the budget deficits that have resulted from
tax cuts and extravagant spending. Nancy Reagan, widow of Ronald
Reagan, has spoken out against cuts in stem-cell research spending by
the federal government. Milton Friedman, originator of monetarism
and a leading proponent of free-market economics, reminds us that
liberty was never meant to be understood as license. The conservative
columnist William Safire inveighs against the vast scope of government material that is now routinely classified as outside the purview
of the Freedom of Information Act because of supposed security concerns. All one way or another find themselves representing a tradition
in American life that is being eroded and derided.

The unraveling began in the 1970s, the decade whose disasters—
defeat in the Vietnam war, Watergate, and an escalating trade

271

deficit—seemed to testify to America's growing vulnerability. In 1974 inflation approached 12 percent, the worst in U.S. history during peacetime; and in 1975 unemployment touched 7.5 percent. All this seemed proof that America must change direction. The fact that the Vietnam war was unwinnable did not take the sting out of what by any standard was a humanitarian and tactical disaster. And it was scant relief that America's trade deficit might be testimony to the emerging economic strength of Europe and Japan, and thus to the success of the postwar policy—led by the United States—of stimulating their economic development. There were two unsuccessful attempts to assassinate President Ford. The Soviet Union invaded Afghanistan. The United States felt on the brink of relative economic, social, and even military decline. The confident Enlightenment center of American politics that had encompassed Eisenhower Republicans and Truman Democrats, the twin architects of the astonishingly successful postwar settlement at home and abroad, was now held responsible for failure by the ideological wings of both parties. For the centrists in the Democratic Party the decisive issue was Vietnam. Even today it is difficult for a Democrat to mount an argument that the original intent of the war was justifiable (communism was a threat and the war did buy a crucial fifteen years in which democracy and capitalism became rooted in Asia) without being decried as an amoral warmonger. Nor could the Democrats cohere around a program for the use of government, regulation, and the role of welfare while taking a credible position on inflation. The Enlightenment core of the party became overwhelmed by the left, by single-issue crusaders, and by proponents of the cultural war against the right. Meanwhile the Enlightenment centrists in the Republican Party could not find a way to defend the role of government, regulation, the legitimacy of taxation, and the redistributive fairness of welfare before the coalition of libertarians, free-market fundamentalists, and antistatists—and they in turn became overwhelmed. A political coalition initially founded as an economic argument has been transmuted into a socially conservative movement centered on cultural propositions concerning the family, abortion, the desirability of prayers in school, religion, and resistance to the sexual revolution. These extreme positions have left the Enlightenment tradition as weakened in the Republican Party as it is in the Democratic Party. The American Enlightenment center has been unable to hold. For thirty years the dynamic element in U.S. politics has been an aggressive conservatism allying itself with a radicalized evangelical movement.

The story is complex. While broad strands of opinion in the public at large have remained stable, there has been an increased unwillingness to look for common ground, with an ideological crystallization, especially on the right. In part this is a reflection of growing inequality in American society (which I discuss later), as Nolan McCarty, Keith Poole, and Howard Rosenthal explain in *Polarized America: The Dance of Ideology and Unequal Riches.* And in part it is a reflection of geography. The arguments of the intellectual right on the economy and society have coincided with the rise of the service industries and the decline of blue-collar manufacturing work. This shift has changed the economic center of gravity—and the center of population growth—from the northeast to the south and west. Between 1959 and 1989 the eight states enjoying the most rapid growth had all belonged to the Confederacy.[1] In these more naturally conservative parts of the country "frontier values" hold sway: self-help, voluntarism, and distrust of government. A cultural suspicion of "elite" liberal positions on social issues has grown.

The south and the west are also home to a disproportionate number of the nearly 100 million evangelical Protestants, who over the last twenty years have become more radicalized. As late as 1987 they split virtually fifty-fifty into Republican and Democrat camps. Now they are more than two to one in favor of Republicans.[2] As the political scientists William Galston and Elaine Kamarck argue in *The Politics of Polarization,* religiosity has become a newly important source of political identification.[3] What has propelled this change is the politicization of evangelical religion, which has become ever more ready to pick fights and oppose what it considers antifaith, anti-American values. The causes are varied. The American evangelical movement has a superabundance of denominations: the United States in 1996 had nineteen Presbyterian denominations, thirty-two Lutheran, thirty-six Methodist, thirty-seven Episcopal or Anglican, sixty Baptist, and 241 Pentecostal, according to one source.[4] These compete for congregations by trying to outdo each other in offering an intense religious experience. This is a sort of evangelical bidding war. Sixteen percent of Americans have changed their faith,[5] and one study reported that half the ministers in the American megachurches had themselves come from another denomination. The Republican Party has harnessed the power of the evangelical right to its political advantage, organizing in the churches and introducing evangelical discourse into its campaigns.

This recruitment of the evangelical right into the Republican base, with little effective resistance from mainstream Republicans, has determined the party's increasingly anti-Enlightenment stance. The Enlightenment center has not managed to marshal an effective counterargument or a majority coalition. American politics and culture have become polarized between a militantly ideological and dominant right, characterized by fervent anti-Enlightenment religiosity, and a more fragmented, less coherent coalition of liberals and centrists who remain loyal to American Enlightenment values and who have reconciled their religious beliefs with modernity. The *National Journal* mapped the ideological loyalties of Democrats and Republicans in 1999 and found for the first time no crossover: the most conservative Democrat was more liberal than the most liberal Republican.[6]

The consequence has been a general diminution of Enlightenment values and processes. Examples include biased new shows in the media, the collapse of labor unionism, and the emasculation of institutions that regulated monopoly, price rigging, accountancy, and corporate governance. The effect in all cases has been the same. The tension between the Enlightenment and the market that, with varying intensity, characterized the United States until the 1980s has been resolved in favor of the market, property, and the rich. This resolution has given the United States its particular character over the last twenty years.

The Economic Vicious Circle

The answer to questions of wages, downsizing, inequality, and declining social mobility is staring the United States and the many critics of free trade in the face, if they care to look. American managers have become more transactional and hawkish in their approach to their stewardship of companies. Over the last twenty-five years they have reconceived their purpose not as building a business but rather as maximizing immediate financial returns to shareholders. They transact, cut, restructure, and downsize rigorously to achieve that objective. The United States has evolved a new business culture. The culture of the first half of the twentieth century, with professional management teams dedicated to creating companies focused on investment, innovation, and R & D, and with a compact between labor and management, has become a financial engineering culture. Raising the share price has become the dominant objective of the CEO, the board, and the wider management team. A new logic holds sway: shareholders own the corporation and put their money at risk, and because the sole purpose of ownership is to maximize profits, the only strategic purpose of the corporation is to maximize the financial returns to shareholders. The share price is God. Everything is consecrated to raising it.

This thesis may be attractive in theory—it provides direction and what is good for the company must be good for the share price. But in practice it leads to destructive "short-termism." Individual savings are increasingly concentrated in funds managed by professional asset managers. The top 100 managers control $6.8 trillion worth of shares—52 percent of the value of the U.S. stock market.[7] These professional managers have become ever more restless in their quest for higher financial returns. The average annual turnover of shares in a portfolio has jumped from 15 percent of the portfolio in the mid-1960s to 100 percent today.[8] Short-term profit drives the buying and selling decisions of the average fund manager. This is true even though—as the analyst and founder of the Vanguard mutual fund group John Bogle (named by *Fortune* as one of the four investment giants of the twentieth century) has pointed out—high-turnover equity mutual funds yield lower financial returns than lower-turnover funds.[9] Fixation on short-term share prices not only destroys investment performance; it destroys the creation of value in business and biases management toward short-term cost strategies rather than long-term growth.

Downsizing and rationalization may be the best way to produce onetime gains through cost reduction, which pleases short-termist fund managers; but sustained growth in productivity is always associated with sustained growth in output and employment. In a revealing paper, Martin Baily and John Haltiwanger, together with Eric Bartelsman for the National Bureau of Economic Research, prove this point by examining the experience of no fewer than 140,000 American manufacturing plants. Theirs is one of the largest analyses of its type.[10] Productivity increased in the plants that expanded output and employment; those that were downsizing experienced mostly decreased productivity. This is one of the oldest truths in economics and business. There is a virtuous circle of growth in output, growth in employment, and growth in productivity; and there is a vicious circle of stagnation in output and employment together with falling productivity.

The takeover of another business—the transaction that, above any other, offers an apparent route to rationalization, reorganization, and cost minimization—in reality generally moves companies from the virtuous to the vicious circle. The scale of mergers, acquisitions, and takeovers in the United States is breathtaking. In the 1960s and 1970s acquisitions ran at between 2 and 4 percent of GDP. Over the last ten years they have averaged about 10 percent of GDP, spiking to over 15 percent of GDP in the late 1990s when the stock market was very bull-ish. In hard cash the cumulative value of deals between 1995 and 2005 was $9 trillion. Of this, $4 trillion occurred 1998 and 2001 alone.[11] In other words, over the last decade such deals have been cumulatively equivalent to nearly 100 percent of GDP. This is the origin of so much downsizing in the United States.

But mergers and acquisitions have proved not to be the route to the promised improvement of either the share price or the efficiency of the underlying assets. *BusinessWeek* conducted a study of 302 deals of more than $500 million between 1995 and 2001.[12] It found that 61 percent of the deals delivered a 25 percent lower rate of return to shareholders than the industry average: buyers consistently overpaid for the companies they bought, overestimated the synergy, found that marrying two disparate businesses was very difficult, and obsessed over trying to cut costs to justify the takeover rather than make the business grow. Bringing together two living social organisms—two companies—is fantastically difficult, as is paying a price that repre-sents a realistic chance of success. The few successful takeovers in the study could not compensate for the scale of overall losses. Nor is the *BusinessWeek* study unusual; every other study of mergers comes to similar conclusions. The management consultant McKinsey's, for ex-ample, reviewing 160 mergers between 1992 and 1999, discovered that only twelve of the merged groups succeeded in lifting organic growth above the trends that that existed before the merger; the other 148 failed.[13] Another management consultant, KPMG, found in a sur-vey of more than 700 cross-border mergers between 1996 and 1998 that only 17 percent of them added value. As many as 53 percent actu-ally destroyed shareholder value, with the remaining 30 percent mak-ing no difference.[14]

The merger of AOL with Time Warner in January 2001 has be-come legendary as an example of why takeovers happen and why they go wrong. On the one hand there was AOL, the Internet com-pany, where the share price had become "the group's mission, a sacred trust."[15] As became obvious after the merger, AOL had sacrificed everything, including business probity, to maintain growth in quarterly earnings. On the other hand, the venerable Time Warner celebrated an Enlightenment value: a free press, the *Time* culture. The two organizations could not be more different, but that did not prevent either CEO from extolling the synergy to be had from merging the best of the new economy with the best of the old. Twelve months later Gerald Levin, Time Warner's CEO, had been forced from office because of the culture clash. He had put journalistic standards before cost-cutting, declaring in one e-mail that after 9/11, *Time* had a "fundamental moral responsibility" to the ideals of journalistic independence and democratic dialogue.[16] Within another twelve months nearly all the senior AOL team had also left, and AOL's business was under a cloud because of accounting irregularities. The synergy that had promised to be so impressive was nonexistent. Thirty months after a merger that had been launched with such fanfare, the organization took $99 billion of write-offs, paid a $300 million fine to the SEC for accounting improprieties, and was facing $3 billion in payments to settle a class action suit. The fall in the share price from about $100 to $11 represented a $200 billion loss for shareholders.

What motivates the orgy of deal making is that it is the CEO's easiest answer to the question from shareholders and boards about how he plans to deliver above-average growth. Of course, the deal will usually also have the happy consequence of sharply increasing his own remuneration. Robert Bruner, professor at Darden Business School and author of *Deals from Hell*—a catalog of American mergers that have gone wrong—says that he talked a lot with senior executives in the course of his research: "They all tell stories about how they are charged with maintaining earnings growth. They can only get to 5 to 6 percent growth organically, yet the CEO has set a target that is much more ambitious, and they make up the difference by acquisitions."[17] The deal will presumably provide synergy; will provide an opportunity for cost-cutting to eliminate irrational duplication of activity; will propel the company to higher market share; and thus will confer the capacity to control prices and margins better. The argument always includes one or all of these points, and it is extraordinarily persuasive—as AOL's Stephen Case and Time Warner's Gerald Levin can ruefully testify.

What turns mere persuasiveness into action—despite the evidence that most deals will end in tears—is a set of interlocking perverse incentives that have no countervailing checks and balances. There are three preconditions for the epidemic. First, most companies no longer have a widespread, diverse ownership consisting of millions of shareholders who are committed to the company for the long term and whom any predator will find difficult, time-consuming, and expensive to convert to his cause. Financial institutions now account for half of all company shares, and as sellers they are addicted to deals, which help their investment performance. Persuade a dozen of them of your case, and you have a deal. Second, today's banks have a hugely enhanced capacity to raise large sums of cash, which can be lent to pay for takeovers by predator companies. Third, as Lucien Bebchuk and Jesse Fried of Harvard argue, as CEOs have become more powerful, because of the weak corporate governance system in the United States, their pay no longer depends on their performance.[18] What matters to a CEO is not whether a deal will succeed but whether it gives him a story to tell about how he will drive up profit; the resulting success or failure does not matter to his remuneration. Failure means a golden handshake, success means more share options. Either way, it is a win-win situation. In addition, as I have argued, deals are easier to finance and it is easier to persuade a few key shareholders to sell. Add the investment bankers, who broker the deals for a handsome commission, and the picture is complete.

Nor are these developments simply accidental. They are part of the retreat from the Enlightenment tradition and its associated belief that enterprise is a mission best pursued by a team of managers and workers who share goals, values, and beliefs. The duty of caring for the whole organization has been abandoned; the only duty is to shareholders. The aim has been to create all-powerful CEOs who want to boost the share price; thus the generous allocations of share options that have increased more than ten times over the last decade.[19] Despite some notable recent efforts, there has been little or no preoccupation with how corporations are governed, how directors are selected and held to account, and how shareholders can constitutionally challenge the power of CEOs.

John Bogle reports that the thousands of publicly traded firms faced an average of just eleven challenges per year during 1996–2002; and for companies with market capitalization exceeding a mere $200 million the average number of challenge was one. The chances of success for a challenge were close to nil.[20] As a result, CEOs have become more able to manipulate companies and corporate strategies to their own advantage.

After the collapse of the American banking system in the 1930s, regulations, checks, and balances were imposed to make sure it would never happen again. These have been steadily eroded. In 1998 the great Glass-Steagall Act of 1933, which sought to separate commercial and investment banking, was repealed. Controls on bank mergers, interstate banking, and interest rates have all been lifted. As a result the flow of credit to finance takeovers has become an avalanche. Accountants, hungry for lavish fees, have been complicit in presenting company accounts in the kindest of lights. Meanwhile, financial savings institutions, mutual funds, and insurance companies have grown rapidly as a result of tax breaks—but they are treated by the law as if they had no more power than individual shareholders. Unable to control or direct the enterprises they own, they have colluded in demanding that the managers simply raise the share price as the overriding goal.

Regulation in general has been allowed to atrophy, and to be captured by those it seeks to regulate. When the American Law Institute has attempted to tighten the procedures of corporate governance and the Financial Accounting Standards Board has tried to make companies account for stock options as a cost of running the business, they have been beaten back by business interests, sometimes unashamedly lobbying Congress.[21] The Securities and Exchange Commission, the widely admired and powerful securities regulator, has been allowed to become progressively poorer and enfeebled. After the Enron crisis it wanted to empower shareholders in poorly performing companies to be able to elect two directors to the board to gain information. The powerful Business Roundtable was fiercely against the idea; it lobbied Bush (as important sources of campaign funds the members of the Roundtable are extremely influential); and the SEC was made to drop the proposal.[22] The idea of regulation as essential to the health of the American economy has been mocked and derided. Challenges to corporate power, to price rigging, and to monopoly have become less and less likely. Corporate America has been encouraged to play the game of takeovers, mergers, monopolies, and downsizing. And play it has.

The Social Vicious Circle

The victim in all this has been the people. Corporate leaders pay lip service to the notion that their greatest asset is their workforce, but every action speaks otherwise. Essentially the injunction is to make higher profits—by downsizing, by outsourcing, by merging, by cutting out duplication, and by lowering wage rates per hour worked. Three of the most distinguished economists in the United States—William Baumol, Alan Blinder, and Edward Wolff—call this the "dirty little secret of downsizing."[23] Looking over the 1990s, they find the same phenomenon as Baily, Haltiwanger, and Bartelsman: that downsizing has not contributed one iota to growth in productivity. Rather, downsized companies have delivered the same or reduced output, but have succeeded in paying less for any given hour worked. In other words, downsizing is merely an effective way of holding down wages and transferring income from labor to capital.

The principal institutional opponent of downsizing is the labor union. American labor unionism has always struggled to find cultural, legal, and social roots; but even as late as the 1970s unions represented one-fourth of all American workers—aided by New Deal legislation and the willingness of much of U.S. business to accept their legitimacy and usefulness. Now in the private sector unions represent only about 8 percent of the workforce, and representation has also declined, though not so sharply, in the public sector. Part of the decline of unionism is due to the decline of large-scale manufacturing plants and of concentrations of white-collar workers in big offices. It is much harder to recruit and organize in much smaller-scale service-sector workplaces such as hotels, garages, and fast-food outlets, where the labor force is much more mobile and less inclined to accept unions' traditional appeals for mutual support. Success in this new economic structure demanded agility and adaptability, which the unions have notably lacked. Overly bureaucratic and locked in internal power struggles, they have presented an unattractive face to the public. The horror stories of corruption and thuggery have been difficult to live down, because they are true. For example, in 1969 the reformer Jock Yablonski of UMW and his family were murdered after he won the union presidency. Not only do potential members recall such acts; potential reformers are afraid of suffering the same fate.

Yet despite these issues, some 40 million workers declare they would like to join a union if given the opportunity.[24] Membership is low because of an ideological onslaught against unions by U.S. business, exploiting the antiunion bias in U.S. labor law. The most obstructive feature of this body of law is that a union will be recognized only if a majority of the workers vote for union representation. Determined employers use many strategies to deter employees from voting yes. For instance, an employer might threaten to move the workplace, though such threats are nominally illegal. Also, employers hire antiunion consultants, an industry that has mushroomed over the last twenty-five years, to make it as difficult as possible for unions to organize. Employers harass union activists and organizers and use temporary or contingent workers who are less likely to join a union. Or an employer might locate in a state with a right-to-work clause that de facto makes organizing a trade union nearly impossible. If an employer finds that there is an existing union, he or she can use federal courts to appeal decisions by the National Labor Relations Board to adjudicate disputes (federal courts are felt to be more pro-employer), thus undermining the purpose of union membership. There are any number of avenues open to a hawkish manager who is motivated by shareholder value and who wants to lower costs by having no union to deal with—and all these avenues have been taken in varying degrees. Nor is there any popular or cultural backlash. In the prevailing environment, to defend a union as a source of Enlightenment-style countervailing power in the workplace is to be branded as antienterprise and hostile to the individual's right to work.

The new insecurity pervades the work experience. Human resource management, for example, is meant to be the organizational discipline responsible for training, developing, and nurturing the company's workforce and fostering a high-performance workplace that supports an organization's goals. But it is a profession in crisis because of the wide gap between its rhetoric and its achievements. The high-performance workplace supposedly consists of strongly motivated, self-managed, autonomous teams with a high level of education and skills that undergo continual "reskilling" to adjust for changing market conditions. In both the United States and Britain, where the tradition of vocational training is weak, it is very difficult to establish the culture of the high-performance workplace. Reskilling has to be done on the job because no wider institutional structure exists for it to be done any differently. Anglo-Saxon management is always tempted by the siren call of transacting its way to short-term cost reduction with a compliant, nonunionized workforce that it directs from the top. Autonomy and high performance are aspirations rather than deliverable reality—hence the crisis in human resources. The trouble is that countervailing forces—unions, workplace regulation, or obligations to train which might lean against the trend to transactionalism and low-performance workplaces—are disappearing. The case for low regulation thereby has become self-fulfilling. In the United States and Britain, regulation of the labor market is at the bottom of the international league table: business interests in both countries insist that it must stay at the bottom.

It is hardly surprising, as the social commentator Richard Sennett writes in *The New Capitalism*, that employees have become distrustful of and cynical about their employers' intentions. Sennett and his researchers interviewed a panel of workers in Britain and America for more than ten years and found a pervasive and growing sense of uselessness. Employees—white-collar, skilled, and less skilled workers—are keenly aware that even if they work hard and acquire skills, they can be laid off through no fault of their own, but simply as a by-product of a merger or reorganization dreamed up to tell a story about future profitability. The idea of work as the progressive development of one's skills, in order to apply one's craft and do a job well in an organization that appreciates experience, is dissolving. Instead, work becomes a series of episodes rather than an evolving narrative about deepening one's professionalism and skill over one's working life. The new injunction is to discard the past and embrace the new. What counts is not what you have done, but the capacity you are judged to have in adapting to the new. In her book *Bait and Switch*, Barbara Ehrenreich observes that applicants for jobs are advised not to submit a résumé that extends more than ten years. Experience is considered a possible obstruction to one's ability to change and move on.[25]

Calls for workers to reskill themselves and educate their children are futile in a system that is systematically biased against the poor and the unskilled. Disadvantage begins at birth and continues in early childhood, now understood to be a critical period for intellectual and emotional development. It is vital for a child's development either to have an adult parent at home full-time, implying forgone income, or alternatively child care, averaging $4,500 a year, which is beyond most working families. Neighborhood determines the wealth of a school, because schools are financed by local property taxes. Scores on the Scholastic Aptitude Test (SAT), which is the passport into the higher education system, closely correlate with family income. International comparisons of standard achievement tell the story. Early education remains of high quality; American fourth-graders do well. But eight years later American students have fallen behind their international peers, especially in mathematics and science. And for those who drop out of the educational or standard vocational route to achievement, there is little likelihood of a second chance. In Germany 80 percent of school dropouts go on to receive some form of vocational degree; in the United States only 54 percent do.[26] Twenty-seven million adult working Americans do not have a high school diploma.

The community college system struggles to carry out its mandate. More than half of its students have full-time jobs; 16 percent are single mothers. Community colleges are democratic and inclusive, but they have increasingly become a second-class system for those who cannot pay their way to academic success. The courses are ill-coordinated with those in the United States' 2,000 corporate universities, and there is no national system to ensure good and rising common standards and curricula. The dropout rate is high, and the standards are increasingly variable. Community colleges fall a long way short of a system that might provide the basis for comprehensive lifelong learning.

In the nineteenth century there was no hesitation about creating a first-class infrastructure of public education for all, funded by the taxpayers. But in the twenty-first century such structures are accused of being a wasteful burden and ineffective because they are public. It is no accident that nineteen of America's top twenty world-class universities are private. In the contemporary United States, universities have used high fees to put themselves in a virtuous circle, from their point of view: these fees enable them to pay for the world's top teachers, researchers, and intellectuals.[27] Annual tuition fees above $30,000 are increasingly common; and tuition together with living expenses means that students can graduate—even allowing for some college, state, and federal grants—with debts in excess of $100,000. Fewer people, especially in the struggling middle class, are entitled to need-based student-aid programs like the Pell grants, which are generally awarded to students whose family income is under $40,000. And even the Pell grants have not kept pace with tuition fees and living costs: they covered 80 percent of the costs at four-year colleges twenty years ago, compared with just 40 percent today. Young people from poorer families are increasingly barred from attending college. Families whose incomes are below the median account for little more than 10 percent of students; families in the top quarter for about three-quarters.[28]

Defenders of the system argue that, at least, the United States is a great job-generating machine. No more. The pace of job creation is dramatically lower in the current economic cycle than in previous cycles.[29] Employment has grown a mere 1.5 percent in the upturn. In the past, growth has grown this feebly only during recessions, near recessions, and the famous jobless recovery of 1992 and early 1993.

As Henry Farber of Princeton University discusses, losing a full-time job in the United States is traumatic despite the good chance of finding new work.[30] Using the Displaced Workers Survey, he finds that nearly half of all Americans who lost their jobs between 2001 and 2003 (at the time of writing in May 2006, the survey for 2003–2005 had not been published) either had not found work (35 percent) or had found only part-time work (13 percent). Moreover, those who found full-time jobs earned about 13 percent less than they had in their old jobs. Those with a college degree lost more earnings than college graduates in the past. Thus for workers in "flexible" labor markets, job loss is not only traumatic but costly. In this atmosphere it is natural to look for a scapegoat. Chinese imports and menacing foreigners come easily to hand.

The Imploding Public Realm

A great democracy should be able to organize a public discourse in which these issues and fears are debated, some resolution is achieved, and remedial action is taken. Of course parties, interest groups, and individuals still fight hard for their ideas, with more or less success. No doubt, some conservatives reading these pages will think that the criticism of American democracy as retreating from its Enlightenment legacy is little more than liberal sour grapes. If the roles were reversed and we were living in a period of liberal hegemony and bias, they might ask, would the criticism be so fierce?

I submit that it would. In the first place, a core Enlightenment concept is a public space where arguments compete freely for acceptance amid the widest public possible on the basis of objective evidence. Free, independent media with access to good resources are crucial in the construction of such a public space and in the development of shared experience. But this concept is under fire in the United States. The "fairness doctrine" was the broadcasters' obligation to report fairly and objectively. It existed since 1929, first as a voluntary principle; later it was built up through a series of rulings by the Federal Communications Commission and the Supreme Court and came to have the force of law. It was abolished in 1987, however; and now the networks have the right to be partisan. It is a concession exploited most aggressively by Fox News, which for all its liveliness runs a news agenda kind to conservatism in general and the Republican Party in particular. It may only be exercising its new right, but to claim its coverage is fair and balanced is a step too far. It betrays the real values of America's great Enlightenment tradition.

This is more than just a controversial marketing ploy; it signifies the general direction in which American news coverage has been moving for more than a decade.[31] The abolition of the fairness doctrine was a turning point. The argument was that individual news and current affairs program no longer had to apply a public-interest notion of balance, fairness, and objectivity. Rather, broadcasting (with the explosion in the number of of broadcast media outlets) could be treated in the same way as newspapers, which have no obligation to be fair. In the 1920s, when radio was dominated by a few monopolistic broadcasters, it had been right to insist on fairness; no more. Listeners and viewers should be allowed to choose the editorial stance they prefer, as they do with newspapers; and balance would be achieved through many media outlets offering a multiplicity of views.

But the broadcast media are not like print. Skim over a printed page, and you will see many more stories and commentaries than the sequential episodes in a news broadcast—which is necessarily linear in the way it must be seen or heard. The reader has the opportunity to read outside his or her original choices and chance on something unexpected or challenging; what we hold in common is broadened. Once the principle of fairness is surrendered in broadcasting, every sequential episode, interview, report, or film can come from the same philosophic viewpoint, with no contrary or offsetting opinion. What is held in common is narrowed to the prejudices we share with one particular minority. Today, Internet news is becoming highly personalized, simultaneously screening out what the user is not interested in and reducing what is held in common. Broadcasting is moving in the same direction.[32]

The sense of media beleaguerment and retreat is palpable. The three network news broadcasts lost 40 percent of their audience between 1981 and 2001; the mission of NBC's *Nightly News,* declared its anchor, Tom Brokaw, in 2000, had become no more than survival.[33] The threat also affects newspapers, whose circulation, editorial self-confidence, and sense of cultural importance are all shrinking. There is a migration to entertainment, as I noted in Chapter 8, and also considerable caution about challenging the prevailing consensus—over the Iraq war, campaign financing, the dot.com bubble, or almost any other journalistic subject. The owners of the media aid the onslaught. Westinghouse owns CBS, GE owns NBC, and Disney owns ABC. The Tribune group of newspapers own—among others—both the *Los Angeles Times* and the *Chicago Tribune.* Institutional shareholders own more than half of the *New York Times* and the *Washington Post.* All adopt the same transactional approach to their media assets as they do to any other assets, seeking to maximize shareholder value, reducing editorial staffs and budgets, and refusing to accept that the media have a special vocation. The *Tribune,* having squeezed the editorial budget of the *Los Angeles Times* ever since the acquisition, insisted on cutting sixty more reporting jobs after the *Times* had won five Pulitzer Prizes in 2004. The editor resigned. CBS News used to have a global network that included fourteen major foreign bureaus, ten minibureaus, and stringers in forty-four countries. Today, CBS only has eight foreign correspondents and three bureaus. Foreign news is increasingly supplied by four of the London-based correspondents voicing over news agency video feeds.[34] And so it goes on. Despite some exceptions, such as the Pulitzer Prize–winning investigation of federal wiretapping of the public's phones, the great muckraking journalism of the early twentieth century is a distant memory.

On radio the talk show has become largely the preserve of aggressively conservative hosts, of whom Rush Limbaugh is the best known. Limbaugh's daily three-hour show, whose agenda in the past has been in sync with the Republican high command, attracts 14 million listeners. Sean Hannity, who cohosts *Hannity and Colmes* on Fox News (which has twice the audience of its rival CNN), has only a slightly smaller audience for his daily radio show.

Opinion has become more important than fact, so that many facts that do not fit an a priori thesis are simply not broadcast. Suddenly one of the core attributes of an Enlightenment civilization—citizens' access to information and evidence on which to debate reasoned public arguments—is seriously undermined. Too many Americans are consuming one-sided opinionated vitriol rather than actual news. Limbaugh routinely complains that the eternal enemy is liberalism. *Air America*, a liberal rejoinder, has come to the game too late. It has a tiny audience and hardly redresses the lopsidedness of coverage. Without the fairness doctrine, the Enlightenment tradition is being eroded—and all the U.S. media are affected.

Ignorance about public affairs, especially among people under forty, is dismaying. As a result, public opinion is becoming more and more manipulable. This is how a new common sense has been established, notwithstanding the facts. America's jobs are under siege from China even when they are not. The war in Iraq is a war against the terrorists who were responsible for 9/11 when there is no evidence of any link between Al Qaeda and Saddam Hussein. There was so much disinformation and so little high-quality journalism about the tax cuts of 2001 and 2003 that only half those polled in 2003 could even recall the tax cut of two years earlier. The more they were informed about tax cuts, the more they opposed any.[35] This is not a media culture that empowers citizens to hold their rulers to account. Rather, it is a media culture that disempowers citizens and empowers the governors.

Unequal Politics

At the heart of the crisis of Enlightenment values lies the United States' political system. The Enlightenment concept of democracy has four bases: accountability; representativeness; respect for the rule of law; and the capacity, through free speech, for debate, exchange, and interaction. By these standards the U.S. system is increasingly compromised. The accountability process is silting up; the spirit and sometimes the letter of the law are evaded; the representativeness of elected officials is declining; and the quality of exchange and debate is chronically poor. The capacity of American democracy to hold political decision makers to account, to represent the people, to contribute to their happiness, and to execute their real wishes is becoming enfeebled.

The starting point is voting. Every citizen's vote is technically equal, but some citizens—the wealthier ones—are more equal than others. Rich people are much more likely to vote than poor people. Because parties and candidates focus on actual voters, the rich have more influence over them than the nonvoting poor.[36] In 2000, 87 percent of the richest third of the population voted, compared to only 60 percent in the poorest third, and the trend has been getting worse. Five million former felons are forbidden to vote for the rest of their lives. The increasing inequality that I mentioned at the end of the last chapter thus extends to voting; the more people are at the bottom of the income distribution, the lower voter turnout is likely to be—and the more the actual voters will be better-off people.

Furthermore, winning elections has become ever more expensive, and so parties have become more reliant on their richer members and on business. In 1974 a candidate successfully challenging an incumbent member of the House of Representatives spent $100,000 in real terms; today the average winning challenger spends more than $1.5 million.[37] This is an invitation for the richer voters to increase their influence. In 2000, one-eighth of American households had annual incomes greater than $100,000, yet these households made up 95 percent of those who gave $1,000 dollars or more to political campaigns that year. Fifty-six percent of those with incomes of $75,000 or more reported making some form of campaign contribution. But only 6 percent of Americans with incomes under $15,000 contributed.[38] And if the campaign contributors are not citizens, they will be local, state, or national lobby groups and businesses—which expect a payback in access and legislation when their candidate is elected.

This puts candidates more and more in thrall to their electoral base; and that trend is exacerbated because increasing inequality in cities and towns is creating polarized districts. Hispanics and blacks, for example, live increasingly in one part of town that becomes a safe Democrat district; well-off white voters live in another part that becomes a safe Republican district. Politicians in both parties have been setting the boundaries of their electoral districts to reflect the socioeconomic character of their base; in effect they have been choosing their voters to capture their district for their party. In 1994 ninety-six congressional races were tight, won by 55 percent of the vote or less; by 2004, there were only thirty tight races. In 2004, three-fifths of the nation's counties gave a supermajority of 60 percent or more to either presidential candidate. In 1996, only two-fifths did. As Mark Gersh, the Washington director of the National Committee for an Effective Congress, observes, "No matter how the voters feel, about 90% of the districts are now preordained to go to a certain party."[39] The most blatant gerrymander was devised by the now disgraced former House majority leader, Tom DeLay, in Texas. The system now works so that if Republicans carry just 45.9 percent of the Texan statewide vote, they hold a majority in the statehouse. And if they carry 51.9 percent of the vote, they win not only 70 percent of statehouse seats but twenty-two out of thirty-two congressional districts—helping to ensure a Republican majority in the House of Representatives.[40]

In a world of gerrymandered and majority-minority districts the key to a congressional seat is winning the primary. And the key to that is to be ideologically purer than one's opponent, to please the base rather than any swing voters. Barry Burden, now at the University of Wisconsin, reports that a primary typically pulls a congressional candidate ten points toward an ideological pole on a scale of zero to 100.[41] The activists, the interest groups, and the talk show hosts create the highly charged ideological atmosphere in which the primary takes place. This would matter less if most congressional districts were subsequently genuinely contested. The problem is that the ideologically sound candidate is virtually wafted into Congress unchallenged— and without having to defend his or her positions in a serious public exchange.

This new environment is kinder to Republicans than Democrats. Because the Republican Party is more inclined to represent the views, policies, and interests of the better-off, it finds itself sailing with the political winds. Its rise has coincided with more ideological militance and coherence from components of the Republican base, and the political system has permitted that trend to have more expression. The Democrats, on the other hand, have faced a harder political task: to find a common program and a leader who can combine the liberal professional classes, increasingly preoccupied with single issues, and the traditional blue-collar base into a cohesively organized, disciplined, and ideologically focused movement. They have not succeeded. The presidential candidacies of a succession of losing Democrats, Bill Clinton aside, testify to the scale of the difficulty; and even Clinton could not hold the coalition together.

The wider national political problem, as the authors of *Off Center* argue, is not that the conservatives control the political agenda; that is the privilege of a winning party and a majority body of opinion in a democracy. Rather, the problem is that they give little evidence of reflecting the values or attitudes of the majority who elected them. They seem to reflect, instead, the values and attitudes of a narrow ideological base that dictates the outcome of the primaries and those who bankrolled them. For despite the conservative ascendancy Americans are no more conservative today than they were thirty years ago. There is no popular groundswell in favor of the notion that government is too powerful. The National Election Survey reports that although 49 percent of respondents agreed with that proposition in the 1970s, the proportion had fallen to only 39 percent in 2000.[42] Nor is there any popular demand for tax cuts. In 2000, 39 percent of Americans wanted to spend more "even it means an increase in taxes"; only 18 percent wanted to spend less. Again, the proportion had if anything moved away from the conservative stance since the early 1990s.[43]

Yet the American political system has been transfixed by the politics of tax cuts. On June 7, 2001, Bush signed into law the Economic Growth and Tax Relief Reconciliation Act, which together with further reductions in 2003 will cumulatively cost more than $4 trillion, if they are extended as their supporters hope. The loss of revenue in 2013 alone will total $430 billion, or 2.4 percent of GDP, equivalent to a 45 percent cut in Social Security benefits or a 53 percent cut in Medicare.[44] Yet there was no great popular demand for reductions of such magnitude. There was certainly no popular demand for 36 percent of the cuts to go to the richest 1 percent of Americans. There will be no popular demand for the cuts in Medicare, Social Security, and education that will need to be made to close the enormous deficit opening up in the public finances. The cuts made little economic sense in terms of stimulating either growth or enterprise; reducing the tax on dividends and capital gains was a much less effective form of economic stimulus or incentive than more general tax cuts—and the most effective stimulus of all would be an increase in educational and vocational investment.

Yet the cuts went ahead. When Paul O' Neill, the treasury secretary at the time, warned privately in autumn 2002 that the budget deficit was mounting dangerously and that there was no case for yet more tax cuts for the wealthy, he was rebuffed. Vice President Cheney replied tellingly: "Reagan proved that deficits don't matter. We won the election. This is our due"[45] Karl Rove told a wavering president, "Stick to the principle"—tax cuts for the better-off. This is not a democratic process that the founding fathers or the Enlightenment tradition would recognize. There was no effective debate or exchange by an informed citizenry, nor an attempt to establish what the citizens wanted and what would be in their interest. Rather, the executive and legislative branches of government were captured by a faction that looks after its own very particular interest group.

Nor is unwanted policy restricted to tax cuts. Similar arguments could be made about climate change, the approach to terrorism, and privatizing Social Security. The political center of gravity is nowhere near the citizenry of what remains essentially an Enlightenment nation. American needs to escape the gathering drift toward closure and xenophobia and rediscover the values of openness, tolerance, and generosity of spirit.

That will not be easy, as Benjamin Friedman argues, without evidence of both growing prosperity and a belief that it is shared. Human beings feel better about themselves and their society if they feel they themselves are getting ahead, and if the general gains are not distributed too unequally. Indeed it is during periods of growth that people are less likely to feel the pangs of relative loss of status, because their own circumstances are improving; thus they are more willing to shoulder their share of paying for policies that promote equality. It is during periods of stagnation, when relative positions can become quickly and irrationally different, that people become fearful and inward-looking.[46] In the United States, great moral advances, such as those of the progressive era (1895–1919) or the civil rights era (1945–1973), have tended to accompany prosperity. Periods of moral retreat, such as the populist era (1880–1895) or the backlash of the

1980s and early 1990s, have been associated with stagnating incomes. Similar patterns hold in France, Britain, and Germany, Friedman argues. If he is right, today's environment of squeezed living standards and insecurity does not augur well.

The risks of a moral retreat are real. Ever since 9/11 there has been a mounting assertion that the only way to achieve national security is to be unilateralist, internationally aggressive against states that might harbor terrorists, and tough on civil liberties. As with tax cuts, it is not obvious that this stance represents what the majority of Americans want or think advisable; but the political system and the media permit very little argument or challenge to the consensual diagnosis. Now there is a wave of nationalist and protectionist sentiment which is rising unchecked toward hysteria, and which, as I have argued in this chapter, is unjustified by the facts. But the democratic process involving the media, the public, intellectuals, and politicians through which such facts might surface is grievously enfeebled. Turning America around is a formidable challenge. It must, however, be attempted.

And It Has Led to Iraq

The repudiation of Enlightenment values and processes reached its disastrous climax in the reaction to 9/11. The United States can no longer depend on deterrence, ran and runs the argument. Rather, it must preempt potential terrorist threats before they emerge. Declaring that "the gravest danger to freedom lies at the crossroads of radicalism and technology," Bush's new strategy cautions that "the United States can no longer rely solely on a reactive posture as we have in the past." In particular, the new National Security Strategy called for "anticipatory action to defend ourselves, even if uncertainty remained as to the time and place of the enemy's attack."[47] Condoleezza Rice, when she was national security adviser, admitted in July 2002 that the decision to invade Iraq was made even before the UN was first consulted in August 2002.[48] George Bush had decided that Iraq merited the new preemptive treatment. The United States was determined to go to war, with or without the authorization of the United Nations. Bush agreed to attempt to get a second UN resolution in the weeks leading up to the invasion in March 2003 only because British Prime Minister Tony Blair wanted to protect his own political position at home—in vain as it turned out. The Bush doctrine of preemption was now in full cry.

People who embrace Enlightenment values and international law find the doctrine of preemption problematic because it offers an open door to lawlessness, arbitrary government, lack of accountability, and warlordism. Within a democracy, preemption gives enormous power to the executive branch of government and the intelligence services charged with establishing whether there is a preemptive threat; the legislative branch of government is necessarily dependent upon the executive for information and therefore is inherently more manipulable. And because so much depends on judgment, there cannot be clear rules about determining when preemption is justified, so that justification—one of the key democratic functions—becomes close to impossible. The same difficulty applies internationally. Obtaining international agreement about what constitutes legitimate preemption is impossible because so much of a threat, unless it is obviously and unambiguously imminent, is based upon perception, so that there is enormous potential for exaggeration. Although there are occasions when a state may feel there is an imminent threat against which it must defend itself, there is inevitably more ambiguity and interpretation with regard to defense against terrorism. The truth of the matter, as Michael Ignatieff writes, is that preemption shades into unilateral aggression, which is illegitimate abroad and undermines the democratic process at home.[49]

The Iraq war is an ample and awesome warning of the dangers of the doctrine of preemption. The UN charter embodies the principle of nonaggression. In order to justify a preemptive war against Iraq, Bush had to characterize Saddam Hussein as presenting "a grave and gathering danger"—as he did in his speech to the UN in September 2002—because Iraq possessed weapons of mass destruction. Many western intelligence services certainly believed that Iraq did possess such weapons, and UN weapons inspector Hans Blix reveals in his memoirs that he did too, even if it is now clear that Iraq did not." [50] But the justification of a preemptive war could not be a matter of belief, suspicion, or an informed guess; the stakes were so high that the intelligence had to prove what the U.S. government wanted. The CIA, like the British MI6, knew in which direction the wind was blowing, as Paul Pillar, a former CIA official, has written, and it knew that unhelpful information would be played down or ignored. [51] A subtle process of politization and self-censorship began in which only the information that is wanted becomes the information that is available.

Actually, the process was not always so subtle. The Policy Counterterrorism Evaluation Group set up by the Pentagon publicly derided the CIA for doubting that there were direct links between Saddam Hussein and Al Qaeda. In such an atmosphere—Tony Blair has acknowledged that in Britain intelligence and policy were "commingled"—intelligence becomes the servant of the executive branch of government, and the justification and accountability process essential to democracy is undermined. [52] The U.S. Congress and the British House of Commons went along with what their executives wanted: without evidence to trump the executive's evidence, it is almost impossible politically to resist. Who wants to be soft on terrorism and put citizens' lives at risk? With three years' hindsight it is obvious that large parts of the democratic infrastructure in the United States and Britain were gravely distorted. Both the CIA and MI6 have been made to look like fools. Both governments' legal infrastructure has been compromised. Even the armed services, sent to war on false pretenses, are encountering a crisis of morale: up to one-fifth of American Iraqi veterans have suffered some form of psychiatric illness. [53] Six former American generals have come together to criticize the manner in which the United States went to war and the quagmire it is now in. [54] Preemption has begun to poison the American state.

Democratic institutions depend upon the rule of law; preemption subverts and pollutes it.

The result in Iraq has been a diplomatic, security, military, and economic disaster. The authors of the United States' foreign policy did not begin to anticipate how the exercise of raw military power—"shock and awe"—in a preemptive strike unsanctioned by international law would be greeted internationally, and how debilitating the consequences would be in the United States' own terms. The United States would be faced with suffering most of the military casualties and paying the enormously expensive reconstruction costs. The administration had suppressed the debate that might have revealed such obvious problems; with better information and openness either the invasion would not have gone ahead or it would have been better planned when it did happen. Iraqis who opposed invasion and occupation were handed a propaganda coup; the United States warranted the condemnation it received in hundreds of Middle Eastern mosques and in the terrorist training camps.

Planners at the Pentagon had anticipated that the United States' military presence could be scaled back to just 25,000 troops six months after the occupation of Baghdad.[55] More than three years later there are over 150,000 U.S. soldiers in Iraq. The underestimation of what was entailed could scarcely have been worse. At the time of writing (July 2006) just more than 2,400 American servicemen and servicewomen have been killed in Iraq and (including Afghanistan) 17,000 wounded.[56] Iraqi civilian dead exceed 35,000. The United States has already spent $251 billion directly (as of December 2005); one estimate forecasts that direct and indirect costs together could reach $2 trillion.[57] An independent audit for the U.S. government says that tens of millions of dollars have been wasted in bungled reconstruction contracts. The treatment of prisoners in Abu Ghraib and Guantánamo has been a legal and public relations disaster for little or no security advantage.

Within Iraq, barbarism has been transmuted into legitimate acts of war in response to the illegal invader. License has been given for systemic disorder and mayhem. The ordinary Iraqi citizen has come to see democracy as synonymous with rationing, fear, murder, and worse living standards than under Saddam Hussein. The economic and security situations are also cloudy. Before the 2003 war, Iraq was pumping about 2.8 million to 3.0 million barrels of oil per day; in February 2006, production had dropped to a low of 1.5 million barrels because of terrorist attacks on exposed oil pipelines, which directly contributed to oil prices approaching $80 per barrel.[58] And there has been an increase in terrorist incidents; the State Department's figures suggest a fourfold increase between 2004 and 2005. Within Iraq alone deaths from terrorism doubled in 2005.

If democratic institutions can be established in Iraq over the long term, it is likely that the country's economic and social performance will improve. A constitution has been agreed to, and 8 million Iraqis went to the polls; more than 500 newspapers have been started, and trade unions are forming.[59] The hope is that the new government will provide stability and begin to stop the slide to civil war. All this only intensifies the sense of tragedy and lost opportunity. Instituting democracy in Iraq was possible; that was why any intervention had to have the full backing of the international community to ensure its legitimacy, and there needed to be a careful plan of reconstruction to prevent the escalation of violent religious conflict between the Shia and Sunni communities of which the CIA had warned. Yet by invading as it did, the United States has set back the cause of Iraqi democracy, set back the potential spread of democracy in the rest of the Middle East, increased the risk of terrorism, and weakened its own capacity to act against the emerging danger of Iran. It has also enfeebled the rule of law within the United States. Failure on this scale demands a fundamental reappraisal of the philosophy that has led the United States into this mess. Enlightenment values count.

Britain is only marginally less compromised. Its reaction to terrorism mirrors that of the United States. Under the Prevention of Terrorism Act (2005) "control orders" can be imposed on terrorist suspects by the home secretary. The accused can be subjected to indefinite house arrest—without the benefit of a trial. Such orders, said Alvaro Gil-Robles, the human rights commissioner for the Council of Europe, were clearly intended to "substitute the ordinary criminal justice system with a parallel system run by the executive.[60] All control orders, he advised, should be subject to judicial authorization and, where necessary, a trial; if the evidence cannot be marshaled the orders should be lifted after twelve months.

Even though this meant that Britain was the only European signatory to defect from the European Convention on Human Rights, the measures encountered virtually no resistance. Apart from some members of the judiciary, a few liberal journalists, and the House of Lords, there was scant objection from civil society to measures that weakened Britain's commitment to fundamental rights—a commitment that had survived world wars and the murderous engagement with the IRA.

This criticism is not to argue that the United States, Britain, and the west should sit by idly against the emergence of fundamantalist Islamic terrorism, whose careless and indiscriminate willingness to murder innocents has been exposed not only by the events of 9/11, but by the outrages in London, Madrid, Mumbai, and Bali. We need a response. The mistake that has been made was to fashion it outside the Enlightenment framework.

The first error was to characterize the response as a war. War is a condition between sovereign states. It is, as Yale professor Bruce Ackerman describes it, a life-and-death struggle to secure a state's will over an area of key national interest when foreign, economic, and diplomatic policies have failed.[61] There is an identifiable enemy and a settlement can be reached by treaty, armistice, or capitulation. War takes place, paradoxically, within a recognized legal framework. Al Qaeda is a terrorist network whose ideology is to contest any such framework and which in any case is not going to invade the United States and Britain.[62] Even if its current leadership agreed to a truce, it could not guarantee control of its members to abide by it. Terrorism is a technique to which its adherents remain wedded in their pursuit of fundamentalist aims; even if agreement is reached with one group it would very probably disband and re-form into a new group.

Thus the United States and its partner Britain are engaged in a war that cannot be won, deploying policies that are self-defeating while undermining democracy at home. However, this suits both governments, in particular the Bush administration. They argue that there is a trade-off between security and legality or, as I would put it, Enlightenment values, and that there has to be a rebalancing in favor of security. To do otherwise is to run unnecessary risks—that political trump card.

A more appropriate response, which in the long run would hold out a genuine prospect of victory, is not to diminish western commitment to the rule of law. Rather it is to recognize that the state may need increased powers of surveillance and detention, and even greater capacity to act preemptively at home and abroad, but that such action must be cast within an Enlightenment, democratic framework. Ackerman suggests that the granting of emergency powers after a terrorist attack must be conceded, but that after a period—certainly within a couple of months and regularly thereafter—the government should be required to ask the legislature to reauthorize its holding of emergency powers. It should then have to secure ever higher majorities for the powers to be continued, thus forcing—in my terms—an Enlightenment process of justification and deliberation. The media, the legislature, and the wider public beyond would be forced into a debate about whether the emergency powers continued to be appropriate. The same rules would apply for increased powers of surveillance and imprisonment. In other words, it would be understood that what was happening was provisional and in response to an emergency rather than a once-and-for-all rebalancing of power to the state and the security forces.

The same logic applies abroad. There should not be a general rule in favor of preemption. Instead the United Nations should accept that preemptive action against terrorism may be required while setting a high bar in terms of proof, and that the particular power taking preemptive action has to come back to the United Nations regularly to regain a mandate. This would force a debate about the appropriateness of the action and a chance to reappraise it if it is wrong. The invasion of Afghanistan would thus have to be rejustified and almost certainly revalidated; and no intervention in Iraq would have been possible. Both would have been better outcomes than what we have.

American hawks will say that this ties the hands of the United States. It does. But the greater gain is legitimacy, both within the eyes of the international community and, more important, with the citizens of the nation against which preemptive action is being taken. The charges of aggressive imperialism will have much less force, and American, coalition, or NATO troops would be able to portray themselves genuinely as liberators—crucial in the fight for hearts and minds that is the key to any successful action on the ground against insurgents who depend on the goodwill of the local people in order to secure safe houses and an infrastructure of support. The aim is to win this struggle, and in ways that are congruent with wider western goals.

The more important challenge of our times remains China. The western interest is for China to supplant communism; build its own Enlightenment institutions, because it comes to understand their crucial value; and become a state that actively wants to uphold the values and processes of international governance. To secure this the United States and Britain would be better advised to live according to their values, including the fight against terrorism, within the international system founded upon the rule of law. They are not. It is a mistake of the first order.

Conclusion

GLOBALIZATION INDUCES SOMETHING CLOSE TO HYSTE-
ria in both its critics and its advocates. The litany of threats is by now
familiar. No unskilled or semiskilled job in the developed world is
safe if it is exposed to international competition, and even jobs that
are not exposed soon will be. Tens of millions of jobs will be sent offshore to India or China. European-style commitment to high levels of
welfare can no longer be afforded; the consequent taxation prices
western workers and producers out of globalizing markets. Governments can no longer provide cradle-to-grave social security; they
must focus solely on education and training. Nothing or nobody is
unaffected. This change cannot be resisted, so the only option is to
accept one's fate as a pawn in the globalizing game.

We need to be less alarmist and more forensic. As I argued in
Chapter 11, globalization is not a juggernaut threatening to crush us
all. Nor is it an experience that can transport us to a free-market
nirvana—or a death that will send us to Hades, depending on your
point of view. As seen from the less developed world, and even from
China, the challenge of globalization is how to compete with the
west. Desperately poor and barely educated peasants, even though
there are billions of them, are hardly in a position to take on western
workers. Actually, the rising affluence that globalization generates
gives the "soft" factors that contribute to economic success a new
importance, so that globalization accentuates rather than levels economic differences. For western producers the global economy is full
of niches and opportunities that are enlarging, not diminishing.

For the last five years Suzanne Berger of MIT has led a team interviewing 500 companies in the United States, Europe, and Asia, in an exhaustive and systematic assessment of how globalization works in practice. The main conclusion from her book *How We Compete* is that wage costs are not the be-all and end-all of economics. A Chinese worker may earn 4 percent of the wage of an American worker but is only 4 percent as productive. What counts is not an absolute wage differential, but the unit wage cost once you have factored in productivity differences. The Americans, Japanese, Germans, and British are highly productive and so can still compete against low-wage Asians. Also, successful companies apply strategies that depend on much, much more than low wage costs. Market responsiveness, for example, means being physically and culturally close to one's markets and thus possessing a critical mass of productive capacity at home.

Berger and her colleagues marshal evidence to prove their point. With regard to productivity, factories are part of a wider economic, social, and value system. Within the factory the capacity of team leaders to solve problems such as fixing a broken machine or finding an alternative source when a supplier breaks a contract—the kind of issues that beset factory managers daily—depend on not just their level of education and training but its character and depth. In other words, the quality of schools and vocational training—built up over decades—is central to factory productivity. McKinsey, for example, estimates that only one-fourth of Indian engineers and one-tenth of Chinese engineers are genuinely equipped to work in multinational companies; and a study at Duke University reports that Indian and Chinese degree programs are significantly less demanding than their western counterparts.[1] Moreover, leadership in a corporate setting is subtle; without an understanding of justification and accountability, it is very difficult for leaders to listen, communicate, seek information from below, and process it effectively—all crucial processes in driving a company forward. In the electronics industry, for example, the world benchmark for overall equipment effectiveness is to achieve utilization rates of 95 percent; even in comparatively well-advanced Taiwan the score is only 84 percent.[2] The gap of 11 percent is the difference between profitability and losses. Taiwanese workers and managers are unable to manage high-tech machinery as effectively as their counterparts in the developed world.

Nor is workforce quality the only problem in low-wage, less developed countries. Weak legal systems mean that theft of intellectual property is rampant, so that multinationals have to be wary that their technology, designs, and processes may be stolen. The lack of density of the local supply chain means that goods have to be imported, so that supply-chain management becomes expensive and time-consuming. Corrupt officials have to be kept sweet, but doing this incurs intense reputational costs at home. Transport costs remain significant. One study of the global garment industry found that when all these factors are included the total costs of direct labor constitute only 3 to 4 percent of the price of a product at the point of being loaded for transport and less than 1 percent of the retail price.[3] Similar results are reported by other studies.

Technology Forecasters, a consulting group, found in sixty case studies that labor averaged only 2 percent of a project's total cost.[4] McKinsey, in a survey of Californian companies, found that high-tech firms would save 0.6 percent by going offshore, plastic firms would save 6 percent, and apparel firms would save 13 percent.[5] For many apparel firms even 13 percent is an insufficient saving to offset the cost of not being close to their markets.

Creating value in a period of affluence is much more sophisticated than just disaggregating production and assembling products where wages are lowest. Rising affluence means a demand for customization of goods and services to suit individual needs, which change and evolve quickly; and more and more sophisticated technology means that every stage of the process of creating value—design, manufacture, distribution, and even finance and marketing—is subject to continual reengineering. This is the heart of the knowledge economy, and firms have to be extremely judicious in how they respond to these powerful forces. According to Berger and her associates, strategies for minimizing costs are essentially short-termist and self-defeating.

Even a company like Dell, which has embraced outsourcing very enthusiastically, is careful to make sure that it retains the ability to customize its equipment with local in-house productive capacity— and its marketing and distribution services are kept very close to its markets. Other electronic companies, like Texas Instruments, pursue a more mixed strategy, keenly aware that they may need to overhaul any stage in the process of creating value; and if they contract it out they risk losing control of the ability to be responsive.

Product cycles are shortening dramatically. It required six years to take a car from concept to production in 1990; now it requires only two years. This phenomenon is general. One study found that the time it took to launch new products or make substantial improvements in products fell from an average of 35.5 months in 1990 to about 23 months in 1995.[6] Firms that outsource too much production too far away from their markets are putting all their eggs in one basket: that is, low wages become the sole determinant of competitiveness. Such firms risk being outcompeted by firms closer to home who can better exploit new technologies and new patterns of demand.

In the face of these challenges many firms choose to remain integrated. Sony and Toshiba in Japan; Samsung in Korea (Samsung is Asia's largest maker of chips and mobile phones); and the clothes manufacturer Zara in Spain are hugely successful companies that have built their performance around keeping some production in-house and sourcing the rest locally. Half of Zara's products come from trusted local suppliers in and around its base in La Coruña.[7] When Ford built its flexible factory in Chicago, it insisted on having suppliers physically close to its new plant. The well-known clusters of high-tech firms in California and Boston in the United States and in Cambridge in Britain are testimony that cluster effects can be more important than low wages. In low-tech textiles in Italy, small-firm clusters outcompete their rivals despite higher wages. Benetton, Safilo, Max Mara, Luxottica, Geox, Tie Rack, and Ermenegildo Zegna, for example, are all globally recognized companies whose production base is still in Italy; they form a critical mass of producers with design genius whose collective output and profitability support trade fairs, design schools, training, and information about foreign markets—all of which feeds back into the productivity of the firms.[8] In fact, despite their high wages they are short of labor; and in Modena, the center of the Italian garment industry, the Chinese have bought into 200 of the 3,200 garment businesses, in order to learn. Low wages, it turns out, are only a small part of contemporary business economics. This confirms common sense and empirical observation. For on top of all the insights about corporate strategies made by Suzanne Berger and colleagues, there are immense cultural, linguistic, and even geographical barriers to trade. Even Canada, so very similar to the United States, trades much more within itself than with the country on the other side of the 49th parallel. The United States is no different. Global integration through trade remains very shallow.

Nor is globalization tearing down the welfare state. Since 1980, according to Peter Lindert of the University of California, social transfers (which he defines as assistance to the poor and the unemployed; pensions for the elderly; and spending on health and public housing) have continued to rise in the industrialized world.[9] He can find no evidence that this trend, or the taxation to finance it, has had any deleterious effect on economic growth rates or been adversely affected by globalization. Indeed there is some evidence that high social spending is good for growth. The critics of social spending make three errors, Lindert argues. First, they bundle it up with all government spending, so that their statistical tests are not focused on what they claim is the significant variable—the relationship between social spending and growth. Second, they assume that governments design and finance welfare states to create disincentives, and that any form of taxation itself is a disincentive. Third, they assume that there can be nothing economically positive about social spending. Lindert holds that they are wrong on all three counts.

First, Lindert separates out social spending from government spending to test the correlation between social spending and growth; he finds no negative correlation.

Second, he finds that countries with high social spending go to great lengths to design the structure of their spending and its financing to avoid disincentives. Indeed, paradoxically, countries with a very tightfisted approach to social spending—countries that use means-testing and withdraw benefits as recipients' circumstances improve—create more disincentives than countries with more generous systems. Nor do countries with high social spending, notably the Scandinavian states, finance it with confiscatory taxes on capital or high incomes. They look for broad-based sources of funding, such as income tax, social insurance, and sales taxes. And they are careful to keep their system economically rational; they encourage unemployed workers to search for work in return for unemployment benefits, and they raise the eligibility age for pensions as life expectancy lengthens.

Third, and most important, social spending, rather than being a ball and chain on the economy, has positive economic effects. It enables a steady growth in consumption by the poor, and it has a strong countercyclical stabilizing influence during recessions. It can also have an amazing effect on employment participation rates and skill levels. Denmark's universal child care system, for example, produces two economic benefits. It allows young mothers to reenter the labor market quickly, and it also ensures that young children from low-income homes have the kind of emotional, social, and intellectual engagement that supports the development of their cognitive skills at a crucial age. All the Scandinavian countries, with similarly high levels of social spending, report high employment participation rates for both men and women, high levels of educational attainment, and a general readiness—because living standards are ensured—to take risks, retrain, and change jobs. The Scandinavian economies are thus win-win. They enjoy all the benefits of a market-based system of incentives for their dynamic, high-productivity private sector; and they also enjoy the benefits of high social spending, which makes it easier rather than harder for workers to accept the sometimes high cost of economic change.[10]

These are pluralist market economies with a strong public realm and a commitment to justification; they also enable ordinary people to develop individual capabilities. In short, they embody contemporary Enlightenment values—as powerful now as two hundred years ago in sustaining the west's economic advantages. If the United States and the EU develop the same powerful commitment, they, too, will have nothing to fear from globalization or China—and everything to gain.

The West Mustn't Panic—It Has the Knowledge Economy

This is a moment when both Americans and Europeans need to keep their confidence about their economic strength and keep their markets open. The knowledge economy is a concept abused by hype, but it does capture a truth about the trajectory of economies with high per capita income. It is banal to observe that the traditional manufacturing and agricultural sectors in advanced industrialized economies now constitute together less than one-fifth of national output and that this proportion will continue to fall; the service sector constitutes the vast preponderance of output and is about to grow yet larger. A less banal observation is that all sectors of the economy in western societies are transmuting because ever more sophisticated consumers are interacting with potential new technologies supported by ever-greater affluence. Essentially western economies and societies are moving up Maslow's hierarchy of needs—away from the basic human needs that can be satisfied by producing commodities and toward more complex preferences that require more nuanced responses. Globalization aids this process but is not its cause. Shoshana Zuboff of Harvard Business School and her husband, James Maxmin, have mapped this new geography of demand in their book *The Support*

Economy.[11] Contemporary consumers, they say, now want psychological self-determination. Today, meeting core material needs is no longer sufficient for happiness—material consumption is seen as an inadequate route to well-being. Consumers want their own voice and feel a need for sanctuary. Rewards, Zuboff and Maxim argue, will fall to businesses that create value not just from efficiently combining material inputs into outputs, but also from helping consumers navigate through complex choices, and from finding answers to consumers' questions about attaining psychological well-being. The choices created by affluence are stunning. From running shoes to soft drinks, television channels to magazines, the range of new goods and services is growing at a mind-boggling rate. All this choice reflects today's flexible capacity to produce customized products, and the sophistication of demand in richer societies. But it also reflects the psychological and emotional needs identified by Zuboff and Maxmin. Ronald Inglehart makes a complementary point when he argues that economic growth and physical security have freed affluent societies from necessity, allowing the emergence of postmaterial values. The new values emphasize autonomy and heterogeneity over tradition and conformity:

> Postmodern values bring declining confidence in religious, political and even scientific authority; they also bring a growing mass desire for participation and self-expression. . . . Today, the spiritual emphasis among mass publics is turning from security to significance; from a search for reassurance in the face of existential insecurity to a search for the significance of life.[12]

This is reflected in the quest for spirituality and happiness, but also in the quest for goods and services that exactly meet the specifications of particular consumers.

The knowledge economy is the economic response. Soft knowledge is becoming as crucial as hard knowledge in the chain of creation of values. By hard knowledge I mean the specific science, technology, and skills that are put into a particular good or service; hard knowledge is needed, for example, to build a new chip or jet engine, devise a distinctive marketing campaign, or invent a new financing vehicle. Soft knowledge is the bundle of less tangible production inputs involving leadership, communication, emotional intelligence, the disposition to innovate, and the creation of social capital that harnesses hard knowledge and permits its effective embodiment in goods and services and—crucially—its customization. Their interaction and combination are the heart of the knowledge economy. While some definitions focus narrowly on technology and science, my own definition extends the concept from high-tech manufacturing to creative industries like advertising and Web design, from investment banking to psychoanalysis—and also includes education and health care. McKinsey has developed the notion of what it calls "tacit interactions" in the workplace—"the exchange of information, the making of judgements with a need to draw on multifaceted forms of knowledge in exchange with coworkers, customers and suppliers" to solve "complex, collaborative problems"—as a way of getting a better understanding of the extent of the current demand for the soft skills inherent in the knowledge economy. It estimates 41 percent of all jobs in the United States now require tacit interactions (45 percent in the United Kingdom), with insurance requiring 63 percent and health care 70 percent.[13]

Ironically, the west feels that its position is precarious when in many respects its advantages—in terms of institutions and processes that take decades or even centuries to build—are ever more marked. These are essential to the infrastructure that supports the knowledge economy and the creation of hard and soft knowledge. As long as the west recognizes and nurtures this asset, its economic strength is guaranteed. There should also be a reality check, especially in the United States. The fear of job insecurity and the reality of mounting inequality should be placed in the context of an American economy with one of the highest employment participation rates in the world. The

United States is the preeminent world economic power. Its technological leadership in many frontier sectors ranging from ICT to biotechnology is years ahead of its competitors. The strength and depth of its universities are unparalleled. American researchers rank at the top in terms of papers published and the rate at which those papers are cited by others.[14] The United States' growth in productivity is beginning to accelerate again, albeit from a low base. In many respects this is a success story against which the rest of the world must compare itself.

The more realistic fear in today's world is the concern of less developed countries that they will be cast as low-knowledge subcontractors for the knowledge-rich developed world, in a new and more subtle form of colonialism. For middle-income, less developed countries like Mexico and Thailand the problem is particularly acute. They have neither the low wages of China nor a sufficiently sophisticated infrastructure to develop a western-style knowledge economy, and so they are between a rock and a hard place—and their relative per capita income has been stagnating.[15] Actually, the concern within China about the label "made in China" rather than "made by China"—indicating China's reliance on foreign producers to deliver Chinese exports and its own inability to develop great Chinese global brands—shows that the Chinese are not immune to this anxiety. Yet despite all the fears, an open global system is of proven, universal benefit. The west has to be brave enough to believe in it, demonstrate the advantages, live by the same rules, and practice what it preaches. What is made can be unmade. If nobody defends globalization, it will cease to be. The costs for everyone would be devastating.

And Then There Is China

At first sight China's explosive growth seems not just challenging but terrifying; China apparently is set to sweep all before it. In the two years between the commissioning of this book in 2004 and its completion in July 2006, China's GDP has grown by one-third. Since 2000

China's fixed investment has tripled from $400 billion to an expected $1.3 trillion in 2006. Over the same period its exports have more than quintupled, to an expected $900 billion in 2006. Recall that these figures have been made possible in the time-honored way.[16] Investment, representing half of China's GDP, has been financed by lending by Chinese banks; this lending has increased by nearly 80 percent in the first five months of 2006 compared with 2005. Exports continue to be manufactured largely by foreign companies. The Chinese trade surplus is now expected to hit $150 billion in 2006 (up from $102 billion in 2005).[17] Foreign exchange reserves will reach $1 trillion in 2006 and grow still more in 2007. Recall again that the United States has already declared that it is unprepared to let China buy what it considers strategic assets, even though the Chinese will feel more pressure to buy American companies as China's trade surplus and foreign exchange reserves increase. The United States may simply refuse to accept mounting Chinese imports, and may decide to wage a trade war—either by unilaterally imposing tariffs or by suspending the privileges China has won in terms of access to the U.S. market through the WTO. In that case globalization will be put in question by its chief leader.

One has to marvel at the China boom. One also has to warn that growth cannot go on at this rate, powered by a near doubling of bank lending to state-owned enterprises every year; the more the Chinese economy grows around contradictions and distortions, the greater the potential problems when the situation unravels. In Chapter 1, I argued that the logic of large numbers alone must soon begin to operate. Who imagines that Chinese investment is going to triple again to $4 trillion by 2012, or that Chinese exports are going to rise to $5 trillion by 2020 or sooner? Neither Chinese enterprises nor Chinese banks are profitable enough to borrow or lend money on the scale required to achieve such investment levels; nor are the savings of rural China going to be sufficient to provide the financial wherewithal. Nor is it probable that Chinese exports will be three and half times higher than the exports from today's leading exporter, Germany, within the next decade. Where are the ships that could move such volumes of goods, the ports through which they could be channeled, or the markets that could comfortably absorb them? And how is the renminbi, which currently keeps Chinese exports so competitive, to be prevented from rising without a dramatic and destabilizing increase in China's money supply? If China is to create the 24 million jobs a year necessary to stop unemployment from soaring, growth rates like those in the recent past have to be supposed with the current economic model continuing to work as it always has worked. My argument is that China is caught in a dilemma. It cannot continue with the current model, which is beset by mountainous contradictions and which sooner or later will fail, because of a banking crisis or simply a crisis of overinvestment and excess supply, or some combination of both. The consequent social reaction will provoke a political crisis, with the risk that the party will resort to nationalism, and perhaps a military adventure in Taiwan, to keep the genie of protest bottled up. But equally, to rebalance China's growth on the basis of more normal levels of investment and consumption, together with fuller participation in the knowledge economy, requires the building of an institutional structure, a welfare system, and property rights—which would be inconsistent with one-party communist rule.

At present the party has reached the limits of reform without creating a genuinely pluralist capitalist economy and society, but hesitating whether it dare. For example, the reform of the capital and labor markets has reached a tipping point. All shares in Chinese enterprises are now to be tradable on Chinese stock markets, but the party still wants to privilege shares held by the state, to give them a special claim over an enterprise's fixed assets. This creates a two-tier stock market. The next stage is to give all shareholders equivalent ownership rights, but that would imply that China's enterprises finally might be genuinely privatized, with the party losing control of them. This is equally true in the labor market. Trade unions have been given the right to sign collective wage contracts; the next stage is genuine collective bargaining. In both areas, as in many others, China can either follow the logic of reform or resist it. Whatever route it takes, China faces convulsions.

The party leadership surveys the scene, keenly aware of the dilemmas. China's Communist Party is not a monolith. The center of gravity remains firmly Dengist, committed to the view that the only way to legitimize the party is for it to be the successful champion of economic development, which implies pro-market, pro-globalization opening to the world. But it is increasingly unstable, beset by a strengthening conservative wing anxious to reaffirm communist verities, alleviate peasant poverty as a priority, intensify party control, and stop the clock on selling even minority shares in state-owned enterprises to the private sector generally and to foreigners in particular. It is hostile to what it views as too large a concession to American liberalism, and is suspicious of American intent. Hu Jintao has tacked toward the conservatives; with the party acutely conscious that it is faced with a crisis of ideological and political legitimacy because of mounting social protests and its own corruption. This is a revolutionary party that no longer practices revolution and has renounced class war; the impact on its ethics and morality is hard to underestimate. Without external sources of accountability to keep party cadres honest, the only weapon to tackle corruption is anticorruption drives— themselves undermined by the corruption of those leading the initiatives. The party's instincts are to promote those who are effective in making the current system work within its own terms rather than those who have experimented with substantial reform.[18]

The fifth generation of leaders who will succeed President and General Secretary Hu Jintao and his team are to be chosen at the Seventeenth Communist Party Congress in autumn 2007, where it will be decided who will occupy the Central Committee and Politburo. The indications are that Hu intends to play it safe, notwithstanding the scale of the dilemmas, and appoint mostly individuals soaked in the party's internal organization and propaganda departments, who have risen through the Chinese Communist Youth League. The so-called *tuanpai* officials—such as Liaoning's party secretary, Li

Keqiang, or Li Zhilun, minister of civil affairs—tend to come from China's poorer, humbler internal provinces; and almost none have experience in foreign trade, finance, or banking.[19] They are party men, and loyal to a conservative vision of Dengist communism; their aim is to sustain Leninist corporatism and the apparatus of a one-party state. One measure of the crisis facing the party is that it feels that it has to look to officials like these essentially to try to hold the line. In the provinces and in particular in cities and large townships, the party is reminiscent of *Animal Farm*. It is seen as turning into the Confucian official class it purported to replace, with even more corruption and with even less opportunity for redress of wrongs. Inequality is conspicuous and growing worse. The danger for the party elite in Beijing is that rather as decollectivization of agriculture came as an unstoppable force from below between 1979 and 1983, there will be an unstoppable insistence by urban citizens that they should have the right to hold officials to account in elections modeled on what has been allowed in the villages. Some form of accountability is the only proven way of tackling corruption and limiting gigantic waste. Yet the shadow of Tiananmen hangs over the country. Everybody knows that if a popular movement for city democracy ever took off, it would be very difficult to resist—not least because those who have power privately recognize the legitimacy and validity of the criticism. A general secretary of the Communist Party, Zhao Ziyang, acknowledged this openly in 1989. Be sure there are others today who think the same thing. The party's only reliable response is thus preemption—the reason why censorship has increased and why the Internet firewall has been erected—coupled with limited institutional improvement, such as attempts to professionalize the judiciary, that are congruent with continued one-party rule. The danger is that this is inadequate, and that China's problems are so serious that the only way for the party to maintain control is through an authoritarian crackdown at home and nationalist aggression abroad. On the other hand the evidence of Chinese history, as Roderick MacFarquhar of Harvard argues, is that shocks of this type—losing the war of 1894–1895 to Japan led to the collapse of the imperial system; the Cultural Revolution preceded Deng—are precursors of reform.[20] China's path to modernity and Enlightenment institutions is unlikely to be smooth.

The west needs to understand the depth of China's problems and the probability of a convulsion as the Chinese seek their resolution. What it must avoid at all costs is a situation in which it forces the Chinese leaders' hand and China retreats toward economic isolation. The challenge to the global trading and financial system would be profound; not only would an important source of global demand be scaled back, but a key source of financing the U.S. trade deficit would be removed. The interest of the west is to help China avoid this fate and encourage a peaceful transition to a pluralist China with a system of accountability that is comfortable with liberal globalization and the rule of law. To describe the goal of policy in this way is demanding enough; more demanding still is to execute it. The simple extrapolations of China's growth, predicting that it will eventually become a one-party colossus, lead to an alarmist climate in which it is easier to justify trade protection or, in the United States, potential military activism. Such a response would be naive. We have to play it long, encourage and help to comanage the change that must come.

The Economic Ship of Fools

The wider background is the growing risks within the international economic system. Both the United States and the United Kingdom are beneficiaries of globalization. About $1 trillion of the United States' GDP—10 percent—depends on it; in the United Kingdom, a more open economy, the proportion is significantly higher.

This phenomenon could not have occurred without an underlying political consensus: states wanted it to happen. In turn, globalization demanded their confidence that multilateral institutions and international laws would allow them to prosper and protect their interests even while they surrendered a measure of sovereignty to international markets and companies. On balance they would benefit from the trade-off. Since World War II, U.S. foreign policy has cleverly constructed an international system of rules and processes that delivers this result; it is transparent and equal for all states that participate, even while—to repeat—the United States is one of the principal beneficiaries and plainly accorded the leadership role. This system of lower tariffs, security for foreign investment, and growing freedom of movement of capital has propelled the growth of the world economy, especially since 1990. Foreign direct investment as a share of world GDP has tripled since then; exports of goods and services have increased by half. As I have argued, it was Deng Xiaoping's genius to see that even China could benefit if it entered the system.

But the system is under increasing strain. It depends on unsustainable, freakishly high Chinese savings to finance unsustainable, freakishly low American savings for the indefinite future. The emergence of a low-saving society is a deep-seated trend. Part of the explanation is that widespread property ownership gives American consumers collateral against which to spend and run down their savings. Another part is that rising affluence has undermined self-control and both the desire and the incentive to defer gratification—an argument made with great persuasiveness by Avner Offer of Oxford University. Individuals in societies where social norms are weakening feel less constrained in demanding, getting, and satiating their wants as soon as they can.[21] Fortunately for the world system, just as this phenomenon has become highly problematic in terms of macroeconomic management, Asia in general and China in particular have emerged to bail the United States out of the consequences—with their own self-interest very much in mind. Some respected commentators argue that the United States is somehow the victim of Asians' high savings and has been compelled to become a spendthrift in order to make the international system work; but this argument is perverse.[22] It is obvious to all but the most purblind that Americans' savings would have fallen whether China was part of the international system or not.

Yet both low American savings and China's compensation for it cannot continue. Just as the law of large numbers suggests the unsustainability of China's position, so it points to similar conclusions about the United States. The United States' current account deficit in 2005 was $804 billion (6.4 percent of GDP), up from $668 billion in 2004; in 2006 it is expected to rise higher. Already the United States has net international debts in excess of $3 trillion. It has staved off the consequences so far in two ways. First, it receives three times more from its investments abroad than it pays out in interest on bonds and treasury bills. That is how the Asians, and especially the Chinese, lend to the United States.[23] However, the scale of its international debts is now eliminating this advantage. Second, China, Japan, and other Asian countries want to peg their currencies to the dollar, both to accelerate their exports to the United States and to make their own exchange-rate relationships within Asia more predictable. By buying dollars indefinitely and building up their dollar reserves, in effect they are lending the United States the savings it needs. So far, both sides are winners. China's exports to the U.S. market propel China's economic growth; and the United States gets cheap imports and the opportunity to live above its means.

But there is an iron law in economics—what is unsustainable is not sustained. I have already argued that China's exports cannot keep on growing at their current rate, and that China cannot afford to acquire an extra $200 billion of foreign exchange reserves every year. The United States faces similar impossibilities. The comforting story offered by many economists and conservative pundits is that the United States can continue to attract savings to finance its high trade deficit because its high productivity and its flexibility guarantee high rates of return on investment. This is a Panglossian doctrine that ignores the logic of the numbers, a point made forcibly by Barry Eichengreen of the University of California.[24] If the United States continues growing and borrowing as it has been doing, eventually its foreign debts will reach 150 percent of its GDP. Then, necessarily, foreigners, with Chinese and Arab investors at the forefront, would own half of the United States' capital stock. Given the reaction to

Dubai Ports World, this trend would provoke a political storm long before such high proportions were actually reached. Even if the U.S. growth rate doubled, the United States' monumental trade deficit would eventually imply foreign ownership of one-third of its capital stock. This is not a politically acceptable outcome.

Nor, Eichengreen argues, does American investment offer such high returns that foreigners would be likely to invest in the United States to such an extent. In any case, they invest in U.S. debt rather than U.S. productive assets or shares, an improbable destination for their investment if it is U.S. productivity that is seducing them into locating their cash in the United States. The Chinese and Japanese central banks are the main providers of foreign saving to the United States, for the old-fashioned mercantilist goal of promoting Chinese and Japanese exports. If the United States' investment were rising as a result of commandeering such a high proportion of world saving, there might be some justification for its stance. Instead, the United States is importing savings to maintain its level of consumer spending.

Here we encounter another set of economic numbers with an impossible logic. The debts of American households, already 125 percent of annual disposable income, cannot continue to grow three times faster than American national output. In 2005, American household saving went negative as American consumers borrowed and spent in unprecedented volumes against the value of equity in their homes, again, a process that cannot continue forever. In an era of low inflation, debts are not inflated away; they are a real and growing burden. The rise in oil prices reduces the growth of real incomes and forces the U.S. Federal Reserve to have a much more cautious policy on keeping money cheap. In short, the United States cannot keep on being the world's growth engine, because there are evident limits to how much American consumers can borrow, and how much international debt the American economy will be allowed to incur. Economics delivers some tough news. There must be a change that is closer to a paradigm shift than a technical correction. The pattern and structure of Chinese and American growth must be rebalanced, as must the interrelationship between these last great powers. The question is not whether but how this change is to be achieved.

In the mid-1980s, when the United States' current account deficit was half its present level, American and international policy makers were keenly aware of the risk that the scale of the emerging imbalances could create mayhem in the international markets. At the Plaza Hotel in New York City on September 22, 1985, Secretary of the Treasury James Baker, after three months of secret financial diplomacy, persuaded Britain, France, Germany, and Japan to agree that an appreciation of their currencies would be "desirable" and that action to bring this about would be "helpful."[25] Baker was working within the multilateral framework of the International Monetary Fund and what was then the Group of Five leading industrialized countries to get the dollar to fall—as it did, spectacularly, on average by 54 percent from its peak in February 1985 to the end of 1987. In the seven years preceding the Plaza accord, American exports had shrunk every year by 0.7 percent; in the eleven years that followed they grew at an average rate of 9.3 percent, one-third faster than the rate between 1950 and 1971, and manufacturing exports doubled from 21 percent to 42 percent of manufacturing value added.[26] The United States still ran a current account deficit during the 1990s, but its position was sustainable. For Japan, however, the appreciation of the yen ended the way the country had grown since the early 1950s and precipitated fifteen years of restructuring, retrenchment, and economic stagnation that have only recently shown signs of ending. The consequence was a domestic disaster; Stephen Jen of Morgan Stanley concludes that the Plaza accord of 1985 was one of the greatest policy mistakes Japan has ever made.[27] But the larger point is that the international system held.

Twenty years later, there is no similar shared urgency or agreement about the action needed to keep the international economic system together. Nor is the United States showing any readiness to reinforce, extend, or even use the multilateral framework to organize a shared way of distributing the burden of painful adjustment. Instead there is a disturbing, careless willingness to test to destruction the capacity of the international system to absorb imbalances. The rationale is that it will be foreigners who get hurt by any fallout; that real Americans do not do deals with lesser countries; and that the domestic political consequences of any belt-tightening in terms of increasing taxes or saving energy—the obvious American share of any adjustment—are impossible to contemplate. Whether the issue is trade, carbon dioxide emissions, or energy use, the position of the U.S. government is now overt self-interest to the point of self-hurt; its aim is to squeeze the lemon as hard as it can for its own immediate advantage. The postwar concern to create global agreements from which the United States was the single largest beneficiary but which nevertheless had legitimacy has vanished in a cloud of neoconservative smoke. This is a dereliction of duty by the U.S. government, which has an obligation both to its citizens and to these agreements. Its dereliction threatens sooner or later to blow up in the face of the United States and the world.

The world in turn has learned from the Americans' lesson in self-interest. Consider the bargain that is now needed over trade. Since the early 1960s average tariffs on imports into industrialized countries have fallen by half, to under 5 percent; tariffs on developing countries' imports have fallen by two-thirds, to just over 10 percent; and China's tariffs have fallen from over 40 percent in 1992 to just over 5 percent today. It is a remarkable achievement, and the world now needs the same to happen in agriculture and services to achieve the same buildup of trade, and thus output growth, in these key areas of the economy. Yet the United States and the EU are resisting, in a game of chicken; nobody wants to be the country that blinked first and began to make concessions without knowing for certain what concessions would be received in return. India, Japan, Brazil, and Russia are following this example, and so the trade talks have been suspended in a destructive standoff. For all of them, especially the middle-income, less developed countries, there is also the fear that if they open to an unreformed China, they could be overwhelmed. Meanwhile the United States piles on more antidumping suits, higher fines, and more aggressive threats of retaliatory trade action. What does not go forward will lose momentum and easily unravel. The great postwar achievement of a rules-bound international trading system on which globalization depends is in peril—at the same time as the scale of international imbalances is reaching new and untested levels.

Not only is this shortsighted in terms of the self-interest of Asia, Europe, and North America; it also has consequences for the rest of the world that are even more serious. The greater Middle East from Morocco to the Central Asian republics has been deglobalized over the last twenty-five years. Between 1979 and 2000 its share of global trade and investment fell by three-fourths while its population nearly doubled, to 600 million. Across the Arab world average per capita incomes fell from $2,300 to $1,600 between 1980 and 2000—this is the background to the anger directed against the west.[28] There is a similar if not quite so dramatic picture in Latin America—economic stagnation and the emergence of a leftist authoritarian populism. Four elected presidents have been forced from office since 2000, and Bolivia's nationalization of its natural gas industry is a signal of where Latin American politics are heading. If the world trading system breaks down, then the direction of Latin American politics and the trajectory of Islamic fundamentalist terrorism are all too obvious.[29]

Alarm bells should be ringing in Washington. The United States is at the center of a delicate worldwide system of economic interdependence that could easily topple into economic dislocation. Three countries—China, Canada, and Mexico—supply the United States with two-fifths of its imports; four more—Germany, South Korea, Britain, and Japan—account for the next one-fifth of imports. All seven are connected through their supply chains to other countries. Nearly 40 percent of consumer demand in the United States is met by foreign producers; if for any reason that demand stagnates or falls, the international, let alone the domestic, consequences will be severe. The biggest risk is a precipitate sell-off of the dollar, forcing U.S. interest rates to rise, with a potential collapse of the inflated prices of American property and bankruptcy for many overextended borrowers. Jochen Sanio, president of the Federal Financial Supervisory Authority, has said that the issue is not whether hedge funds as currently regulated will cause a disaster; "the only question is when." [30] The most likely answer is that this will occur during the financial aftereffects of an unexpected sell-off of the dollar, when unregulated and overextended hedge funds will find they are unable to settle their debts, and will therefore precipitate a financial crisis.

This brings us back to China. As I have argued, it must be carefully managed, rather than forced into a retreat from global markets or into a nationalist response—at worst a face-saving invasion of Taiwan. Of course, consistent pressure for change needs to be maintained, and an example set of how to behave. But not to the point of hurting ourselves more than them. The United States could find itself confronting an Asian war, a financial crisis, and economic recession simultaneously. Preemptive unilateralism with regard to terror and a parallel policy with regard to the international economic system will have landed the country and the world in a debacle that was all too foreseeable. But nothing was done in better times to avert the risk.

To Conclude

The west needs to stand by its values and institutions at home and reproduce them internationally, to give the rest of the world a genuine opportunity to catch up and to recast its domestic organization around Enlightenment principles—inevitably a slow task. Yet the international institutions are hardly exemplars of Enlightenment values. The IMF, World Bank, and World Trade Organization, for example, all have grievous deficiencies in their accountability, representation, and mandate. They may be better than nothing; they may be subjected to unrealistic criticism; but at least they have kept the show running so far. But even their defenders have to acknowledge that they resemble a rich men's club and fall far below the standards we would expect of domestic institutions. [31] For example, the behind-the-scenes "green room" process in the World Trade Organization, in which the EU and the United States essentially broker a common position behind closed doors, is an affront to the rest of the world—as is the notion that the head of the IMF should always be a European and the head of the World Bank an American irrespective of merit. Financial decision making should obviously include China, India, Brazil, and representatives from Africa and the Middle East alongside the traditional group of seven industrialized countries and Russia. The IMF should, plainly, be more than a debt collector for western banks and an enforcer of economic stringency. Similarly, the World Bank should have the financial resources to be a serious development institution. Yet the deficiencies have been allowed to continue for decades.

The charitable view is that these are design flaws that can be readily addressed with sufficient political will; a tougher appraisal is that they reflect mainly the power struggles that beset the creation of the institutions and have persisted ever since. There should be little surprise at the widespread perception that these institutions are no more than vehicles for western power—indeed U.S. power—with inherent biases, because essentially the perception is correct. The broad political, economic, and social agenda for such reform may be understood and even favored by some within the IMF and World Bank, but it conflicts with their institutional bias to favor efficiency over equity, to favor transactional market incentives rather than justification and accountability mechanisms, and to suspect social spending rather than understand its value.

The reform agenda is not hard to outline. There should be wider membership in the governing councils of every international institution, just as the UN Security Council should now include Japan, Germany, India, and Brazil. International institutions should be able to finance themselves from the taxation of global "bads," such as carbon dioxide emissions. There should be higher standards of transparency and accountability. There should be a bias toward what, for want of a better term, I have called the Enlightenment agenda. Necessarily it will have a proper skepticism about legitimizing doctrines of preemptive action against perceived threats, terrorist or otherwise. There should be a broadening of the treaty and institutional network to regulate climate change, the arms race, and the harboring of terrorists and to ensure better auditing and less tax evasion. There needs to be a drive for higher literacy, higher numeracy, and better health standards.

If the need for such institutions is pressing in terms of global security and economic soundness, then the environmental need is no less urgent. During 2003 the concentration of carbon dioxide in the atmosphere hit the highest level in 420,000 years.[32] Winter temperatures in some of the world's coldest places—western Canada, eastern Russia, and Alaska—have risen by three to four degrees Celsius over the last 50 years.[33] Few scientists dispute the link between burning fossil fuels, increased carbon dioxide emissions, and the rise in temperatures. Yet the International Energy Agency projects that over the next twenty-five years coal use will rise by 51 percent, oil by 57 percent, and natural gas by 89 percent. Together, those increases will bring a 62 percent rise in carbon dioxide emissions unless fuel efficiency improves remarkably or carbon use is capped.[34]

The impact on the global ecosystem is already evident and will worsen. The great ice sheets and glaciers melt, sea levels rise, ocean currents change their velocity and temperature, and the weather and distribution of rainfall change. The Greenland ice sheet would not survive a rise in world temperatures of three degrees Celsius, now within the range of projections for 2100. If the Greenland ice sheet was lost, world sea levels would rise twenty-three feet, with incalculable consequences.[35] China and India are already, with current weather patterns, chronically short of water; so is sub-Saharan Africa. In 2005 the Millennium Ecosystem Assessment, a four-year project involving 1,300 researchers and scientists from ninety-five countries, announced that 60 percent of the world's ecosystem services have been degraded and that species extinction is anywhere up to 1,000 times the normal background rate. According to Jared Diamond, environmental despoliation has killed civilizations as disparate as the Khmer of Angkor Wat, the Norse Greenlanders, and the Easter Islanders.[36] Ecosystems are part of what makes the earth habitable. The concern to preserve them is not the kooky preoccupation of the green brigade; it is the concern of every human being alive. Unless we take care, we will follow other species to extinction.

We urgently need a concerted, redoubled international effort to lower carbon dioxide emissions through taxation, regulation, and greater efficiency. We also need to replace the Kyoto Treaty—a commitment to reduce carbon dioxide emissions by 2012 to 95 percent of 1990 levels—with something much tougher and more encompassing. The EU has signed and ratified the treaty; the United States, which produces one-fourth of the world's carbon dioxide, has not—because it wants less developed countries to share the pain, and because Bush believes that lowering carbon dioxide emissions might damage the U.S. economy. The United States wants to ride free and do nothing itself, while the rest of the world rises to the environmental challenge.

To progress, we need a belief in international action legitimized by a multilateral commitment to the rule of law, and we need a self-confident rather than a defensive, anxious west—precisely what we do not have. Within the EU twenty years of high unemployment in Italy, Germany, and France have undermined confidence in liberal capitalism and in the case for European integration around a commitment to enlarge four great freedoms of movement—of goods, people, money, and services. There is a dangerous introspection, a desire to protect, and a turning away from even the limited process of European governance that exists today. The French and Dutch "No" votes in their referenda in 2005 on the proposed EU constitution were but further evidence of the malaise. It is all the more tragic in that the European Union is the most successful experiment with multilateral governance the world has ever seen; and as a social model—as I have argued above—it is not only attractive but eminently viable. The Nordic countries in particular have an enviable record of high and growing productivity, high employment, innovativeness, and high social spending that belies the conventional criticism of the EU. Parts of it work astonishingly well. Even the three large countries plagued by high unemployment enjoy as high if not higher productivity than the United States and, unemployment aside, good social outcomes.

In the western effort to sell globalization and manage China, the EU has a crucial role: it offers a model of capitalism that is more attractive than the American and more sympathetic to Chinese concerns about equity and social solidarity. Yet the EU is mired in doubt and fearfulness. Meanwhile in the United States the same mood that brought preemptive unilateralism and extralegal detention without trial is informing the attitude toward multilateral institutions and international initiative. Global governance can go hang.

To urge the overcoming of these impulses is almost purposeless without a recognition of the deeper roots of what is happening today. Trying to solve China's economic catch-22 without acknowledging its ideological crisis would be equally pointless. If class war is over from a party that now includes capitalists in its ranks, what is the ideological justification of one-party rule? Communism aimed to be more than a political creed: it sought, and for a period it succeeded, in offering an answer to the universal question of how to live a life well. It does no longer. Simply put, it is a moral and ideological empty vessel. Of course a precondition for any movement is political will, but there needs to be something more. Political leaders need to feel that they speak for a majority and that there is a consensus regarding values. In the west it is the dismaying lack of consensus over Enlightenment values—indeed whether to believe in the Enlightenment at all—that lies beneath the surface of today's malaise, creates uncertainty, and is the root cause of political immobility. Rationalism and justification are under assault because they do not answer the question "why." As the fundamentalisms of flag, tribe, nation, and religion becomes ever more primitive and visceral, western politicians become ever more nervous about continuing to argue for a politics based on rational law, multilateral institutions, and collaboration. The attacks on stem-cell research and Darwinian theories of natural selection are important not only because they are attacks on the willingness to accept evidence as proof of truth, the very core of the Enlightenment. They are also important because they dramatize the gulf that has opened between the world of the secular and rational and the world of the believer. The bitter divisions within the United States between the crusading Christian fundamentalists and a more secular civil society are but one expression of this phenomenon; another is the rise of militant Islamic fundamentalism; another is the rise of nationalism within Europe and resistance to further European integration; another is the conservative faction in China wanting to stop the clock on the reform program and return to old communist and nationalist verities. Reason is at loggerheads with faith and the ties of blood.

The German philosopher Jürgen Habermas, in his exploration of the future of human nature, insists that the emerging battle between faith, instinct, and belief on the one hand and secularism, rationality, and empiricism on the other is useless and self-destructive. The essence of human nature is to need both. It is impossible, he says, to try to box human nature into scientific rationalism, the logic of market transactions, and justice based on no more than rational human principles. It is not that this universe is wrong or should be qualified in any way; it is that human nature also needs the richness of the morality and understanding of how knowledge is used that can be derived from religion. Equality, for example, can be a more powerful notion if it is understood that equality before our Maker is more profound than equality with any other basis. Similarly, morality can be better comprehended if we can find a language that differentiates between what is wrong and what is evil.[37] Religiously formed morality can have a power that secular morality lacks.

Even the justification process—which I have argued is one pillar of the Enlightenment commitment to the rule of reason—is not just a rational process of claim and counterclaim; it is animated, Habermas argues, by a sense of what ought to or should take place. You do not necessarily have to be a believer or have faith to recognize the debt western moral sensibility owes religion. Only when both parties to this debate within western societies can respect each other's traditions and understand their contribution to the whole will we construct a basis for mutual respect—and then show the rest of the world the complexity of our own struggle to come to terms with the two impulses. To understand and present the west to others in these terms will be more persuasive, Habermas argues, than simply praising the rule of the market while threatening to use overwhelming military force against those who dare challenge us. Our roots, as well as the times, demand that we do better than this.

Habermas's thesis is closely related to the core of this book. "Hard" economics, politics, and social realities need to be complemented, corrected, and enriched by countervailing "soft" forces. When the west creates and manages this interaction well, it is the heart of our genius; but too frequently we do not grasp its nature, and today we are neglecting it at our peril. Suddenly the stakes of this failure have become higher. China, riven with contradictions and full of potential menace, is coming to terms with the bankruptcy of communism and the logical impossibility of continuing to grow as it has been growing. It should borrow from rather than be opposed to the west. We have to enable this process rather than hinder it. Equally, the world is racked by crazy economic imbalances and imprudently regulated financial institutions. We must challenge the doctrine that these should be left untouched because the primacy of the private and the market should always be respected. Imbalances as severe as those today need to be managed, and high-risk financial institutions need to be regulated. The world's ecosystems are in peril; an international reaction is vital. Overshadowing everything is the war on terror, and the fear that as Islamic terrorism cannot be beaten we should retreat into our national strongholds. Even there we will not be safe, though, for the world has never been more interdependent. Both the benefits of cooperation and the costs of noncooperation have never been greater. There is an accident waiting to happen unless we find an accommodation over values, which is the precondition for action within this cooperative framework that needs to be newly invigorated. And then we must act. The writing is on the wall.

Acknowledgments

I OWE TWO PEOPLE AND ONE ORGANIZATION, ABOVE ANY others, thanks for this book. The first person is Ed Victor, my agent, who suggested the concept after reading my first column on China after my weeklong lecture tour in Beijing and Shanghai in the autumn of 2003 and who persisted in arguing that I could take on this vast subject despite my misgivings. Nine months later he overcame my doubts, and this book is the result. Ed has a deserved reputation as one of the best in the business, and his conviction and gentle persistence have led me into territory that I have found endlessly interesting and rewarding. I know a great deal more about China—and the United States—than I did eighteen months ago!

The second person is Philippe Schneider, who joined me as a Mandarin-reading researcher in December 2004 and who worked with me right to the last minute of the very last missed deadline. It was one of the best hires of my life. We became firm companions in an intellectual and political odyssey—as we joked, an "Enlightenment" project in its own right. The depth and range of Philippe's reading, the quality of his background papers, and the catholicism of his intellectual interests sometimes took my breath away and were never less than excellent. He ensured, as a great researcher should and must, that I was fully aware of the literature on every subject I wrote about; and the evidence is in the exhaustive list of references. He was indefatigable and a relentless chaser after facts and theories alike. He was also firmly committed to my ambition for the book, and his enthusiasm carried me along when sometimes it just seemed an ambition too far. This book and I owe him an enormous debt of gratitude.

331

And the organization is the British Council. China Regional Director Michael O'Sullivan, Gary Hallsworth in Beijing, Jeff Streeter in Shanghai, Ruth Gee in Hong Kong, and Christine Skinner in Guangzhou together arranged two programs of visits and briefings that would have been impossible had I attempted them by myself. My thanks to them all. Nor should I forget Peng Yanni, the project manager in Beijing who so carefully shepherded Philippe and me through our schedule. I compressed an enormous amount into my two journeys, and I was hugely impressed with the affection and regard with which the British Council is held in China—and the depth and range of its contacts. And thanks to Michael for his suggestion that we visit the Qing tombs—much farther from Beijing than the Ming tombs but more than worth the journey. Thanks also to my fixer in Beijing, Liang Yan (Edera); and the researcher Li Jialin. Edera's wide range of potential interviewees from her contact book was essential, and Li Jialin's helpful overview papers were balanced and thorough.

In no particular order I would like to thank Jeremy Sargent, Wang Ershan, Zhu Hui, Lui Siewying, Professor Lin Jiang, Li Yongning, Yang Zaigao, Yin Ningyu, Lu Tong, Neil Blakeman, Patrick Powers, Li Zhaoxi, Yang Dongning, Wang Jiangping, Hu Shuli, Professor Ding Ding, Stephen Green, Cong Yan, Professor Lin Shangli, Kong Quiyun, Professor Lu Feng, Fu Jun, Li Bozhong, Professor Hu Angang, David Concar, Robin Porter, Huang Ping, Ambassador Sir Christopher Hum, Professor Shi Yinhong, Mao Yushi, Joseph Cheng, Dr. Eden Woo, Stephen Bradley, Michael Elliott, Nic Dean, Hong Kong's Vision 2047 for their breakfast, Sherman Hung, Phil Chan, Zandra Mok, and many others for the time they gave up to see me in China. The usual disclaimers about my being solely responsible for the opinions expressed here apply with even more force.

I also made a research trip to the United States in January 2006. I would like to thank Tony Saich, Dwight Perkins, Liz Perry, Richard Cooper, Dani Rodrik, Richard Lester, Iain Johnston, Yasheng Huang, Kevin Lanzit, commissioners Bill Reinsch and Larry Wortzel, Minxin

Pei, Anatol Lieven, Rob Atkinson, Frank Jannuzi, Shahid Yusuf, Kaoru Nabeshima, Fred Bergsten, James Lilley, William Galston, Stephen Roach, Adam Segal, and Walter Russell Mead for the time they freely gave. Sidney Blumenthal's comments arrived just in time to let me make some important changes. In London Geoff Mulgan, Peter Nolan, Howard Davies, and Susan Lawrence all made helpful suggestions about people I should approach in China, while David Held, Philip Dodd, Chris Patten, and Jonathan Fenby have also contributed to the cause; Jonathan's detailed comments on the first three chapters were especially constructive. In addition Howard Davies offered insightful comments on an early draft. Thanks to them all, and once again the same disclaimer.

Then, thanks to my editors at Little, Brown in London and Free Press (Simon & Schuster) in New York. Richard Beswick has been supportive and engaged throughout, resisting various suggestions for titles until I hit on this one and feeding back comment on the chapters as I sent them. Similarly, Fred Hills in New York—one of the great figures in American publishing—gave me a good sense of how Americans will react to the thesis. After he retired at Easter 2006, his successor, Emily Loose, took up the challenge with dedication, great professionalism, and commitment. In London Phillippa Harrison read every chapter and made typically shrewd and insightful remarks; my thanks to her as well. Andrew Bevan, an anonymous proof editor at Simon & Schuster, and my daughter Alice all contributed to the editing process.

I also benefited from a two-month sabbatical from the *Observer* and a three-month semisabbatical from The Work Foundation; thanks to the *Observer*'s editor Roger Alton and The Work Foundation's chairman Peter Ellwood for their support. My colleagues at The Work Foundation have been encouraging when I flagged, and did not raise their eyebrows too often as I became progressively more harassed toward the end. Sarah Holden operated beyond the call of duty in helping with the logistics of the trips, to the United States and China; and Steve Bevan's and Aine O'Keefe's reaction—along with that of other colleagues at The Work Foundation at a midterm seminar—kept my spirits up.

And last, as every author knows, writing imposes a terrible strain on one's family. My two daughters followed the drama away from home, but Andrew (brainstorming for a title) and especially Jane had to experience it firsthand. She has now been through three of these exercises (*The State We're In* and *The World We're In* being numbers one and two). The love and support she offers—along with the occasional but never overly accusatory groan at another lost weekend or evening—is indispensable. And if inadvertently I have left anyone out, an apology. I shall make sure you are included in the next edition (if there is one)!

Will Hutton, June 6, 2007

Notes

CHAPTER 1

1. Scott C. Bradford, Paul L. E. Grieco, and Gary Clyde Hufbauer, "The Payoff to America from Global Integration," in Fred Bergsten, ed., *The United States in the World Economy,* Institute for International Economics, Washington, D.C., 2005, p. 105.
2. For the most bullish assessment, see *Dreaming with the BRICs: The Path to 2050,* Goldman Sachs Global Economics Paper No. 99, 2003.
3. Angus Maddison, The World Economy: A Millennial Perspective, OECD Development Center, Paris, 2001, table B-20. Maddison computes the rise in U.S. GDP as a proportion of the world total from 8.9 percent in 1870 to 19.1 percent in 1913. China's GDP as a share of world output was 4.6 percent in 1973 and rose to 11.5 percent in 1998. I compute a further rise to about 16 percent in 2006.
4. Martin Ravaillion and Shaohua Chen, *China's (Uneven) Progress against Poverty,* World Bank Policy Research Working Paper No. 3408, September 2004. Ravaillon and Chen use the following poverty lines: 850 yuan (about $102 at current exchange rates) a year for rural areas and 1,200 yuan ($145) a year for urban areas, both at 2002 prices. Across China in 2001, the number of people living in extreme poverty had been reduced by about 400 million since twenty years previously. Between 1981 and 2001, the proportion of the Chinese population living in poverty fell from 53 percent to 8 percent.
5. See, for instance, *China 2020: Development Challenges in the New Century,* World Bank, Washington, D.C. 1997; Ravallion and Chen, op. cit.; OECD, *Economic Survey: China,* 2005; and *Zhongguo tongji nianjian* (Statistical Yearbook of China), 2000 and various other years.
6. OECD, *Economic Survey: China,* 2005, p. 30.
7. U.S. Department of Defense, *Quadrennial Defense Review Report,* February 6, 2006, p. 29.

8. When we adjust for its low prices and wages in a measurement called purchasing power parity (PPP). China is now unambiguously the world's second largest economy—worth $7.3 trillion. By comparison, the United States is worth $11.6 trillion and Japan $3.8 trillion.

9. In his speech at the Sixeenth Chinese Communist Party Congress, Jiang Zemin defined the "three represents" as follows: "Viewing the course of struggle and the basic experience over the past eighty years and looking ahead to the arduous tasks and bright future in the new century, our party should continue to stand in the forefront of the times and lead the people in marching toward victory. In a word, the party must always represent the requirements of the development of China's advanced productive forces, the orientation of the development of China's advanced culture, and the fundamental interests of the overwhelming majority of the people in China."

10. Zhao Suisheng, *A Nation-State by Construction: Dynamics of Modern Chinese Nationalism,* Stanford University Press, Stanford, Calif., 2004.

11. Peak Oil Netherlands Foundation, "World Oil Production and Peaking Outlook," 2005, table 1, p. 7.

TABLE 1. WORLD OIL PEAKING ESTIMATES AS OF OCTOBER 2005

Source of Projection	Projected date	Source of Projection	Projected date
Individual Experts		**Governments**	
A. Bakthiari	2006–2007	Dutch Government (IEA HI copy)	After 2030
M. Simmons	2007–2009	French Government	2020–2030
C. Skrebowski	2007–2010		
K, Deffeyes	2005–2009	**Analyst Firms**	
J. Laherrère	2010–2020	IHS Energy*	2011–2020
P. Odell	2060	Douglas Westwood	2010–2020
B. Pickens	2005–2007	Energy Files	2010–2020
M. Lynch	After 2030	PFC Energy	2014–2025
C. Campbell	2010		
S. Al-Husseini	2015	**Energy Advisory Organizations**	
J. Gilbert	2010	World Energy Council	After 2020
T. Petrie	Before 2010	Energy Research Center Netherlands	2010–2035
		CERA	After 2020
Oil Companies		ASPO	2010
CNOOC	2005–2010	IEA deferred investment scenario	Around 2020
Total	2020–2025	IEA high resource case	After 2030
Shell	After 2025		
BP	We cannot know	**Other Organizations**	
Exxon-Mobil	After 2030	Volvo	2010–2015
		Ford	2005–2010

* Prediction means that the demand of oil will probably not be met.

12. Cited by Dr. Gal Luft in his statement to U.S.-China Economic and Security Review Commission, Hearing on China's Future Energy Development and Acquisition Strategies, July 21, 2005.

13. The investment bankers Morgan Stanley estimate that since the beginning of the "China boom" in 1978. American consumers have cumulatively saved $100 billion by paying China's prices rather than what they would have paid otherwise.

14. Letter from the president to senators Hagel, Helms, Craig, and Roberts, March 13, 2001.

15. *BusinessWeek,* Top 100 Brands, 2005.

16. "The Day Nothing Much Changed," *Foreign Policy,* September–October 2006, p. 25.

17. Alistair Iain Johnston, "Chinese Middle Class Attitudes towards International Affairs: Nascent Liberalization?" *China Quarterly,* Vol. 179, No. 1, 2004. However, Johnston does not look directly at attitudes toward Taiwan.

18. Clyde Prestowitz, *Three Billion New Capitalists,* Basic Books, New York, 2005, p. 76.

19. Oded Shenkar, *The Chinese Century: The Rising Chinese Economy and Its Impact on the Global Economy, the Balance of Power, and Your Job,* Wharton School Publishing, 2004.

20. John Maynard Keynes, "National Self-Sufficiency," *Yale Review,* Vol. 22, No. 4, June 1933, pp. 755–769.

21. Harold James, *The End of Globalization: Lessons from the Great Depression,* Harvard University Press, Cambridge, Mass., 2001, p. 8.

22. Ibid, p. 11.

23. Michael D. Bordo, Barry Eichengreen, and Douglas A. Irwin, *Is Globalisation Today Really Different from Globalisation a Hundred Years Ago?* NBER Working Paper No. 7195, table 3 (Average Tariffs on Imported Manufactured Goods).

24. Ibid, table 6.

25. Ibid.

26. Maddison, op. cit.

27. "China and the World Economy: From T-Shirts to T-Bonds," *Economist,* July 28, 2005. For a more modest account, see Steven B. Kamin, Mario Marazzi, and John W. Schindler, *Is China "Exporting Deflation"?* Board of Governors of the Federal Reserve System, International Finance Discussion Papers No. 791, January 2004.

28. Nouriel Roubini and Brad Setser, "The U.S. as Net Debtor: The Sustainability of U.S. External Imbalances," November 2004, pages.stern .nyu.edu/~nroubini/papers/Roubini-Setser-U.S.-External-Imbalances .pdf. For a slightly different perspective, see Charles Dumas and Diana Choyleva, *The Bill from the China Shop: How Asia's Savings Glut Threatens the World Economy*, Profile, London, 2006.

29. Richard Freeman, "Doubling the Global Labour Force," Centre for Economic Performance, October 2004. Freeman estimates that there are also 400 million new additions to the global workforce from India and 200 million from the former Soviet Union; ultimately, these will double the world's effective labor force.

30. Jiang Zemin's speech at the Sixteenth Chinese Communist Party Congress.

31. David Hale, "China's Growing Appetites," *National Interest*, Summer 2004.

32. World Economic Forum on East Asia, Security, and Sustainability, Tokyo, Japan, June 15–18, 2006. Available at www.weforum.org/pdf/ SummitReports/eastasia2006/security.htm.

33. David Zweig and Bi Jianhai, "China's Global Hunt for Energy," *Foreign Affairs*, September–October 2005.

34. Communications from the localities to Party Central and State Council. See Zhang Liang in Andrew J. Nathan and Perry Link, eds., *The Tiananmen Papers: The Chinese Leadership's Decision to Use Force against Their Own People—In Their Own Words*, Public Affairs, New York, 2001, p. 398, This book gives a remarkable account of the whole episode.

35. See Bruce Gilley, *China's Democratic Future: How It Will Happen and Where It Will Lead*, Columbia University Press, New York, 2004.

36. Nathan and Link, op. cit.

37. Wang Hui, *China's New Order: Society, Politics, and Economy in Transition*, ed. Theodore Huters, Harvard University Press, Cambridge, Mass., 2003.

38. Nathan and Link, op. cit.

39. Quoted in Nicholas Kristof and Sheryl Wu Dunn, *China Wakes*, Times Books, New York, 1994, p. 82.

40. There is considerable dispute over the exact figures. For example, see Kristof and Wu Dunn, op. cit. These two authors, who are Beijing correspondents of the *New York Times*, estimate that up to 800 unarmed

people were killed and several thousand injured. Western news agencies at the time offered a range of numbers. My figures are from Nathan and Link, op. cit.

41. Hu Angang, *Great Transformations in China*, Oxford University Press, Oxford, 2006, table 4.1. The computations are based on purchasing power parity (PPP).

42. According to the Chinese Bureau of National Statistics, the gini coefficient has risen from 0.403 in 1998 to 0.465 in 2004. It excludes corrupt income going to officials, so the calculation is almost certainly too low.

43. *Financial Times* China Supplement, November 8, 2005. Xie Fuzhan, deputy director of the Development Research Council, is quoted: "We need to create about 20 million new jobs a year." See also Tony Saich, *China: Sociopolitical Issues, 2005–2010,* Kennedy School of Government, Harvard University, Cambridge, Mass., 2005. Saich quotes Lu Zhongyuan, also of the Development Research Council, as saying that China will need 24 million jobs a year.

44. Saich, op. cit., p. 6.

45. Hu Angang, op. cit., p. 259.

46. "China in 2005: Hu in Charge," *Asian Survey,* Vol. 46, No. 1, January–February 2006, p. 42.

47. See Richard McGregor, "Power, Not Socialism in Today's Chinese Ideology," *The Financial Times,* July 25, 2006.

48. Xinhua News Agency, "China Becoming Growth Engine for World." Hu Jintao's speech to the 2005 Fortune Global Forum, http://www .china.org.cn/english/2005/May/128956.htm (accessed August 13, 2005). See also Ira Kalish, *The World's Factory: China Enters the Twenty-first Century,* Deloitte Research Consumer Business Study, 2003.

49. Hu Angang, op. cit.

CHAPTER 2

1. Jonathan D. Spence, *The Quest for Modern China,* Norton, New York, 1999.

2. Max Weber, *The Religion of China,* Free Press, New York, 1968. See also Max Weber, *The Protestant Ethic and Other Writings,* Twentieth Century Classics, Penguin, London, 2005.

3. Douglass C. North, "The Paradox of the West." in Richard W. David, ed., *The Origins of Modern Freedom,* Stanford University Press, Stanford, Calif., 1995, pp. 7–34.

4. Robert Finlay, "China, the World, and World History in Joseph Needham's 'Science and Civilisation,'" *Journal of World History*, Vol. 11, No. 2, 2000.

5. Peter C. Perdue, *China Marches West*, Belknap-Harvard University Press, Cambridge, Mass., 2005.

6. Angus Maddison, *The World Economy: Historical Statistics*, OECD, Paris, 2004.

7. Kent Deng, *The Premodern Chinese Economy*, Routledge, London, 2003, pp. 46–47.

8. Erik Ringmar, *The Mechanics of Modernity in Europe and East Asia*, Routledge, London, 2005, p. 159.

9. Richard Tawney, *Land and Labour in China*, George Allen and Unwin, London, 1937.

10. Deng, op. cit.

11. Mark Elvin, *The Pattern of the Chinese Past*, Stanford University Press, Stanford, Calif., 1973.

12. Deng, op. cit., p. 164. From the Song to the Qing, on average, government tax revenue represented 7.1 to 9.3 percent of the agricultural GDP and 5 to 7 percent of the total GDP.

13. Li Bozhong, *Agricultural Development in Jiangnan, 1620–1850*, Palgrave-Macmillan, Basingstoke, 1998.

14. Deng, op. cit., p. 170.

15. Gu Yanwu was a seventeenth-century Confucian scholar who personified this tradition.

16. American Council on Education, *China and Europe, 1500–2000*, 2004.

17. Deng, op. cit.

18. Ibid., p. 68.

19. Erik Ringmar, *The Mechanics of Modernity in Europe and East Asia*, Routledge, London, 2005, p. 150. In the late Ming dynasty some 2,000 officials were dismissed as a result of one inspection by the censorate.

20. Deng, op. cit., p. 110.

21. Ibid., p. 222.

22. John Fairbank, *The United States and China*, American Foreign Political Library, Harvard University Press, Cambridge, Mass., 1989.

23. Jurgen Habermas, *The Structural Transformation of the Public Sphere*, Polity, Cambridge, 1999. See also C. A. Bayly, *The Birth of the Modern World 1780–1914*, Blackwell, London, 2004.

24. Joel Mokyr, "The Enduring Riddle of the European Miracle: The Enlightenment and the Industrial Revolution," Northwestern University, Mimeo, 2002.

25. Ibid.

26. Jared Diamond, *Guns, Germs, and Steel: A Short History of Everybody for the Last 13,000 Years,* Vintage, New York, 1998.

27. Charles Tilly, *Coercion, Capital, and European States, A.D. 990–1990: Studies in Social Discontinuity,* Blackwell, London, 1993. See also Eric L. Jones. *The European Miracle: Environments, Economies, and Geopolitics in the History of Europe and Asia,* Cambridge University Press, Cambridge, 2003.

28. Daron Acemgolu, Simon Johnson, and James Robinson, "The Rise of Europe: Atlantic Trade, Institutional Change, and Economic Growth," *American Economic Review,* Vol. 95, No. 3, June 2005, pp. 546–579. The balance of power between competing groups lies at the heart of their account of democratization. See also the following. Daron Acemoglu and James Robinson, *Economic Origins of Dictatorship and Democracy,* Cambridge University Press, Cambridge, 2006. Michael Johnston, *Syndromes of Wealth: Wealth, Power, and Democracy,* Cambridge University Press, Cambridge, 2005, pp. 216–219.

29. Having examined various competing explanations, Perdue reaches this conclusion. He maintains that conflict-driven innovation essentially stopped when the Qing finally put down the last nomadic empire in 1760. Peter C. Perdue, "Constructing Chinese Property Rights: East and West," in Huri Islamoglu, ed., *Constituting Modernity: Private Property in the East and West,* IB Tauris, London, 2004.

30. Fernand Braudel, *Civilization and Capitalism, Fifteenth–Eighteenth Century,* Vol. 2, *The Wheels of Commerce,* University of California Press, Berkeley, 1992.

31. J. M. Keynes, *A Treatise on Money,* Vol. 2, Palgrave-Macmillan, Basingstoke, 1971.

32. Ringmar, op. cit.

33. This point is made by Mokyr, *The Enduring Riddle of the European Miracle,* op. cit.

34. Joel Mokyr, "The Great Synergy: The European Enlightenment as a Factor in Modern Economic Growth," keynote address, European Association for Political and Evolutionary Economics, Maastricht, November 2003.

35. Angus Maddison, *Growth and Interaction in the World Economy: The Roots of Modernity,* Washington, D.C.: AEI Press, 2005, p. 18.

36. At this point in brief histories of China, it is traditional, indeed ritualistic, to quote Emperor Qian Long's famous retort to Lord Macartney's trade mission to China in 1793: China has "not the slightest need for your country's manufactures." I have spared readers this ritual in my main text, but I include the quotation here because it remains a telling insight into the Chinese mentality at the time.

37. See Kent Deng, *Statebuilding: The Original Push for Institutional Changes in Modern China, 1840–1950,* Working Paper No. 0104, Global Economic History Network, London School of Economics, February 2004. Deng quotes a work of 1990 by D. Zhang.

CHAPTER 3

1. R. Keith Schoppa, *Revolution and Its Past: Identities and Change in Modern Chinese History,* Prentice Hall, Saddle River, N.J., 2002.

2. Ibid.

3. Ibid. See also Jonathan D. Spence, *The Quest for Modern China,* Norton, New York, 1999.

4. Marc Blecher, *China Against the Tides,* 2nd ed., Continuum International, London, 2003, p. 21.

5. Jonathan Fenby, *Generalissimo: Chiang Kai-shek and the China He Lost,* Simon & Schuster, New York, 2003.

6. Spence, op. cit.

7. Ibid.

8. Brantly Womack, ed. *Contemporary Chinese Politics in Historical Perspective,* Cambridge: Cambridge University Press, 1991. In particular, see his contribution "In Search of Democracy: Public Authority, and Popular Power in China."

9. Quoted in Spence, op. cit., p. 495.

10. John Fairbank, Edwin Reischauer, and Albert M. Craig, *China: Tradition and Transformation,* Allen and Unwin, London, 1989.

11. Quoted in Blecher, op. cit., p. 23.

12. Chris Bramall, *Sources of Chinese Economic Growth 1978–1996,* Oxford University Press, Oxford, 2000.

13. Mark Selden, *The Political Economy of Chinese Development,* Socialism

and Social Movements Series, Sharpe, Armonk, N.Y., 1992. These self-reinforcing dynamics are a theme in Roderick MacFarquhar, *Origins of the Cultural Revolution,* 3 vols., Oxford University Press, Oxford, 1974, 1983, 1999.

14. Blecher, op. cit., pp. 52–72.

15. It is uncertain how many people died as a result of the Great Leap Forward. Estimates range from 16.5 million to a more debatable 40 million. The *Cambridge History of China* offers a narrower range, between 16 million and 27 million. See also Jung Chang and Jon Halliday, *Mao: The Unknown Story,* Random House, London, 2005; these authors offer a figure of 37 million. Computer modeling by U.S. Bureau of the Census has yielded an estimate of 30 million that is widely though not universally accepted; see http://countrystudies.us/china/33.htm.

16. Min C. Tsang, "Education and National Development in China," *China Review,* 2000, p. 6.

17. Justin Yifu Lin, Fang Cai, and Zhou Li, *The China Miracle,* Chinese University Press, Hong Kong, 2003.

18. Bramall, op. cit., p. 137.

19. Ibid., p. 158. In analyzing the Indian experience, the Nobel laureate Amartya Sen also praises this aspect of China's development. See, for instance, Jean Dreze and Amartya Sen, *India: Economic Development and Social Opportunity,* Oxford University Press, Oxford, 1995, especially pp. 85–86.

20. Qian Yingyi "The Process of China's Market Transition (1978–1998): The Evolutionary, Historical, and Comparative Perspectives," paper prepared for a symposium of *Journal of Institutional and Theoretical Economics,* "Big-Bang Transformation of Economic Systems as a Challenge to New Institutional Economics," June 9–11, 1999, Wallerfangen/Saar, Germany.

21. Shahid Yusuf, Kaoru Nabeshima, and Dwight Perkins, *Under New Ownership,* World Bank, 2006, p. 50.

22. Chang and Halliday, op. cit.

23. Zhao Suisheng, *A Nation-State by Construction: Dynamics of Modern Chinese Nationalism,* Stanford University Press, Stanford, Calif., 2004, p. 241.

24. Maurice Meisner, *The Significance of the Chinese Revolution in World*

History, Working Paper No. 1, Asia Research Centre, London School of Economics and Political Science. See also Maurice Meisner, *Marxism, Maoism, and Utopianism: Eight Essays,* University of Wisconsin Press, Madison, 1982.

25. Max Weber, "Politics as Vocation," in H. H. Gerth and C. Wright Mills, trans. and eds., *From Max Weber: Essays in Sociology,* Oxford University Press, New York, 1946, pp. 77–128.

26. May 16, 2006, was the fortieth anniversary of the start of Cultural Revolution. Officially, the event remains shrouded in silence; this is characteristic of the Chinese Communist Party, which is unwilling to grapple with its own ambiguous history. See, for instance, "China Ignoring the Past," *Economist,* May 18, 2006.

27. Barrington Moore, *Social Origins of Dictatorship and Democracy: Lord and Peasant in the Making of the Modern World,* Penguin, London, 1991.

28. Karl Polanyi, *The Great Transformation,* Octagon, New York, 1980.

29. Andrew Neil, Fourteenth Annual Friedrich Hayek Lecture, November 28, 2005.

CHAPTER 4

1. Cited in Qian Yingyi, "The Process of China's Market Transition (1978–1998): The Evolutionary, Historical, and Comparative Perspectives," paper prepared for a symposium of *Journal of Institutional and Theoretical Economics,* "Big-Bang Transformation of Economic Systems as a Challenge to New Institutional Economics," June 9–11, 1999, Wallerfangen/Saar, Germany.

2. Made on Deng's southern tour (January 18–February 21, 1992).

3. Barry Naughton, "Deng Xiaoping: The Economist," in Lin Chun, ed., *China,* Vol. 2, *The Transformation of Chinese Socialism,* Ashgate-Dartmouth, Burlington, Vt., 2000, p. 388.

4. Richard Baum, *Burying Mao: Chinese Politics in the Age of Deng Xiaoping,* Princeton University Press, Princeton, N.J., 1996.

5. Ibid.

6. Barry Naughton, *Growing Out of the Plan: Chinese Economic Reform, 1978–1993,* Cambridge University Press, Cambridge, 1997. See also William Byrd, *The Market Mechanism and Economic Reforms in China,* Sharpe, Armonk, N.Y., 1991.

7. Shahid Yusuf, Kaoru Nabeshima, and Dwight H. Perkins, *Under New Ownership: Privatizing China's State Owned Enterprises*, World Bank, 2005, table 1.2.
8. F. Modigliani and Shi Larry Cao, "The Chinese Saving Puzzle and the Life-Cycle Hypothesis," *Journal of Economic Literature*, Vol. 42, March 2004, pp. 145–170.
9. Jeffrey Sachs and Wing Thye Woo, *China's Transition Experience, Reexamined*, World Bank, 1996. See also Jeffrey Sachs and Wing Thye Woo, "The Real Reasons for China's Growth," *China Journal*, January 1999.
10. Qian Qingyi, op. cit.
11. Naughton, "Deng Xiaoping: The Economist," op. cit.
12. Yusuf, Nabeshima, and Perkins, op. cit.
13. Ibid., table 1.3.
14. Qian Yingyi, "The Institutional Foundations of China's Market Transition," paper prepared for World Bank Development Conference of April 1999.
15. Ibid., p. 8.
16. *Economist* China Survey, March 23, 2006.
17. Professor Li Bozhong showed me thousands of property titles, dating from the seventeenth century, that had been used in Anhui province to reclaim land.
18. Chris Bramall, *Sources of Chinese Economic Growth 1978–1996*, Oxford University Press, Oxford, 2000, pp. 250–251.
19. Naughton, "Deng: The Economist," op. cit., p. 19.
20. Qian Yingyi, op. cit.
21. Chong-en Bai, David D. Li, and Yijiang Wang, "Thriving on a Tilted Playing Field," in Nicholas C. Hope, Dennis Tao Yang, and Mu Yang Li, eds., *How Far across the River?*, Stanford University Press, Stanford, Calif., 2003.
22. Jean Oi, *Rural China Takes Off: Institutional Foundations of Economic Reform*, University of California Press, Berkeley, 1999. See also Susan Whiting, *Power and Wealth in Rural China: The Political Economy of Institutional Change*, Cambridge University Press, Cambridge, 2000.
23. Edward Steinfeld, *Forging Reform in China: The Fate of State-Owned Industry*, Cambridge University Press, Cambridge, 1998.
24. This characterization seems to surface in some of the arguments of Jean Oi, whose work is otherwise very illuminating.
25. Joe Studwell, *The China Dream*, Profile, London, 2005.

26. Kellee Tsai, *Back Alley Banking,* Cornell University Press, Ithaca, N.Y., 2002. ch. 4.

27. Liu Yaling, "Reform from Below: The Private Economy and Local Politics in the Rural Industrialization of Wenzhou," *China Quarterly,* Vol. 130, June 1992.

28. Dali Yang, *Remaking the Chinese Leviathan: Market Transition and the Politics of Governance in China,* Stanford University Press, Stanford, Calif., 2004.

29. Yasheng Huang, "Institutional Development and Private Sector Development," in *China,* Wilson Centre Asia Report Series No. 129, July 2005.

30. Lee Branstetter and Nicholas Lardy, "China's Embrace of Globalisation," in *China,* Wilson Centre Asia Report Series No. 129, July 2005.

31. Studwell, op. cit., p. 15.

32. Ibid., p. 75.

33. Wanda Tseng and Harm Zebregs, *Foreign Direct Investment in China: Some Lessons for Other Countries,* IMF Policy Discussion Paper No. PDP/02/03, 2002.

34. "Keeping Tabs on China's Growth," *BusinessWeek,* http://www.businessweek.com/globalbiz/content/may2006/gb20060524_346105.htm?chan=globalbiz_asia_today%27s+top+story.

35. OECD, *Economic Survey: China,* 2005, fig. 1.1.

36. Yasheng Huang, *Selling China: Foreign Direct Investment during the Reform Era,* Cambridge University Press, Cambridge, 2003, table 8.1 (Export Shares of FIEs of Total Exports in Three Countries: Taiwan, China, and Indonesia).

37. Ira Kalish, *The World's Factory: China Enters the Twenty-first Century,* Deloitte Research, 2004.

38. "The Debate of China's Becoming a World Factory," Academy of China's Economic Reform and Development, Renmin University, 2004.

39. Peter Nolan, *China at the Crossroads,* Palgrave-Macmillan, Basingstoke, 2004.

40. Yasheng Huang, *Selling China,* op. cit.

CHAPTER 5

1. Some of these themes are mentioned in Zheng Yongnian, *Globalization and State Transformation in China,* Cambridge University Press, Cambridge, 2004.
2. Martin Ravallion and Shaohua Chen, *China's (Uneven) Progress against Poverty,* World Bank Policy Research Working Paper No. 3408, September 2004.
3. Joshua Ramo, former foreign editor of *Time* magazine, coined this phrase in *The Beijing Consensus,* Foreign Policy Centre, 2004.
4. Jiang Zemin, "Promote the Building of a Clean Government (2000)," in *On the "Three Represents,"* Foreign Languages Press, Beijing, 2002, pp. 119–147.
5. Nicholas Lardy, cited in Dali L. Yang, "Economic Transformation and State Rebuilding in China," in Barry Naughton and Dali L. Yang, eds., *Holding China Together,* Cambridge University Press, Cambridge, 2004.
6. Dali L. Yang, *Remaking the Chinese Leviathan,* Stanford University Press, Stanford, Calif., 2004.
7. Marc Blecher, *China against the Tides,* Continuum International, London, 2003, p. 106.
8. Barry Naughton and Dali L. Yang, eds., "Holding China Together: Diversity and National Integration in the Post-Deng Era," Cambridge University Press, Cambridge, 2004, p. 8.
9. Blecher, op. cit., p. 106.
10. Yang, *Remaking the Chinese Leviathan,* op. cit.
11. Zhiyue Bo, "The Institutionalisation of Elite Management," in Barry Naughton and Dali L. Yang, eds., *Holding China Together,* Cambridge University Press, Cambridge, 2004, p. 86.
12. Yang, *Remaking the Great Leviathan,* op. cit.
13. Sun Yan, "Corruption, Growth, and Reform: The Chinese Enigma," *Current History,* Vol. 104, No. 683, September 2005, pp. 257–263. For a fuller account, see Sun Yan, *Corruption and Market in Contemporary China,* Cornell University Press, Ithaca, N.Y., 2004.
14. Samuel Huntingdon, *Political Order in Changing Societies,* Yale University Press, New Haven, Conn., 1968.
15. Xiaobo Lu, *Cadres and Corruption: The Organizational Involution of the Chinese Communist Party,* Stanford University Press, Stanford, Calif., 2001.

16. *Observer,* June 26, 2005. See also Susan Rose-Ackerman, *Corruption and Government: Causes, Consequences, and Reform,* Cambridge University Press, Cambridge, 1999.

17. James Kynge, *China Shakes the World: The Rise of a Hungry Nation,* Weidenfeld and Nicolson, London, 2006, pp. 153–154.

18. Ibid., pp. 158–159.

19. Andrew Wedeman, "Anticorruption Campaigns and the Intensification of Corruption in China," *Journal of Contemporary China,* Vol. 14, No. 42, February 2005, pp. 93–116.

20. Stanley B. Lubman, *Bird in a Cage: Legal Reform in China after Mao,* Stanford University Press, Stanford, Calif., 2000. See also William Alford, "Double-Edged Swords Cut Both Ways: Law and Legitimacy in the People's Republic of China," *Daedalus,* March 22, 1993; Alford is skeptical about the Chinese Communist Party's "instrumental" approach to law. For a more upbeat assessment that is still sensitive to the contradictions, see Randall Peerenbloom, *China's Long March toward Rule of Law,* Cambridge University Press, Cambridge, 2002.

21. Shandong Xinhuanet, cited in "Enforcement of Civil Judgments: Harder Than Reaching the Sky," *China Law and Governance Review,* December 13, 2003.

22. Minxin Pei, Director, China Program, Carnegie Endowment for International Peace, statement to Senate Foreign Relations Committee, June 7, 2005.

23. "Enforcement of Civil Judgments," op. cit.

24. Minxin Pei, op. cit.

25. Ye Zhang, *China's Emerging Civil Society,* Working Paper, Center for Northeast Asian Policy Studies, Brookings Institution, 2003.

26. Guo Zhenglin and Thomas Bernstein, "The Impact of Elections on the Village Structure of Power: The Relations between the Village Committees and the Party Branches," *Journal of Contemporary China,* Vol. 13, No. 39, May 2004, pp. 257–275. See also Bjorg Alpermann, "The Postelection Administration of Chinese Villages," *China Journal,* Vol. 46, July 2001, pp. 45–68.

27. "Back on the Leash," *Economist,* August 18, 2005.

28. John G. Palfrey, Jr., Executive Director, Berkman Center for Internet and Society, Harvard Law School, evidence to the U.S.-China Economic and Security Review Commission, April 14, 2005. For a com-

plete study of Internet filtering in China, as of 2005, see http://www
.opennetinitiative.net/china/.

29. Karl Taro Greenfeld, "The Viral Hunters," *Foreign Policy,* March
    2006.

30. Ibid., p. 8.

31. Isabel Hilton, "Beijing's Media Chill," *Open Democracy,* February 15,
    2006; available at http://www.opendemocracy.net/democracy-china/
    chill_3272.jsp.

32. Minxin Pei, *China's Trapped Transition,* Harvard University Press,
    Cambridge, Mass., 2006.

33. Ibid., pp. 92–95.

34. Bruce Dickson, *Red Capitalists in China: The Party, Private Entrepre-
    neurs, and Prospects for Political Change,* Cambridge University Press,
    Cambridge, 2003.

35. Ru Xin, Lu Xueyi, and Li Peilin, eds., *Zhongguo shehui xingshi fenxi yu
    yuce 2005* (Analysis and Forecast of China's Social Development,
    2005), Social Sciences Academic Press, Beijing, 2004.

36. Richard Baum, "China's State Control Mechanism and Methods," evi-
    dence to U.S.-China Economic and Security Review Commission,
    April 14, 2005.

37. Murray Scott Tanner, "China's State Control Mechanism and Meth-
    ods," evidence to U.S.-China Economic and Security Review Commis-
    sion, April 14, 2005.

38. George J. Gilboy and Eric Heginbothan, "The Latin Americanization
    of China," *Current History,* September 2004, p. 258.

39. Cited in Tony Saich, "Satisfaction with Government Performance:
    Public Opinion in Rural and Urban China," May 2005, p. 8 (mimeo-
    graph).

40. Described in Elizabeth Perry, *Challenging the Mandate of Heaven:
    Social Protest and State Power in China,* Sharpe, Armonk, N.Y., 2002.

41. Minxin Pei derives rankings from the raw numbers in World Bank,
    Governance Matters III. See Minxin Pei, *Trapped Transition,* op. cit.,
    pp. 5–6.

42. Quoted in Minxin Pei, *Trapped Transition,* op. cit., p. 4.

43. Baum, op. cit.

44. Ibid.

CHAPTER 6

1. Martin Wolf, *Why Globalization Works,* Yale University Press, New Haven, Conn., 2005, p. 144.

2. OECD, *Economic Survey of China,* 2005, p. 96.

3. Shahid Yusuf, Kaoru Nabeshima, and Dwight H. Perkins, *Under New Ownership: Privatizing China's State Owned Enterprises,* World Bank, 2005.

4. "The Struggle of the Champions," *Economist,* January 6 2005.

5. For a foreign perspective, see "Over the Wall," *Economist,* November 3, 2005.

6. Carl E. Walter and Fraser J. T. Howie, *"To Get Rich Is Glorious": China's Stock Markets in the 1980s and 1990s,* Palgrave-Macmillan, Basingstoke, 2001, pp. 36–43.

7. According to the 2006 ISS Global Institutional Investor Study, which interviewed 322 multinationals worth a combined $27 billion, the market value of all listed companies in China dropped by 50 percent between 2001 and 2005. "China told to refine corporate governance," *FT,* April 16, 2006.

8. Yusuf, Nebeshima, and Perkins, op. cit., p. 90.

9. Guy Liu and Pei Sun, "China's Public Firms: How Much Privatisation?" in Stephen Green and Guy Liu, eds., *Exit the Dragon? State Control and Privatisation in China,* Blackwell, Oxford, 2005. But see also, in the same book, Stephen Green, "The Privatization Two-Step at China's Listed Firm," pp. 125–144. Green (like some other contributors to this work) believes that these structures are inherently transitory and the movement is toward increased privatization, though he concedes that increased regulation may be required to inhibit a tendency to strip assets.

10. Michael E. Porter, Klaus Schwab, and Augusto Lopez-Claros, *The Global Competitiveness Report 2005–2006: Policies Underpinning Rising Prosperity,* Palgrave-Macmillan, Basingstoke, 2005.

11. Yasheng Huang, *Selling China,* Cambridge University Press, Cambridge, 2003.

12. Heytens and Karacadag, quoted in Yusuf, Nebeshima, and Perkins, op. cit. p. 14.

13. OECD, op. cit., p. 96.

14. Ibid., p. 52.
15. Minxin Pei, "The Dark Side of China's Rise," *Foreign Policy*, March-April 2006.
16. "The Myth of China Inc.," *Economist*, September 1, 2005.
17. Edward Steinfeld, *Forging Reform in China: The Fate of State-Owned Industry*, Cambridge University Press, Cambridge, 1998.
18. OECD, op. cit.
19. "A healthy financial sector requires enterprises that deserve financing," Davin A. McKenzie to Conference on Financial Sector Reform in China, September 2001. See also David L. Wank, *Commodifying Communism: Business, Trust, and Politics in a Chinese City*, Cambridge University Press, Cambridge, 1999.
20. *Asia Times*, August 10, 2005. See also "The Myth of China Inc.," op. cit.
21. "The Myth of China Inc.," op. cit.
22. Ibid.
23. George Gilboy, "The Myth behind China's Miracle," *Foreign Affairs*, July-August 2004.
24. Edward Steinfeld, "China's Shallow Integration: Networked Production and the New Challenges for Late Industrialization," Commission on U.S.-China Economic and Security Review, September 25, 2003.
25. Ibid.
26. Sandra Poncet, "Measuring Chinese Domestic and International Integration," *China Economic Review*, Vol. 14, No. 1, 2003, pp. 1–21.
27. Ibid., p. 17.
28. Y. Rao, B. Lu, and C. Tsou, "Transition from Rule by Man to Rule by Merit: Comments on National Planning of Science and Technology," *Nature*, Vol. 432, No. 7015, November 18, 2004.
29. Adam Segal and Ernest J. Wilson III, "Trends in China's Transition toward a Knowledge Economy," *Asian Survey*, Vol. 45, No. 6, November-December 2005, p. 893.
30. Elizabeth Economy, "China's Environmental Challenge," *Current History*, Vol. 104, September 2005. See also Elizabeth Economy, *The River Runs Black: The Environmental Challenge to China's Future*, Cornell University Press, Ithaca, N.Y., 2004 (monograph).
31. Economy, "China's Environmental Challenge," op. cit., p. 279.
32. Nathan Nankivell, "China's Pollution and Its Threat to Domestic and Regional Stability," *Jamestown Review, China Brief*, Vol. 5, Issue 22,

October 25, 2005, http://jamestown.org/publications_details.php? volume_id=408andissue_id=3505andarticle_id=2370389. However, Elizabeth Economy puts the figure at just over 300,000.

33. Nathan Nankivell, "The National Security Implications of China's Emerging Water Crisis," *Jamestown Review, China Brief*, Vol. 5, Issue 17, August 2, 2005, http://jamestown.org/publications_details.php?vol ume_id=408andissue_id=3422andarticle_id=2370095.

34. Economy, "China's Environmental Challenge," op. cit., p. 279.

35. Yusuf, Nebeshima, and Perkins, op. cit., pp. 6–8.

36. For a general overview of the challenges and responses, see Yasheng Huang, Tony Saich, and Edward Steinfeld, eds., *Financial Sector Reform in China*, Harvard University Press, Cambridge, Mass., 2005.

37. The classic account is Nicholas R. Lardy, *China's Unfinished Economic Revolution*, Brookings Institution, Washington, D.C., 1998.

38. Joe Studwell, *The China Dream*, Profile, London, 2005. Studwell notes the findings of Stu Fulton, a financial systems specialist working with PWC. After three years in the field, he concluded that 50 percent of total portfolios were NPLs; in some branches, the proportion rose as high as 70 to 80 percent.

39. "A Great Big Banks Gamble," *Economist*, October 27, 2005.

40. Ibid.

41. Richard Podpiera, *Progress in China's Banking Sector Reform: Has Bank Behavior Changed?* IMF Working Paper No. WP/06/71, 2006.

42. *Financial Times*, May 3, 2006.

43. *Financial Times*, May 31, 2006.

44. Yusuf, Nebeshima, and Perkins, op. cit.

45. Hu Angang, *Great Transformations in China*, Oxford University Press, Oxford, 2006, table 3.1.

46. Qu Hongbin and Sophia Ma Xiaoping, *China Economic Insight*, Vol. 25, *Balancing Act*, HSBC Global Research, 2006.

47. Ibid.

48. Ibid. These authors recount the anecdote and also describe how the local government of Jian in Guangxi province has built an ultramodern eight-lane highway in the city center, even though there are only 200,000 people and fewer than 10,000 cars.

49. Olivier Blanchard and Francesco Giavazzi, *Rebalancing Growth in China*, MIT Working Paper No. 05-32, November 2005. These authors say that the RMB is 30 percent undervalued, and in support quote un-

published work by Haussman and Rodrik. Morris Goldstein of the Institute for International Economics in Washington also calculates, in a paper of December 2005 for the Cato Institute, that the RMB is 30 percent undervalued.

50. Blanchard and Giavazzi, op. cit.

51. Edward Lim, Michael Spence, and Ricardo Hausmann, "China and Global Economy: Medium Term Issues and Options," Center for International Development Working Paper, No. 126, Harvard University, 2006.

52. Minxin Pei, *China's Trapped Transition: The Limits of Developmental Autocracy,* Harvard University Press, Cambridge, Mass., 2006, p. 173.

53. Ibid.

54. Ibid.

55. Ibid., p. 174.

56. Tony Saich, "Development and Choice in Asia's Giants," in Bruce Gilley and Edward Friedman, eds., *Comparing China and India,* Palgrave-Macmillan, Basingstoke, 2005, p. 231.

57. Minxin Pei, *Trapped Transition,* op. cit., p. 171.

58. Ibid., p. 170.

59. Cheng Li, *Hu's Policy Shift and the Tuanpai's Coming-of-Age,* China Leadership Monitor No. 15, 2005, pp. 4–5, available at www.chinalead ershipmonitor.org.

60. This point is made in Thomas Palley, "External Contradictions of the Chinese Development Model: Export-Led Growth and the Dangers of Global Economic Contraction," *Journal of Contemporary China,* Vol. 15, No. 46, 2006.

61. David Metcalf and Jianwei Li, "Chinese Unions: Nugatory or Transforming? An Alive Analysis," CEP Discussion Paper No. 708, December 2005.

CHAPTER 7

1. Dani Rodrik, "Good-Bye Washington Consensus, Hello Washington Confusion?" 2006, http://ksghome.harvard.edu/~drodrik/Lessons%20of%20the%201990s%20review%20_JEL_.pdf.

2. Jared Diamond, *Guns, Germs, and Steel: A Short History of Everybody for the Last 13,000 Years,* Vintage, New York, 1998. For instance, Diamond attributes delays in food production and their effects on eco-

nomic, political, and military organization to a lack of domesticated animals. Eurasia's native cows, sheep, goats, horses, and pigs, which were relatively docile, cheap to feed, and capable of being bred in captivity, were important to its development. The same was not true of Africa: the African buffalo, zebra, bush pig, rhino, and hippopotamus were violent and difficult to keep in captivity.

3. David Bloom and Jeffrey D. Sachs, *Geography, Demography, and Economic Growth in Africa,* Brookings Papers on Economic Activity No. 2, 1998, pp. 207–273.

4. Wing Thye Woo, "The Washington Consensus: Misunderstanding the Poor by the Brightest," paper presented at a conference organized by FONDAD, "Stability, Growth, and the Search for a New Development Agenda: Reconsidering the Washington Consensus," 2004.

5. Ibid., p. 17. Woo cites a work by John Williamson, "What Should the World Bank Think about the Washington Consensus?"

6. World Economic Forum, Global Competitiveness Report No. 2005–5, Palgrave-Macmillan, Basingstoke, 2005.

7. Dani Rodrik, "Institutions for High-Quality Growth: What They Are and How to Acquire Them," paper prepared for IMF Conference on Second Generation Reform, 1999.

8. Amartya Sen, *Freedom as Development,* Oxford University Press, Oxford, 1999.

9. Nicholas Stern, Jean-Jacques Dethier, and F. Halsey Rogers, *Growth and Empowerment: Making Development Happen,* MIT Press, Cambridge, Mass., 2005. See also David Ellerman, *Helping People Help Themselves: From the World Bank to an Alternative Philosophy of Development Assistance,* University of Michigan Press, Ann Arbor, 2006.

10. Joseph Stiglitz compares Latin America's average 2.7 percent growth rate during the 1990s with 5.4 percent during the 1960s and attributes it to a different policy approach and mix.

11. James C. Scott, *Seeing Like a State: How Certain Schemes to Improve the Human Condition Have Failed,* Yale University Press, New Haven, Conn., 1998.

12. "The Geopolitics of Sexual Frustration," *Foreign Policy,* March-April 2006.

13. Ibid.

14. These comments are drawn from Yanzhong Huang and Dali L. Yang,

"Population Control and State Coercion in China," in Barry Naughton and Dali L. Yang, eds., *Holding China Together*, Cambridge University Press, Cambridge, 2004; and from Sen, op. cit.

15. For a typology of unintended consequences of intervention, see Sam D. Sieber, *Fatal Remedies: The Ironies of Social Intervention*, Plenum, New York, 2001.

16. Sen, op. cit.

17. Ibid., pp. 221–223.

18. Tom R. Tyler, *Why People Obey the Law*, Yale University Press, New Haven, Conn., 1990.

19. Morton H. Halperin, Joseph T. Siegle, and Michael M. Weinstein, *The Democracy Advantage: How Democracies Promote Prosperity and Peace*, Routledge, London, 2005.

20. Ibid. See especially ch. 1, "Exposing a 50-Year-Old Myth"; and ch. 2, "Setting the Record Straight."

21. Ibid., p. 13.

22. Ibid. See especially ch. 4, "Democracy and Security."

23. Cass Sunstein, *Why Societies Need Dissent*, Oliver Wendell Holmes Lectures, Harvard University Press, Cambridge, Mass., 2003.

24. James Surowiecki, *The Wisdom of Crowds: Why the Many Are Smarter Than the Few and How Collective Wisdom Shapes Business, Economies, Societies, and Nations*, Doubleday, Garden City, N.Y., 2004.

25. For a synthesis of case studies, see John Kay, *The Truth about Markets: Their Genius, Their Limits, Their Follies*, Allen Lane, London, 2003.

26. Richard Florida and Gary Gates, *Technology and Tolerance*, Brookings Institution Survey Series, June 2001.

27. The BBC introduced the waterholing technique in the early 2000s under its director general, Greg Dyke. For an account of how it works and its success, see *Creativity*, Work Foundation, 2005.

28. Richard K. Lester and Michael J. Piore, *Innovation: The Missing Dimension*, Harvard University Press, Cambridge, Mass., 2004.

29. Barry Lynn, "Up to the Old-Fashioned Power of the New Oligopolies," *Financial Times*, February 14, 2006. For a more historically informed discussion, see Barry Lynn, *End of the Line: The Rise and Coming Fall of the Global Corporation*, Doubleday, Garden City, N.Y., 2005.

30. John Zaller, "Market Competition and News Quality," paper prepared for annual meetings of American Political Science Association, Atlanta,

Ga., 1999. See also Manuel Castells, *The Power of Identity: The Information Age—Economy, Society, and Culture,* 2nd ed., Blackwell, London, 2004, Vol. 2.

31. Andrew Dunsire, "Tipping the Balance: Autopoiesis and Governance," *Administration and Society,* Vol. 28, No. 3, November 1996. See also the following. Colin Scott, "Analysing Regulatory Space: Fragmented Resources and Institutional Design," *Public Law,* Summer 2001. Albert Hirschman, "Pillars of Order: Social Conflicts as Pillars of Democratic Market Society," *Political Theory,* Vol. 22, No. 22, May 1994.

CHAPTER 8

1. Arjun Appadurai, "The Capacity to Aspire: Culture and the Terms of Recognition," in Vijayendra Rao and Michael Walton, eds., *Culture and Public Action,* Stanford University Press, Stanford, Calif., 2004.

2. Robert Schiller, *The New Financial Risk in the Twenty-First-Century Order,* Princeton University Press, Princeton, N.J., 2003. This work is quoted in Roger C. Altman, Peter R. Orszag, Jason E. Bordoff, and Robert E. Rubin, *An Economic Strategy to Advance Opportunity, Prosperity, and Growth,* Brookings Institute Hamilton Project, 2006, p. 13.

3. John Armour and Douglas Cumming, *The Legal Road to Replicating Silicon Valley,* Centre for Business Research, Cambridge University, Working Paper No. 281, http://www.cbr.cam.ac.uk/pdf/WP281.pdf.

4. Marcus Noland and Howard Pack, *The East Asian Industrial Policy Experience: Implications for the Middle East,* Institute for International Economics, Working Paper No. 05-14, December 2005. In discussing the historical relevance of the east Asian experience for the Middle East, Noland and Pack make an argument similar to the one offered in my text. Partly because of this, they are skeptical about popular arguments that stress an activist industrial policy and the strategy of picking winners.

5. Hernando de Soto, *The Mystery of Capital: Why Capitalism Triumphs in the West and Fails Elsewhere Else,* Black Swan, London, 2001.

6. Many commentators object strongly to this figure. See Christopher Woodruff, "Review of de Soto's *The Mystery of Capital*," *Journal of Economic Literature,* Vol. 39, December 2001. Woodruff argues that the unrealized price of peasant property is $3.6 trillion, which would be

further reduced by translating collateral into loans. Even so, the figure remains large.

7. De Soto, op. cit.

8. See, for instance, David Dyzenhaus, "Form and Substance in the Rule of Law," in C. Forsyth, ed., *Judicial Review and the Constitution,* Hart, Oxford, 2000, p. 141. See also David Dyzenhaus, "Law as Justification: Étienne Mureinik's Conception of Legal Culture," *South African Journal on Human Rights,* Vol. 14, 1998, p. 11.

9. For an overview, see Jerry Evensky, *Adam Smith's Moral Philosophy: A Historical and Contemporary Perspective on Markets, Law, Ethics, and Society,* Cambridge University Press, Cambridge, 2005.

10. Richard Wilkinson, *The Impact of Inequality: How to Make Sick Societies Healthier,* New Press, London, 2005. See also Richard Sennett, *The Culture of the New Capitalism,* Yale University Press, New Haven, Conn., 2005.

11. Alan Greenspan, "Capitalizing Reputation," at Financial Markets Conference of the Federal Reserve Bank of Atlanta, Sea Island, Georgia, April 16, 2004. Cited in John C. Bogle, *The Battle for the Soul of Capitalism,* Yale University Press, New Haven, Conn., 2005.

12. Herbert Gintis, Samuel Bowles, Robert Boyd, and Ernst Fehr, eds., *Moral Sentiments and Material Interests,* MIT Press, Cambridge, Mass., 2005 (a collection of essays).

13. Gintis et al., ibid., distinguish between what they call *weak reciprocity,* cooperation premised on the expectation that individuals will obtain future benefits (as associated with the work of the evolutionary biologist Robert Trivers); and *strong reciprocity,* "the disposition to cooperate with others and to punish those who violate norms of cooperation, at personal cost, even when it is implausible to expect that these costs will be repaid either by others or at a later date."

14. Ibid., p. 12.

15. Robert Axelrod, *The Evolution of Cooperation,* Penguin, London, 2004.

16. For a discussion of how humans differ from other animals, see, e.g., Jeffrey R. Stevens and Marc D. Hauser, "Why Be Nice? Psychological Constraints on the Evolution of Cooperation," *Trends in Cognitive Sciences,* Vol. 8, No. 2, February 2004, pp. 60–65.

17. In so doing, they build on the kind of work developed by Antonio

Damasio. See, e.g., A. R. Damasio, *Descartes' Error: Emotion, Reason, and the Human Brain,* Putnam, New York, 1996.

18. See Stephen Pinker, *The Blank Slate: The Modern Denial of Human Nature,* London: Viking Penguin, 2001, p. 271.

19. Leda Cosmides and John Tooby, "Better Than Rational: Evolutionary Psychology and the Invisible Hand," *American Economic Review,* Vol. 84, No. 2, 1994, p. 239. See also Jerome H. Barkow, Leda Cosmides, and John Tooby, *The Adapted Mind: Evolutionary Psychology and the Generation of Culture,* Oxford University Press, Oxford, 1992.

20. Dan M. Kahan, "The Logic of Reciprocity: Trust, Collective Action, and Law," *Michigan Law Review,* Vol. 102, 2003, p. 71.

21. Richard Wilkinson, "Social Corrosion, Inequality, and Health," in Anthony Giddens and Patrick Diamond, eds., *The New Egalitarianism,* Polity, Cambridge, 2005, p. 191.

22. William Easterly, Jo Ritzen, and Michael Woolcock, *Social Cohesion, Institutions, and Growth,* 2005, www.nyu.edu/fas/institute/dri/DRIW P17.pdf. See also William Easterly, Jo Ritzen, and Michael Woolcock, *On "Good" Politicians and "Bad" Policies: Social Cohesion, Institutions, and Growth,* World Bank Policy Research Working Paper No. 2448, 2000.

23. S. Knack and P. Keefer, "Does Social Capital Have an Economic Payoff? A Cross-Country Investigation," *Quarterly Journal of Economics,* Vol. 112, No. 4, 1997, pp. 1251–1288. See also Hilton L. Root, *Capital and Collusion: The Political Logic of Global Economic Development,* Princeton University Press, Princeton, N.J., 2006.

24. Alexis de Tocqueville, *Democracy in America,* Hackett, Indianapolis, Ind., 2000; cited in Wilkinson, op. cit., p. 1.

25. James C. Collins and Jerry I. Porras, *Built to Last,* Random House, New York, 1998, pp. 72–73.

26. Ibid., p. 81. Collins and Porras describe how profits are not the "why" of Boeing; the "why" of Boeing is "aviation pioneering, adventure, challenge and contribution."

27. Unilever Annual Report, 2004.

28. Collins and Porras, op. cit., p. 58.

29. *Cracking the Performance Code,* Work Foundation, July 2005.

30. On the Asian financial crisis, see François Godement, *The Downsizing of Asia,* Routledge, London, 1998. For the debate over Asian values, see Randall Peerenbloom, *Beyond Universalism and Relativism: The*

Evolving Debates about "Values in Asia," Research Paper No. 02-23, Los Angeles School of Law, University of California (available from SSRN). See also Lucien W. Pye, "The Asian Values Ballyhoo: Patten's Common Sense on Hong Kong and Beyond," *Foreign Affairs,* November-December 1998. Pye puts the debate in its rather contingent political context.

31. An example of this tendency is Daniel A. Bell and Hahm Chaibong, eds., *Confucianism for the Modern World,* Cambridge University Press, Cambridge, 2003.

32. Kim Dae-Jung, "Is Culture Destiny? The Myth of Asia's Anti-Democratic Values," *Foreign Affairs,* November-December 1994.

33. See, e.g., Richard Katz, *The System That Soured: The Rise and the Fall of the Japanese Miracle,* Sharpe, Armonk, N.Y., 1998; and Gavan McCormack, *The Emptiness of Japanese Affluence,* Sharpe, Armonk, N.Y., 2001.

34. Jeff Kingston, *Japan's Quiet Revolution: Social Change and Civil Society in the Twenty-first Century,* Routledge, London, 2004, p. 54

35. Ibid, pp. 70–94.

36. *Economist,* Survey: Japan, "The Sun Also Rises," October 6, 2005.

37. Amartya Sen, *The Argumentative Indian: Writings on Indian History, Culture, and Identity,* Penguin, London, 2005.

38. Ibid, p. 23.

39. In a survey of twenty-five emerging market economies conducted in 2000 by Crédit Lyonnais Securities Asia, India ranked sixth in corporate governance; China ranked nineteenth.

40. Cited in Yasheng Huang and Tarun Khanna, "Can India Overtake China?" *Foreign Policy,* Vol. 137, 2003, pp. 74–81. See also the following. Prasenjit K. Basu, "India and the Knowledge Economy: The 'Stealth Miracle' Is Sustainable," in *India as a New Global Leader,* Foreign Policy Centre, London, 2005. Edward Friedman and Bruce Gilley, *Asia's Giants: Comparing China and India,* Palgrave-Macmillan, Basingstoke, 2005. Friedman and Gilley provide a spritely, judicious reassessment of India's institutional advantages.

41. This point is made in Meghnad Desai, *India and China: An Essay in Comparative Political Economy,* IMF Conference on India and China, New Dehli, 2003.

42. UNDP, Human Development Report. Statistics available at http://hdr .undp.org/statistics/data/.

43. For evidence, see K. Hoff and B. Pandey, *Belief Systems and Durable In-*

equalities: An Experimental Investigation of Indian Caste, World Bank Policy Research Working Paper No. 3351, 2004.

44. Joshua Cooper Ramo, *The Beijing Consensus: Notes on the New Physics of Chinese Power,* Foreign Policy Centre, London, 2004.

CHAPTER 9

1. Quoted in Avery Goldstein, *Rising to the Challenge: China's Grand Strategy and International Security,* Stanford University Press, Stanford, Calif., 2005. See also Christopher R. Hughes, *Chinese Nationalism in the Global Era,* Routledge, London 2006.

2. Quoted in Wu Xinbo, "China: Security Practice of Modernizing and Ascending Power," in Muthiah Alagappa, ed., *Asian Security Practice: Material and Ideational Influences,* Stanford University Press, Stanford, Calif., 1998.

3. For an account of Li Hongzhang's efforts at modernization, see Jonathan Spence, *The Search for Modern China,* 2nd ed., Norton, New York., 1999.

4. Quoted in Zhao Suisheng, *A Nation State by Construction: Dynamics of Modern Chinese Nationalism,* Stanford University Press, Stanford, Calif., 2004.

5. The full text of Li Zhaoxing's press conference of March 7, 2004, is available at http://english.people.com.cn/200403/07/eng20040307_136794.shtml.

6. Zheng Bijian, "China's Peaceful Rise to Great Power Status," *Foreign Affairs,* September-October 2005.

7. John Mearsheimer, *The Tragedy of Great Power Politics,* Norton, New York, 2001.

8. Goldstein, op. cit.

9. Thomas J. Christensen, "Looking beyond the Nuclear Bluster: Recent Progress and Remaining Problems in PRC Security Policy," *China Leadership Monitor,* No. 15, http://www.chinaleadershipmonitor.org/20053/tc.html.

10. Louisa Lombard, "China's Africa Card," *Foreign Policy,* May 2006, http://www.foreignpolicy.com/story/cms.php?story_id=3419.

11. Confirmed by the author at the time, in conversations with Jonathan Fenby, editor of *South China Post;* and with Chris Patten, governor of

Hong Kong. See also Jonathan Dimbleby, *The Last Governor: Chris Patten and the Handover of Hong Kong,* Time Warner, New York, 1998.

12. Freedom House, *Freedom in the World: The Annual Survey of Political Rights and Civil Liberties,* 2001–2002.

13. Interview by author, February 2, 2006.

14. Report to Congress of the U.S.-China Economic and Security Review Commission, 2005, p. 19.

15. Ibid., pp. 44–45.

16. *Economist,* February 18, 2006.

17. See http://usinfo.state.gov/eap/Archive/2006/Apr/04-929128.html.

18. Edward M. Graham and David M. Marchick, *U.S. National Security and Foreign Direct Investment,* Institute of International Economics, Washington, D.C., 2006, p. 102

19. Ibid, n17.

20. "Pricey Oil's Path to Your Pocket," *BusinessWeek,* April 27, 2005, http://www.businessweek.com/bwdaily/dnflash/apr2005/nf20050427_2905.htm (accessed October 10, 2005).

21. Statement by Dr. Gal Luft at USCC hearing on China's Future Energy Development and Acquisition Strategies, July 21, 2005.

22. Cited in "The Breaking Point," *New York Times,* August 21, 2005.

23. "The Future of Oil," Institute for the Analysis of Global Security, www.iags.org/futureoil.html (accessed March 3, 2006).

24. "The List: The Top Five Global Chokepoints," *Foreign Policy,* May 8, 2006.

25. Ibid.

26. Michael L. Ross, "Does Oil Hinder Democracy?" *World Politics,* Vol. 53, April 2001, pp. 325–361.

27. Jeffrey D. Sachs and Andrew M. Warner, *Natural Resource Abundance and Economic Growth,* NBER Working Paper No. W5398, 1995. See also see Paul Collier and Anke Hoeffler, *On Economic Causes of Civil War,* Oxford Economic Papers No. 50, 1998, pp. 563–573.

28. Paul Collier and Anke Hoeffler, *Greed and Grievances in Civil War,* World Bank, 2001.

29. Christopher Hitchey, "The Oil Shield," *Foreign Policy,* May–June 2006, pp. 37–40.

30. Michael T. Klare, "The Twilight Era of Petroleum," *Tomdispatch,* August 4, 2005.

31. David Zweig, "The Foreign Policy of a Resource-Hungry State," Center

of China's Transnational Relations, Hong Kong University of Science and Technology, www.cctr.ust.hk, 2005. (Dr. Zweig is director of this center.)

32. Li Zhibiao, a researcher at CASS, is quoted in *Financial Times,* February 23, 2006: "China wants to have diversified channels in case of disruptions. It's the same as the U.S. policies [on oil]."

33. Quoted in David Zweig and Bi Jianhai, "China's Global Hunt for Energy," *Foreign Affairs,* September-October 2005, p. 34.

34. Ibid. See also *China Brief: The Jamestown Foundation,* Vol. 5, Issue 21, October 13, 2005.

35. Zweig and Bi, op. cit.

36. Vincent Wei-cheng Wang, "Democratic Consolidation or Electioneering Nationalism? The 2004 Taiwan Presidential Election and Its Implications," statement to USCC hearing on China's Military Modernization and Cross-Strait Balance, September 15, 2005. See also "Turning Taiwanese," *Economist,* January 13, 2005.

37. Emile C. J. Sheng, "Cross-Strait Relations and Public Opinion on Taiwan," *Issues and Studies,* Vol. 38, No. 1, March 2002, pp. 17–46.

38. Eric A. McVadon, evidence to U.S.-China Economic and Security Review, September 15, 2005.

39. U.S. Department of Defense, "The Military Power of the People's Republic of China," Annual Report to Congress, 2005.

40. Ibid.

41. Kent E. Calder, "China and Japan's Simmering Rivalry," *Foreign Affairs,* March-April 2006.

42. Cited in Ted Galen Carpenter, *America's Coming War with China: A Collision Course over Taiwan,* Palgrave-Macmillan, Basingstoke, 2006, p. 153.

43. Robert Zoellick, speech to National Committee on U.S.-China Relations, September 21, 2005.

44. Eric Heginbotham and Christopher P. Twomey, "America's Bismarckian Asia Policy," *Current History,* Vol. 104, No. 683, September 2005.

45. Roo had only a forty-five-minute audience with Bush; Koizumi was given the five-star treatment at the Bush ranch.

46. Jeff Kingston, *Japan's Quiet Revolution: Social Change and Civil Society in the Twenty-first Century,* Routledge, London, 2004, p. 227.

47. The textbooks in question remain highly controversial. According to an article in *Asahi Shinbun,* September 2005, they have been adopted in

only 0.04 percent of Japan's junior high schools since their introduction in 2001. The "penetration target" that the Japanese Society for History Textbook Reform had set itself was 10 percent. My thanks to Yoko Enomura for helping track down much of the Japanese material.

48. The ten members of ASEAN are Brunei, Myanmar, Cambodia, Indonesia, Thailand, Vietnam, Singapore, Malaysia, Phillipines, and Laos.

49. Hu Angang, *Great Transformations in China*, Oxford University Press, Oxford, 2006, p. 50.

50. Zhao Suisheng, op. cit. See also the following. Howard French, "China's Textbooks Twist and Distort History," *New York Times*, December 6, 2004. Edward Friedman, "Chinese Nationalism and American Policy," statement to USCC hearing on State Control Mechanisms and Methods, April 14, 2005.

51. Peter Hay Gries, "Chinese Nationalism: Challenging the State," *Current History*, Vol. 104, No. 683, September 2005.

52. Edward Friedman, "Preventing War between China and Japan," in Edward Friedman and Barrett L. McCormick, eds., *What If China Doesn't Democratize?* Sharpe, Armonk, N.Y., 2000.

53. Heginbotham and Twomey, op. cit., p. 250.

CHAPTER 10

1. Joan Robinson, *Aspects of Development and Underdevelopment*, Cambridge University Press, Cambridge, 1978.

2. Paul Bairoch, *Economics and World History: Myths and Paradoxes*, Wheatsheaf, Brighton, 1993, p. 40, table 3.3.

3. Liah Greenfield, *The Spirit of Capitalism*, Harvard University Press, Cambridge, Mass., 2003.

4. Ibid., p. 417.

5. Douglas Irwin, "Tariffs and Growth in Late Nineteenth Century America," *World Economy*, Vol. 24, No. 1, 2001, pp. 15–30. As Irwin notes, correlation is not causation.

6. The period was one of acute deflation. This was due to a variety of factors, including ongoing technological and organizational change.

7. Walter LaFeber, *The New Empire: An Interpretation of American Expansion, 1860–1898*, Cornell University Press, Ithaca, N.Y., 1963.

8. Niall Ferguson, *Colossus: The Rise and Fall of the American Empire*,

Penguin, London, 2004. See also Fareed Zakaria, *From Wealth to Power: The Unusual Origins of America's World Role,* Princeton University Press, Princeton, N.Y., 1999.

9. Charles A. Maier, *Among Empires: American Ascendency and Its Predecessors,* Harvard University Press, Cambridge, Mass., 2006, p. 78.

10. Alfred T. Mahan, *The Influence of Sea Power upon History, 1660–1783,* Dover, New York, 1987.

11. David Lake, *Power, Protection, and Free Trade: International Sources of U.S. Commercial Strategy, 1887–1939,* Cornell University Press, Ithaca, N.Y., 1988. For a discussion of the relationship between free trade and security interests, see Joanne Gowa, *Allies, Adversaries, and International Trade,* Princeton University Press, Princeton, N.J., 1995.

12. Alfred E. Eckes, Jr., and Thomas W. Zeiler, *Globalization and the American Century,* Cambridge University Press, Cambridge, 2003. See also Aaron Forsberg, *America and the Japanese Miracle: The Cold War Context of Japan's Postwar Economic Revival, 1950–1960,* University of North Carolina Press, Chapel Hill, 2000.

13. X, "The Sources of Soviet Conduct," *Foreign Affairs,* 1947.

14. Cited in Jeffrey A. Frieden, *Global Capitalism: Its Fall and Rise in the Twentieth Century,* Norton, New York, 2006, p. 267.

15. In Chalmers Johnson, *Blowback: The Costs and Consequences of American Empire,* Time-Warner, New York, 2002.

16. Eckes and Zeiler, op. cit., p. 139.

17. William J. Drake and Kalypso Nicolaidis, "Ideas, Interests, and Institutionalization: Trade in Services and the 'Uruguay Round,' " *International Organization,* Vol. 46, No. 1, Winter 1992, pp. 37–100.

18. David Reynolds, *One World Divisible: A Global History since 1945,* Norton, New York, 2001, p. 517.

19. John Braithwaite and Peter Drahos, *Information Feudalism: Who Owns the Knowledge Economy,* Norton, New York, 2003.

20. Between 1980 and 2001, the United States brought 856 suits, compared with 784 brought by the European Union. Maurizio Zanardi, "Antidumping: A Problem in International Trade," June 2005, http://darkwing.uoregon.edu/%7Ebruceb/adpage.html, U.S. Antidumping Database and Links. For information on dumping since the inception of WTO, see http://www.wto.org/english/tratop_e/adp_e/adp_e.htm.

21. Bruce A. Blonigen, *Evolving Practices of U.S. Antidumping Activity,* NBER Working Paper No. 9625, 2003.

22. Claude Barfield,. *High-Tech Protectionism: The Irrationality of Anti-dumping Laws,* American Economic Institute, Washington, D.C., 2003.

23. Jagdish Bhagwati and Douglas Irwin, "The Return of the Reciprocitarians: U.S. Trade Policy Today," *World Economy,* Vol. 10, June 1987, pp. 109–130. (Reprinted in Kevin O'Rourke, ed., *The International Trading System: Globalization and History,* Edward Elgar, Aldershot, 2005.)

24. "America's Place in the World 2005: Opinion Leaders Turn Cautious, Public Looks Homeward," Pew Research Center for the People and the Press and Council on Foreign Relations, November 17, 2005.

25. "Bush Approval Falls to 33 Percent, Congress Earns Rare Praise," Pew Research Center for the People and the Press, March 15, 2006, http://people-press.org/reports/display.php3?ReportID=271.

26. Ibid.

27. Edward Glaeser and Andrei Shleifer, "The Rise of the Regulatory State," *Journal of Economic Literature,* Vol. 41, No. 2, June 1, 2003, pp. 401–425.

28. Benjamin M. Friedman, *The Moral Consequences of Economic Growth,* Knopf, New York, 2005, p. 107.

29. James Kloppenberg, *The Virtues of Liberalism,* Oxford University Press, New York, 1998.

30. Claudia Goldin and Lawrence F. Katz, *The "Virtues" of the Past: Education in the First Hundred Years of the New Republic,* NBER Working Paper No. 9958, 2003. See also Claudia Goldin, "The Human-Capital Century and American Leadership: Virtues of the Past," *Journal of Economic History,* Vol. 61, No. 2, June 2001, pp. 263–292.

31. "Closing the Growth Gap," *Economist,* October 27, 2005.

32. Goldin, "The Human-Capital Century," op. cit., p. 275–276.

33. Matthew Gentzkow, Edward Glaeser, and Claudia Goldin, *The Rise of the Fourth Estate: How Newspapers Became Informative and Why It Matters,* NBER Working Paper No. 10791, 2004.

34. Glaeser and Shleifer, op. cit.

35. Alfred Chandler. *The Visible Hand,* Harvard University Press, Cambridge, Mass., 1977.

36. Glaeser and Shleifer, op. cit.

37. Adolf A. Berle and Gardiner C. Means, *The Modern Corporation and Private Property,* Harcourt, Brace, and World, New York, 1968. (Originally published 1932.)

38. Jordan Schwarz, *The New Dealers: Power Politics in the Age of Roosevelt,* Knopf, New York, 1993. See also Gary Brechin, "Keeping the Faith," *San Francisco Chronicle,* December 27, 2005, http://www.sfgate.com/cgi-bin/article.cgi?file=/chronicle/archive/2005/12/27/EDG2IGCO ES1.DTL (accessed February 20, 2006).

39. Many innovations owe their creation to government support. For a comprehensive overview, see http://www.nsf.gov/od/lpa/nsf50/nsfout reach/htm/home.htm.

40. I adapted this idea from Stephen Jenkins and Frank Cowell, *Dwarves and Giants in the 1980s,* Department of Swansea Discussion Paper No. 93-03. The (rough) calculations are based on a study of class by the *New York Times* and on numbers from the U.S. Internal Revenue Service regarding tax returns.

41. Louis Uchitelle, *The Disposable American: Layoffs and Their Consequences,* Knopf, New York., 2006.

42. Muriel Siebert, "To Encourage Recovery, Encourage Investors," *New York Times,* August 6, 2002; cited in Thomas A. Kochan, *Restoring the American Dream: A Working Families' Agenda for America,* MIT Press, Cambridge, Mass., 2005.

43. *How Many People Lack Health Insurance and for How Long,* Congressional Budget Office Report, May 2003; cited in Kochan, op. cit.

44. According to the Employment Policy Institute Report, 2005, the middle-earning group of households—defined as those with half to twice the median income—shrank to 60.7 per cent in 2002, from 68 percent in 1979.

45. Thomas Piketty and Emmanuel Saez, *The Evolution of Top Incomes: A Historical and International Perspective,* NBER Working Paper No. 11955, 2006.

46. Stephen Roach, *Globalization's New Underclass,* Global Economic Forum, http://www.morganstanley.com/GEFdata/digests/20060303-fri.html (accessed February 4, 2006).

47. "Minding the Gap," *Wall Street Journal,* March 6, 2006, http://on line.wsj.com/public/article/SB114182443308492484.html (accessed March 14, 2006).

48. Gosta Esping-Andersen, "Inequality of Incomes and Opportunities," in Anthony Giddens and Patrick Diamond, eds., *The New Egalitarianism,* Polity, Cambridge, 2005.

49. Computation by Ton Hertz, from University of Michigan survey.

Cited in David Wessel, "Moving Up: Challenges to the American Dream," *Wall Street Journal,* May 13, 2005.

50. "The World Value Survey (1983–1997)," in Alberto Alesina and Edward Glaeser, *Fighting Poverty in the U.S. and Europe: A World of Difference,* Oxford University Press, Oxford, 2004.

51. Interview, *Mother Jones,* February 7, 2005.

52. *American Prospect,* March 27, 2006.

53. Scott C. Bradford, Paul L. E. Grieco, and Gary Clyde Hufbauer, "The Payoff to America from Global Integration," in Fred Bergsten, ed., *The United States and the World Economy,* Institute for International Economics, Washington, D.C., 2005, p. 105.

54. According to an estimate by EPI, 11,120 jobs are embedded in every net $1 billion of trade deficit with China; thus the trade deficit of $202 billion in 2005 would imply 2.24 million cumulative lost job opportunities. See also I. Thomas Palley, *Trade, Employment, and Outsourcing: Some Observations on U.S.-China Relations in Offshoring and the Internationalisation of Employment,* ILO, 2006.

55. Palley, op. cit., pp. 82–84.

56. Uchitelle, op. cit.

57. Bradford, Grieco, and Hufbauer, op. cit.

58. Data in this paragraph are from Frank Levy and Richard Murnane, *The New Division of Labor: How Computers Are Creating the Next Job Market,* Princeton University Press, Princeton, N.J., 2004.

59. Ian Dew-Becker and Robert Gordon, "Where Did the Productivity Growth Go? Inflation Dynamics and the Distribution of Income," paper for Eighty-first Meeting of the Brookings Panel on Economic Activity, 2005, p. 2.

60. Paul Krugman, "Graduates versus Oligarchs," *New York Times,* February 27, 2006.

CHAPTER 11

1. Nolan McCarthy, Keith T. Poole, and Howard Rosenthal, *Polarized America: The Dance of Ideology and Unequal Riches,* MIT Press, Cambridge, Mass., 2006, p. 47.

2. "Will White Evangelicals Desert the GOP?" Pew Research Center Commentary on Public Opinion, May 2, 2006.

3. William G. Galston and Elaine C. Kamarck, *The Politics of Polarization: The Third Way Middle Class Project,* October 2005.

4. Kevin Phillips, *American Theocracy,* Viking, New York, 2006, p. 105. Phillips cites a work by Mark Noll, *The Old Religion in a New World.*

5. John Micklethwait and Adrian Wooldridge, *The Right Nation: Why America Is Different,* Penguin, London, 2005, p. 325.

6. Cited in Thomas Gallagher, "Politics and the Economy," in Thomas R. Keene, ed., *Flying on One Engine: Fourteen Views of the World Economy,* Bloomberg, New York, 2005.

7. John C. Bogle, *The Battle for the Soul of Capitalism,* Yale University Press, New Haven, Conn., 2005, p. 74.

8. Ibid., p. 94.

9. Ibid., p. 96.

10. Martin N. Baily, Eric J. Bartelsman, and John Haltiwanger, "Downsizing and Productivity Growth: Myth or Reality?" *Small Business Economics,* Vol. 8, No. 4, 1996, pp. 259–278. (Reprinted in David G. Mayes, ed., *Sources of Productivity Growth,* Cambridge University Press, Cambridge, 1996.)

11. See Mergerstat and *BusinessWeek,* "Mergers: Why Most Big Deals Don't Pay Off," October 14, 2002, http://www.businessweek.com/magazine/content/02_41/b3803001.htm (accessed March 2, 2006).

12. Ibid.

13. Matthias M. Bekier, Anna J. Bogardus, and Tim Oldham, "Is the Belief That Mergers Drive Revenue Growth an Illusion?" *McKinsey Quarterly,* No. 4, 2001.

14. "Unlocking Shareholder Value: The Key to Success," *KPMG,* January 2001.

15. Nina Munk, *Fools Rush In: Steve Case, Jerry Levin, and the Unmaking of AOL Time Warner,* HarperCollins, New York, 2004. See also Alec Klein, *Stealing Time: Steve Case, Jerry Levin, and the Collapse of AOL Time Warner,* Simon and Schuster, New York, 2004.

16. Matthew T. Bodie, *AOL Time Warner and the False God of Shareholder Primacy,* Hofstra University Legal Studies Research Paper No. 05–21, August 8, 2005. (Available at SSRN: http://ssrn.com/abstract=776228.)

17. Quoted in Gretchen Morgenson, "What Are Mergers Good For?" *New York Times,* June 5, 2005.

18. Lucien A. Bebchuk and Jesse M. Fried, *Pay without Performance,* Dis-

cussion Paper No. 528, John M. Ohlins Discussion Series, Harvard, October 2005. See also Lucien A. Bebchuk and Jesse M. Fried, *Pay without Performance: The Unfulfilled Promise of Executive Compensation,* Harvard University Press, Cambridge, Mass., 2004.

19. Will Hutton, *The World We're In,* Little, Brown, London, 2002.

20. John Bogle, *The Battle for the Soul of Capitalism,* Yale University Press, New Haven, Conn., 2005.

21. Mark Roe, *The Inevitable Instability of American Corporate Governance,* Working Paper, Harvard Law School, 2004.

22. Ibid.

23. William J. Baumol, Alan S. Blinder, and Edward N. Wolff, *Downsizing in America: Reality, Causes, and Consequences,* Russell Sage Foundation, New York, 2003.

24. Richard B. Freeman and Joel Rogers, *What Do Workers Want?* Cornell University ILR Press, Ithaca, N.Y., 1999. See also Seymour Martin Lipset, Noah M. Meltz, Rafael Gomez, and Ivan Katchanovski, *The Paradox of American Unionism: Why Americans Like Unions More Than Canadians Do, but Join Much Less,* Cornell University ILR Press, Ithaca, N.Y., 2004.

25. Barbara Ehrenreich, *Bait and Switch: The (Futile) Pursuit of the American Dream,* Metropolitan Books, New York, 2005.

26. Hutton, op. cit. See also OECD, *Economic Surveys: China,* Paris, 2005.

27. See, generally, William G. Bowen, Martin A. Kurzweil, and Eugene M. Tobin, *Equity and Excellence in American Higher Education,* University of Virginia Press, Charlottesville, 2005.

28. Robert L. Woodbury, "Social Contracts Erode at Colleges," http://www.utexas.edu/conferences/africa/ads/1392.html (accessed April 2, 2006).

29. In 2005, 2 million new jobs were created, representing a gain of 1.5 percent: less than half of the average growth rate of 3.5 percent for the same stage of previous business cycles that lasted as long. See Lee Price, *Why People Are So Dissatisfied with Today's Economy,* Employment Policy Institute Issue Brief No. 219, January 27, 2006.

30. Henry Farber, *What Do We Know about Job Loss in the United States? Evidence from the Displaced Workers Survey, 1984–2004,* Princeton Working Paper No. 498, January 2005.

31. New America Foundation, "Decline of Broadcasters' Public Interest Obligations," Policy Backgrounder, March 29, 2004.

32. For a discussion of the role of the Internet in this transformation, see Cass Sunstein, *republic.com*, Princeton University Press, Princeton, N.J., 2002.

33. Jacob. S. Hacker and Paul Pierson, *Off Center: The Republican Revolution and the Erosion of American Democracy*, Yale University Press, New Haven, Conn., p. 176.

34. Michael Massing, "The Press; The Enemy Within," *New York Review of Books*, Vol. 52, No. 20, December 15, 2005. See also Michael Massing, "The End of News," *New York Review of Books*, Vol. 52, No. 19, December 1, 2005.

35. Larry Bartels, "Homer Gets a Tax Cut: Inequality and Public Policy in the American Mind," *Perspectives on Politics*, Vol. 3, No. 1, March 2005, pp. 15–31. See also Jacob S. Hacker and Paul Pierson, "Abandoning the Middle: The Bush Tax Cuts and the Limits of Democratic Control," *Perspectives on Politics*, Vol. 3, No. 1, March 2005, pp. 32–53.

36. Richard Freemen, *What Me, Vote?* NBER Working Paper 9896, 2003.

37. American Political Science Association Supported by the Russell Sage Foundation, *American Democracy in an Age of Rising Inequality*, 2006, p. 7.

38. Ibid.

39. Cited in Hacker and Pierson, *Off Center*, op. cit.

40. Ibid.

41. Barry Burden, "Candidate Positioning in U.S. Congressional Elections," *British Journal of Political Science*, Vol. 34, No. 2, 2004, pp. 211–227.

42. Hacker and Pierson, *Off Center*, op. cit.

43. Ibid.

44. William G. Gale and Peter R. Orszag, "Sunsets in the Tax Code," *Tax Notes*, June 9, 2003, pp. 1553–1561.

45. Ron Suskind, *The Price of Loyalty: George W. Bush, the White House, and the Education of Paul O'Neill*, Simon & Schuster, New York, 2004.

46. Benjamin M. Friedman, *The Moral Consequences of Economic Growth*, Knopf, New York, 2005.

47. "Introduction," *The National Security Strategy of the United States of America*, September 2002: available at http://www.whitehouse.gov/nsc/nss.html.

48. Nicholas Lemann, "How It Came to War: When Did Bush Decide That He Had to Fight Saddam?," *The New Yorker*, March 31, 2005.

49. Ignatieff, op cit.

50. Hans Blix, *Disarming Iraq: The Search for Weapons of Mass Destruction,* Bloomsbury, 2004.

51. Paul R. Pillar, "Intelligence Policy and the War in Iraq," *Foreign Affairs,* March–April 2006.

52. Ibid.

53. Quoted in the *Observer,* May 14, 2006, p. 8.

54. They include retired Army Maj. Gen. Charles Swannack, former Central Command chief Marine Gen. Anthony Zinni, Army Maj. Gen. Paul Eaton, Marine Lt. Gen. Gregory Newbold, and Army Maj. Gen. John Batiste.

55. George Packer, *The Assassin's Gate,* cited by Francis Fukuyama, "After Neoconservatism," *New York Times,* February 19, 2006.

56. "Iraq Body Count: War Dead Figures," BBC News, May 15, 2006. Available at http://news.bbc.co.uk/1/hi/world/middle_east/4525412.stm.

57. *Project Syndicate: The True Costs of the Iraq War,* February 2006. http://www.projectsyndicate.org/commentary/stiglitz67. Joseph Stiglitz and Linda Bilmes, a budget expert at Harvard, estimate that the Iraq war's overall costs are likely to settle in a range of $1 trillion to $2 trillion, vastly higher than official estimates.

58. "Conflict Contributes to Rising Insecurity over Energy Supply," *The Times,* March 7, 2006. Available at http://www.timesonline.co.uk/article/0,,5-2072761,00.html.

59. "Iraqi Voters Defy the Bombers," *The Guardian,* January 31, 2005.

60. Report by Alvaro Gil-Robles, Commissioner for Human Rights, on his visit to the United Kingdom, November 4–12, 2004

61. Bruce Ackerman, *Before the Next Attack: Preserving Civil Liberties in an Age of Terrorism,* Yale University Press, New Haven, Conn., 2006.

62. Ibid.

CONCLUSION

1. Quoted in Guy de Jonquieres, "The Critical Skills Gap," *Financial Times,* June 12, 2006, http://www.ft.com/cms/s/733ea3c8-fa38-11da-b7ff-0000779e2340.html.

2. Suzanne Berger, *How We Compete,* Doubleday, Garden City, N.Y., 2005, p. 120.

3. David Birnbaum, *Birnbaum's Guide to Winning the Great Garment*

War, Third Horizon Press, Hong Kong, 2000; cited in Berger, op. cit, p. 124.

4. Berger, op. cit, p. 125.

5. Ibid., p. 260.

6. Robert D. Atkinson, *The Past and Future of America's Economy,* Edward Elgar, Cheltenham, 2004, p. 124.

7. Berger, op. cit, p. 169.

8. Ibid., p. 68.

9. Peter Lindert, "Growing Public: Is the Welfare State Mortal or Exportable?" University of California-Davis, April 17, 2005.

10. Jeffrey D. Sachs, *Lessons from the North,* Project Syndicate, April 2006. On the benefits of child-centered redistribution, see Gosta Esping-Anderson, "Inequality of Incomes and Opportunities," in Anthony Giddens and Patrick Diamond, eds., *The New Egalitarianism,* Polity, Cambridge, 2005.

11. Shoshana Zuboff and James Maxmin, *The Support Economy: Why Corporations Are Failing Individuals and the Next Episode of Capitalism,* Viking Penguin, New York, 2002.

12. Ronald Inglehart, *Modernization and Postmodernization: Cultural, Economic, and Political Change in Forty-Three Societies,* Princeton University Press, Princeton, N.J., 1997; cited in Zuboff and Maxmin, op. cit, p. 96.

13. "Competitive Advantage from Better Interactions," *McKinsey Quarterly,* 2006, No. 2.

14. David A. King, "The Scientific Impact of Nations," *Nature,* Vol. 430, 2004, pp. 311–316.

15. Geoffry Garrett, *The Three Worlds of Globalization: Market Integration, Economic Growth, and the Distribution of Income in High-, Middle-, and Low-Income Countries,* UCLA Working Paper, February 2004.

16. Stephen Roach, "Scale and the China Challenge," Morgan Stanley Global Economic Forum, June 19, 2006, http://www.morganstanley.com/GEFdata/digests/20060619-mon.html.

17. International *Herald Tribune,* http://www.iht.com/articles/2006/06/12/bloomberg/sxchitrade.php.

18. Qiu He—who has excelled at old-fashioned mobilization to the detriment of more lasting institution-building—had, as of this writing, recently been promoted to deputy governor of Jiangsu province. See Joseph Fewsmith, *China Leadership Monitor,* No. 17, 2006.

19. Cheng Li, "Hu's Policy Shift and the Tuanpai's Coming-of-Age," *China Leadership Monitor,* No. 15, 2005.

20. Roderick MacFarquhar, " 'Rotting from the Inside Out': FP Roundtable—Tale of Two Chinas," *Foreign Policy,* May–June 2006, pp. 71–72. See also Bruce Gilley, *China's Democratic Future: How It Will Happen and Where It Will Lead,* Columbia University Press, New York, 2004. The thesis of shock as a precursor of reform is the centerpiece of Gilley's crystal-ball-gazing in this work.

21. Avner Offer, *The Challenge of Affluence: Self-Control and Well-Being in the United States and Britain since 1950,* Oxford University Press, Oxford, 2006.

22. Charles Dumas and Diana Choyleva, *The Bill from the China Shop: How Asia's Savings Glut Threatens the World Economy,* Profile, London, 2006.

23. Howard Davies, lecture on financial reform at the London School of Economics, 2005. Davies cited Andrew Sheng, chairman of the Hong Kong Securities and Futures Commission, who claims that the annual return on U.S. foreign direct investment (FDI), mostly equity, is 12 to 15 percent, compared with the long-term annual return on U.S. treasuries, 4 percent.

24. Barry Eichengreen, "Global Imbalances: The New Economy, the Dark Matter, the Savvy Investor, and the Standard Analysis," *Journal of Policy Modeling,* March 2006.

25. James M. Boughton, *Silent Revolution: The International Monetary Fund 1979–1989,* IMF, 2001, p. 208.

26. Robert Brenner, *The Boom and the Bubble: The United States in the World Economy,* Verso, London, 2003, p. 64.

27. Stephen Jen, "The Plaza Accord, Japan, and Lessons for China," Morgan Stanley Global Economic Forum, July 4, 2005, http://www.morganstanley.com/GEFdata/digests/20050704-mon.html.

28. Charlene Barshefsky, "With or without Doha," *Foreign Affairs,* WTO Special Edition, December 2005.

29. Ibid.

30. Jochen Sanio, "Should Hedge Funds Be Regulated?" Goldman Sachs conference, "Ten Top Financial Risks to the World Economy," September 30, 2005.

31. Joseph E. Stiglitz, "The Overselling of Globalization," in Michael M. Weinstein, ed., *Globalization: What's New?* Columbia University Press,

New York, 2005. See also, generally, David Held, *Global Covenant: The Social Democratic Alternative to the Washington Consensus,* Polity, Cambridge, 2004.

32. James Gustave Speth, "Afterword," in *Red Sky at Morning: America and the Crisis of the Global Environment,* Yale University Press, New Haven, Conn., March 2005, p. 3. (This afterword was prepared especially for the paperback edition.)

33. Ibid., p. 4.

34. Cited ibid., p. 9.

35. Ibid., p. 5.

36. Jared Diamond, *Collapse: How Societies Choose to Fail or Survive,* Penguin, London, 2005.

37. Jürgen Habermas, "Faith and Knowledge," in *The Future of Human Nature,* Polity, Cambridge, 2003.

Bibliography

Acemoglu, Daron. "Technical Change, Inequality, and the Labor Market," *Journal of Economic Literature*, Vol. 40, March 2002, pp. 7–72.

Acemoglu, Daron, Simon Johnson, and James Robinson. "The Rise of Europe: Atlantic Trade, Institutional Change, and Economic Growth," *American Economic Review*, Vol. 95, No. 3, June 2005, pp. 546–579.

Acemoglu, Daron, and James A. Robinson. *Economic Origins of Dictatorship and Democracy.* Cambridge: Cambridge University Press, 2006.

Ackerman, Bruce. *Before the Next Attack: Preserving Civil Liberties in an Age of Terrorism,* New Haven, Conn.: Yale University Press, 2006.

Aghion, Philippe, and Steven N. Durlauf, eds. *Handbook of Economic Growth,* Vol. 1A, B, London: Elsevier North-Holland, 2005.

Alagappa, M., ed. *Asian Security Practice: Material and Ideational Influences.* Stanford, Calif.: Stanford University Press, 1998.

Albert, Michel. *Capitalism against Capitalism.* London: Whurr, 1993.

Alesina, Alberto, and Edward L. Glaser. *Fighting Poverty in the U.S. and Europe: A World of Difference.* Oxford: Oxford University Press, 2004.

Alford, William. "Double-Edged Swords Cut Both Ways: Law and Legitimacy in the People's Republic of China," *Daedalus,* March 22, 1993.

Alpermann, Bjorg. "The Postelection Administration of Chinese Villages," *China Journal,* Vol. 46, 2001, pp. 45–68.

Amsden, Alice. *The Rise of "The Rest": Challenges to the West from Late-Industrialising Economies.* Oxford: Oxford University Press, 2001.

Ansolabehere, Stephen, Roy Behr, and Shanto Iyengar. *The Media Game: American Politics in the Television Age.* New York: Macmillan, 1993.

Aoki, M., et al., eds. *The Role of Government in East Asian Economic Development: Comparative Institutional Analysis.* Oxford: Clarendon, 1997.

Arendt, Hannah. *The Human Condition.* New York: Doubleday Anchor, 1958.

Arrighi, Giovanni. *The Long Twentieth Century.* London: Verso, 1994.

Arrighi, Giovanni, Takeshi Hamashita, and Mark Selden, eds. *The Resurgence of East Asia: 500-, 150-, and 50-Year Perspectives.* London: Routledge, 2003.

Asian Development Bank. *Country Economic Review: People's Republic of China CEP-PRC 2000–2009,* 2000.

Atkinson, Robert D. *The Past and Present of America's Economy.* Cheltenham: Edward Elgar, 2004.

Autor, David H., Lawrence F. Katz, and Melissa S. Kearney. "Trends in U.S. Wage Inequality: Reassessing the Revisionists," September 2005. (Unpublished.)

Axelrod, Robert. *The Evolution of Cooperation.* London: Penguin, 2004.

Baily, Martin N., Eric J. Bartelsman, and John Haltiwanger. "Downsizing and Productivity Growth: Myth or Reality?" *Small Business Economics,* Vol. 8, No. 4, 1996, pp. 259–278. (Reprinted in David G. Mayes, ed., *Sources of Productivity Growth,* Cambridge: Cambridge University Press, 1996.)

Bairoch, Paul. *Economics and World History: Myths and Paradoxes.* Brighton: Wheatsheaf, 1993.

Barber, Benjamin R. *Jihad versus McWorld: Terrorism's Challenge to Democracy.* New York: Ballantine, 2001.

Bardhan, Pranab. *Scarcity, Conflicts, and Cooperation: Essays in the Political and Institutional Economics of Development.* Cambridge, Mass.: MIT Press, 2005.

Barfield, Claude. *High-Tech Protectionism: The Irrationality of Antidumping Laws.* Washington, D.C.: American Economic Institute, 2003.

Barkow, Jerome H., Leda Cosmides, and John Tooby. *The Adapted Mind: Evolutionary Psychology and the Generation of Culture.* Oxford: Oxford University Press, 1992.

Barry, Brian. *Why Social Justice Matters.* Cambridge: Polity, 2005.

Barshefsky, Charlene. "With or without Doha," *Foreign Affairs,* December 2005. (WTO Special Edition.)

Bartels, Larry. "Homer Gets a Tax Cut: Inequality and Public Policy in the American Mind," *Perspectives on Politics,* Vol. 3, No. 1, March 2005, pp. 15–31.

Basu, Prasenjit K. "India and the Knowledge Economy: The 'Stealth Miracle' Is Sustainable." In *India as a New Global Leader.* London: Foreign Policy Centre, 2005.

Bates, Robert H., Avner Greif, Margaret Levi, Jean-Laurent Rosenthal, and Barry R. Weingast. *Analytic Narratives.* Princeton, N.J.: Princeton University Press, 1998.

Bauer, Joanne R., and Daniel A. Bell. *The East Asian Challenge for Human Rights.* Cambridge: Cambridge University Press, 1999.

Baum, Richard. *Burying Mao: Chinese Politics in the Age of Deng.* Princeton, N.J.: Princeton University Press, 1994.

Baumol, William L. *The Free Market Innovation Machine: Analyzing the Growth Miracle of Capitalism.* Princeton, N.J.: Princeton University Press, 2004.

Baumol, William J., Alan S. Blinder, and Edward N. Wolff. *Downsizing in America: Reality, Causes, and Consequences.* New York: Russell Sage Foundation, 2003.

Bayly, C. A. *The Birth of the Modern World 1780–1914.* Oxford: Blackwell, 2004.

Bebchuk, Lucien A., and Jesse M. Fried. *Pay without Performance: The Unfulfilled Promise of Executive Compensation.* Cambridge, Mass.: Harvard University Press, 2004.

Beck, Ulrich, *The Brave New World of Work.* Cambridge: Polity, 2001.

Beck, Ulrich, Anthony Giddens, and Scott Lash, eds. *Reflexive Modernization: Politics, Tradition, and Aesthetics in the Modern Social Order.* Stanford, Calif.: Stanford University Press, 1994.

Beisner, Robert L. *From the Old Diplomacy to the New,* 2nd ed. Arlington Heights, Ill.: Harlan Davidson, 1986.

Bell, Daniel A., and Hahm Chaibong, eds. *Confucianism for the Modern World.* Cambridge: Cambridge University Press, 2003.

Benabou, Roland. "Unequal Societies: Income Distribution and the Social Contract," *American Economic Review,* Vol. 90, 2000, p. 96–129.

Ben-Ner, Avner, and Louis Putterman. *Economics, Values, and Organization.* Cambridge: Cambridge University Press, 1999.

Berger, Suzanne. *How We Compete: What Companies around the World Are Doing to Make It in Today's Global Economy.* Garden City, N.Y.: Doubleday, 2005.

Bergsten, Fred, ed. *The United States and the World Economy.* Washington, D.C.: Institute for International Economics, 2005.

Berle, Adolf A., and Gardiner C. Means. *The Modern Corporation and Private Property.* New York: Harcourt, Brace and World, 1968. (Originally published 1932.)

Bernstein, Peter L. *Against the Gods: The Remarkable Story of Risk.* New York: Wiley, 1996.

Bhagwati, Jagdish. "From Seattle to Hong Kong," *Foreign Affairs,* December 2005. (WTO Special Edition.)

Bhagwati, Jagdish, ed. *Going Alone.* Cambridge, Mass.: MIT Press, 2002.

Bhagwati, Jagdish, and Douglas Irwin. "The Return of the Reciprocitarians: U.S. Trade Policy Today," *World Economy,* Vol. 10, June 1987, pp. 109–130. (Reprinted in Kevin O'Rourke, ed., *The International Trading System: Globalization and History,* Aldershot: Edward Elgar, 2005.)

Blanchard, Olivier, Francesco Giavazzi, and Filipa Sa. "The U.S. Current Account and the Dollar," *Brookings Papers on Economic Activity,* Vol. 1, 2006, pp. 1–49.

Blanchard, Olivier, Jean Pisani-Ferry, and Charles Wyplosz. *L'Europe Déclassée.* Paris: Flammarion, 2005.

Blecher, Marc. *China against the Tide: Restructuring through Revolution, Radicalism, and Reform.* London: Continuum International, 2003.

Blinder, Alan. "Offshoring: The Next Industrial Revolution," *Foreign Affairs,* Vol. 85, No. 2, March-April 2006.

Blonigen, Bruce A. *Evolving Practices of U.S. Antidumping Activity,* NBER Working Paper No. 9625, 2003.

Bloom, David, and Jeffrey D. Sachs. "Geography, Demography, and Economic Growth in Africa," *Brookings Papers on Economic Activity,* Vol. 2, 1998, pp. 207–273.

Bobbitt, P. *The Shield of Achilles: War, Peace, and the Course of History.* London: Allen Lane, 2002.

Bogle, John C. *The Battle for the Soul of Capitalism.* New Haven, Conn.: Yale University Press, 2005.

Boltanski, Luc, and Eve Chiapello. *The New Spirit of Capitalism.* London: Verso, 2005.

Bordo, Michael D., Barry Eichengreen, and Douglas A. Irwin. *Is Globalization Today Really Different Than Globalization a Hundred Years Ago?* NBER Working Paper No. 7195, 1999.

Boughton, James M. *Silent Revolution: The International Monetary Fund 1979–1989.* Washington, D.C.: IMF, 2001.

Bowen, William G., Martin A. Kurzweil, and Eugene M. Tobin. *Equity and Excellence in American Higher Education.* Charlottesville: University of Virginia Press, 2005.

Braithwaite, John, and Peter Drahos. *Information Feudalism: Who Owns the Knowledge Economy.* New York: Norton, 2003.

Bramall, Chris. *Sources of Chinese Economic Growth 1978–1996.* Oxford: Oxford University Press, 2000.

Braudel, Fernand. *Civilization and Capitalism, Fifteenth–Eighteenth Century,* Vol. 2, *The Wheels of Commerce.* Berkeley: University of California Press, 1992.

Bronfenbrenner, Kate, and Stephanie Luce. "The Changing Nature of Corporate Global Restructuring: The Impact of Production Shifts on Jobs in the U.S., China, and around the Globe." Submitted to U.S.-China Economic and Security Review Commission, October 2004.

Burden, Barry. "Candidate Positioning in U.S. Congressional Elections," *British Journal of Political Science,* Vol. 34, No. 2, 2004, pp. 211–227.

Buss, David M. *Evolutionary Psychology: The New Science of the Mind.* Boston: Allyn and Bacon, 1999.

Buzen, Barry, and Rosemary Foot. *Does China Matter? A Reassessment.* London: Routledge, 2004.

Card, David, and John E. DiNardo. "Skill-Biased Technological Change and Rising Wage Inequality: Some Problems and Puzzles," *Journal of Labor Economics,* Vol. 20, October 2000, pp. 733–783.

Carpenter, Ted Galen. *America's Coming War with China.* Basingstoke: Palgrave-Macmillan, 2006.

Castells, Manuel. *The Rise of the Network Society: The Information Age— Economy, Culture, and Society,* 2nd ed., Vol. 1. Oxford: Blackwell, 2000.

Castells, Manuel. *The Power of Identity: The Information Age—Economy, Culture, and Society,* 2nd ed., Vol. 2. Oxford: Blackwell, 2004.

Castells, Manuel. *End of Millennium: The Information Age—Economy, Culture, and Society,* 2nd ed., Vol. 3. Oxford: Blackwell, 2000.

Chan, Sylvia. *Liberalism, Democracy and Development.* Cambridge: Cambridge University Press, 2002.

Chandler, Alfred. *The Visible Hand.* Cambridge, Mass.: Harvard University Press, 1977.

Chandler, Alfred, and James W. Cortada, eds. *A Nation Transformed by Information.* Oxford: Oxford University Press, 2000.

Chang, Ha-Joon. *Kicking Away the Ladder: Development Strategy in Historical Perspective.* London: Anthem, 2002.

Chang, Jung, and Jon Halliday. *Mao: The Unknown Story.* London: Random House, 2005.

Chang, Maria Hsia. "The Thought of Deng Xiaoping," *Communist and Post-Communist Studies,* Vol. 29, No. 4, 1996, pp. 371–394.

Chen, An. "The New Inequality," *Journal of Democracy,* Vol. 14, No. 1, January 2003.

Chen, Jie. "Assessing Political Support in China," *Journal of Contemporary China*, Vol. 6, No. 16, 1997, pp. 551–567.

Christensen, Clayton M. *The Innovator's Dilemma*. Boston: Harvard Business School Press, 1997.

Cline, William R. "Doha and Development," *Foreign Affairs*, December 2005. (WTO Special Edition.)

Cohen, Daniel. *Globalization and Its Enemies*. Cambridge, Mass.: MIT Press, 2006.

Cohen, Edward S. *The Politics of Globalization in the United States*. Washington, D.C.: Georgetown University Press, 2001.

Collier, Paul. *Economic Causes of Civil Conflict and Their Implications for Policy*. Washington, D.C.: World Bank, 2000.

Collins, Jim, and Jerry I. Porras. *Built to Last: Successful Habits of Visionary Companies*. New York: HarperBusiness, 1994.

Corak, Miles, ed. *Generational Income Mobility in North America and Europe*. Cambridge: Cambridge University Press, 2004.

Deng, Kent. *The Premodern Chinese Economy: Structural Equilibrium and Capitalist Sterility*. London: Routledge, 2003.

Desai, Meghnad. *India and China: An Essay in Comparative Political Economy*. IMF Conference on India and China, New Delhi, 2003.

De Soto, Hernando. *The Mystery of Capital: Why Capitalism Triumphs in the West and Fails Everywhere Else*. London: Black Swan, 2001.

Destler, I. M. *American Trade Politics*, 4th ed. Washington, D.C.: Institute for International Economics, 2005.

Dew-Becker, Ian, and Robert Gordon. "Where Did the Productivity Growth Go? Inflation Dynamics and the Distribution of Income." Paper presented at Eighty-First Meeting of Brookings Panel on Economic Activity, 2005, p. 2.

Diamond, Larry. "Thinking about Hybrid Regimes," *Journal of Democracy*, Vol. 13, No. 2, 2002, pp. 21–35.

Dickson, Bruce. *Red Capitalists in China: The Party, Private Entrepreneurs, and Prospects for Political Change*. Cambridge: Cambridge University Press, 2003.

Dixit, Avinash K. *Lawlessness and Economics: Alternative Modes of Governance*. Princeton, N.J.: Princeton University Press, 2004.

Drake, William J., and Kalypso Nicolaidis. "Ideas, Interests, and Institutionalization: Trade in Services and the 'Uruguay Round,' " *International Organization*, Vol. 46, No. 1, Winter 1992, pp. 37–100.

Dreze, Jean, and Amartya Sen. *India: Economic Development and Social Opportunity.* New York: Oxford University Press, 1995, p. 85.

Drifte, Reinhard. *Japan's Foreign Policy for the Twenty-First Century.* Basingstoke: Palgrave-Macmillan, 1998.

Dumas, Charles, and Diana Choyleva. *The Bill from the China Shop: How Asia's Savings Glut Threatens the World Economy.* London: Profile, 2006.

Dunn, John. *Setting People Free: The Story of Democracy.* London: Atlantic, 2005.

Dunsire, Andrew. "Tipping the Balance: Autopoiesis and Governance," *Administration and Society,* Vol. 28, No. 3, November 1996.

Dutton, William, Brian Kahiw, Ramon O'Callaghan, and Andrew W. Wycoff. *Transforming Enterprise: The Economic and Social Implications of Information Technology.* Cambridge, Mass.: MIT Press, 2005.

Easterly, William. *The Elusive Quest for Growth: Economists Adventures and Misadventures in the Tropics.* Cambridge, Mass.: MIT Press, 2001.

Easterly, William. *The White Man's Burden: Why the West's Efforts to Aid the Rest Have Done Much Ill and So Little Good.* New York: Penguin, 2006.

Easterly, William, Jo Ritzen, and Michael Woolcock. "Social Cohesion, Institutions, and Growth," 2005. (Unpublished paper.)

Eckes, Alfred E., Jr., and Thomas W. Zeiler. *Globalization and the American Century.* Cambridge: Cambridge University Press, 2003.

Economy, Elizabeth. *The River Runs Black: The Environmental Challenge to China's Future.* Ithaca, N.Y.: Cornell University Press, 2004.

Ehrenreich, Barbara. *Bait and Switch: The (Futile) Pursuit of the American Dream.* New York: Metropolitan, 2005.

Eichengreen, Barry. "Global Imbalances: The New Economy, the Dark Matter, the Savvy Investor, and the Standard Analysis," *Journal of Policy Modeling,* March 2006.

Ellerman, David. *Helping People Help Themselves: From the World Bank to an Alternative Philosophy of Development Assistance.* Ann Arbor: University of Michigan Press, 2006.

Evensky, Jerry. *Adam Smith's Moral Philosophy: A Historical Perspective and Contemporary Perspective on Markets, Law, Ethics, and Culture.* Cambridge: Cambridge University Press, 2005.

Fairbank, John. *The United States and China.* American Foreign Political Library. Cambridge, Mass.: Harvard University Press, 1989.

Fairbank, John King. *China: A New History.* Cambridge, Mass.: Harvard University Press, 1992.

Farber, Henry. *What Do We Know about Job Loss in the United States? Evidence from the Displaced Workers Survey, 1984–2004.* Princeton Working Paper No. 498, January 2005.

Fenby, Jonathan. *Generalissimo: Chiang Kai-shek and the China He Lost.* New York: Simon & Schuster, 2003.

Feng, Yi. *Democracy, Governance, and Economic Performance: Theory and Evidence.* Cambridge, Mass.: MIT Press, 2005.

Ferguson, Niall. *The Cash Nexus: Money and Politics in Modern History, 1700–2000.* London: Penguin, 2002.

Ferguson, Niall. *Colossus: The Rise and Fall of the American Empire.* London: Penguin, 2004.

Finlay, Robert. "China, the World, and World History in Joseph Needham's 'Science and Civilisation,' " *Journal of World History,* Vol. 11, No. 2, 2000.

Florida, Richard. *The Rise of the Creative Class.* New York: Basic Books, 2002.

Florida, Richard, and Gary Gates. *Technology and Tolerance.* Brookings Institution Survey Series, June 2001

Fogel, Robert William. *The Fourth Great Awakening and the Future of Egalitarianism.* Chicago: University of Chicago Press, 2000.

Forsberg, Aaron. *America and the Japanese Miracle: The Cold War Context of Japan's Postwar Economic Revival, 1950–1960.* Chapel Hill: University of North Carolina Press, 2000.

Fortin, Nicole M., and Thomas Lemieux. "Institutional Changes and Rising Wage Inequality: Is there a Linkage?" *Journal of Economic Perspectives,* Vol. 11, No. 2, 1997, pp. 75–95.

Frank, Robert H., and Philip Cook. *The Winner-Take-All Society.* New York: Free Press, 1995.

Frankel, Jeffrey. "Globalization and the Economy." In J. Nye and J. Donahue, eds., *Governance in a Globalizing World.* Washington, D.C.: Brookings Institution, 2002.

Freeman, Richard B., and Joel Rogers. *What Do Workers Want?* Ithaca, N.Y.: Cornell University ILR Press, 1999.

Frieden, Jeffrey A. *Global Capitalism: Its Fall and Rise in the Twentieth Century.* London: Norton, 2006.

Friedman, Benjamin M. *The Moral Consequences of Economic Growth.* New York: Knopf, 2005.

Friedman, Edward, and Barrett L. McCormick, eds. *What If China Doesn't Democratize? Implications for War and Peace.* Armonk, N.Y.: Sharpe, 2000.

Friedman, Thomas L. *The World Is Flat: The Globalized World in the Twenty-First Century.* London: Penguin, 2005.

Fukuyama, Francis. *After the Neocons: America at the Crossroads.* London: Profile, 2006.

Galbraith, J. K. *American Capitalism: The Concept of Countervailing Power.* Boston: Houghton Mifflin, 1952.

Gale, William. "Effects of Recent Tax Cuts on Marginal Tax Rates." Tax Policy Center: Urban Institute and Brookings Institution, February 2005.

Galston, William A. *Public Matters: Politics, Policy, and Religion in the Twenty-First Century.* Lanham, Md.: Rowman and Littlefield, 2005.

Galston, William A., and Elaine C. Kamarck. *The Politics of Polarization.* Third Way Middle Class Project, October 2005.

Garrett, Geoffrey. *The Three Worlds of Globalization: Market Integration, Economic Growth and the Distribution of Income in High, Middle and Low Income Countries.* UCLA Working Paper, February 2006.

Gates, Hill. *China's Motor: A Thousand Years of Petty Capitalism.* Ithaca, N.Y.: Cornell University Press, 1996.

Gentzkow, Matthew, Edward Glaeser, and Claudia Goldin. *The Rise of the Fourth Estate: How Newspapers Became Informative and Why It Matters.* NBER Working Paper No. 10791, 2004.

Giddens, Anthony, and Patrick Diamond, eds. *The New Egalitarianism.* Cambridge: Polity, 2005.

Gilboy, George. "The Myth behind China's Miracle," *Foreign Affairs,* July-August 2004.

Gilboy, George J., and Eric Heginbothan. "The Latin Americanization of China," *Current History,* September 2004.

Gilley, Bruce. *China's Democratic Future: How It Will Happen and Where it Will Lead.* New York: Columbia University Press, 2004.

Gilpin, Robert. *The Challenge of Global Capitalism.* Princeton, N.J.: Princeton University Press, 2001.

Gilpin, Robert. *Global Political Economy: Understanding the International Order.* Princeton, N.J.: Princeton University Press, 2001.

Gintis, Herbert, Samuel Bowles, Robert Boyd, and Ernst Fehr. *Moral Sentiments and Material Interests: The Foundation of Cooperation in Economic Life.* Cambridge, Mass.: MIT Press, 2005.

Gittings, John. *The Changing Face of China: From Mao to Market,* Oxford: Oxford University Press, 2005.

Glaeser, Edward, and Andrei Shleifer. "The Rise of the Regulatory State," *Journal of Economic Literature*, Vol. 41, No. 2, June 1, 2003, pp. 401–425.

Godement, François. *The Downsizing of Asia*. Oxford: Routledge, 1998.

Goldin, Claudia, and Lawernce F. Katz. "Decreasing (and Then Increasing) Inequality in America: A Tale of Two Half-Centuries." In F. Welch, ed., *The Causes and Consequences of Increasing Income Inequality*. Chicago: University of Chicago Press, 2001.

Goldin, Claudia, and Lawrence F. Katz. *The "Virtues" of the Past: Education in the First Hundred Years of the New Republic*. NBER Working Paper No. 9958, 2003.

Goldstein, Avery. *Rising to the Challenge: China's Grand Strategy and International Security*. Stanford, Calif.: Stanford University Press, 2005.

Goodman, David S., and Gerald Segal. *China Deconstructs: Politics, Trade, and Regionalism*. London: Routledge, 1995.

Goody, Jack. *East in the West*. Cambridge: Cambridge University Press, 1996.

Goos, Maarten, and Alan Manning. "Lousy and Lovely Jobs: The Rising Polarization of Work in Britain." Center for Economic Performance, London School of Economics, September 2003. (Unpublished paper.)

Gowa, Joanne. *Allies, Adversaries, and International Trade*. Princeton, N.J.: Princeton University Press, 1994.

Gray, John. *False Dawn: The Delusions of Global Capitalism*. New York: New Press, 1999.

Gray, John. *The Moral Foundations of Market Institutions*. London: IEA Health and Welfare Unit, 1992.

Green, Stephen, and Guy S. Liu, eds. *Exit the Dragon? Privatization and State Control in China*. Oxford: Blackwell, 2005.

Greenfield, Liah. *The Spirit of Capitalism*. Cambridge, Mass.: Harvard University Press, 2003.

Greider, William. *One World, Ready or Not: The Manic Logic of Global Capitalism*. New York: Touchstone, 1998.

Greider, William. *The Soul of Capitalism: Opening Paths to a Moral Economy*. New York: Simon & Schuster, 2003.

Gries, Peter Hay. "Chinese Nationalism: Challenging the State?" *Current History*, No. 683, September 2005, pp. 251–256.

Guo Yong and Angang Hu. "The Administrative Monopoly in China's Economic Transition," *Communist and Post-Communist Studies*, Vol. 37, 2004, pp. 265–280.

Guo Zhenglin and Thomas Bernstein. "The Impact of Elections on the Village Structure of Power: The Relations between the Village Committees and the Party Branches," *Journal of Contemporary China*, Vol. 13, No. 39, May 2004, pp. 257–275.

Habermas, Jürgen. *The Future of Human Nature*. Cambridge: Polity, 2003.

Habermas, Jürgen. *The Structural Transformation of the Public Sphere*. Cambridge: Polity, 1999.

Hacker, Jacob S., and Paul Pierson. *Off Center: The Republican Revolution and the Erosion of American Democracy*. New Haven, Conn.: Yale University Press, 2005.

Halperin, Morton H., Joseph T. Siegle, and Michael M. Weinstein. *The Democracy Advantage: How Democracies Promote Prosperity and Peace*. New York: Routledge, 2005.

Hanser, Amy. "Made in the P.R.C.: China's Consumer Revolution," *Current History*, No. 683, September 2005, pp. 272–277.

Hardin, Russell. *One for All: The Logic of Group Conflict*. Princeton: Princeton University Press, 1995.

Hart, Oliver. *Firms, Contracts, and Financial Structure*. Oxford; Clarendon, 1995.

He Qinglian. *Zhongguo de Xianjing* (China's Pitfall). Hong Kong: Mingjing Chubanshe, 1998.

Heginbotham, Eric, and Christopher P. Twomey. "America's Bismarckian Asia Policy," *Current History*, No. 683, September 2005, pp. 243–250.

Held, David. *Global Covenant: The Social Democratic Alternative to the Washington Consensus*. Cambridge: Polity, 2004.

Held, David, and Anthony McGrew, eds. *The Global Transformations Reader*, 2nd ed. Cambridge: Polity, 2003.

Hirschman, Albert. *The Passion and the Interests: Political Arguments for Capitalism before Its Triumph*. Princeton, N.J.: Princeton University Press, 1997.

Hirschman, Albert. "Pillars of Order: Social Conflicts as Pillars of Democratic Market Society," *Political Theory*, Vol. 22., No. 22, May 1994.

Hiscox, Michael J. *International Trade and Political Conflict: Commerce, Coalitions, and Mobility*. Princeton, N.J.: Princeton University Press, 2002.

Holsti, Ole R. *Public Opinion and American Foreign Policy*. Ann Arbor: University of Michigan Press, 1997.

Hope, Nicholas C., Dennis Tao Yang, and Mu Yang Li. *How Far across the River?* Stanford, Calif.: Stanford University Press, 2003.

Hu, Angang. *Guoqing yu Fazhan* (The National Condition and Development). Beijing: Qinghua Daxue Chubanshe, 2005.

Hu, Angang. *Yuanzhu yu Fazhan* (Support and Development). Beijing: Qinghua Daxue Chubanshe, 2005.

Huang, Yasheng. *Selling China: Foreign Investment during the Reform Era.* Cambridge: Cambridge University Press, 2002.

Huang, Yasheng, Tony Saich, and Edward Steinfeld, eds. *Financial Sector Reform in China.* Cambridge, Mass.: Harvard University Press, 2005.

Hughes, Christopher R. *Chinese Nationalism in the Global Era.* London: Routledge, 2006.

Hughes, Jonathan, and Louis Cain. *American Economic History,* 8th ed. Boston: Addison-Wesley, 2002.

Hughes, Neil C. "A Trade War with China?" *Foreign Affairs,* July-August 2005.

Huntington, Samuel. *Political Order in Changing Societies.* New Haven, Conn.: Yale University Press, 1968.

Hussain, Athar. "Repairing China's Social Safety Net," *Current History,* No. 683, September 2005, pp. 268–271.

Ignatieff, Michael. *The Lesser Evil: Political Ethics in an Age of Terror.* Princeton, N.J.: Princeton University Press, 2004.

Inglehart, Ronald, and Christian Weizel. *Modernization, Cultural Change, and Democracy: The Human Development Sequence.* Cambridge: Cambridge University Press, 2005.

International Institute for Strategic Studies. *Military Balance 2005–2006.* London: Routledge, 2005.

International Monetary Fund. *World Economic Outlook: Building Institutions.* Washington, D.C.: IMF, 2005.

International Monetary Fund. *World Economic Outlook: Globalization and External Balances.* Washington, D.C.: IMF, 2005.

Irwin, Douglas A. *Free Trade under Fire.* Princeton, N.J.: Princeton University Press, 2002.

Irwin, Douglas A. "Tariffs and Growth in Late Nineteenth Century America," *World Economy,* Vol. 24, No. 1, 2001, pp. 15–30.

Isaacs, Harold. *Scratches on Our Mind: American Views of China and India.* Armonk, N.Y.: Sharpe, 1958.

James, Harold. *The End of Globalization: Lessons from the Great Depression.* Cambridge, Mass.: Harvard University Press, 2001.

James, Harold. *The Roman Predicament: How the Rules of International Order Create the Politics of Empire*. Princeton, N.J.: Princeton University Press, 2006.

Johnson, Chalmers A. *Blowback: The Costs and Consequences of American Empire*. New York: Time Warner, 2002.

Johnson, Chalmers A. *MITI and the Japanese Miracle*. Stanford, Calif.: Stanford University Press, 1982.

Johnston, Alistair Iain. "Chinese Middle Class Attitudes towards International Affairs: Nascent Liberalization?" *China Quarterly*, Vol. 179, No. 1, 2004.

Johnston, Alistair Iain. *Cultural Realism: Strategic Culture and Grand Strategy in Chinese History*. Princeton, N.J.: Princeton University Press, 1998.

Johnston, Alistair Iain, and Robert Ross, eds. *Engaging China: The Management of an Emerging Power*. London: Routledge, 1999.

Johnston, Michael. *Syndromes of Corruption: Wealth, Power, and Democracy*. Cambridge: Cambridge University Press, 2005.

Jones, Eric L. *Cultures Merging: A Historical and Economic Critique of Culture*. Princeton, N.J.: Princeton University Press, 2006.

Jones, Eric L. *The European Miracle: Environments, Economies, and Geopolitics in the History of Europe and Asia*. Cambridge: Cambridge University Press, 2003.

Kagan, Robert, and William Kristol. *Present Dangers: Crisis and Opportunity in American Foreign and Defense Policy*. San Francisco: Encounter, 2000.

Kahan, Dan M. "The Logic of Reciprocity: Trust, Collective Action, and Law," *Michigan Law Review*, Vol. 102, 2003, pp. 71–103.

Katz, Richard. *The System That Soured: The Rise and the Fall of the Japanese Miracle*. Armonk, N.Y.: Sharpe, 1998.

Kaufmann, Daniel, Aart Kraay, and Massimo Mastuzzi. *Governance Matters, 4, Governance Indicators for 1996–2004*. World Bank Working Paper No. 3630, 2005.

Kay, John. *The Truth about Markets: Their Genius, Their Limits, Their Follies*. London: Allen Lane, 2003.

Keene, Thomas R., ed. *Flying on One Engine: Fourteen Views of the World Economy*. New York: Bloomberg, 2005.

Keynes, J. M. *A Treatise on Money*, Vol. 2. Basingtoke: Palgrave-Macmillan, 1971.

Kim Dae-Jung. "Is Culture Destiny? The Myth of Asia's Anti-Democratic Values," *Foreign Affairs 73,* pp. 189–96, 1996.

King, Desmond. *The Liberty of Strangers: Making the American Nation.* Oxford: Oxford University Press, 2005.

Kissinger, Henry. *Does America Need a Foreign Policy? Toward a Diplomacy for the Twenty-First Century.* New York: Touchstone, 2002.

Klare, Michael. *Blood and Oil: How America's Thirst for Petrol Is Killing Us.* London: Penguin, 2005.

Kletzer, Lori. *Imports, Exports, and Jobs: What Does Trade Mean for Employment and Job Loss?* Kalamazoo, Mich.: Upjohn Institute for Employment Research, 2002.

Kloppenberg, James. *The Virtues of Liberalism.* New York: Oxford University Press, 1998.

Knack, S., and P. Keefer. "Does Social Capital Have an Economic Payoff? A Cross-Country Investigation," *Quarterly Journal of Economics,* Vol. 112, No. 4, 1997, pp. 1251–1288.

Kochan, Thomas A. *Restoring the American Dream: A Working Families' Agenda for America.* Cambridge, Mass.: MIT Press, 2005.

Kornai, Janos, and Susan Rose-Ackerman. *Building a Trustworthy State in Post-Socialist Transition.* Basingstoke: Palgrave-Macmillan, 2004.

Kynge, James. *China Shakes the World: The Rise of a Hungry Nation.* London: Weidenfeld and Nicolson, 2006.

LaFeber, Walter. *The Cambridge History of American Foreign Relations,* Vol. 2, *The American Search for Opportunity, 1865–1913.* Cambridge: Cambridge University Press, 1995.

LaFeber, Walter. *The New Empire: An Interpretation of American Expansion, 1860–1898.* Ithaca, N.Y.: Cornell University Press, 1963.

Lake, David. *Power, Protection, and Free Trade: International Sources of U.S. Commercial Strategy, 1887–1939.* Ithaca, N.Y.: Cornell University Press, 1988.

Lampton, David. *Same Beds, Different Dreams: Managing U.S.-China Relations 1989–2000.* Berkeley: University of California Press, 2002.

Landau, Ralph, Timothy Taylor, and Gavin Wright, eds. *The Mosaic of Economic Growth.* Stanford, Calif.: Stanford University Press, 1996.

Landes, David. *The Wealth and Poverty of Nations.* New York: Norton, 1998.

Lardy, Nicholas. *China's Unfinished Economic Revolution.* Washington, D.C.: Brookings Institution, 1998.

Lardy, Nicholas. *Integrating China into the Global Economy.* Washington, D.C.: Brookings Institution, 2001.

Lee, David S. "Wage Inequality in the U.S. during the 1980s: Rising Dispersion or Falling Minimum Wage?" *Quarterly Journal of Economics,* Vol. 114, August 1999, pp. 977–1023.

Leifer, Michael, ed. *Asian Nationalism.* London: Routledge, 2000.

Lemieux, Thomas. "Decomposing Changes in Wage Distributions: A Unified Approach," *Canadian Journal of Economics,* Vol. 35, No. 4, November 2002, pp. 646–688.

Lester, Richard K., and Michael J. Piore. *Innovation: The Missing Dimension.* Cambridge, Mass.: Harvard University Press, 2004.

Levy, Frank, and Richard J. Murnane. *The New Division of Labor: How Computers Are Creating the Next Job Market.* Princeton, N.J.: Princeton University Press, 2004.

Lewis, William W. *The Power of Productivity: Wealth, Poverty, and the Threat to Global Stability.* Chicago: University of Chicago Press, 2004.

Li Bozhong. *Agricultural Development in Jiangnan, 1620–1850.* Basingstoke: Palgrave-Macmillan, 1998.

Lieberthal, Kenneth. *Governing China: From Revolution through Reform.* New York: Norton, 1995.

Lieven, Anatol. *America: Right or Wrong.* London: HarperCollins, 2004.

Lin, Chun, ed. *China,* Vol. 2, *The Transformation of Chinese Socialism.* Burlington, Vt.: Ashgate, 2000.

Lin, Justin Yifu, Fang Cai, and Zhou Li. *The China Miracle.* Hong Kong: Chinese University Press, 2003.

Lin, Yimin. *Between Politics and Markets: Firms, Competition, and Institutional Change in Post-Mao China.* Cambridge: Cambridge University Press, 2002.

Lind, Michael. *Made in Texas: George Bush and the Southern Takeover of American Politics.* New York: Basic Books, 2004.

Lind, Michael. *Vietnam, the Necessary War: A Reinterpretation of America's Most Disastrous Military Conflict.* New York: Simon & Schuster, 2002.

Lindert, Peter H. "Voice and Growth: Was Churchill Right?" *Journal of Economic History,* Vol. 63, 2003, pp. 315–350.

Lindert, Peter H. *Growing Public: Social Spending and Economic Growth since the Eighteenth Century,* Vol. 1, *The Story.* Cambridge: Cambridge University Press, 2004.

Lipset, Seymour Martin, Noah M. Meltz, Rafael Gomez, and Ivan Katchanovski. *The Paradox of American Unionism: Why Americans Like Unions More Than Canadians Do, but Join Much Less.* Ithaca, N.Y.: Cornell University ILR Press, 2004.

Liu Yaling. "Reform from Below: The Private Economy and Local Politics in the Rural Industrialization of Wenzhou," *China Quarterly,* Vol. 130, June 1992.

Lorsch, Jay W., Leslie Berlowitz, and Andy Zelleke. *Restoring Trust in American Business.* Cambridge, Mass.: MIT Press, 2005.

Lovett, A. William, Alfred E. Eckes, Jr., and Richard L. Brinkman. *U.S. Trade Policy: History, Theory, and the WTO,* 2nd ed. Armonk, N.Y.: Sharpe, 2004.

Lu, Xiaobo. *Cadres and Corruption: The Organizational Involution of the Chinese Communist Party.* Stanford, Calif.: Stanford University Press, 2001.

Lubman, Stanley B. *Bird in a Cage: Legal Reform in China after Mao.* Stanford, Calif.: Stanford University Press, 2000.

Lynn, Darry. *End of the Line: The Rise and Coming Fall of the Global Corporation.* New York: Doubleday, 2005.

MacFarquhar, Roderick. *Origins of the Cultural Revolution,* 3 vols. Oxford: Oxford University Press, 1974, 1983, 1999.

Maddison, Angus. *The World Economy: A Millennial Perspective.* Paris: OECD Development Center, 2001.

Maddison, Angus. *Growth and Interaction in the World Economy: The Roots of Modernity.* Washington, D.C.: AEI Press, 2005.

Mahbubani, Kishore. *Can Asians Think?* Singapore and Kuala Lumpur: Times Books International, 1998.

Maier, Charles A. *Among Empires: American Ascendancy and Its Predecessors.* Cambridge, Mass.: Harvard University Press, 2006.

Mankiw, Gregory N., and Phillip L. Swagel. "Antidumping: The Third Rail of Trade Policy," *Foreign Affairs,* December 2005. (WTO Special Edition.)

Mansfield, Edward D. *Power, Trade, and War.* Princeton, N.J.: Princeton University Press, 1994.

Maravall, Jose M., and Adam Przeworski. *Democracy and the Rule of Law.* Cambridge: Cambridge University Press, 2003.

Marglin, Stephen A., and Juliet B. Schor. *The Golden Age of Capitalism: Reinterpreting the Postwar Experience.* Oxford: Clarendon, 1990.

Marquand, David. *Decline of the Public.* London: Polity, 2004.

Maslow, A. *Motivation and Personality.* New York: Harper and Row, 1987.

Massing, Michael. "The End of News," *New York Review of Books,* Vol. 52, No. 19, December 1, 2005.

Massing, Michael. "The Press: The Enemy Within," *New York Review of Books,* Vol. 52, No. 20, December 15, 2005.

Mayer, Frederick W. *Interpreting NAFTA: The Science and Art of Political Analysis.* New York: Columbia University Press, 1998.

McCarty, Nolan, Keith T. Poole, and Howard Rosenthal. *Polarized America: The Dance of Ideology and Unequal Riches.* Cambridge, Mass.: MIT Press, 2006.

McCormack, Gavan. *The Emptiness of Japanese Affluence,* 2nd ed. Armonk, N.Y.: Sharpe, 2001.

McCormick, Barrett, and Jonathan Unger, eds. *China after Socialism: In the Footsteps of Eastern Europe or East Asia?* Armonk, N.Y.: Sharpe, 1995.

McNeil, John Robert, and William H. McNeil. *The Human Web: A Bird's Eye of World History.* New York: W. W. Norton, 2004.

Mead, Walter Russell. *Power, Terror, Peace, and War: America's Grand Strategy in a World at Risk.* New York: Vintage, 2005.

Mead, Walter Russell. *Special Providence: American Foreign Policy and How It Changed the World.* New York: Knopf, 2001.

Mearsheimer, John. *The Tragedy of Great Power Politics.* New York: W. W. Norton, 2001.

Meisner, Maurice. "China's Communist Revolution: A Half-Century Perspective," *Current History,* September 1999, pp. 243–248.

Meisner, Maurice. *Mao's China and After: A History of the People's Republic,* 3rd ed. New York: Free Press, 1999.

Meisner, Maurice. *Marxism, Maoism, and Utopianism: Eight Essays.* Madison: University of Wisconsin Press, 1982.

Menand, Louis. *The Metaphysical Club.* London: Flamingo, 2002.

Metcalf, David, and Jianwei Li. *Chinese Unions: Nugatory or Transforming? An Alice Analysis.* CEP Discussion Paper No. 708, December 2005.

Micklethwait, John, and Adrian Wooldridge. *The Right Nation: Why America Is Different.* London: Penguin, 2005.

Modigliani, F., and Shi Larry Cao. "The Chinese Saving Puzzle and the Life-Cycle Hypothesis," *Journal of Economic Literature,* Vol. 42, March 2004, pp. 145–170.

Mokyr, Joel. *The Gifts of Athena: The Historical Origins of the Knowledge Economy.* Princeton, N.J.: Princeton University Press, 2004.

Mokyr, Joel. "The Great Synergy: The European Enlightenment as a Factor in Modern Economic Growth." Keynote address, European Association for Political and Evolutionary Economics. Maastricht, November 2003.

Mokyr, Joel. *The Lever of Riches: Technological Creativity and Economic Progress.* Oxford: Oxford University Press, 1990.

Moore, Barrington. *Social Origins of Dictatorship and Democracy: Lord and Peasant in the Making of the Modern World.* Boston: Beacon, 1993.

Moore, Mike. *A World without Walls: Freedom, Development, Free Trade, and Global Governance.* Cambridge: Cambridge University Press, 2003.

Morgan Stanley. *Global Restructuring: Lessons, Myths, and Challenges.* International Investment Research, 1998.

Morgan Stanley. *India and China: A Special Economic Analysis.* Equity Research, Asia/Pacific, 2004.

Mueller, John. *Retreat from Doomsday: The Obsolescence of Major War.* New York: Basic Books, 1989.

Mulgan, Geoff. *Good and Bad Power: The Ideals and Betrayals of Government.* London: Penguin, 2006.

Narayan, Deepa, ed. *Measuring Empowerment: Cross-Disciplinary Perspectives.* Washington, D.C.: World Bank, 2005.

Nathan, Andrew J. "Authoritarian Resilience," *Journal of Democracy,* Vol. 14, No. 1, January 2003.

Nathan, Andrew J., and Bruce Gilley. *China's New Rulers: The Secret Files.* London: Granta, 2002.

Nathan, Andrew J., and Perry Link. *The Tiananmen Papers: The Chinese Leadership's Decision to Use Force against Their Own People—In Their Own Words.* New York: Public Affairs, 2001.

Naughton, Barry J. *Growing Out of the Plan: Chinese Economic Reform, 1978–1993.* Cambridge: Cambridge University Press, 1995.

Naughton, Barry J., and Dali Yang. *Holding China Together: Diversity and National Integration in the Post-Deng Era.* Cambridge: Cambridge University Press, 2004.

Nee, Victor, and Richard Swedberg, eds. *The Economic Sociology of Capitalism.* Princeton, N.J.: Princeton University Press, 2005.

Nivola, Pietro S. *Thinking about Political Polarization.* Brookings Institution Policy Brief No. 139, January 2005.

Nolan, Peter. *China at the Crossroads.* Cambridge: Palgrave-Macmillan, 2004.

Nolan, Peter. *China and the Global Business Revolution.* Basingstoke: Palgrave-Macmillan, 2001.

Nolan, Peter. *China and the Global Economy.* Basingstoke: Palgrave-Macmillan, 2001.

Noland, Marcus. *Religion, Culture, and Economic Performance.* Working Paper 03-8, September 2003.

Noland, Marcus, and Howard Pack. *The East Asian Industrial Policy Experience: Implications for the Middle East.* Institute for International Economics, Working Paper No. 05-14, December 2005.

North, Douglas C. *Understanding the Process of Economic Change.* Princeton, N.J.: Princeton University Press, 2005.

Nye, Joseph S. *Soft Power: The Means to Success in World Politics.* New York: Public Affairs, 2005.

Nye, Joseph S., Phillip D. Zelikow, and David C. King. *Why People Don't Trust Government.* Cambridge, Mass.: Harvard University Press, 1997.

O'Brien, Kevin J. *Reform without Liberalization: China's NPC and the Politics of Institutional Change.* Cambridge: Cambridge University Press, 1990.

Obstfeld, Maurice, and Kenneth Rogoff. *The Unsustainable U.S. Current Account Position Revisited.* NBER Working Paper No. 10869, October 2004.

OECD, *Dynamising National Innovation Systems.* Paris: OECD, 2002.

OECD. *Economic Surveys: China,* Vol. 2005/13. Paris: OECD, 2005.

Offer, Ayner. *The Challenge of Affluence: Self-Control and Well-Being in the United States and Britain Since 1950.* Oxford: Oxford University Press, 2006.

Ohmae, Kenichi, ed. *The Evolving Global Economy: Making Sense of the New World Order.* Boston: Harvard Business School Press, 1995.

Oi, Jean. *Rural China Takes Off: Institutional Foundations of Economic Reform.* Berkeley: University of California Press, 1999.

Olson, Mancur. *The Rise and Decline of Nations.* New Haven, Conn.: Yale University Press, 1982.

Panagariya, Arvind. "Liberalizing Agriculture," *Foreign Affairs,* December 2005. (WTO Special Edition.)

Patten, Chris. *East and West.* London: Pan Books, 1999.

Patterson, James T. *Restless Giant: From Watergate to Bush v. Gore.* Oxford: Oxford University Press, 2005.

Peak Oil Netherlands Foundation. *World Oil Production and Peaking Outlook.* Netherlands, 2005.

Peerenbloom, Randall. *Beyond Universalism and Relativism: The Evolving Debates about "Values in Asia."* University of California, Los Angeles School of Law, Research Paper No. 02-23, 2002.

Peerenbloom, Randall. *China's Long March toward Rule of Law.* Cambridge: Cambridge University Press, 2002.

Pei, Minxin. *China's Trapped Transition: The Limits of Developmental Autocracy.* Cambridge, Mass.: Harvard University Press, 2006.

Perdue, Peter C. *China Marches West: The Qing Conquest of Eurasia.* Cambridge, Mass.: Belknap-Harvard University Press, 2005.

Perdue, Peter C. "Constructing Chinese Property Rights: East and West." In Huri Islamoglu, ed., *Constituting Modernity: Private Property in the East and West,* London: I. B. Tauris, 2004.

Perlstein, Rick. *Before the Storm: Barry Goldwater and the Unmaking of the American Consensus.* New York: Hill and Wang, 2001.

Perry, Elizabeth. *Challenging the Mandate of Heaven: Social Protest and State Power in China.* Armonk, N.Y.: Sharpe, 2002.

Perry, Elizabeth, and Mark Selden, eds. *Chinese Society: Change, Conflict, and Resistance.* London: Routledge, 2000.

Phillips, Kevin. *American Theocracy.* New York: Viking, 2006.

Piketty, Thomas, and Emmanuel Saez. *The Evolution of Top Incomes: A Historical and International Perspective.* NBER Working Paper No. 11955, 2006.

Podpiera, Richard. *Progress in China's Banking Sector Reform: Has Bank Behavior Changed?* IMF Working Paper No. WP/06/71, 2006.

Polanyi, K. *The Great Transformation.* New York: Octagon, 1980. (Originally published 1944.)

Pomeranz, Kenneth. *The Great Divergence: China, Europe, and the Making of the Modern Economy.* Princeton, N.J.: Princeton University Press, 2000.

Poncet, Sandra. "Measuring Chinese Domestic and International Integration," *China Economic Review,* Vol. 14, No. 1, 2003, pp. 1–21.

Porter, Michael E., Klaus Schwab, and Augusto Lopez-Claros. *The Global Competitiveness Report 2005–2006: Policies Underpinning Rising Prosperity.* Basingstoke: Palgrave-Macmillan, 2005.

Prestowitz, Clyde. *Rogue Nation: American Unilateralism and the Failure of Good Intentions.* New York: Basic Books, 2003.

Prestowitz, Clyde. *Three Billion New Capitalists: The Great Shift of Wealth and Power to the East.* New York: Basic Books, 2005.

Putnam, R. D. *Bowling Alone.* New York: Touchstone, 2000.

Qian Yingyi. "The Process of China's Market Transition (1978–1998): The Evolutionary, Historical, and Comparative Perspectives." Paper prepared for a symposium of the *Journal of Institutional and Theoretical Economics*, "Big-Bang Transformation of Economic Systems as a Challenge to New Institutional Economics," June 9–11, 1999, Wallerfangen/Saar, Germany.

Ravallion, Martin, and Shaohua Chen. *China's (Uneven) Progress against Poverty.* World Bank Policy Research Working Paper No. 3408, September 2004.

Rawski, T. G. "Will Investment Behavior Constrain China's Growth?" *China Perspectives,* Vol. 38, 2001, pp. 28–35.

Resnick, Mitchel. *Turtles, Termites, and Traffic Jams: Explorations in Massively Parallel Microworlds.* Cambridge, Mass.: MIT Press, 1997.

Reynolds, David. *One World Divisible: A Global History since 1945.* London: Norton, 2001.

Ridley, Matt. *The Origins of Virtue.* London: Penguin, 1997.

Ringmar, Erik. *The Mechanics of Modernity in Europe and East Asia.* London: Routledge, 2005.

Robinson, Joan. *Aspects of Development and Underdevelopment.* Cambridge: Cambridge University Press, 1979.

Rodrik, Dani. *Feasible Globalizations.* NBER Discussion Paper No. 9129, 2002.

Rodrik, Dani. "Where Did All the Growth Go? External Shocks, Social Conflict, and Growth Collapses," *Journal of Economic Growth,* December 1999.

Rodrik, Dani, ed. *In Search of Prosperity: Analytic Narratives on Economic Growth.* Princeton, N.J.: Princeton University Press, 2001.

Rodrik, Dani. *Goodbye Washington Consensus, Hello Washington Confusion?* Harvard University, 2006 (MIMEO).

Roe, Mark J. *The Inevitable Instability of American Corporate Governance.* Discussion Paper No. 493, John M. Olin Center for Law, Economics, and Business, Harvard, 2004.

Rose-Ackerman, Susan. *Corruption and Government: Causes, Consequences, and Reform.* Cambridge: Cambridge University Press, 1999.

Rosecrance, Richard. *The Rise of the Trading State: Commerce and Conquest in the Modern World.* New York: Basic Books, 1986.

Rothschild, Emma. *Economic Sentiments: Adam Smith, Condorcet, and the Enlightenment.* Cambridge, Mass.: Harvard University Press, 2001.

Roubini, Nouriel, and Brad Setser. "The U.S. as a Net Debtor: The Sustainability of the U.S. External Imbalances." Stern School of Business, New
York University, 2004. (Unpublished manuscript.)

Rowe, W. T. *Hankow: Commerce and Society in a Chinese City, 1796–1889.*
Stanford, Calif.: Stanford University Press, 1984.

Ru Xin, Lu Xueyi, and Li Peilin, eds. *Zhongguo shehui xingshi fenxi yu yuce
2005* (Analysis and Forecast of China's Social Development, 2005).
Beijing: Social Sciences Academic Press, 2004.

Sabel, Charles, and Joshua Cohen. "Directly Deliberative Polyarchy," *European Law Review,* Vol. 3, No. 4, December 1997, pp. 313–340.

Sachs, Jeffrey D., and Andrew M. Warner. *Natural Resource Abundance and
Economic Growth.* NBER Working Paper No. W5398, 1995.

Sachs, J., and W. T. Woo. "Structural Factors in the Economic Reforms of
China, Eastern Europe and the Former Soviet Union," *Economic Policy,*
Vol. 9, No. 18, 1994, pp. 101–145.

Saich, Tony. *Governance and Politics of China,* 2nd ed. Basingstoke: Palgrave-
Macmillan, 2004.

Sapir, André, et al. *An Agenda for a Growing Europe: The Sapir Report.* Oxford: Oxford University Press, 2004.

Schedler, Andreas, Larry Diamond, and Marc F. Plattner. *The Self-
Restraining State: Power and Accountability in New Democracies.* Boul-
der, Colo.: Lynne Rienner, 1999.

Schiller, Robert. *The New Financial Risk in the Twenty-First-Century Order.*
Princeton, N.J.: Princeton University Press, 2003.

Schoppa, R. K. *Revolution and Its Past: Identities and Change in Modern
Chinese History.* Englewood Cliffs, N.J.: Prentice Hall, 2002.

Schuck, Peter H. *The Limits of Law: Essays on Democratic Governance.* Boul-
der, Colo.: Westview, 2000.

Schwarz, Jordan. *The New Dealers: Power Politics in the Age of Roosevelt.* New
York: Knopf, 1993.

Scott, Colin. "Analysing Regulatory Space: Fragmented Resources and Institutional Design." *Public Law,* Summer 2001, pp. 329–353.

Scott, James C. *Seeing Like a State: How Certain Schemes to Improve the
Human Condition Have Failed.* New Haven, Conn.: Yale University
Press, 1998.

Segal, Adam. *Digital Dragon: High-Technology Enterprises in China.* Ithaca,
N.Y.: Cornell University Press, 2002.

Segal, Adam, and Ernest J. Wilson, III. "Trends in China's Transition toward a Knowledge Economy," *Asian Survey,* Vol. 45, No. 6, November-December 2005, pp. 886–906.

Selden, Mark. *The Political Economy of Chinese Development.* Socialism and Social Movements Series. Armonk, N.Y.: Sharpe, 1992.

Sen, Amartya. *Identity and Violence: The Illusion of Destiny.* New York: W. W. Norton, 2006.

Sen, Amartya. *The Argumentative Indian.* London: Penguin, 2005.

Sen, Amartya. *Freedom as Development.* New York: Knopf, 1999.

Sennett, Richard. *The Culture of the New Capitalism.* New Haven, Conn.: Yale University Press, 2005.

Setser, Brad. "The Chinese Conundrum: External Financial Strength, Domestic Financial Weakness." Paper for CESifo Conference, "Understanding the Chinese Economy," November 15, 2005.

Shambaugh, David, ed. *The Modern Chinese State.* Cambridge: Cambridge University Press, 2000.

Shang-Jin Wei and Arvind Subramanian. *The WTO Promotes Trade Strongly, but Unevenly.* NBER Working Paper No. 10024, October 2003.

Sheng, Emile C. J. "Cross-Strait Relations and Public Opinion on Taiwan," *Issues and Studies,* Vol. 38, No. 1, March 2002, pp. 17–46.

Shevchenko, Alexei. "Bringing the Party Back In: The CCP and the Trajectory of Market Transition in China," *Communist and Post-Communist Studies,* Vol. 37, 2004, pp. 161–185.

Shiller, Robert. *The New Financial Order: Risk in the Twenty-First Century.* Princeton, N.J.: Princeton University Press, 2003.

Shleifer, Andrei, and Lawrence Summers. "Breach of Trust in Hostile Takeovers." In A. Auerbach, ed., *Corporate Takeovers: Causes and Consequences.* Chicago: University of Chicago Press, 1988.

Shleifer, Andrei, and Robert. W. Vishny. *The Grabbing Hand: Government Pathologies and Their Cures.* Cambridge, Mass.: Harvard University Press, 1999.

Silverstein, Michael J., and John Butman. *Treasure Hunt: Inside the Mind of the New Consumer.* New York: Portfolio Books, 2006.

Skocpol, Theda. *Diminished Democracy: From Membership to Management in American Civil Life.* Norman: University of Oklahoma Press, 2003.

Skocpol, Theda. *The Missing Middle: Working Families and the Future of American Social Policy.* New York: W. W. Norton, 2000.

Spence, Jonathan. *The Search for Modern China,* 2nd ed. New York: W. W. Norton, 1999.

Speth, James Gustave. *Red Sky at Morning: America and the Crisis of the Global Environment.* New Haven, Conn.: Yale University Press, 2005.

State Statistics Bureau. *Zhongguo tongji nianji* (China Statistical Yearbook). Beijing: China Statistics Press, 2003.

Steinfeld, Edward. *Forging Reform in China: The Fate of State-Owned Industry.* Cambridge: Cambridge University Press, 1998.

Stephenson, Hugh, ed. *Challenges for Europe.* Basingstoke: Palgrave-Macmillan, 2004.

Stern, Nicholas, Jean-Jacques Dethier, and F. Halsey Rogers. *Growth and Empowerment: Making Development Happen.* Cambridge, Mass.: MIT Press, 2005.

Stevens, Jeffrey R., and Marc D. Hauser. "Why Be Nice? Psychological Constraints on the Evolution of Cooperation," *Trends in Cognitive Sciences,* Vol. 8, No. 2, February 2004, pp. 60–65.

Stewart, Thomas A. *The Wealth of Knowledge: Intellectual Capital and the 21st Organization.* New York: Doubleday, 1997.

Stiglitz, Joseph. *Globalization and Its Discontents.* London: Allen Lane, 2002.

Stiglitz, Joseph. "The New Development Economics." In G. M. Meier and J. E. Rauch, eds., *Leading Issues in Economic Development,* 7th ed., New York: Oxford University Press, 2000, pp. 352–355.

Studwell, Joe. *The China Dream: The Elusive Quest for the Greatest Untapped Market on Earth.* London: Profile, 2005.

Sunstein, Cass. *republic.com.* Princeton, N.J.: Princeton University Press, 2002.

Sunstein, Cass. *Why Societies Need Dissent.* Oliver Wendell Holmes Lectures. Cambridge, Mass.: Harvard University Press, 2003.

Surowiecki, James. *The Wisdom of Crowds: Why the Many Are Smarter Than the Few and How Collective Wisdom Shapes Business, Economies, Societies, and Nations.* Garden City, N.Y.: Doubleday, 2004.

Suskind, Ron. *The Price of Loyalty: George W. Bush, the White House, and the Education of Paul O'Neill.* New York: Simon & Schuster, 2004.

Sutton, John. *Technology and Market Structure.* Cambridge, Mass.: MIT Press, 2001.

Tabb, William K. *Economic Governance in the Age of Globalization.* New York: Columbia University Press, 2004.

Tamanaha, Brian Z. *On the Rule of Law: History, Politics, Theory.* Cambridge: Cambridge University Press, 2004.

Tanner, Murray. *The Politics of Lawmaking in Post-Mao China: Institutions, Processes, and Democratic Prospects.* Oxford: Oxford University Press, 1999.

Tawney, Richard. *Land and Labour in China.* London: George Allen and Unwin, 1937.

Taylor, Charles. *Modern Social Imaginaries.* Durham, N.C.: Duke University Press, 2004.

Thompson, Edward P. *Whigs and Hunters.* London: Penguin, 1976.

Tilly, Charles. *Coercion, Capital, and European States, A.D. 990–1990.* Cambridge: Blackwell, 1990.

Tsai, Kellee S. *Back Alley Banking: Private Entrepreneurs in China.* Ithaca, N.Y.: Cornell University Press, 2002.

Tseng, Wanda, and Harm Zebregs. *Foreign Direct Investment in China: Some Lessons for Other Countries.* IMF Policy Discussion Paper No. PDP/02/03, 2002.

Tucker, Nancy B., ed. *Dangerous Strait: The U.S.-Taiwan-China Crisis.* New York: Columbia University Press, 2005.

Turner, Adair. *Just Capital: The Liberal Economy.* Basingstoke: Macmillan, 2001.

Tyler, Tom. *Why People Obey the Law.* New Haven, Conn.: Yale University Press, 1990.

Uchitelle, Louis. *The Disposable American: Layoffs and Their Consequences.* New York: Knopf, 2006.

UNDP. *Human Development Report.* Oxford: Oxford University Press. (Various years.)

Verba, Sidney, et al. *Elites and the Idea of Equality: A Comparison of Japan, Sweden and the United States.* Cambridge, Mass.: Harvard University Press, 1987.

Walder, A., and J. Oi, eds. *Property Rights and Economic Reform in China.* Stanford, Calif.: Stanford University Press, 1999.

Waldron, Jeremy. *The Dignity of Legislation.* Cambridge: Cambridge University Press, 1999.

Walt, Stephen M. *Taming American Power: The Global Response to U.S. Primacy.* New York: W. W. Norton, 2005.

Walter, Carl E., and Fraser J.T. Howie. *To Get Rich Is Glorious: China's Stock Markets in the 1980s and 1990s.* Basingstoke: Palgrave-Macmillan, 2001.

Wank, David L. *Commodifying Communism: Business, Trust, and Politics in a Chinese City.* Cambridge: Cambridge University Press, 1999.

Warsh, David. *Knowledge and the Wealth of Nations: A Study of Economic Discovery.* New York: W. W. Norton, 2006.

Weber, Max. "Politics as Vocation." In H. H. Gerth and C. Wright Mills, trans. and eds., *From Max Weber: Essays in Sociology.* New York: Oxford University Press, 1946, pp. 77–128.

Weber, Max. *The Protestant Ethic and Other Writings.* Twentieth-Century Classics. London: Penguin, 2005.

Wedeman, Andrew. "Anticorruption Campaigns and the Intensification of Corruption in China," *Journal of Contemporary China,* Vol. 14, No. 42, February 2005, pp. 93–116.

Weinstein, Michael M. *Globalization: What's New?* New York: Columbia University Press, 2005.

Whiting, Susan. *Power and Wealth in Rural China: The Political Economy of Institutional Change.* Cambridge: Cambridge University Press, 2000.

Wilkinson, Richard. *The Impact of Inequality: How to Make Sick Societies Healthier.* London: New Press, 2005.

Williamson, Oliver E. *The Economic Institutions of Capitalism.* New York: Free Press, 1985.

Wilson, Edward O. *Consilience: The Unity of Knowledge.* London: Abacus, 1998.

Wolf, Charles, Jr., et al. *Fault Lines in China's Economic Terrain.* Santa Monica, Calif.: Rand, 2003.

Wolf, Martin. *Why Globalization Works.* London: Yale University Press, 2004.

Womack, Brantly, ed. *Contemporary Chinese Politics in Historical Perspective.* Cambridge: Cambridge University Press, 1991.

Wong, R. Bin. *China Transformed: Historical Change and the Limits of the European Experience.* Ithaca, N.Y.: Cornell University Press, 1997.

Woo, Wing Thye. "The Washington Consensus: Misunderstanding the Poor by the Brightest." Paper presented at a conference organized by FONDAD, "Stability, Growth, and the Search for a New Development Agenda: Reconsidering the Washington Consensus," 2004.

Wood, Adrian. *North-South Trade, Employment, and Inequality: Changing Fortunes in the Skill-Driven World.* Oxford: Clarendon, 1994.

Wood, Gordon S. *The Radicalism of the American Revolution.* New York: Vintage, 1993.

World Bank. *The Right to Tell: The Role of Media in Economic Development.* Washington, D.C: World Bank, 2002.

World Bank. *The State in a Changing World.* Oxford: Oxford University Press, 1997.

Wrigley, E. A. *Continuity, Chance, and Change.* Cambridge: Cambridge University Press, 2001.

Wrong, Brian. *The Problem of Order: What Unites and Divides Society.* Cambridge, Mass.: Harvard University Press, 1995.

Xiao, Geng. *What Is Special about China's Reforms?* World Bank Research Paper Series, No. 23, 1991.

Xiao, Gongqin. "The Rise of the Technocrats," *Journal of Democracy,* Vol. 14, No. 1, January 2003.

Yahuda, Michael B. *The International Politics of the Asia-Pacific since 1945.* London: Routledge, 2004.

Yan Sun. *Corruption and Market in Contemporary China.* Ithaca, N.Y.: Cornell University Press, 2004.

Yang, Dali. *Remaking the Chinese Leviathan: Market Transition and the Politics of Governance in China.* Stanford, Calif.: Stanford University Press, 2004.

Yergin, D., and J. Stanislaw. *The Commanding Heights: The Battle between Government and Marketplace That Is Remaking the World.* New York: Touchstone, 2000.

Yusuf, Shahid, Kaoru Nabeshima, and Dwight Perkins. *Under New Ownership.* Washington, D.C.: World Bank, 2006.

Zakaria, Fareed. *From Wealth to Power: The Unusual Origins of America's World Role.* Princeton, N.J.: Princeton University Press, 1998.

Zaller, John. "Market Competition and News Quality." Paper prepared for presentation at the 1994 Annual Meetings of the American Political Science Association, Atlanta, Ga., 1999.

Zhao Suisheng. *A Nation State by Construction: Dynamics of Modern Chinese Nationalism.* Stanford, Calif.: Stanford University Press, 2004.

Zheng Yongnian. *Globalization and State Transformation in China.* Cambridge: Cambridge University Press, 2004.

Zuboff, Shoshana, and James Maxmin. *The Support Economy: Why Corporations Are Failing Individuals and the Next Episode of Capitalism.* New York: Viking Penguin, 2002.

Zweig, David. *Internationalizing China: Domestic Interests and Global Linkages.* Ithaca, N.Y.: Cornell University Press, 2002.

Zweig, David, and Bi Jianhai. "China's Global Hunt for Energy," *Foreign Affairs,* September-October 2005, pp. 25–38.

Index